BOUNDARIES OF THE SOUL

June Singer is an analyst, practicing in Palo Alto, California. She holds a diploma in Analytical Psychology from the C. G. Jung Institute in Zurich, and a Ph.D. from Northwestern University. Her books include *Androgyny: The Opposites Within*, *The Unholy Bible: Blake, Jung, and the Collective Unconscious*, *Love's Energies*, and *Seeing Through the Visible World*.

BOUNDARIES OF THE SOUL

THE PRACTICE OF JUNG'S PSYCHOLOGY

JUNE SINGER

ANCHOR BOOKS

DOUBLEDAY

NEW YORK LONDON TORONTO SYDNEY AUCKLAND

AN ANCHOR BOOK

PUBLISHED BY DOUBLEDAY

a division of Bantam Doubleday Dell Publishing Group, Inc.
666 Fifth Avenue, New York, New York 10103

ANCHOR BOOKS, DOUBLEDAY, and the portrayal of an anchor
are trademarks of Doubleday, a division of Bantam Doubleday
Dell Publishing Group, Inc.

You would not find out the boundaries of the soul, even by travelling along every path: so deep a measure does it have.

HERACLITUS

I am indebted to the following: to Dr. Werner H. Engel, whose encouragement was present at the conception of this book and helped immeasurably throughout the writing; to Dr. Leland H. Roloff, whose discerning comments helped me to enliven the style; to James B. Martin, who corrected the final copy; and to Mary Kennedy, who prepared the typescript with care and devotion. Finally, I am grateful to my analysands, who allowed me to share in their experience and so to deepen my own understanding.

June Singer
Chicago, 1972

CONTENTS

INTRODUCTION

In teaching and lecturing and also in analytic practice I have heard again and again the question: "Why doesn't somebody write a book about the Jungian analytic process and how it works?" Thoughtful people are recognizing that Jung provides a bridge in our time between the scientific-intellectual aspects of life and the religious-nonrational aspects. Jung has faced the apparent dichotomy between abstraction and generalization on one side and the experience of immediate knowing on the other. Our culture, steeped in the principles of Aristotelian logic, finds it difficult to accept paradoxical thinking as valid. Too often it seems necessary to make a choice between the rationalistic-academic way of life or the anti-intellectual camp. Jung's greatness is in that he saw both of these as aspects of the same reality, as polar opposites on a single axis. The challenge has been put to me to describe how Jung came to his position, and to explain how Jung's concepts have been integrated into my work as an analytical psychologist.

One of the comments I heard when I first began attending courses at the C. G. Jung Institute for Analytical Psychology in Zurich was, "You cannot really understand the psychology of Jung through merely reading him. You have to assimilate his concepts into yourself and live them actively." While I have come to agree that the most direct way of doing this is through a guided tour, that is to say, through the analytic process, I am convinced that this is not the only way. And it is of course fortunate that it is *not* the only way, for Jung's teachings have much to offer to the troubled world in this last third of the twentieth century, and there are not nearly enough Jungian analysts to meet the need, the interest, and the demand. There are still less than five hundred members of the International Association of Analytical Psychologists in the world, though the number has been growing rapidly in recent years. Multiply this number by the small number of patients any analyst is able to see during a given period of time, and it becomes immediately apparent how very few people can be given direct exposure to Jung's ideas through the analytic process.

Often when Jungian analysts have spoken out to the general public about the experience of the analytic way—the "way of individuation"—small groups of people have sprung up spontaneously to meet and discuss the words and work and the life of Jung, and to try to understand all this in terms of their own personal experience. Furthermore, the teachings of Jung are beginning at last to find their way into the universities. More often than not the demand for Jung comes from the students rather than from faculty members. Typically, students have come across references to Jung in their readings in philosophy or personality psychology, or in the works of such men as Tillich or Fromm or Rollo May, cr Buber, Mircea Eliade or Claude Lévi-Strauss, Alan Watts or Aldous Huxley, Hesse or Freud—men who have read Jung or known Jung, and who have never been the same afterward. Remarks these men have made, taking issue with Jung, never quite resolving their differences with him, leave their readers with the misty awareness that Jung had the capacity to touch something essential in the human soul which needs to be touched or needs to be healed, in order to be made whole.

Mentally acquisitive people have been led by their own curiosity to find out what manner of man Jung was, and why he left his imprint upon the work of so many of the great minds of our century, despite the fact that he himself was often put down as too much of a mystic, unscientific, inconsistent, and wordy; and also to question why, on occasion, he has been vilified and discredited by those who needed to deify the gods of rationalism. The students among these people, today in a position where they are being listened to more and more at the universities and accorded a voice in the determination of the curricula, have asked for Jung.

One reason for the rather late renascence of Jung may be that his *Collected Works* only began to be published in English in 1953. Only a few of his books, miscellaneous collections of papers and lectures, and isolated essays have been available to the English-speaking public for a much longer time. Still today, the *Collected Works* have not been published in their entirety—volumes have been coming out one by one, and volumes published earlier are being reprinted.

There does not yet exist an all-inclusive index to Jung's writings, classifying the wide range of subject matter and fields of exploration essayed by this remarkable man. Therefore, it is difficult to follow his development along a certain line of direction over his lifetime of eighty-six years. Furthermore, there does not yet exist a complete annotated bibliography of Jungiana. Much has been written about this man, in many lands and by many people, scholars and psychologists, poets and playwrights, musicians and nuclear physicists. Some of the best works on the psychology of Jung have been written by Jungian analysts, who have formulated the theoretical approach in terms of their own experiences—as therapists and as human beings—living in an active relationship with the unconscious. It is understandably hard to get at Jung in any methodical way. And, where "methods" have been devised, they tend to schematize the abstractions at which Jung arrived, without maintaining the vitality of the flesh-and-blood experiences from which his theories were generalized. Such writings often lack a real understanding of the struggles of thinking people whose orientation is toward the future, and who rail against a social system which fails to offer sustenance for their spiritual lives while it surfeits them with things and concepts and methodologies.

The one book which has broken through all of this to give the public a glimpse into the private world of the psyche through Jung's eyes is *Memories, Dreams, Reflections*.[1] Jung began it in 1957, when he was already in his eighties. This book has been called Jung's "autobiography" for want of a better designation. But, if an autobiography is a chronicle of a man's life and his impact upon the world, his successes and his failures, then *Memories, Dreams, Reflections* is not an autobiography. It is rather the confession of a man concerning his observations of those aspects of living that may be called the "inner life." This is that part of life which all men experience to greater or lesser degrees but which, it is self-understood, they rarely share with other people. These matters Jung did share shortly before his death with his collaborator, longtime assistant, and trusted friend, Aniela Jaffé. While he wrote much of the book himself and approved all of it, much material was communicated to Mrs. Jaffé, who talked it through with him, recorded it, edited it, and then submitted it to Jung for further discussion and clarification before it was at last incorporated into the book. Like all of Jung's work it bears his unique imprint. It was not the product of his isolation from humanity, but rather the product of his interaction with another human being. At the same time it was the product of his interplay with the unconscious: not "his own" unconscious, but that collective mystery most of which must remain forever hidden from consciousness with only occasional glimpses offered to anyone whose attitude is open enough to receive it.

Close to the beginning of *Memories, Dreams, Reflections* there is a short passage which establishes for the reader the basic attitude with which Jung approached his life, and with which Jung approached the phenomenon of *Life*, and it is this which has seized so many readers and refused to let them go until they had lived with Jung for a long enough time to make him the friend of their soul. The passage follows:

> Life has always seemed to me like a plant that lives on its rhizome. Its true life is invisible, hidden in the rhizome. The part that appears above the ground lasts only a single summer. Then it withers away—an ephemeral apparition. When we think of the unending growth and decay of life and civilizations, we cannot escape the impression of absolute nullity. Yet I have never lost a sense of something that lives and endures underneath the eternal flux. What we see is the blossom, which passes. The rhizome remains.[2]

Students in universities today engage too much in the contemplation and dissection of the blossom. Psychology courses insist that all that counts is man's behavior, which can be broken down into operations to be observed and measured, predicted, conditioned and manipulated. I agree that behavior merits considerable concern. But I am with many thinking people today who are not altogether satisfied with studying what it is, or to be more accurate, "what it appears to be." The bloom of existential psychology is beginning to fade, for it is not fulfilling to find all of one's meaning in *this moment* and in the often terrifying experience of *this moment*. We are torn between two extremes: on the one hand is the existential ultimatum that we are here in this frightful or fabulous present, and nowhere else, nor will we ever be anywhere else; and on the other hand is the Freudian dilemma that we are where we are because of where we were and what happened to us in infancy, and all efforts must be devoted to overcoming that past which can never be changed, and which casts its long shadow across the future. Many concerned people are disenchanted with both extremes.

Some seek to escape by not thinking at all. In place of serving the demand to "think" (which has been put upon their heads since ever there were such institutions as universities), they have listened lately to the Pied Pipers who lure them with the cry that "thinking is out," no longer allowable. What you must do now is to "feel," to "sense," to "touch," and all that this implies, without bothering to recognize the disciplined partner to the emotional experience that rational thinking provides.

Others go beyond sensing, into the various kinds of drug experiences, in which their perceptive mechanisms are so altered as to distort their impressions of the objective world—thus leading to the dangerous conclusion that if that world can be changed subjectively through changing the eye that sees it, it need not be changed objectively by correcting the flaws that actually exist "out there."

Currently in the world of the student, as well as in the world of the dropout, other approaches to an understanding of man and his place in the eternal scheme have been sought. For many young people, Jung has provided some answers and, more than that, some directions in which to carry on the search. They have become aware that . . . "Yes, the blossom is important, but so is the rhizome." It is not a matter of making a choice: either-or. Both are necessary to the existence of the plant and to its growth. But in today's hurried world, where the blossom is all too easily seen, enjoyed, and knocked off its stem when it begins to wither and decay, the rhizome is all too often overlooked. We forget that it carries the source of tomorrow's blossom. I admit that Jungian psychology may lay too much emphasis on the rhizome, and not enough on the blossom. Jung has often enough been criticized for that. But just *because* institutional psychology has dealt with the observable phenomena, and dealt with it relatively adequately within the limitations of its methods, it has not been necessary for Jung or for Jungians to dwell overlong upon grounds that have been competently tended by others. Therefore, at the risk of appearing one-sided in my approach, I will follow Jung's way and stress the importance of the unconscious rather than of consciousness, the mysterious rather than the known, the mystical rather than the scientific, the creative rather than the productive, the religious rather than the profane, the meaning of love rather than the techniques of sex.

I have found that this is what many young people are looking for, to round out the one-sided views of life they are fed on most campuses, in most churches, and elsewhere. I have found this out in my own analytic practice, where I listen to the concerns of undergraduate and graduate students, professors, clergymen, and those others who have turned their backs on school and church and have looked for a different way. They have come, not *to* me, but *through* me to Jung, and to what they hope will be a clarification of what they have somewhat dimly understood yet recognized as a great personal value *in potentia* for themselves in Jung's work, and in his life.

By way of introduction to the analytic process, I will review some important moments and motifs of Jung's early life. I will proceed much as a therapist must do with a patient, that is, I will attempt to see the man in the context of his life history, with particular reference to the patterns that were established in youth, and which determine to a large degree his subsequent attitudes and activities.

Born in 1875 in Kesswil, Switzerland, Jung came to manhood just at the turn of the century. His interests had been varied during his student years, but they divided naturally between his philosophical, humanistic and religious concerns, and his fascination with science. To the latter category belonged archaeology, the subject that most intrigued him. He wrote in his autobiography, *Memories, Dreams, Reflections*[3] that he was intensely interested in everything Egyptian and Babylonian. As we know from his later writings and the course of his life, this interest was not in the shards and stones so much as it was in the mysteries that inspired ancient peoples to tell and preserve their myths and legends about how the world was created and the nature of the forces that animated it.

The autobiography reveals Jung's early awareness of two quite distinct aspects of his own personality. Each one held sway over its own sphere of interests, and each one had its own style of functioning. I suppose that co-existing trends exist in many people, especially in childhood when the direction of their lives is not yet focused, and the demands of society and practical necessity have not yet made themselves felt. How many of us in childhood enjoy fantasies of what we will be when we grow up, pursue daydreams in which we imagine ourselves as heroes and conquerors, magicians or scientists or great inventors, and are torn between this or that hero of our secret life until there comes a time when we must decide what role to assume, what may be possible and what impossible in terms of our resources and limitations! Yet in most of us the awareness of these "personalities *in potentia*" is vague and diffuse, and is often disregarded instead of being consciously thought through and resolved.

What was unusual about Jung's "two personalities" was that from early childhood he reflected upon them. Gradually he came to know each one of them in its uniqueness and watched the development of each from the standpoint of the other. His fine capacity to differentiate the varied, apparently autonomous aspects of the psyche came to him intuitively when he was very young. It is possible to trace back his theory of the structure of the psyche to his early observations about his own functioning from his first experiences of self-awareness. It is interesting to note that Jung has often been criticized because of his lack of interest in the psychology of the child and his alleged exclusive interest in the psychology of the adult. It is true that in his published scientific writings he did not stress the developmental stages of the child, particularly of the infant, as did Freud. He did not theorize about the feelings, the subjective experiences of childhood, from the "objective" stance of the adult. Instead, he was able to re-enter the delicate web of childhood. He writes of recollections of his own life beginning with his second or third year. He remembers seeing the sun glittering through the leaves and blossoms of the bushes as he looked upward from his buggy when the hood had been left up one splendid summer day; again, he recalls becoming aware of the pleasant taste and characteristic smell of warm milk as, sitting in his high chair, he spooned it up with bits of bread broken up in it.

He re-experiences "separation anxiety" as he tells of his illness at the age of three, and his dim awareness that it had something to do with a temporary separation of his parents. His mother had to spend several months in a hospital in Basel a few miles from his home. While she was gone he was

cared for by an elderly and none too sympathetic aunt and
he was deeply troubled by his mother's absence. He wrote that
for a long time thereafter he felt distrustful when the word
"love" was spoken and he associated a feeling of innate un-
reliability with women. His father stood for reliability, but he
also represented powerlessness. Jung lets us know that these
early impressions were revised over the course of time, for he
says, "I have trusted men friends and been disappointed by
them, and I have mistrusted women and not been disappointed."

He writes of his early fears, particularly fears of the night,
when his vivid imagination peopled the blackness of the room
with forms that shaped themselves out of nearly invisible
patches of light. In the muted roar of the Rhine Falls outside
his window were drowned the voices of those unfortunates
who had been claimed by the water-swirled rocks. Also, out
of the same sound, he sometimes thought he could discern
his father's distant clerical voice as he intoned funereal
phrases.

In those tense nights of early childhood, dreams became
a living myth for Carl Jung and, as with all living myths, he
did not recognize their true nature when they first came upon
him. His autobiography tells us that the earliest remembered
dream occurred when he was between three and four years
of age, and that it was to occupy him all his life. Those who
have said of Jung that he undervalued the importance of
sexual symbolism in the infant have not heard of this dream
and the tremendous import it had for him.

*The dream took place in the big meadow behind the vic-
arage where he lived with his family. While aimlessly wandering he suddenly discovered a dark, rectangular stone-lined
hole in the ground with a stone stairway within, leading down.
He descended with fear and hesitation, and found himself
standing before a doorway with a round arch closed off by a
heavy and sumptuously brocaded curtain. This he pushed
aside and, amazed, saw before him a large throne room all
of stone with a red carpet leading to a golden throne, a magnificent throne such as would be used by the king in a fairy*

tale. Something was standing upon the throne which he took at first to be a tree trunk twelve to fifteen feet high and about one-and-a-half to two feet thick, of a curious composition: made of naked flesh and skin. On top was something like a rounded head with no face and no hair but with a single eye on the top, gazing motionlessly upward. Above the head was an aura of brightness. The child was paralyzed with terror, feeling that the thing might crawl off the throne at any moment and creep toward him. Suddenly, in the background, he heard his mother's voice calling out, "That is the man-eater!"

The towering phallus of the dream was a subterranean God, "not to be named," Jung felt. Looking back upon that shattering sight in later years, he came to believe that through that dream he had originally conceived the idea that sexuality is a symbolized form for the creative potency of the Deity. How great a contrast to the classic psychoanalytic view that religion and ideas of Deity are sublimations for qualities of maleness, such as sexuality, fatherhood, authority.

The mysteries implicit in religion held so great a fascination for Jung as a child that his openness to this aspect of life seemed nearly to be predestined. He relates, concerning a time before he was six when he could not yet read, that his mother read aloud to him from *Orbis Pictus*, which contained accounts of exotic religions. He was especially interested in Hinduism, and the illustrations of Brahma, Vishnu and Shiva fascinated him. As his mother later told him, he returned to these particular pictures again and again; but what his mother did not know was that he nourished an obscure feeling for their relatedness to the earlier phallic dream. This was a secret which he kept, knowing that there was something "heathen" about the idea that his mother would never accept.

In the beginning of analysis the analyst usually will ask the analysand to tell him about his dreams. The dream is an important diagnostic tool. It is much more than that, but in the very first sessions the special value of the dream is that it gives the analyst an impression which comes directly from the unconscious and is not modified by any conscious wishes or desires on the part of the analysand. Presented as he is with the image that the analysand puts forth, largely for his own conscious purposes and with certain intentions to create an image, the analyst wants to gain access to a view that takes him beyond this. Often, the patient brings an "initial dream" to the first session or two, a dream which may lay open the whole psychic process as it takes place in the individual. In the absence of such a dream, or even as an adjunct to it, the analyst will frequently ask for a dream that has recurred frequently, or for a dream of early childhood, the earliest that can be recalled. Such a dream, having persisted through many years in some borderline area of consciousness from which it can be snatched back readily, has the import of a personal myth. It carries, in allegorical or metaphorical terms, the story by which a man lives, just as a tribal mythology is often the symbolic form of the way in which a people lives.

For this reason, I have called attention to the phallic-mystery dream of Jung's early childhood. That it remained with Jung into the ninth decade of his life suggests its importance. We will see how threads which have their beginning here will emerge time and again throughout Jung's life, in his *Weltanschauung*, in his writing, and in the practice of Jungian psychotherapy. It was this early (although Jung of course had at the time not the slightest awareness of it) that sexuality and spirituality were unalterably fused together as essential aspects of a single concept of human nature. The image of God and the image of the phallus were no more separate and distinct for Jung than they were for the pre-Hellenic Arcadians who raised ithyphallic shrines to Hermes, the giver of fertility—or to architects of those fabled temples of southern India, the façades of which depict the sexuality of the gods as the prototype of the creative power in nature and in men, who are seen as small fragments of the created and creating world.

Jung had learned early in his childhood that reality had to be discriminated in order that one could separate what could be lived out and talked about, from what had to be reserved and thought about. One ear had to be tuned to an outer world, which might be parents or school or community, and the other to an inner world which has its own way of knowing and growing, based on innate or spontaneously arising images and on individual developmental patterns.

During his school years, the secret, introspective life remained important to Carl Jung. When he was a student, much as it is today, independent thought and fantasy were rarely encouraged in the classroom. The way to get along in school was to accept what you had been taught without questioning it too much and to repeat what you had heard at examination time. This was well and good for Jung when it came to history and languages, because they did not really deal with the direct experience of the learner. But when it came to mathematics, specifically algebra, he could not accept the concepts at all. He enjoyed his studies of flowers and fossils and animals, because these were observable, but he was unable to say what numbers really were; he could not imagine quantities that resulted from merely counting. When it then came to algebra he was unable to recognize that different letters amounted to the same thing; to him "a" and "b" had to be different. He objected to rote learning; an idea was only valid for him when he could discover it himself.

An unhappy incident for Jung, but a fortunate one for posterity, occurred and temporarily resolved the academic problem for the young scholar. One day Carl was given a shove by another boy that knocked him off his feet and against the curbstone, so that he almost lost consciousness and for about a half hour afterward was a little dazed. He recalls that at that moment the thought that he would now not have to go to school any more flashed through his mind, and that he remained lying there on the sidewalk somewhat longer than was necessary contemplating the possibility. After receiving more than his share of solicitous attention from maiden aunts and worried parents, he began to have fainting spells from time to time, especially when he had to return to school or when homework became particularly irksome. He managed to stay away from school for months at a time, and during these periods he happily engaged himself in pursuing his own interests in the mysterious worlds of trees, stones, shaded pools, and the swamp near his home teeming with tiny animals and plants. There was also his father's library with books on the classics and philosophy which often absorbed him for hours. There were times when he busied himself making drawings of whatever amused or interested him, or haunted his fantasies. Although much time passed in loafing, collecting, reading and playing, he was not altogether happy. The vague feeling persisted that he was not really living, but rather escaping from the challenges and excitement of life.

One day a shocking realization came when he overheard his father confiding to a friend his worries about his young son, who might have epilepsy or some other incurable disease and might never be able to earn a living or take care of himself. The boy was at this moment suddenly struck with the import of the results of his malingering. He recognized that the moment had arrived for him to put away his childish games and return to his studies. Again and again fighting the growing tendency to faint, he refused to give in, and within a few weeks he was able to return to school. He writes, "I . . . never suffered another attack, even there. The whole bag of tricks was over and done with! That was when I learned what a neurosis was."[4]

In later life, Jung was to recognize that a neurosis is often a rebellion of the unconscious psyche against forces which it perceives as threatening to its specific individual nature. The unconscious psyche has at its deeper levels little concern with the demands of parents or teachers or society in general—but it seeks its own survival as an entity, as well as the survival of its offspring: thoughts and feelings. It has its particular tendencies, its "genius" in the less common sense of the word, meaning a strong leaning or inclination, a peculiar, distinctive or identifying character or spirit, which is often personified or embodied as "a tutelary spirit." It would seem that Jung's tutelary spirit had been kept reasonably well under control during his primary years, getting enough attention so that it would not intrude itself overmuch into the disciplines of study. His resistance to certain types of study were dealt with by conscious efforts of the will. But when the threshold of consciousness was lowered, as it was when Jung's head hit the curbstone, the "genius" found an opportunity to come forth.

This suggests the classic story of the genie (same root word) who streams out of the bottle when the stopper is released, and performs for the individual his every secret wish. It may be compared to the conduct of the neurotic who responds to every impulse, until at last the consequences of his acts begin to come down upon his head and he cannot cope adequately with them. It is then that he runs with his neurosis to the psychotherapist, as the possessor of the genie in fabled times ran to the magician to ask him to put the genie back into the bottle.

Carl Jung managed to get under control his tendency to function in other ways than those approved by his school-masters. It was often a struggle, however, and remained so until he learned to come to terms with it, and to give the genii of the unconscious their due. Throughout his school years, Jung continued his studies in a wide variety of fields, and he also continued to observe his own developing mind in process. He noted his growth in two rather distinct directions which would alternate with one another for dominance. The first was the now industrious schoolboy, deep into the classics and the natural sciences, building up a fund of knowledge through voracious reading. The second was concerned with the mysteries of ultimate things, given to questioning the nature of God and of reality, to brooding, to silence and to secrets. He spoke of his number one and his number two "personalities,"— one oriented toward the objective world "out there" and the other toward the subjective world of the psyche. No matter which aspect of personality was in the forefront of conscious-ness, the other was never very far away. This dual experiencing of reality produced at times a rare richness of approach, at other times a gloomy obscurantism, and sometimes confusion and anxiety. This characteristic "divisible" quality of per-sonality exists in varying degrees in everyone and is the basis of many unconscious conflicts, as dynamic psychiatry has well understood. Jung's extraordinary gift was in his willingness to take up these conflicts within himself and to follow them wherever they might lead, despite his feelings of insecurity and his sometime fear, his sometime awe. Thus, almost without knowing it, he was from a very early age committed to a position of exploring the psyche from its own depths. Only later would the way to do it become clear to him.

Jung made the decision to enter medical school rather quickly, after a period of indecision at the end of his student years. He was still hoping to enter the university to study in the natural sciences, despite the fact that archaeology was his most compelling interest. He had not yet learned what it was in this science which summoned him, although the call was clear. But family finances were such that he could not study anywhere except in nearby Basel, and the University of Basel did not offer the curriculum he wanted. Also, though he had by now grown tall and strong, he had never forgotten his father's fears that poor, sickly Carl would never be able to earn his living. Medicine seemed to be a practical solution, for it provided a number of specialities and the possibility of research, and in the meantime offered the chance of a comfortable livelihood. And so, in the last days before matriculation, he enrolled in the faculty of medicine.

Medical school was difficult and demanded a great deal of concentration. Special training in anatomy and pathology demanded precise attention to objective realities and factual knowledge, and what he called his "number two personality" had little time or occasion to assert itself, until the summer of 1898, when several very curious happenings occurred which were to lead Jung's attention astray into an entirely new direction.

The first of these experiences took place during the summer vacation while Jung was at home poring over his textbooks. His mother was seated in an armchair in the adjoining room, knitting. Suddenly a report like a pistol shot was heard. Jung jumped up from his work and ran to his mother, to find her flabbergasted in her armchair, the knitting fallen from her hands. "It was right beside me!" she cried out, and Jung, following her eyes, saw that the sturdy round table which had come from the dowry of his paternal grandmother and was now about seventy years old, had split from the rim straight through to the center and beyond, not following any joint. He could not understand it—how could a table of solid walnut that had dried out for seventy years now suddenly split on a summer's day in the relatively high humidity of the Swiss climate? He was thinking to himself that it could have been conceivable in winter next to a heating stove but at this time —what in the world could have caused such an explosion? As if in answer to the unverbalized question, Jung's mother said, "Yes, yes, that means something." When Jung related the incident later, he recalled that against his will he was impressed and annoyed with himself at not having anything to say.

The next very curious happening occurred about two weeks later. Jung had arrived at his home about six in the evening to find the household upset and excited. There had been another shattering noise about an hour earlier. Jung searched all about for the cause of it and, finding no cracks in any of the furniture, began to examine the interiors of various pieces in the room where the sound had been heard. At last he came upon a cupboard containing a breadbasket with a loaf of bread in it, and beside it lay the bread knife. The blade had snapped off into several pieces; the handle lay in one corner of the rectangular basket and each of the other corners held a piece of the broken blade. The knife had been used a couple of hours earlier during afternoon tea and had been replaced in the cupboard intact, and the cupboard had not been opened since. The next day Jung took the pieces of the knife to one of the best cutlers in town who examined them with a magnifying glass. The cutler stated: "There's no fault in the steel. Someone must have deliberately broken it piece by piece. It could be done, for instance, by sticking the blade into the crack of the drawer and breaking off a piece at a time. Or else it could have been dropped on stone from a great height. But good steel can't explode."

Again, Jung had no answer. He kept the pieces of the knife

as long as he lived. He had sought to penetrate the mystery, not necessarily to explain it, and certainly not to explain it away. As he did not discard the knife, so Jung never did push away any of the unanswerable problems that beset his life. Perhaps that was a reason for many of his difficulties, as well as a cause of his greatness. When faced with the unknowable, he was never willing to say simply, "That is out of my province, I will not allow myself to be concerned with it or side-tracked by it." Rather, his attitude was, "I will try to understand it, but if I cannot, I will keep it always near me, and hope that one day the meaning that is concealed in the mystery may be in some measure revealed."

Perhaps something of the uneasy mood still pervaded the atmosphere when, a few weeks later, Jung heard of certain relatives who had been engaged in table-turning, and also about a young medium in the group who was said to be producing some peculiar trance states during which she would relay messages from spirits of departed persons. Jung immediately connected the strange manifestations that had so recently occurred in his house with the conversations he was hearing from members of his family about the fifteen-and-a-half-year-old girl, S.W. Out of curiosity he began attending the regular Saturday evening séances which were held by his relatives. For about two years Jung followed these séances, observing instances of what purported to be communications from the beyond, tapping noises from wall and table, and some highly interesting verbal messages relating to what appeared to be a reconstruction of a long bygone past.

Toward the end of this time Jung was preparing for the examinations which would conclude his formal medical education. He had not found the usual lectures and clinics in psychiatry particularly interesting and so had put off until last his preparations for the examination in that subject. In those days psychiatry was held in contempt rather generally by the medical profession. Insane asylums for the most part were isolated in the country and the doctors lived there with the patients, remote from the rest of the world. Mental illness was considered to be a hopeless and fatal disease, and the psychiatrist a fool to want to devote his life to such a thankless cause. So, when Jung picked up the *Textbook of Psychiatry* by Krafft-Ebing[5] he was not at all prepared for the effect that it would have upon him.

Jung describes in his autobiography the strong impression made on him by these words in the preface, "It is probably due to the peculiarity of the subject and its incomplete state of development that psychiatric textbooks are stamped with a more or less subjective character." And when, a few lines further on, the author referred to the psychoses as "diseases of the personality," Jung became aware, in what he called later "a flash of illumination," that psychiatry was the only possible goal for him. Here was a field in which the two streams of his interests could run together. It was the one empirical field which encompassed all that was known about the biology of man and also all that was known about his spiritual nature. In psychiatry it could all be combined. The "subjective character" of psychiatric textbooks of which Krafft-Ebing spoke provided a welcome concurrence with Jung's own awareness of the importance of subjective experiential perception as a vital factor in the acquisition of all knowledge. He informed his professor of internal medicine, who had fully expected Jung to follow in his footsteps, that he had made the decision to study psychiatry. No amount of persuasion from his teacher or from colleagues and friends could dissuade him from embarking upon the career that they all assured him would be a bypath to obscurity.

He completed his examinations successfully and on December 10, 1900, took up his post as resident at Burghölzli, the cantonal mental hospital of Zurich. There Jung's attitude took on a quality of profound intention, consciousness, duty and complete responsibility. He became committed to a stern regime within the walls of the hospital: studying, reading, learning to make diagnoses, observing the patients, observing his colleagues—and reflecting again upon the S.W. notes he had made during the two years in medical school. These notes, which he had laid aside not knowing what to make of them, now took on new meaning in the perspective of a doctor occupied with severely neurotic and psychotic patients. Jung began now to acquire some objectivity as to the meaning of the manifestations which had occurred at the séances. He was at this time sufficiently removed from the actual experience of being present at the séances so that he could also view their subjective aspects: the feelings and experiences as they seemed to the medium herself, as well as how they appeared to the person who viewed them from a medical standpoint. Therefore, at the turn of the century, when the dichotomy was becoming ever clearer between the rational thinkers in the emerging sciences of behavior and the "mystics," he early expressed his "way of individuation" by becoming intrigued with the challenge of exploring the never-never land between science and mysticism, to gain an understanding of how man thinks and feels, and why he behaves as he does.

Jung has asserted that his observations of the altered states of consciousness in S.W., and his subsequent interpretative writing about them, wiped out his earlier philosophy and made it possible for him to achieve a psychological point of view. Through this, he became interested in the subjective aspect of experience, that is, the realization that what happens in the objective world is highly colored by the factors present in the individual to whom it is happening. Understanding these subjective factors gives the event a whole new dimension of reality. This dimension he did not underestimate thereafter, for he realized that all that we know comes to us through the agency of the psyche—what is perceived must be seen in the context of the total field of the perceiver before it can have any existential meaning and before it can be given any valid interpretation.

Psychic reality is not the same as objective reality. Psychic reality refers to immediate reality as we experience it, and what we perceive are the psychic contents which crowd into the field of consciousness. In his own words:

> All that I experience is psychic. Even physical pain is a psychic image which I experience; my sense impressions—for all that they

force upon me a world of impenetrable objects occupying space—
are psychic images, and these alone constitute my immediate
experience, for they alone are the immediate objects of my
consciousness. My own psyche even transforms and falsifies
reality, and it does this to such a degree that I must resort to
artificial means to determine what things are like apart from
myself. Then I discover that a sound is a vibration of air of
such and such a frequency, or that a colour is a wave of light
of such and such a length. We are in truth so wrapped about
by psychic images that we cannot penetrate at all to the essence
of things external to ourselves. All our knowledge consists of
the stuff of the psyche which, because it alone is immediate, is
superlatively real.[6]

Interestingly enough, Jung was making these discoveries for
himself about the nature of *psychological reality* at just about
the same time that important and not unrelated discoveries
in the physical world were being formulated and presented
to a skeptical public view. It was in the summer of 1900 that
the physicist Max Planck entered into the intense theoretical
work which led to results so different from anything known in
classical physics that Planck himself could hardly believe his
own findings. His son tells that his father spoke to him about
his new ideas on a long walk through the woods near Berlin,
explaining that he had possibly made a discovery of first rank,
comparable only to the discoveries of Newton. He must have
realized at this time that his formula had touched the foundations of our description of nature, and that these foundations
would soon start to move from their traditional location toward a new and as yet unknown position of stability. In December of 1900, Planck published his quantum hypothesis.[7]
Werner Heisenberg, in reviewing the history of quantum
physics, said of this great advance of Planck's, "In classical
physics science started from the belief—or should one say from
the illusion?—that we could describe the world or at least
parts of the world without any reference to ourselves. . . .
It may be said that classical physics is just that idealization
in which we can speak about parts of the world without any
reference to ourselves. Its success has led to the general ideal

of an objective description of the world. Objectivity has become the first criterion for the value of any scientific result. . . . Certainly quantum theory does not contain genuine subjective features, it does not introduce the mind of the physicist as a part of the atomic event. But it starts from the division of the world into 'object' and the rest of the world. . . . This division is arbitrary and historically a direct consequence of our scientific method; the use of the classical concepts is finally a consequence of the general human way of thinking. But this is already a reference to ourselves and in so far our description is not completely objective."[8]

But also in the year 1900, another epoch-making event in the exploration into the subjective aspects of man and his world took place: Sigmund Freud published his *Interpretation of Dreams*. In this momentous volume, Freud published the results of his years of study and inquiry into the meaning of dreams, his own and those of his patients. One of his guiding principles was that the dream could not be studied properly apart from the mind of the dreamer, nor the mind of the dreamer apart from his dreams. Subject and object had to be seen in their relationship to one another. And, when the subject was man the dreamer, and the object was the man in the dream, a degree of clarity and differentiation was demanded that presented the analyst with a whole new series of dilemmas.

Jung, the medical student, read the new book *Interpretation of Dreams* by the controversial Viennese doctor when it first came out. He later wrote, "I had laid the book aside, at the time, because I did not yet grasp it."[9] The book, like many of the impressions that were making their mark on the mind of Jung during these crucial years, all but dropped out of consciousness. But all the while these matters were constantly being turned over and over again in the unconscious, mixing with other contents, and gathering power for their emergence at a later time when the ground would be better prepared for them.

In 1900, too, Jung wrote his doctoral dissertation *On the Psychology and Pathology of So-Called Occult Phenomena* and, in the process, made order of the chaotic supply of material he had gathered during the previous year when he had attended the séances. Jung began his dissertation with the traditional scientific approach, that is, a review of the literature up to the time of his observations dealing with "certain rare states of consciousness."[10] He identified and defined terms whose meanings had not yet been agreed upon by the various authors: "narcolepsy" (a tendency to fall asleep for no apparent reason), "somnambulism" (activity in a trance state), "lethargy," "*automatisme ambulatoire*" (automatic walking while seeming to be awake), and "periodic amnesia," in which there is no remembrance upon awakening of the strange events which were described during the trance state. He also described a condition called "double-consciousness" in which the subject is at one time aware of the external conditions surrounding him and able to communicate to those present the description of a totally different dimension of awareness, in respect to both time and space. And lastly, he discussed the states of pathological dreaming and pathological lying, in which the subject is not aware of his departure from what seems to be normal for most people.

The characteristic that interested Jung in all these conditions is that they did not seem to be limited to any specific set of psychiatric syndromes. He observed that they occur in people who are otherwise quite normal and who carry on their work and their relationships to other people in an unremarkable manner. The peculiar departure from the usual state of consciousness, which occurs in every one of us from time to time, was seen by Jung to stem from a *complex*, which is nothing more than an idea filled with emotionally charged contents, which interrupts our attention and redirects our thinking and often our behavior.

The idea of the complex led Jung to a search through the labyrinthine maze of the human psyche, to seek out those incomprehensible elements which erupt into consciousness from unknown sources and interfere with our plans and hopes, our intentions and desires. The trail of the complex led backward toward its sources in those basic elemental tendencies of the human personality which produce certain specific kinds of thinking patterns common to the entire human species. These Jung named the *archetypes*.

The complexes led Jung in another direction also, toward the images which man creates or discovers—as expressions of the not-yet-known. These he called *symbols*. And so it was that Jung occupied himself for much of his life with the mysteries that all men sense but only a fascinated few explore.

Because of this intense preoccupation with the unknowable, Jung has been called a mystic by some critics. They point out where he differs from Freud—Freud was interested in reducing all psychic processes to rational explanations, while Jung was content to let his speculations run free as he entered into the realm of the mysterious without attempting to concretize the ineffable experience. He had many arguments with Freud about this, and most were never resolved. The questions were crucial in bringing about the separation of Freud and Jung—although many, more practical, reasons for their disagreements were advanced. Yet as Freud grew older, and as his experience deepened and was tempered by his own suffering, his thinking approached closer to Jung's in these matters. The two men influenced each other significantly, in the areas of their disagreement as well as in the areas of their agreement.

It is not my intention to present a study of Jung's life, or of the history of his relationship with Freud. This material has been dealt with fully by others. In this work I will only touch upon such areas of Jung's personal experience and his relationship with Freud as are needed to explain the basic Jungian concepts and how they developed. My primary purpose here will be to present these concepts as clearly as I can, and to show how they function in the analytic process and also in the course of everyday living.

I have not done extensive research, in the ordinary sense, in the preparation of this book. A good part of what I have come to believe and tried to communicate was distilled in the alembic of my own analytic experience. For this, I am deeply grateful to those analysts with whom I had my training in Zurich, Dr. Liliane Frey and Dr. Heinrich K. Fierz. I have returned to them from time to time since I completed the formal program in Zurich, and have been privileged to refresh at the springs of their wisdom.

There is another debt to acknowledge, though there are hardly words to express my gratitude for the contributions made by my analysands to my learning experience and to the substance of this book. These men and women have shared with me their sorrows and their desires, their secret shames, their fears, their doubts of self and others, and also some rare moments of understanding and deeply-rooted joy. Their concerns have served to provide the illustrative material which gives depth and meaning to the descriptions of various aspects of analytic practice. I have changed the names and many of the circumstances connected with the incidents described. Sometimes I have used a dream in an entirely different context from that in which it occurred. Certain of the characters are composites rather than individuals. On the whole, the persons who provided these examples expressed their willingness to allow the use of their case material, recognizing that the scientific study of Analytical Psychology, or any other psychological discipline for that matter, depends on the sharing and communication of the data of experience. In those rare cases where there were objections, the case material has, of course, not been used.

Another source has been my students. They have listened to me, argued with me, forced me to rethink and refine my ideas. They have contributed many ideas of their own. In the process we together have tried to update some of the approaches to psychological understanding to suit the rapidly changing needs and interests of men and women living in the United States in the 1970's.

At all times I have had the sense that an old wise man was standing behind me, meditating with closed eyes, his gold-rimmed glasses perched up on his balding forehead.

I have not agreed with Dr. Jung in all things—and I do not believe he would have wanted that, for he saw as an important goal not slavish imitation, but each person's realization of his own individuality. When I describe what I do in psychotherapy, I am not saying that this is *the Jungian way*, nor is it necessarily representative of what other Jungian analysts do, or ought to do. Because the analytic process is so personal, I can only offer material from my own experience, as examples of possibilities that exist in the practice of Analytical Psychology. And yet, as Jung taught, there are certain experiences which are common to all mankind, with which we can empathize and from which much can be learned. A blending of individuality and commonality structures the human personality. This constant and ever-changing interplay of the individual psyche and the collective psyche forms the background for the work of the analytic process: the search for self-knowledge, and for knowledge of the wider Self, as carried on in the spirit of C. G. Jung.

1

ANALYST
AND
ANALYSAND

The state of science today has been characterized by the term "information explosion." This is a condition which is surely evident in the field of psychology, where a new approach to the human psyche bursts forth from the laboratories and the clinics every few months or so, and filters through the mass media to the attention of the man in the street. The general reader admits his ignorance of technical fields in which he has had no special training, but in psychology he feels qualified to read a few articles, or watch the latest "in" psychologist on the late-night talk shows and to pass judgment as though he were an expert. After all, he may reason: if psychology is what its name implies, the study of the human psyche—that is, the "mind" as it experiences itself—why should not my view of what is happening or can happen in the psyche be as valid as anyone else's? After all, I have a "mind," whatever that is, and I know what I feel and what I experience at least as well as anyone who may practice psychology upon me.

And so Multi-media Man, the contemporary successor to Renaissance Man, has taken up successively Freudian or psychoanalytic therapy, Reichian bio-energetics, the neo-Freudian social psychologies, Rogerian client-centered therapy, Rational therapy, Reality therapy, behavior modification therapy, existential therapy, hypnotherapy, chemotherapy, psychodrama, encounter groups and sensitivity training with all their variations, and even transcendental meditation as a quick way to bliss on earth. Abandonment of emotional controls is cited as the way to mental health in Primal therapy; while the ability to gain control by the mind over the body, including the autonomic nervous system, through bio-feedback training is held by others to be the magic key.

Many of these schools claim, or have claimed at one time or another, to have found the secret to mental or emotional health, a secret which can be universally applied for the benefit of all mankind. Each new panacea is presented by its creator in lucid and persuasive terms—it is not unusual to see on the dust jacket of the book "X Therapy: *The* Cure for Neurosis." Next month it will be Y therapy that is *the* cure, and the following month, Z.

Why then should there be still another book about still another approach to the problem of the human psyche, and especially an approach which is not very current, not very popular, and which does not promise a "cure" to anybody—much less to everybody? I refer to the work of the Swiss psychiatrist Carl G. Jung, work which is a "psychology" only in the broadest sense of the word, for it deals with human experience of every kind as it is experienced through that mysterious and hypothetical—if you will—organ which no one has ever seen or weighed or measured: the psyche. Jung's "Analytical Psychology" (the name he gave to his approach at the time of his break with Freud, in order to distinguish his work from that of the founder of "psychoanalysis") includes and is subject to the discipline of the scientific method, but it is not limited to the traditional methodology of science. It includes and is subject to the insights of religion, but is not limited to the forms of traditional religious expression. Furthermore, Analytical Psychology concerns itself with the kernel of art which is the functioning of the creative process, but it is not bound by the techniques of any of the arts.

Dealing with such broad and extensive fields of human endeavor, Jung's psychology consequently appears vast and complex. In some of his writings Jung is mercifully clear and direct, but in many of his works he is difficult and abstruse, often seeming to be carried along by his thought processes instead of consciously directing them. It is in this latter type of work that he is at his best in weaving a richly textured and intricately patterned fabric, and yet he is here most difficult to understand. It is said often of certain of Jung's books that the first time you read some of them they seem to be absolutely incomprehensible, except for a few sections of unusual clarity which stand out with more of a promise than an explication. The next time you read him the area of light enlarges, the shadows are not quite so deep. And it is the experience of many who read Jung that with each successive reading a whole new view of his meaning is revealed, so that in time his writing uncovers the living experience of the psyche. The meaning of Jung's life and work and its implications for psychotherapy cannot be grasped easily.

Why then, in these days when claims for instant enlightenment are competing against claims for instant intimacy on the current scene, is the psychology of Jung slowly but certainly gaining in adherents—and this without any special publicity or proselytizing? Why is Jung just now beginning to be taught in universities, a century after his birth? Why is Jungian analysis gradually attracting more and more people, despite the fact that its appeal is admittedly limited to those who are willing to submit themselves to a long and difficult process which must of necessity disturb the very premises upon which their lives are based? Why are people willing to set aside the equilibrium with which they have lived for many years more or less successfully, and chance a journey through the mysterious realms of the hidden recesses of the psyche, a journey which Jung called "the way of individuation"? Why have they taken this path with all its potential dangers, the agonizing slowness of the process, the requirements for a great investment of time and energy, and the absence of the familiar unconditional guarantee of success?

The problem of the multiplicity of psychologies was anticipated by Jung at least as early as 1933 when, in an essay called "Problems of Modern Psychotherapy" he wrote:

> Since the mind is common to mankind it may seem to the layman that there can be only one psychology, and he may therefore suppose the divergences between the schools to be either a subjective quibbling, or else a commonplace disguise for the efforts of mediocrities who seek to exalt themselves upon a throne. . . . The many-sidedness and variety of psychological opinions in our time is nothing less than astonishing. . . . When we find the most diverse remedies prescribed in a textbook of pathology for a given disease, we may confidently assume that none of these remedies is particularly efficacious. So, when many different ways of approaching the psyche are recommended, we may rest assured that none of them leads with absolute certainty to the goal, least of all those advocated in a fanatical way. The very number of present-day "psychologies" amounts to a confession of perplexity. The difficulty of gaining access to the mind is gradually borne in upon us. . . . It is small wonder therefore, that efforts to attack this elusive riddle are multiplied, first from one side and then from another.[1]

How much more true this is today, forty years after Jung wrote those words!

Jung believed that the well-being of the psyche is directly connected with a man's conscious or unconscious philosophy of life, so that his way of looking at things is actually of supreme importance to him and to his mental health. The important fact about a situation or thing, from a psychological standpoint, is not so much *how it objectively is*, as it is *how we see it*. That which is unbearable may become acceptable if we can give up certain prejudices and change our point of view. This philosophy of life—a *Weltanschauung*, as Jung called it—is developed step by step through every increase in experience and knowledge. As a man's image of the world changes, so a man changes himself. Jung, writing on "Analytical Psychology and *Weltanschauung*," illuminates his entire approach to the human psyche:

> A science can never be a *Weltanschauung*, but merely a tool with which to make one. Whether a man takes this tool in hand

or not depends on the sort of *Weltanschauung* he already has. For no one is without a *Weltanschauung* of some sort. At worst he has at least that *Weltanschauung* which education and environment have forced upon him. If this tells him, to quote Goethe, that "the highest joy of man should be the growth of the personality," he will unhesitatingly seize upon science and its conclusions, and with this as a tool will build himself a *Weltanschauung* to his own edification. But if his inherent convictions tell him that science is not a tool but an end in itself, he will follow the attitude that has become more and more prevalent during the last hundred and fifty years and has increasingly shown itself to be the decisive one. Here and there single individuals have desperately resisted it, for to their way of thinking the meaning of life culminates in the perfection of the human personality and not in the differentiation of techniques, which inevitably leads to an extremely one-sided development of a single instinct, for instance the instinct for knowledge. If science is an end in itself, man's *raison d'être* lies in being a mere intellect. If art is an end in itself, then its sole value lies in the imaginative faculty, and the intellect is consigned to the woodshed. If making money is an end in itself, both science and art can quietly shut up shop. No one can deny that our modern consciousness, in pursuing these mutually exclusive ends, has become hopelessly fragmented. The consequence is that people are trained to develop one quality only; they become tools themselves.[2]

The inevitable conclusion is that the many psychological theories become rationales for psychotherapies, rationales which are in turn merely tools designed to fashion a certain type of personality, whatever type is considered valuable by the originator of the system. Thus for one system the achievement of maturity might be the crowning goal, freedom from symptoms for another, self-understanding for a third, or adjustment to the norms of society, or realization of potential for growth, or learning to accept responsibility, or reducing existential *Angst*, or simply "being real," and so on *ad infinitum*. There are psychological "tools" to open you up, calm you down, adjust you and readjust you. Each one deals with one or more aspects of the human personality, and many focus

on a single problem or a single type of problem, or seek to
reduce all human psychological ills to a single explanation.

While Jung's psychology may be many things to many people, of one thing we may be certain, it is not a "tool." Unlike
many other well-known psychologists, Jung never presented
a psychological theory in the strict sense of a theory: that
is, a body of generalizations and principles developed in association with the practice of psychotherapy and forming its content as an intellectual discipline. Unlike the leaders of other
psychological schools, Jung does not offer a methodology, a
technique for procedure, a series of "applications" that the
Jungian analyst can use from the insights and formulations
of the master. For what is essential in the psychology of Jung
is the requirement that each individual develop consciously
his own *Weltanschauung*, his own "philosophy of life," if you
will, in accordance with the "given" factors of his personality
which are present at birth, and unfold according to their genre
and in their own time, and also those "acquired" factors which
include the environment into which he is born and the circumstances which surround him through the days of his life. I
see this philosophy as one which must transcend the fragmentary approaches to the human psyche that are currently
subject of so much literature and discussion. It must envision
man as a unitary and total being—encompassing everything
that every psychological approach says that man is, even
though some of those approaches may be in direct opposition
to some others.

Jung has wisely said that if you are able to observe a quality
that is characteristic of a man, you may be quite certain that
somewhere in him the opposite is equally true. I believe that
the greatness of Jung rested in his ability to accept the paradox
as a fact of man's psychological being. And the great paradox
of Jung's work is that it is highly individual—it depends very
much on the particular nature of the individual who conceived
it, while at the same time it reaches into general principles
drawn from the history of human consciousness and experience and thus is applicable to a wide spectrum of human
nature.

My colleagues all function in their individual ways; their analytic training has in no way recast them into a single mold. Some are extremely liberal in dealing with patients, quite permissive in terms of relationships—others have developed a relatively formalized structure. Some follow the medical model and occasionally use drugs as an adjunct to analytic treatment. Others insist that Jung's psychology is a "cure of souls" and properly falls close to, if not actually within, the area of religion. Still others say it is a way of educating a man for a better life, and as such belongs within the purview of academic psychology. And one Jungian analyst has suggested that "Before the work of Jung can be carried further . . . analysts will have to free themselves from those remains of theology, of academic psychology, and especially of medicine which still clutter the ground and which are false markers for an analytical psychology."[3] Thus it is clear why it is so difficult to attempt to explain in a general way exactly how Jungian analysis works. On the other hand, it seems a more practical undertaking to write about Jungian analysis and how it works *for me*. In such an undertaking it will be possible to discuss some of Jung's basic principles, how he discovered them, and how an understanding of what he has illuminated makes it possible for the Jungian analyst, specifically *this* Jungian analyst, to function.

This writing project has been over a dozen years in the deep freeze, and only now begins to thaw out. It had its inception with the first course I attended at the Jung Institute in Zurich, given by Jolande Jacobi, one of the foremost interpreters of Jung. The subject was "Masculine and Feminine Psychology" or, as familiarly called in Jungian circles, "Anima and Animus."[4] I discovered that what Dr. Jacobi had to say had direct reference to me personally, and to problems in my own marriage which had grown out of failure to understand some of the basic differences between the ways in which men and women approach one another. Jung's explications of the mysterious unconscious workings which give rise to certain of our sex-oriented attitudes came to me as an overwhelming experience of what seemed to be "prior knowledge," as

though somewhere within me I had always been aware of
these differences, although I had never been able to formulate
them.

At the beginning, I resisted the idea of analysis for myself.
I could quite easily see the advantages of this for *other* people
because I could see that *they* had obvious psychological problems which required attention. But I could not see that I
personally had any such problems. To embark upon the analytic experience would be an admission that there might be
something wrong with me, something that needed correction.
However, as I began to get some feel for a new attitude toward
the psyche, I came to recognize that the best way to experience the transformation about which Jung spoke would be
to undergo personal analysis. And so this intensive experience
was started.

At the same time, I was reading Jung. I found his work
sometimes beautifully and strikingly clear. But in some places
it was complicated, convoluted, rambling, and unorganized.
Jung made no complete systematic presentation himself, and
the interpreters I read who sought to systematize his writing
tended toward essays that were overschematized, that somehow failed to capture the spirit of Jung. I asked around, "Why
doesn't somebody write a clear, simple book about Jung, explaining how his theories are applied in analytic practice?"

I never received a satisfactory answer. Many "Jungians"
would say, "Just wait till you've been around here a while,
then you'll understand." Or "Jung can't be explained in simple
terms. One has to live Jung, not just read Jung." Or, "It takes
the kind of devoted study that these books require, in order
to come to a real appreciation." Or "to explain Jung is to
destroy Jung." Nevertheless, as I heard the lectures and participated in discussions, and proceeded with my personal
analysis, I kept feeling that much of what I was learning could
be written about in a clear and non-technical manner. As time
went on, however, I began to have my doubts. It seemed
to be necessary to travel Jung's labyrinthine path in order
to approach anywhere near the center. The "way of individuation" was described as a lifelong journey, and the more I read

of Jung, the more I realized that I would devote many years before I could approach the insights of this great man with a true measure of understanding.

At the end of the course of studies, with my head crammed full of information, and a sense of having come to terms with my own personal psychology to the degree that I would now be able to carry on my developmental progress independently of my analyst, I appeared for final examination. I shall never forget what happened to me when I sat before the examiner and the two experts for my oral examination on The Individuation Process, which is the essence of analysis. I had prepared for this in a most elaborate manner, and was ready to show how the analytic process has its parallel in the alchemical literature of the Middle Ages, in Tantric yoga, in the Hebrew Scriptures and elsewhere. I was ready to illustrate and document all statements I would be asked to make. I appeared. I was informed that there would be only one question for this examination, that is, for this section of the six-part examination. The question that was put to me was the following, "If you were asked to explain the Individuation Process to one of the fellows who sweeps the streets of Zurich with a faggot broom, during the time it takes to wait for the tram, what would you tell this man?" I don't need to tell you that I was taken aback by the question!

I cannot recall whether my first reaction was more one of shock or fury. In any case, I flashed to my own background the story of Rabbi Hillel, who had been asked a similar question. The question put to him was, "Can you explain the essence of Judaism while I am standing on one foot?" Hillel had answered, "Do not do unto your neighbor what you would not have your neighbor do unto you. That is the essence of Judaism. All the rest is commentary."

Quieted by this thought, I had a momentary vision of something I had been doing the day before, taking a sailing lesson on the Zürichsee, the Lake of Zurich. It was as though the unconscious had presented me at the right moment with an image of the Process. I began to speak. "It is as though you were sitting in a little sailing boat in the middle of the

Zürichsee, and had no idea how to manage a sailboat. If the current was right and the wind was right, you might get to where you were going sooner or later. Or, you might bob around indefinitely and get nowhere. Or a storm could come up and you could be overturned and the whole project could end in disaster. But begin the Process, guided by another who has been through it himself and coped with the difficulties and found ways to solve them, and it is all different. You learn to take into account the structure of the boat itself, how it is made and how it responds to the water and the wind. The boat is comparable to your own personality. You learn about the currents in the lake; these correspond to the realities of life in which you are situated and which are somewhat predictable. You learn about the winds, which are invisible and less predictable, and these correspond to those spiritual forces which seem to give direction to life without ever showing themselves. In learning to sail you do not change the current of the water nor do you have any effect on the wind, but you learn to hoist your sail and turn it this way and that to utilize the greater forces which surround you. By understanding them, you become one with them, and in doing so are able to find your own direction—so long as it is in harmony with, and does not try to oppose, the greater forces in being. You may still have to face dangers—there may be swift currents or wild winds at times, but somehow you do not feel helpless any longer. In time, you may be able to leave your guide and sail alone, and one day you may even become a guide for others. You are not helpless any more."

I remembered well the first hour of my own analysis. I was not sure why I was there, except that I was no longer young and the hopes and promise of earlier years were still unfulfilled. It seemed to me that my life was narrowing down, closing in, that there were fewer and fewer possibilities for development with the passing years. I felt that whatever little I had possessed of talent or skill was falling away, but I could not put my finger on what was wrong with me. I could see that plenty was wrong in my daily life, but most of it was "not my fault." My analyst asked me what I hoped to gain

personally from analysis. I found that this was a question
that had not even occurred to me! But then some thoughts
did come up, and I replied that I wished that I were able
to express myself better, more articulately, to be able to say
what I mean, and not to be afraid to take a strong position.
As a child I had been more verbal than most, but over the
years I had become more and more inhibited in expressing
myself in conversation. Of course I found reasons for it, I
could blame it on external circumstances, and I did, without
the slightest realization of what the "symptom" of my painful
shyness was pointing to, in terms of real need. The analyst
took me at my word and we began with my own perception
of my situation. She was fully aware of something that I had
yet to learn, that the problems which the analysand brings
to the analyst in the beginning are not the real problems,
though they often contain the real problems in a cryptic form.

What is seen in the beginning by the analysand and is
presented to the analyst as "problems" consists of what is already in consciousness. By consciousness, I mean that level
of awareness that is achieved by the individual through his
perceptions and understanding of his world and of himself.
My consciousness consists of myself and my world, and the
relationship between them as it appears to me. It is clear
enough that the psyche is not identical with consciousness,
and that any understanding of the psyche must begin with
an understanding of the role of the unconscious and the relations between consciousness and the unconscious. The starting
point of understanding the analytic process is the concept of
the psyche as a self-regulating system in which consciousness
and the unconscious are related in a compensatory way.[5] Anything psychic, that is any experience when it comes into awareness, will take on the quality of consciousness; otherwise it
remains unconscious. The organ of awareness is called the
ego, and as such the ego functions as the center of consciousness. The field of consciousness then refers to all contents
that are related to the ego; a whole other sphere lies outside
the ego. This can be characterized the non-ego field, the unconscious. The psyche consists of consciousness and the un-

conscious, but the critical point is that these are not two separate systems, but rather two aspects of one system, with the exchange of energy between consciousness and the unconscious providing the dynamic for growth and change. This growth and change takes place throughout life in a natural way, with unconscious contents constantly being fed into consciousness and assimilated. At the same time, conscious contents are constantly being repressed, forgotten, or just overlooked, and losing their energic charge, they fall into the unconscious.

It is with this constant interplay between consciousness and the unconscious that the analytic process deals, attempting to improve the nature of the dynamic interchange in the direction of bringing order out of disorder, purpose out of aimlessness, and meaning out of senselessness. Toward this end we need to see the unconscious as potentially constructive, offering a constant stream of information to compensate the limitations of conscious awareness. The analytic process is a means of systematically drawing upon the resources of the unconscious and progressively integrating these contents into consciousness; at the same time "letting go" of those conscious contents, attitudes, modes of behavior, that are no longer necessary or desirable.

The goal of treatment, which is rarely understood at the beginning, and then only in an intellectual way, is the shift of psychic balance from the area of consciousness with the ego as its center, to the totality of the conscious and unconscious psyche. This "totality" has its own center, which Jung has called the "self," in contradistinction to the "ego." How this shift of balance develops, and what it means in terms of the changes in the lives of individuals undergoing analysis, can best be understood through a discussion of actual situations in analytic practice.

The importance of the analysand's first interview is that it establishes the patterns and expectations for the future analytical work and for the analyst-analysand relationship. To begin with, the attitude of the analyst toward his patient will be immediately apparent to the patient, and will have its effect from the first moment on their relationship.

The Jungian, as psychotherapist, approaches each new patient with interest, curiosity, and wonder. Here is the great mystery of humanity: that every man and woman, though he shares in the evolutionary history of mankind, is yet unique! "In thine own breast dwell the stars of thine own fate," Jung was fond of quoting. Each person speaks a different language— although the patient uses the same words that I do, he means something subtly different by them. His ways of being, his ways of thinking and feeling and perceiving and knowing are distinctly his, based on his particular constellation of archetypal foundations, the sum total of his experiences, and the behavior patterns that have been shaped by the interaction between the internal and external factors. No one has ever been exactly like this person who sits with me—I must regard him well, for there will never be another like him.

In my experience, I have found that a person rarely enters into analysis with the stated purpose of confirming that individuality which was born in him as a potential, and which has somehow gotten lost in the pursuit of the practical goals of his life. More often he had gone along well enough until some crisis arose which tested all his abilities and resources and still could not be dealt with in any satisfactory way. He feels frustrated, hurt, or desperately alone in an alien or hostile world. If he is young, he may feel blocked in achieving some career goal; he knows he should be able to get beyond the point where he is stuck, but he cannot. Or, if he is in the second half of life, he may reflect upon himself and find that for all his strivings he has had precious little satisfaction; life has become empty, meaningless, boring. Success or failure are alike to him. The years should have brought him a sense of reward, but there is only a revulsion with overindulgence in the face of spiritual poverty. He asks himself: "Isn't there more than this?"

Most schools of psychotherapy maintain that people are and should be individuals. I agree, they say so. But I am not so sure that all really function in complete devotion to this principle, or that they even believe it is a good thing that we are all so different, both in terms of our psychological constitution as well as our way of dealing with the world. Too many believe, or act as if they believed, that the function of psychotherapy is to smooth off the rough edges of differences and induce or persuade the individual to adapt to the demands or requirements of the situation in which he finds himself. To be "normal" means to many the same as being able and willing to conform to some sort of a socially produced "norm," an "accepted" standard of behavior.

This attitude is nowhere so evident as in the question so often raised by professionals who practice one or another form of psychotherapy, but who have never themselves completed a successful analysis. The question, usually raised in the popular magazines, is: "How can you evaluate analysis anyway?" Each writer who poses this question makes the assumption that there are certain norms that characterize the outcome of "good therapy." It takes only a little insight to recognize that the goals of many of today's "gods" in the high places of psychotherapy are to create man in their own image. In the words of the incomparable Henry Higgins, "Why can't a woman/ be more like me?" Thus, for instance, for one group facilitator a desirable outcome of psychotherapy could be absence of inhibition in the area of sexuality, while a clergyman would be more likely to push for "self-mastery" or "impulse control," a Primal therapist for freedom from Pain,[6] a Reality therapist for "responsible" behavior, and a Behavior therapist for extinction of a particular phobia or compulsive ritual.[7]

The danger is that the psychotherapist who has not had analysis himself tends to get *his* way confused with *the* way, and consequently in his work finds himself living out his own unconscious needs *through* the patient and *using* the patient to prove his own efficacy as a therapist. This is, of course, an ego trip, and precisely what the analytic process as I understand it is careful to avoid. It is for this reason that a prospective analyst, as part of his training, must go through a personal, therapeutic analysis. He must undergo the experience of facing and dealing with the manifestations of his own unconscious through intense involvement with the analyst until, at the end, through disengagement from the analyst-as-a-person he achieves his independence while retaining the meaning of the analytic relationship.

Everything that happens in the course of analysis may be regarded as being of potential importance. The analyst must of course sort out and determine what he will deal with in any given moment and what he will exclude. Otherwise the analysis would never proceed very far, and surely it would never terminate. The patient, also will make similar decisions, but often for different reasons. Even at the very start, in that fateful phone call in which a stranger informs the analyst that he has learned of this analyst in this or that way and that he would like to make an appointment to come in and talk with him—or to consider the possibility of undergoing analysis—or simply to discuss a certain problem. Obviously the analyst will not be able to interview everyone who thinks he might like to come in, and so there is a need to learn right then whether this may be an individual with whom the analyst may be able to work. A few questions can reveal much: How is it that the person on the phone has selected *this* analyst and not another? Has he ever had any psychotherapy or analysis? If so, when? And with whom? And for how long? What does he expect from the interview or therapy that he is requesting? Is he aware of some practical considerations?

I cannot speak for my colleagues, but I find it helpful to do the initial telephone screening myself. I get a feeling for the level of awareness in the individual with respect to what he is actually seeking, also for his degree of anxiety or urgency, and sometimes even for his capacity for insight. All of this can occur in a very brief conversation, in which I generally try not to get into the nature of the presenting problem itself. This topic is reserved for the initial interview, when analyst and patient meet face to face for the first time, exposed to each other in as near a condition of psychic nakedness as is possible.

On the phone some patients come right to the point. Others

begin to ramble, not knowing what to say, and starting off in all directions: "I've heard a lot about you, Dr. Singer," "I was reading this book by Jung," and so on—so I have to help the person focus in—by saying something that brings him directly into the moment—perhaps like, "How did you happen to decide to call me *just now?*" Another may launch into a long and complicated story—"I was an only child and . . ." and on and on. Here again, I must try to see if the person can be brought to some sort of focus out of the diffusion—for instance by saying, and at the same time showing that the person on the other end of the line is a person to me, "And just how may *I* be of help to *you?*" If these simple attempts to get an idea of at least the precipitating factor fail to work, I may quickly realize that this may be a person who is unable to come into contact with the requirements of reality, and I will seriously question whether the analytic approach, with its strenuous demands for a concentration of consciousness, is going to serve the needs of this individual. Experience has taught me to determine very quickly whether it makes sense to offer an appointment to the patient, or to suggest that something else may be indicated.

When an appointment is made, I note the questions that the prospective patient asks or fails to ask. Does he ask how to get to my office, and whether he can find a place to park? If so, does he ask in a dependent, helpless way, or in a manner which indicates that he is cool and efficient and wants to save the time of blundering about? Does he ask whether he should prepare anything for the initial meeting? If so, I often suggest that if the patient has any dreams between now and the appointment, that he might write them down and bring them in to the initial session. I never speak of the *first* session, because that implies that there is to be a second, a commitment which neither I nor the patient can be prepared to make before an actual meeting, so I speak in terms of an *initial* session. Also, I never tell a beginning patient in which form he should bring in the dreams, because the way he chooses will tell me a great deal about his attitude toward his dreams. It says quite a different thing to me if a patient brings in a dream scrawled on a piece of scratch paper, or typewritten with a few errors, or impeccably typed by his office secretary. Yes, people do that, too, as if they were submitting them for publication! Some bring in a beautifully hand-bound book which they have made, while others write on the backs of pages which were once mimeographed for some other purpose and left over. Such *little* things can tell the therapist a lot. That is, if the therapist is watching what is happening and not busily trying to follow a set of procedures.

The first telephone conversation may also offer clues as to how much the caller knows about what he may be getting into. For instance, if he asks how long it will take, I can be pretty sure he doesn't have much of an idea of what analysis may involve, and I know that it will be necessary to spell everything out very carefully. Other questions will show his reality-orientation and sense of practicality: questions concerning my hours, fees, what happens if he has to cancel the appointment, and so on. Ordinarily these do not come up in the first phone call, but sometimes they do, and I have to be prepared to answer them in a way that will convey my own way of working. All the while I am also learning about the prospective patient from the questions he raises.

Suppose now the appointment has been made and the hour has come. Does the person arrive early, on time, or late? I note this, because as a therapist I will want to find out what this signals. Some people automatically allow themselves an extra few minutes to go to a place where they have never been—"time to get lost." Others invariably come with "I didn't realize the traffic was so heavy at this time of day," or "I couldn't find a place to park"—and then there are the ones who get lost, or who simply didn't leave in time. And always, there are the compulsive ones who push the doorbell at the exact stroke of the hour. They are all telling me something about themselves, whether they realize it or not. And as therapist, I had better get the message.

Sitting in my office, I hear a knock on my door. Is it timid, indecisive? Is there another tentative rap, in case I didn't hear? Or a fast, crisp clack? Or an aggressive bang bang bang? Before

I see the patient he has transmitted a signal. I had better hear it. The door is opened and there is the first eye contact. Therapists of some schools believe in stress situations to test out the patient. I do not. Life is stressful enough, in my opinion. I am not there to manipulate the patient, not even "for his own good." I am there to befriend him, and not to antagonize him or deliberately mobilize his defenses. It seems to me that if I am to be privileged to gain access to the dark reaches of the unconscious, it is my role to provide an atmosphere of trust and freedom in which the new patient will be helped to face hidden aspects of himself that he may fear. I am to help open wide the doors that have long been shut, the doors which have long kept out the dangerous and stormy thoughts and feelings which he did not dare to meet alone. Now I am to be fully present to him; and I must get this fact across to him. It begins at the threshold of my consulting room.

When our eyes meet for the first time, I pronounce his name. He is an individual to me, I look squarely at him so that I will see him as a person, and I let him see me. I introduce myself. I bring him into my office, my place as I have arranged it; a place which expresses me, my likes and dislikes, my totems and talismans, my pictures and the great antique roll-top desk that dominates the room.

One reason I prefer private practice to working in an institution is that here I am able to establish my own environment. It is a place of symbolic separation from the world, which makes it possible to view the world in a special way—outside of its pressures and its immediacy. I believe that the unconscious does not perform well before an audience. Perception of it becomes contaminated with all sorts of cultural values and needs for approval. This is what I try to minimize in my way of being-with a patient, and I can do it less self-consciously if I know that in my work I am not answerable to anyone except to the person who sits with me, and to myself.

I am not unaware of the value of cross-fertilization that comes when one works with other professionals. In a group setting much may be gained in breadth from discussion of cases and sharing experiences and especially problems. Still, it is difficult enough to understand another person and to formulate your ideas and responses concerning him, when you work together with him in intimate communion; how unreasonable then it is to expect that someone who does not know the patient but depends only on selected bits of data in a report could give valid counsel on the handling of a case? While a therapist is being trained there is no question that adequate supervision is necessary, but all the more it must be remembered that the presence of the tape recorder or the one-way mirror, or the patient's knowledge that his case will be discussed in conference cannot help having its effect on what transpires between patient and therapist. It is a calculated risk; perhaps in a training situation the value outweighs the disadvantages, but I am not sure.

The privacy of the analytic hour is offered to the patient in exchange for his confidence in and personal commitment to the process. Another thing which he is offered is the freedom to be himself. The only restriction I apply is that he must allow me, also, to be myself, and that means to function within the limits of my own self-concept. That reserves for me the privilege of talking about my own personal life and my feeling reactions only to the point where I feel comfortable with it and where it appears to me to be relevant to the task in which we are mutually engaged.

The initial session begins, and I have been as receptive as I know how to all the non-verbal messages that have come my way: the patient's general appearance indicating his self-image, his voice and posture and his walk. He decides which of the chairs in my office he will sit in, or perhaps he waits for me to make the choice for him. Many such minute matters as these combine to give an impression which will form a base for what will happen later on. Until now, the approach has been consistent with that of most therapists who utilize "depth psychology," that is, psychology in which unconscious material is a primary consideration.

One distinctive feature of the Jungian approach is the analyst's openness about himself and his own reactions. His involvement in the process is active—he is not merely an observer, nor even a participant-observer, but he is an active partner in a mutual endeavor. Receptivity to the patient continues—as he is now in this moment—and to all that he brings to recount as he discusses the details of the situation which has brought him to therapy. The analyst listens attentively so that he may understand what the patient is saying and hear the feeling behind the words. He will be continually checking with the patient to make sure he is getting the message intended. As he listens he will be evaluating the nature of the problem and the patient's motivations and capacity for carrying on therapy or analysis.

Up to this point I have used the words "therapy" and "analytically oriented therapy" and "analysis" more or less interchangeably. "Therapy," an abbreviated form of "psychotherapy," refers to "the use of any psychological technique for the treatment of mental disorder or maladjustment" performed by a professionally trained person.[8] Analysis is a specific form of psychotherapy which deals chiefly with unconscious materials such as dreams, fantasy, visions, creative productions and, in the orthodox psychoanalytic framework, with free association. The analyst will utilize an approach based on his understanding of the unconscious processes, even though he may not in all cases interpret the unconscious material to the patient. Analysis is a specifically dialectical process in which the analyst and analysand are together engaged in attaining an understanding of unconscious material.

Interpretations arise out of the analyst's experience in his personal and training analysis and out of his experience in analyzing others. In the Jungian framework, based as it is upon a familiarity with archetypal material, the analyst needs to have at his disposal familiarity with mythology and comparative religions and other fields which contribute to a knowledge of a variety of symbols of the collective unconscious. How far he will go in his interpretations depends very much on his own background, plus the kind of material that appears in individual cases, and the ability of the analysand to deal with this sometimes highly charged matter. Sometimes the symbols have not to be interpreted at all, but rather taken "as is," or for what they evoke, and observed in that spirit. At first the analyst will reserve interpretation for the most part, waiting to see what effect the raising of newly emerged contents to a conscious level will have on the patient, and what he will do spontaneously with his material—so that the analyst does not "direct" the process. It is important to let the unconscious have its say.

Two matters have to be dealt with specifically in the first sessions. One concerns the patient's understanding of his role in the analysis, and the second concerns his understanding of the role of the analyst. The patient needs to recognize why he has come to analysis: he has found himself in a conflict situation that appears insoluble, and this discrepancy is between the conscious attitude he holds and unconscious factors which interfere with his carrying through on the intentions which correspond with his conscious attitude. He needs to know, too, that his task will be to make himself accessible to whatever unconscious material may present itself, and to face it as honestly as he can. By unconscious material, I will explain to him, we mean the dreams, the fantasies, and other expressions of thought and behavior which do not seem to originate with his own will or awareness—those things which seem to happen to him to cross his plans and hopes and prevent him from fulfilling his commitments. He has to realize that the conflict between consciousness and the unconscious cannot be resolved by advice from the analyst or even through the willingness of the patient to co-operate, but only through the patient's trying to understand the unconscious material as it comes up, and moreover to carry his insights with him when he leaves the consulting room and returns to the field of his daily living.

The second matter that needs to be discussed is the attitude of the analyst. Since the patient is identified with his own conscious attitudes, it may be necessary at times for the analyst to take his position on the side of the unconscious, as the advocate for the point of view of the unconscious. This means that the analyst will be charged with helping the patient to uncover material which has either long remained repressed in the unconscious, or material that has not yet come to consciousness and stays "underground" to all intents and purposes, in a state of potentiality. Thus in some ways the analyst becomes the adversary of certain of the patient's conscious attitudes.

I let the analysand know from the beginning that he will face the dark, ugly, and tawdry aspects of his life which he has been avoiding, and that since these contents are and have long been unacceptable to him, that something in him will take every possible means to frustrate their disclosure. As for the positive, developmental trends which up to now have remained unconscious, these by their revolutionary nature have the capacity to disturb the established patterns he currently has; hence, they too, will be resisted.

The beginning analysand will say that he understands, and that he is willing to go through all this, but in fact he does not yet understand what it will be like, and when it comes to going through it he will fight it with all the intensity of his being. Yet I will have to warn him about potential resistance. Later in the analysis when he has fought his way through it, he will probably say, "Now I understand what you meant by resistance, whereas I did not really understand before." The only possible way to know what is real is to discover, first, what has been unreal.

Sometimes the new analysand will bring a dream to the initial interview; sometimes the first dream does not appear until after the first session, or after several sessions. It is not at all unusual for the initial dream to be a significant one, putting into focus either the condition of the patient or else his feelings about the analysis or the analyst.

Gina, a young woman of Roman Catholic religion, came into analysis in a desperate situation. She was about five months pregnant by the first man with whom she had had sexual relations. He had no intention of marrying her. She was the sort of woman who seemed ideally suited for the role of wife and mother, but circumstances were against it, and she blamed her own impetuousness for not having avoided the pregnancy. Yet she felt that she was unwilling to compound her guilt by adding murder to her crime of carelessness. She would have the child, and she would have to find an attitude toward it that would be consistent with what she understood as the meaning of her life. This did not permit the negation of a life for which she was responsible, her firstborn. Gina brought the following dream to the first analytic session: *I was thinking about coming to you. I had a guide. She said you do all sorts of weird things. She said you told one lady to throw her car into the water. She said you told another lady to jump into the cold icy water of the lake and swim across.*

This dream contained Gina's fears of the analytic process. The whole thing was mysterious to her. She expected to have demands made which would be extremely difficult for her to meet. In the course of our discussion of the dream I asked her what a car meant to her. Her car was her most valuable possession; she had worked very hard to pay for it. It was a source of great pleasure. When I questioned further, the car turned out to be the place where she and her friend had had sexual intercourse. So, evidently, the car represented the treasure (her sexuality) that she felt she had misused, and therefore it would have to be sacrificed. All her guilt was bound up in this painful realization. Her guilt also resulted in her having withdrawn her tender feelings into herself as she had become somewhat hardened to the world. This was understandable in the face of what she expected to find in the attitudes of friends and relatives.

The second lady in the dream represented to her the absence of sensitivity to emotion that she was experiencing. "It is as though all my feelings have gotten turned off and I feel nothing for anyone, I just don't care. And still I miss my feelings, painful as they are, and wish I could get them back." Jumping into the icy water would be a great enough shock, she said, to make her *feel* again. The analyst would demand that from her, and the analysis would be like icy water. The dream shows her attitude: the sacrifice will have to be made, the risk will have to be taken, and the hope is that she will be made whole with her feelings once more.

The beginnings of *transference* are also present in this initial dream. Gina brings into her analysis an unconscious relationship to the analyst, upon whom she had placed the image of a stern task-mistress. Since she had not yet met me, these expectations had to come from within herself; they were reflections of her own unresolved conflicts, unconscious emotions and problems with relationships. These were activated at the prospect of entering a new and intense relationship. Transference means that something from elsewhere is transferred or redirected into the analytic relationship. Thus we have attitudes and behaviors coming up in analysis which carry with them more emotional charge than would seem to belong to the situation being explored. Behind the façade of the analytic dialogue, however, stands the life history of the patient, with all its personalities and conflicts and the feelings associated with them. The experiences of the individual and, more than these, the bases upon which the life experience takes place, namely the archetypal foundations of the personality, all infuse the analytic confrontation.

I want to return to the first session with Gina because it contained not only an important initial dream, which illustrates how transference can be present even before the analysis begins, but because another very important aspect of analysis entered into this case in an especially dramatic way. This concerned the attitude of the analyst to the patient, an attitude which, like that of transference, has a strong unconscious aspect. *Countertransference* is the term used to describe the unconscious analyst-analysand relationship as experienced subjectively from the side of the analyst.

In the case of Gina, I had a very powerful emotional reaction to her in the first moment I saw her. Gina's youth and her long straight brown hair, her dark eyes with the mod glasses, reminded me with excruciating sharpness of my only daughter who had died just a few months before. My daughter had been newly married, and had no child, and so my hopes ever to have a grandchild had been demolished. Now Gina's coming, wondering whether to keep her child, hit me very strongly; I felt rising in me a determination that she should not under any circumstances give up her child for adoption. Because I am close enough to my own unconscious, I could feel the "mother-tiger" rising within me. So all the while as I was listening to and speaking with Gina, I was dealing with the uproar in my own unconscious.

I had to recall what I had learned in my own analysis when I had been training, shortly after I had begun to work with my first cases under supervision. I was, like all neophytes, exceedingly eager to achieve a successful outcome, and I tended to become quite active in leading, rather than gently guiding the process. My training analyst had gently tried to restrain me, but when that failed she shocked me one day by saying, "You are not supposed to want the patient to get well!"

At first I could not quite believe this, for I surely did not understand her meaning. But gradually as it sank in I was able to see that if I acted out of my desire to heal the patient, I was setting myself up as the miracle worker. I would be doing it for my own satisfaction, for the joy of success, and maybe for the approval of my training analyst. My own needs would be in the foreground then, and the patient's needs would revert to the secondary position. Besides, the possibility for healing lies in the psyche of the patient, the place where the disunion or split exists. The psyche, as Jung has taught, is a self-regulating system, containing within it all the elements which are necessary both to produce a neurosis and to transform the neurosis into a constructively functioning element. If I, as analyst, impose my concepts of the direction into which the analysis should go and what the outcome should be, I am doing violence to the potential unity of the patient's psyche. My task is to use myself as a vehicle for clarifying the patient's dilemmas and for helping him learn to interpret his unconscious production. My task is not to contaminate the analysis with my own problems. And it is for this reason that I constantly need to be aware of my own needs and my own biases.

The twin problems of transference and countertransference

in the psychology of Jung are given a position of great importance in the analytic process. In this, analytical psychologists are in full agreement with analysts of other schools. Jung
has stated in "The Psychology of the Transference," "that almost all cases requiring lengthy treatment gravitate round the
phenomenon of transference, and that the success or failure
of the treatment appears to be bound up with it in a very
fundamental way."[9]

The nature of the transference in Jungian analysis develops
along with the style of the analysis, and especially as fostered
by the individuality of the analyst. Jung long ago "took analysis off the couch," with all the meaning that implies, symboli-
cal as well as otherwise. "The couch, with the analyst sitting
behind the patient, clearly aims at establishing as far as possible (I don't believe it is very far, in fact) an 'impersonal,'
'objective' analyst figure. That it also forms one of the defense
mechanisms used by analysts for self-protection is evident,"
we are told by a Jungian critic of the couch technique.[10]
In the Jungian analysis, the analyst and analysand sit face
to face on the same level. This gives greater flexibility to the
analytical situation and to the active interchange that goes
on between the two participants. I, as analyst, am exposed
and I expose myself deliberately to the observing and scrutiniz-
ing view of the analysand. This puts us immediately on the
same plane, and we are therefore part and parcel of a mutual
relationship.

Jung has warned the analyst with respect to countertransference:

> Even the most experienced psychotherapist will discover again
> and again that he is caught up in a bond, a combination resting
> on mutual unconsciousness. And though he may believe him-
> self to be in possession of all the necessary knowledge con-
> cerning the constellated archetypes, he will in the end come to
> realize that there are very many things indeed of which his
> academic knowledge never dreamed. Each new case that re-
> quires thorough treatment is pioneer work, and every trace of
> routine then proves to be a blind alley. Consequently the higher
> psychotherapy is a most exacting business and sometimes it sets

tasks which challenge not only our understanding or our sympathy, but the whole man. The doctor is inclined to demand this total effort from his patient, yet he must realize that this same demand only works if he is aware that it also applies to himself.[11]

The analysis of the transference is the crux of the analyst-analysand relationship, for the unconscious patterns come into play here where we can see them directly and do not have to rely on the patient's recital of things past. Transference material is presented spontaneously by dreams, and so in looking at the dreams we can see the outcroppings of unconscious processes, disengaged from any conscious purposes of the analysand. In this way the analysis of the dream has a certain advantage over the analysis of the defenses and resistances; for the latter may be all mixed in with the will and other conscious notions.

In my own experience I have found that the transference material is not necessarily disguised to the degree that it becomes necessary to interpose concepts like that of a "dream censor" who twists the message of the dream into something quite different, even opposite from what appears. Some transference dreams can be taken quite literally, for their meaning is evoked by images and symbols with beautiful clarity.

For example, a homosexual schoolteacher who is bound to his mother by hate and fear, and who occasionally takes a hallucinogenic drug, brought the following dream: *I am visiting the zoo and am in a giant outdoor bird cage there looking at plants and birds. I wander down a steep path and find Dr. S. cooking what smells to be chocolate fudge. There, in an earthen room below the birds, are twelve huge vats of gurgling, bubbling chocolate candy. She tells me that it is a kind of a grain candy, completely non-sugared and very non-habit-forming. She then offers me some and I taste it, remarking that it tastes like regular fudge to me. She says, "See, what did I tell you about drugs?" I leave to walk out of the bird cage, and my mother is there, fat and ugly. She starts wrestling me, saying, "You're going to stay in the cage, you're going*

*to stay in the cage," in a singsong kind of way. I grab her
and begin shaking her. As I shake her I keep saying to myself
the same thing I once thought when I really shook a student
in my class, hard, "Migod, you're shaking the shit out of this
kid!"*

Bill, the dreamer, feels encapsulated. His life is like a big
cage, so large that he can go about with apparent freedom,
but go too far and he suddenly finds out where the bars are.
That is the limitation that his underdeveloped sexuality places
upon him. In my view, his homosexuality is not a matter
of constitutional disposition (as is thought to be the case with
certain homosexuals). Rather, Bill might be said to be re-
tarded in his sexual development, so that now he is functioning sexually on a twelve- or thirteen-year-old level, although
intellectually he is quite adult.

As a young child he had been surrounded by prohibitions
against enjoying any sensual pleasures. He was informed in
no uncertain terms that his body and everything that came
out of it was filthy and untouchable. He recalls his mother
standing over him and shaming him when he was two or three,
but can't remember why. He must have repressed suddenly
all the good feelings associated with the "making" of warm,
soft, pungent feces. Bill recalled that he was kept at home
a great deal of the time with minor ailments while the other
children were out playing. He had no early experience of body
contact or sex play with other children. It seemed to him
that wherever he went, his mother was watching him, that
he was never out of her sight. He grew extremely shy and,
not surprisingly, failed to form any close attachments outside
of the family. Much of his time was spent in solitary activity:
practicing the cello, reading, and compulsive masturbation surrounded by guilt feelings and fear of divine retribution. All
through his growing years Bill was dogged by a sense of failure
in personal relationships. As a young adult he related to others
mostly on a superficial "talky" level, without any sense of concern about the other, and without ever feeling that he himself
was held in high regard.

In his analytic "confession" he described his masturbatory

fantasies; they were homosexually oriented and full of unend-
ing streams of urine and inundations of feces; there were all
sorts of scenes of sexual abuse being heaped on him, or performed by him on other people. I listened to it all without
much comment, primarily interested in understanding what
it meant to him. Since there was no blame from my side,
he had felt freer in going ahead to explore his actual relationships of various kinds. These were brief impersonal homosexual encounters.

My appearance in his dreams showed that he experienced
me as being involved with him and committed to the process
in which we were both engaged (were we not in the same
huge bird cage?). My acceptance and participation in his reliv-
ing of his repressed experiences allowed him to convert the
disgust he had learned back into its original context of something natural—to him that was sweet and delicious, like "regular fudge." But the old suspicion was not gone from him;
he felt that my acceptance of him could not be altogether
real, it must carry a moral judgment, perhaps referring to my
having questioned his sometime use of LSD or mescaline. He
associated me in his mind with the image of the criticizing
mother. In other words, he had projected that image onto
me. So even while consciously and rationally he saw me as
myself, on an unconscious level he saw mother—and he transferred his feelings of fear and distrust of his mother to me.
Therefore, in the dream he tried to escape (and in reality
this preceded his attempt to flee from analysis because of the
tensions it produced), and then we were able to see what
it was that he was resisting. I was really his mother after
all, it appeared, and he saw any attempt on my part to hold
him within the discipline of the process as a ruthless effort
to control him, which he must avoid by a counterattack. The
aggressive behavior which could not be lived out with his
mother, except in dreams, had found its way into his daily
life, where he had taken on the mother role himself and found
himself "shaking the shit out of this kid." The permissiveness
which my activity in the dream symbolizes is something he
missed in his childhood and would have liked to attain now,

but he was unable to because he could not trust it. It will
be a task in the analysis to give him the opportunity to test
out freer attitudes and to discover that these attitudes, which
appear in his dreams, represent not only elements of unfulfilled wishes or incest fantasies, but a still more important
element in them.

The other element of the dream, which we have not yet
considered, is that which is suggestive of the potential for
future development of the dreamer. In this case the symbol
of the cooking provides the clue, for obviously "cooking" here
is not the ordinary occupation of whipping up a batch of
fudge in the kitchen. The cooking is an extraordinary procedure, taking place on a subterranean level which has to be
approached by going down a steep path and entering an
earthen room. Here, in the place that symbolizes the depths
of the unconscious, twelve huge vats are boiling and gurgling.
Cooking means changing or transforming a substance from
one form into another to make it edible, that is, assimilable.
It is as though the dream were saying, "Look here, there is
a tremendous job to be done, but look, this substance has
within it all that is needed to produce something valuable
and highly desirable!"

Often in the process of analysis the unconscious yields up
symbols of transformation, like this one. The appearance of
the symbols does not mean that a transformation of the personality is imminent; it only means that it is a possibility.
For some individuals, if these symbols appear at a time of
psychological readiness, they may be taken as a challenge to
advance beyond the stage of concern with neurotic symptoms
and their causes, and to begin to consider the deeper meaning
of the symptoms, that is, their constructive aspect. A constructive view of a symptom means trying to see what it is that
the symptom is symbolically attempting to accomplish—to
what psychological need is it responding?

Looking at a symptom in this way corresponds to Jung's
"purposive view" of neurosis. Jung accepted first of all the
important psychoanalytic precept that neurotic and psychotic
symptoms rest on a base of conflict between the instinctive

nature of man and the demands imposed upon him by the society in which he lives. He then moved on another step. He was not content only to analyze every neurotic and psychotic symptom from the point of view of determining where it came from, why it got started, and how it worked, as he perceived that Freud had done. Jung also wanted to know where the symptoms might be leading the patient, that is, what unconscious purpose might be operating. He believed that the way to uncover meaning in events and developments was to observe the direction in which they were pointing, that is, to look for the purposive aspect of the symptom.

Thus Jung was willing to consider and probe the early history of the child, not as an end in itself, and not even to discover clues leading back to traumatic events that, being repressed, acted to sensitize points in the psyche which would form the grounds for later psychic disturbances. His major interest in infantile experience was to discern in it patterns which, established at a very early age, proceeded to give form to future thought and behavior. His concern was not alone to establish the *causes* of neuroses, but rather to be able to find in them some hint as to the *direction* in which they were leading the patient. The "cure" of the symptoms was not necessarily the most essential matter. In Bill's case, for example, his homosexuality might have been regarded by some as the symptom that needed to be cured. I would have regarded his withdrawal from homosexual relationship at a time when he was just beginning on that road as anything but "cure," even if it could have been accomplished. Rather, I felt that by regarding that kind of relationship as a necessary stage of development—out of his isolation from all human relationships in-depth toward a state of being willing to offer himself openly to another person—as something positive, the way was left open for possible heterosexual development in the future. In any case one would say that the neurosis had a purposive aspect, namely to lead him out of his social alienation; therefore it could be allowed to play itself out until such time as it would no longer be needed.

I made the statement earlier that the reasons a person gives

for wanting to enter analysis are rarely the true reasons. They
are, without a doubt, the conscious reasons, and the would-be
analysand is completely sincere in advancing them. Whether
he offers marital problems, or coming to terms with the death
of a member of his family, or not being able to succeed in
his work, or drinking too much, or sexual impotence, or a
generalized feeling of anxiety—it all boils down to a truth
which seems deceptively simple but is in fact complicated and
all-encompassing. It is that he has looked at himself and does
not like the person he has become, and that he believes that
somewhere there is in him the possibility of being another
sort of person, the one he was meant to be.

That second entity was united with the first at some point
in time, perhaps in early childhood, perhaps in adolescence
under the aegis of an admired friend or an inspiring teacher.
It may have been recognized as a peaceful way of being, or
a way of seeing the world that was wide and full of wonder;
or it may have been seen in terms of devotion to some idea,
some purpose. In the struggle for material possessions, for personal achievement, for social position or for the favors of an
entrancing lover, the second entity was sacrificed—the birthright for the mess of pottage. For some this meant the determined putting away of the dreams of youth, and sometimes
that unique entity of personality simply slipped away unnoticed, leaving a sense of quiet despair, which primitive people have termed the "loss of soul." Those people of an ancient
tribal culture would try by their own means to call back that
mysterious entity that gave life its zest and energy but, failing
this, they would seek out the witch-doctor or shaman for help.
Such a man, or woman in some cases, was one who had been
chosen for a life of dedication to the world of non-corporeal
reality—chosen for this not by any group but by some psychic
or spiritual manifestation of a particular quality of being that
set him apart from the other members of the tribe. It could
be an illness, a physical impairment, an ability to see visions.
He had to be prepared for his vocation by undergoing an
arduous period of isolation and personal sacrifice, taking into
himself the sufferings of his people and living them through.

Contemporary man experiences something very like the feelings of ennui, lowered vitality, being "boxed-in" that sent the primitive in search of the wise one of the tribe to get back his soul. Today, there are many self-proclaimed wise ones, from the Pied Pipers of instant intimacy to the purveyors of instant salvation. Yet how many are willing to involve themselves with one suffering individual for as long as it takes to help him come together again, and to reunite the splintered fragments?

Besides, the task is not merely to restore what is lost. In becoming lost, the "soul" (I do not know a better word for that central guiding aspect of the unconscious, the nature of which we may have only a dim awareness) has ceased to be the connecting ribbon of a road between a man as he knows himself and the vast unknown and unknowable. It needs not only to be restored to what it was before, but it needs to serve as a travelers' highway in which a continuous and busy intercourse between the ego and the unconscious may take place. In this active and reciprocal relationship neither the ego nor the unconscious will remain as it was in the past.

The change that may be brought about in the analytic process, the dialectic between the ego and the unconscious, may come close to its true potential; if so, it will result in a transformation of the personality. This transformation is not achieved through the efforts of an outside agent; the analyst, for instance, does not "make it happen." Rather, the analyst is there to help in enabling the self-regulating aspect of the psyche to function. He will take the side of the unconscious when the ego of the analysand is in the foreground attempting to control everything. On the other hand, when the analysand is floundering out of control in the grip of overwhelming unconscious material, the analyst may align himself on the side of the ego, and offer whatever strength may be needed to enable the totality of the personality to survive.

The intervention of the analyst, however, is a subtle matter, for he may not allow the initiative to be taken from the analysand. He is there, with his strength, when the situation demands more than the analysand is able to muster. But, for the most part, the process is carried on by the analysand, and by following the leads provided from his unconscious as well as from the data of his daily living experience. Contrary to what many people believe when they enter analysis, the analysand is encouraged to lead the process in his own way. Analysis is not something that an analyst "does to" a person. I am reminded of an initial dream which was brought by a patient to his second analytical session: *I was lying on a huge butcher's block, naked, with my hands tied to the corners above my head and my feet tied to the opposite corners. Someone was standing over me with a great knife, poised to draw and quarter me.* This dream suggests that the would-be analysand conceived of analysis on the medical model, with psychotherapy as a form of treatment—a radical form to say the least!

Another initial dream was more optimistic, yet to the point: *I had bought a new car, but I did not know how to drive it. A woman told me to get behind the wheel and she would show me what to do. At first I was frightened, but she said, "We will go slowly at first until you get used to it, and after a while you will get the feel of it." I followed her instructions until I was convinced that I would soon be in control. After a while she said, "Now it is time for us to look under the hood."*

Gradually throughout the analytic process, the analysand learns to recognize the many and varied aspects of himself that were unconscious before. These vary in their acceptability—those which come from the dark repressed side may be fought intensely, while those which offer promise may be embraced with joy. The excitement of analysis is that one never knows what may be presented—but this fact is sure, the most evil and disgusting images are capable of being redeemed, while the treasures that were hard to attain may easily be lost again to the unconscious. Perhaps this suggests one reason why the analysand at times exerts so much resistance to the analytic process.

Resistance disguises itself behind many masks: they range from minor symptomatic actions such as being late or missing appointments, to raising spurious arguments to rationalize behavior, forgetting to bring dreams or swamping the analyst with dreams, tight-lipped silences or compulsive talking, rejecting the analyst's interpretations out of hand or accepting everything the analyst says like a "good pupil" who is looking for teacher's approval.

Psychotherapists of certain schools confront the patient immediately and excoriate him for his resistance to the therapeutic process. I would hesitate before doing so. I often wonder, when I become aware of resistance in the patient and find in myself the tendency to call him to account, whether it is possible that secretly I feel rejected by the patient. Could I, unconsciously of course, be asking myself, "How can this person who is so disturbed and who functions so uncertainly feel anything but eagerness to listen to me and learn from my wisdom? He *has* to be broken of this dastardly habit." I hope I am able to avoid this hubris at all costs, and if I sometimes do, it is only that I am acutely aware that I could easily commit this sin were I to forget for a moment that I am fully capable of it!

It seems to me that I, as analyst, must regard my analysand as though I were an anthropologist, and he a native, exploring the unknown regions of his psyche, where the territory is as yet unmapped. As psychotherapist, I may have a wide variety of experience gained from other expeditions, and I may know in general what sort of equipment to take, and what kinds of dangers I must be on the lookout for. But the person with me is the one who knows, and knows in depth, the terrors of his particular wilderness, and where they may be lurking. Therefore, I as psychotherapist, am open to being led by my patient, to allowing my patient ample opportunities to structure the forays. There will be a preliminary period in which each participant in the search must learn the rudiments of the other's language, in order that we may communicate to each other the ways in which each of us may contribute to the joint endeavor. Sometimes a patient, inexperienced in leading the search, may be reluctant to expose the secret places. I must accept in my own mind the reality that the native has been there a long time, and knows all the paths

and the terrain, also all the places to hide. The native may
have his own way of doing things, and one day he may not
arrive at the appointed time at the anthropologist's hut, with
his burden balanced on his head. What then?

A therapist, with this image before him, will ask himself
while he is waiting for the knock at the door, why is he still
not here when it is so late? Is there something in *his life*
which is distracting him from our arranged appointment? Or
is it possible that I may have done something to put him
off? Did I frighten him last time? Did I ask too much from
him? Did I in some way insult him? Did I fail to give him
credit when he cleared a new path? Did I fail to take his
hand when he reached out to me? So then the therapist does
not approach the patient next time only with the questions:
Why did *you* make yourself late; or dodge an interpretation;
or forget to bring your dreams. He will also ask, What could
I have done to bring this about? He will seek out information
from the patient at such times as to how he reacted to the
last session, what he took away from it, how he understood
what occurred, and what happened in the interim between
the sessions.

There is a time in the process of analysis, when resistance
on the part of the patient may be a welcome sign for the
analyst. This is a fact that I did not learn from any book, but
from one of my analysands. I was discussing the question of
resistance with a perceptive young woman, and I was saying
that I did not think the analyst needs to be in a hurry to
break down the patient's resistance. To this she heartily
agreed, and added: "What the patient often is resisting is a
therapist's attempt to get him to give up his independent
responsibility for how he conducts his life, and his independent standpoint."

2

COMPLEXES BY DAY
AND
DEMONS BY NIGHT

I find that Jung's "complex theory" and the related ideas concerning psychic energy are not easy to comprehend from an exclusively pragmatic point of view. On the other hand, if one can admit to being open-minded enough to allow for the possible existence of demons, many difficulties in understanding the nature of complexes can be overcome.

What Jung has called *complexes* are certain constellations of psychic elements (ideas, opinions, convictions, etc.) that are grouped around emotionally sensitive areas. I understand the complex as consisting of two factors. First, there is a nuclear element which acts as a magnet, and second, there is a cluster of associations that are attracted to the nucleus. I see the nuclear element itself as made up of two components. One is determined by experience, and so is causally related to the environment. The other is determined by the disposition of the individual in question, and is innate; its foundation is basic to the structure of the psyche. When the disposition of the individual at some point in his life confronts an experiential situation which he can in no way handle, a psychic trauma occurs. It is as though you bump up against an object—most times there is enough resilience so that no harm is done or, if you are temporarily out of balance, your equilibrium is quickly regained. But if the bump is hard

enough, and if you were totally unprepared for it, you may
be cut or bruised or broken, and the area may remain sensitive. Then every time you touch it, you will feel the hurt;
you will favor it and try to protect it by your behavior. If,
nevertheless, someone hits you on the same spot, you will
cry out in pain. A psychic wound acts in somewhat the same
way, but the whole process is largely, if not totally, unconscious. Therefore you feel its effects, even though you do not
know the meaning and the cause of the suffering. When in
analysis I trace the predisposing factor to its roots, I am likely
to discover an elemental characteristic of the individual's nature, a *given*. It is not the superficial psychic jolts and bumps
that occur which give rise to the formation of complexes, but
only those wounds which lay bare the vital, pattern-forming
elements of the psyche, the elements which Jung has called
the *archetypes*. Those experiences which threaten our deepest
beliefs—in our gods and in ourselves—those are the ones which
give rise to complexes.

Jung proposed that the nuclear element of the complex is
characterized by its feeling-tone, the emphasis arising from
the intensity of the emotion involved. This emphasis, this
intensity, can be expressed in terms of energy, a value quantity. In direct relation to the amount of energy, the energic
quantity, is the capacity of the nucleus to draw associations
to it, thereby forming a complex. The more energic quantity,
the more associations, hence the more material from everyday
life experiences gets drawn into the complex.

Only when you are experiencing a complex can you evaluate
its feeling tone, and then only to the degree that the nuclear
element itself is *conscious*. Ordinarily, with some awareness
of what in your nature and what in your life experiences have
led to this psychic sensitivity, it is possible for you as an
individual to make a reasonably good adaptation to a complex. You may either structure your life so as to avoid situations which contribute to the production of excessive psychic
tension or, if that is not possible or desirable, you may learn
how to deal with the tensions that the complex-laden situation
produces. But if, as frequently occurs, the nuclear element

is *unconscious*, then it becomes impossible to achieve a subjective awareness of the feeling-tone in the experience through which you as an individual must move.

As a complex becomes conscious, little by little it is possible to disengage its components and so to defuse the bomb, as it were. The bomb is still there, or at least its component parts are there, but it is not now so dangerous. An unconscious complex continues to add more and more to its nucleus and associated contents, thus building up increasing pressure in the volatile bundle. I believe that it is this sense of intolerable pressure that brings people into psychotherapy, although when they express the feeling-tone of the complex to me it is most likely to come out in terms of a specific problem or symptom.

The concept of the complex was Jung's original contribution to psychotherapy, and Freud acknowledged his debt to his younger colleague. In his 1901 study *The Psychopathology of Everyday Life*, where Freud described the way in which "complexes" interfere with our conscious intent by causing embarrassing slips of the tongue, misreadings, forgetting of people's names and other errors and bungled actions, he used the explanatory expression "circles of thought." The word "complexes," replacing this in the 1907 edition, marks the beginning of Jung's influence on Freud.[1] The primary complex upon which Freud concentrated his efforts throughout his work was the well-known "Oedipus complex," centering around the mother-son relationship. The ramification of this complex is seen in the "castration concept" with which Freud dealt extensively, and the "Elektra complex" which describes the problems in the father-daughter relationship paralleling the Oedipus complex. Alfred Adler, in his use of this concept, focused his attention on the "inferiority complex" with all its associated "power complexes," these latter conceived of as neurotic means of overcoming inferiority feelings. Jung carried the concept of the complex much further than either Freud or Adler, pointing out its damming effects in many and various phases of life. He paid particular attention to the "mother-daughter complexes" which he specifically described

in his essay on "Psychological Aspects of the Mother Archetype."[2] He also called attention to the complex of "possession" which often manifests itself in a belief in spirits:
"Spirits are complexes of the collective unconscious which
appear when the individual loses his adaptation to reality, or
which seek to replace the inadequate attitude of a whole people by a new one. They are therefore either pathological fantasies or new but as yet unknown ideas."[3] Other complexes,
according to Jung, are ideas with which people identify themselves and their endeavors, hence the "saviour complex," the
"healer complex," and the "prophet complex," to name only
a few. Even the ego, according to Jung, might better be called
the "ego complex" as it is a specific self-concept with which
the individual identifies himself and which draws to itself
certain very specific ideas. A list of complexes could be extensive, for it would cover every type of feeling-toned idea
that tends to create a highly charged atmosphere of thought
or behavior.

Some of the more abstruse papers in Analytical Psychology
have been written on the subject of complexes, dealing with
principles which, I readily confess, I have found difficult to
integrate intellectually. Experiencing the complex is much
easier in the analytic session, when you recognize its presence
in unconscious material. Dreams often provide access to these
apparently split-off portions of the psyche which make their
appearance as separate entities, often in some non-human or
mythological form. Sometimes they point the way to long-
buried experiences which, although forgotten, have retained
their power to create neurotic disturbances and interfere with
the natural functioning of the psychic life of the individual.

Such was the experience of Cecelia, a bright young college
woman. When I began analysis with her she was living with a
man who was rather limited in personality and quite immature. Cecelia had been "lost" in the hippie-psychedelic world
since she dropped out of college two years before in her first
semester. Her story is so commonplace these days that it need
not be repeated in detail. She was the daughter of upper-
middle-class parents who were themselves unhappy and un-

loving. The mother was a self-righteous woman who always knew how things should be done and said so, expecting all members of the family to conform to her requirements in everything from what to wear to what political opinions to hold. The father, quiet, introverted, and beaten-down, said little at home, except now and then when he tried impotently to modify the strenuous demands of his wife. With Cecelia he was always patient, permissive, and non-directive.

The year before, a crisis had occurred. Cecelia was caught smoking marijuana by her mother. Her father admitted he had known about it for a long time, that he didn't regard it as terrible. His attitude only infuriated the mother. She severely reprimanded Cecelia, calling her all sorts of degrading names. Soon after this, Cecelia ran away from home, and shortly became involved with an older man who was deep in the drug scene. This man introduced her to acid, mescaline, group sex. Cecelia had some bad trips and became disoriented and paranoid. When her parents finally caught up with her they consigned Cecelia to a mental hospital. A couple of months later she came out sullen, angry at the world, but convinced that there had to be a better way to live than the way she had been living for the past year.

In the course of the drug experience, by a circuitous route she had found her way to reading Jung. While entranced by the visionary world she had glimpsed under LSD, she had come across the book *The Psychedelic Experience, a manual based on the Tibetan Book of the Dead* by Timothy Leary, Ralph Metzner, and Richard Alpert. The authors included in their introduction tributes to three men: Dr. W. Y. Evans-Wentz, Tibetan scholar and translator of the *Book of the Dead*, Lama Anagarika Govinda, one of the world's leading interpreters of Tibetan Buddhism, and Carl G. Jung. Cecelia's introduction to the drug world may have provided her with instant ecstasy, but as time went on she discovered that instant ecstasy is not necessarily followed by instant enlightenment. She wanted to find out what others had to say about enlightenment. She began to read Jung, and discovered that his way to a deeper understanding of the mysterious processes

of the unconscious was far from instantaneous, but that it
offered a slow and painstaking way of entering into a productive relationship with those processes. She also found in her
reading that not only Jung but also Evans-Wentz and Lama
Govinda were men who had gone through the discipline of
academic study, learning the techniques of discrimination and
order which are necessary to transform a creative flash into
a creation of substance.

After the "easy way" did not work for Cecelia, she decided
to come into analysis and submit herself to the difficult developmental way. She returned to college, studying, often
chafing at some of the requirements, but expressing her discomfort by talking about her problems in a *responsible* way
(by this I mean seeking out the facts in the situation rather
than blustering about in generalities and baseless opinions),
writing poetry and prose, and doing some interesting painting.

She continued to have paranoid feelings at times, and she
would become angry when her wandering thoughts became
temptations that distracted her from doing what she felt was
necessary to rebuild her life. The young man with whom she
was then living was a fellow student whom she met recently at
the university. He wanted to marry her. On one level she was
all for the marriage, but she would frequently pick fights with
him so that it seemed as though she were trying to alienate
him. Whenever she was encouraged to reflect on the apparent
inconsistency of her behavior, she would insist that she was
doing everything possible to improve the relationship. Cecelia
found his presence supportive at the time, but she was not
sure she wanted to live her life with him.

One night she had the following dream: *There is a big
black she-bear. She is fighting with a man. The man, with the
help of another man, stuffs the bear down in a hole. Then I
go and get a gun. One of the men shoots the bear over and
over. They drag her out of the hole and she is still a little bit
alive, so they shoot her again. There is blood all over the
bear. Then there is a large wedding. Everyone is there. The
bride comes out. She is very ugly and she is sneezing. Her*

mother puts a fake fur dress and coat in brown and black over her wedding dress.

Cecelia's dream expressed her feeling of the heavy and threatening power that constantly opposed her conscious wishes. The power was female and inexorable—whatever you did it could not be done away with. The power of the masculine element in her life was of little use against the dreadful she-bear. Cecelia tried to help by getting a gun. She thought that she could destroy the rough and cruel animal but, since it was a part of her, she could not do so without jeopardizing the totality of herself. Stuffing the bear down a hole was symbolic of trying to get rid of some element in life that could not be tolerated. In this case the she-bear image may have referred on one level to the girl's mother, in her menacing aspect. But the mother-complex had over the years drawn to it so many experiences and feelings and attitudes that it was now well covered over, and the original image that attracted these contents was no longer recognizable. A whole complex of ideas relating to the terrible power, Mother, her cruelty, and her blind-instinctive protectiveness of her young, was represented by this brutal creature. The rebellious aspects of the girl, the runaway who attempted to deal with the problem by avoidance, were symbolized by the men who shot the bear while she was down in the hole.

The effort to drag the bear to the surface suggests the analytic process of bringing up that which is hidden. Here, again, the purpose seemed to be to demolish the destructive complex. Living with the young man, in direct opposition to the mother's wishes was a bloody business, and all the more when we see how the young man's personality resembled in some ways the girl's weak and ineffectual father. In the end of the dream the bride came out and was very ugly and sneezing. The *negative-mother-complex* interfered with the expression of that beautiful femininity which is the traditional quality associated with a bride on her wedding day. Sneezing is said to be an age-old tactic for getting rid of devils or demons— which is why we say "God bless you" whenever one of those infernal creatures is supposedly let loose. The mother complex, as expressed by the image of the mother of the bride, had not been done away with, only transformed into a different image, but she still went about her nefarious business, attempting to hang onto the girl the empty bearskin, trappings of the cruel and dominating female.

After working through the negative-mother-complex with Cecelia for some time, it began to come clear that the bear symbolized that inner aspect of her nature which had never been sufficiently fed with warmth and affection, and therefore continued to demand what it needed in an unreasonable way. The angry devouring quality which had become associated with Cecelia's own personality had to be given what is required—and Cecelia had to learn to pay attention to it. She began to take an interest in her home, making it a very personal expression of her own interests and skills. She renewed her interest in painting and her works were hung where she could enjoy them. She designed a beautiful mural for her wall, in the form of a sun-circle which represented to her a new cycle of life, a new day and a new chance every morning. She enjoyed her courses in eastern religions and English literature, and wrote some very good term papers. Now and then she composed a poem, just for herself. The creative-maternal began gradually to overcome the destructive-maternal.

Some may say of her that she was using her art and her craft to sublimate her neurotic tendencies. But I would not tell her that. I cannot imagine that she would settle for that, she who has fought the battle for deliverance from the terrible mother.

Anyone familiar with Freud's *Interpretation of Dreams* will readily see that Cecelia's dream could as easily have been interpreted in the traditional psychoanalytic manner. Her difficulty in relating sexually to her young man could have been seen in purely personal terms, rather than in terms of the devouring mother who negates the creative-maternal aspect of the feminine. Cecelia might have been described as being in a regressed psychosexual stage, still living in a pregenital state and unable to progress beyond an oral dependency on her mother. The details of the interpretation that might be offered are not important here. What is important is the difference in thrust that occurs, depending on whether you emphasize the cause of the complex and so solve the problem of etiology (i.e., origin, especially of a disease), or whether you see the complex as a dynamic indicator pointing toward the potential development of the dreamer.

Jung discovered the complex very early in his career, while he was working at the Burghölzli Clinic in Zurich as a resident in psychiatry. When he arrived at the Clinic in 1900, he was already engaged in the writing of his doctoral dissertation, *On the Psychology and Psychopathology of So-Called Occult Phenomena*.[4] During the day he was engaged in seeing patients and in working on a research project under the direction of his chief, Dr. Eugen Bleuler, whose great contribution to psychiatric history was the monograph *Dementia Praecox or The Group of Schizophrenias*. By night Jung was absorbed in the problems of S.W., the young lady who had produced the amazing séances and the aberrant behavior which had been of such great interest to him in his medical-school years.

As Jung described S.W., she had a pale face with large dark eyes that gave out a peculiar, penetrating look. Although her body was slight and of delicate construction, she appeared to be in good health. Her typical behavior for the most part was quite reserved, but there were times when she would become engulfed in the most exuberant joy or exaltation. Her education was extremely limited. She came from a home where there were few books about and where the members of the family were all artisans or business people with very limited interests. Furthermore, she was of average or slightly below average intelligence, with no special talents. She enjoyed handwork or just sitting around daydreaming, when there were no chores to be done. So, superficially at least, there was nothing remarkable about this teen-ager which would give rise to expectations that she would become a "visionary" living as much in a strange world beyond the ordinary senses as in the usual world.

But there were differences. A pattern existed in her family

which would suggest the acceptance as normal of what we would probably call paranormal phenomena. A young child tends to accept as a matter of course the behavior of members of its family, however outlandish that behavior may appear to outsiders. Thus, S.W. had no way of knowing that waking hallucinations were peculiar, to say the least. How could she, when her paternal grandfather, a very intelligent clergyman, frequently recounted his visions in the form of whole dramatic scenes complete with dialogues? Or when her paternal grand-mother was subject to fainting fits that were nearly always followed by trance states during which she uttered prophe-cies? Her father is described by Jung in his case history as "an odd, original person with bizarre ideas," and two of his brothers were much the same. All three had waking hallucina-tions and were given to premonitions. Her mother was a bor-derline psychotic, one sister a hysteric and called a "visionary," and another sister had a heart condition that was described as having a strong psychosomatic element.

In a household such as S.W.'s, the rational aspects of life must have existed side by side with the non-rational, or even the irrational. Missing—or, at best, faulty—would have been the barriers which early training and education erect between fact and fantasy in a child's mind. Inner vision must have been granted at least equal validity with experience in the objective world. No one would say to the child who "saw" shapes in the dark, "Don't worry, darling, they aren't really there, they're *just* imaginary." On the contrary, the images of the night would have been reinforced with great interest by the parents, and perhaps even with the suggestion that they surely belonged to a world of spirit which sometimes became manifest to a chosen few. In S.W.'s family, the possibility of contacting the "spirit world" was looked upon as a very special gift, rather than as potentially dangerous. S.W. was, as I have indicated, a girl of little education or cultural achievement. The intellectual world was fairly closed to her. But the door to the non-rational events of life was wide open. She saw them as events which simply occurred; it did not seem to require any special effort on her part to experience them.

This "spirit world" is one with which many conventionally educated Americans have a great deal of trouble. Most young children have imaginary playmates, look for images in the clouds, are careful not to offend the spirits ("Step on a crack, you break your mother's back"), and have countless other ways of paying respects to the non-rational part of life. But early childhood education is a brainwashing carried on mostly under the influences of child-development experts schooled in watered-down Freudian concepts that seek to explain superstitions as the result of certain unconscious conflicts—as if perhaps on an unconscious level an aggressive, rebellious child sometimes really does want to break his mother's back, while at the same time loving that mother dearly and needing her. The demonic tendency in the unconscious has to be split off from consciousness because the child cannot admit to the conflict within himself. Therefore the spirit would have to be seen on the outside, and it would have to be propitiated.

Our rational parents, having been well indoctrinated with the belief that every event has a cause, believe that they have understood the causes of superstitions and fantasies. These "causes" can be traced back to undesirable tendencies existing in the individual. A rational education roots out these tendencies, exposes them as destructive aspects of the unconscious, as if exposure or even understanding makes an end of them. Freud's essay on "Determinism, Belief in Chance and Superstition," in *The Psychopathology of Everyday Life* was instrumental in promoting the view that it could. Its influence has been tremendously important in changing the course of education. It translated into psychological terms the voices of the Enlightenment that called for the elimination of the superstitious, the mystical, and the non-rational in the Western intellectual tradition.

S.W. had been exposed to none of this new thought. It is not surprising that when she heard at home and from friends about table turning that she would take an interest in it and ask to be allowed to take part in the experiments. Half jokingly and half seriously, she joined the circle of family and friends, sat in the darkness and felt movement in the table around which they were all seated. In the midst of all this she announced that she was receiving communications, and that these were being transmitted to her through the spirit of her grandfather. Those present, and among them the medical student, were surprised by the clerical tone of the messages, which seemed to be "in character" with the old man. We piece together some of what must have taken place from Jung's dissertation, based on his notes taken after returning home from the séances.

He described the trance state, which he called "somnambulism," after his first observation in August 1899. He spoke of the event as an "attack" and apparently regarded the whole matter as the manifestation of a psychiatric illness. Whatever else it might be, he did not feel free to conjecture at that time.

At the onset of the attack, S.W. would grow pale, slowly sink to the floor or into a chair, and close her eyes. Then she would assume the state of suspended animation and have apparent loss of voluntary control, clinically known as catalepsy. When she at last began to speak, she would be generally relaxed, her eyelid reflexes remaining normal, as well as her sense of touch, so that when someone brushed against her unexpectedly she would start as though frightened. At this stage she was no longer aware of her usual personality, as evidenced by her failure to react when called upon by her name. She took the roles of various dead friends and relatives and carried them off with astounding accuracy, according to those present. Gradually her performances built up into whole dramatic scenes full of passion and glowing rhetoric. Sometimes she would even expound with great fluency in literary German, a language which she spoke with hesitation and fumbling in her normal state. Her speeches would be accompanied by grandiloquent gestures; sometimes they would erupt into ecstatic fervor. Invariably she spoke of herself in the third person, and when she used first person it was only to prophesy another outburst.

S.W.'s mediumistic performances followed a pattern familiar to anyone who has read occult literature. It would not be unexpected that they might occur in a girl of her background. Especially interesting to Jung, however, were certain visionary experiences which she described to him in their private meetings. She told him that between being awake and falling asleep as she lay in bed, she would experience a light flooding the room. Shining white figures would detach themselves from the brightness around them. The women wore flowing robes girdled at the waist and turbans wrapped about their heads. As time went on she had begun to find that the spirits were already there when she went to bed. After that she began seeing them in the daylight, though only for fleeting moments. The visions filled her with a feeling of unearthly bliss. Only on rare occasions, and then at night, did she see terrifying images of a demonic character.

Jung became convinced that S.W.'s visions had a reality of their own, the nature of which he could only surmise. As the weird experiences developed they seemed perfectly natural to her, and she told him, "I do not know if what the spirits say and teach me is true, nor do I know if they really are the people they call themselves; but that my spirits exist is beyond question. I speak to them about everything I wish as naturally as I'm talking to you. They must be real." Yet the young girl who was seeing the apparitions was quite different from the one who lived a normal unremarkable life in between times. Jung saw that she was leading a "double life" with two personalities existing side by side or in succession, each continually striving for mastery.[5]

Jung's interpretations of the girl's activities in her trance states were made under scientific conditions which included meticulous observation and classification of data. He described in detail all the symptoms: the headaches that preceded the attacks, the cold pallor associated with them, and lapses of attention suggestive of epileptoid disorder. He also described the various manifestations: in addition to the visions there were automatic writing, glossolalia (speaking in strange incomprehensible tongues) and cryptomnesia (the appearance in consciousness of memory images which are not recognized as such—but which appear as original creations).

His participation, however, had to go beyond the objective, scientific approach, for he felt that he would have to involve himself more fully in order to get a feeling for what was happening. He entered into the table turning himself, noting the effect of verbal suggestion on the subject. He also experimented with the even more potent effect of a very slight push or a series of light rhythmical taps of his own. The movement of the table would grow stronger and continue even when he had stopped applying the stimulus. Jung explained this as a partial hypnosis and compared it to methods often used by hypnotists to produce an exhibition of automatism.

He took the factor of suggestibility into account, as well as the questionable mental health of the subject. All of this could explain well enough some aspects of the alteration of the states of consciousness, but he still knew nothing about the sources of the *content* of what S.W. spoke about. As her condition became more extreme, it appeared that she was developing a highly systematized "mystic science." She began to hint that the spirits had revealed to her the nature of strange forces in the world and the Beyond.

She decided that she could trust Jung, and after a while she offered him a sheet of paper upon which she had written numerous names. These were neologisms purporting to describe the nature of the forces which guide the universe, these being both material and spiritual forces acting upon man and the physical world. Jung diagramed the entire system according to her instructions, and traced her patterns of word association that may have led to the coining of the words. They were a conglomeration of word fragments from physics, astrology and mythology. At the same time he was interested in the construction of the system itself, as an example of the way unconscious processes lent themselves to an attempt to decipher the mysteries of the creation and functioning of our world. He knew from his classical studies that myths of cosmogony arise in every culture, and often lay the basis for the way in which the culture develops. Could his fascination with the communications of S.W. have had to do with his recognition that myths occur not only in a collective setting, but that they can also arise spontaneously in an individual? Perhaps even some of his personal experiences, for example his recollection of his childhood dream of the phallus enthroned, may have prepared him for the emergence of the mythic where the person is not bound by the constraints of a conventional consciousness.

S.W. produced other extravaganzas. One featured a frivolous gentleman with a North German accent who attempted to charm all the ladies present. Another was the report of the instructions of the spirits on the subject of the geography of Mars where, she learned, everyone travels by flying machines which have long been in existence there. (This is especially interesting in view of the fact that this report preceded by several years the Wright brothers' first flight in a power-driven, heavier-than-air machine.) Reincarnation also played its role in the complex systems she related, through a spiritual being called "Ivenes," who embodied herself about every two hundred years all the way back to biblical days. She wove a complicated tapestry of narration which involved all members of her family in their present and previous existences, surprising and baffling Jung and the others with her "amazing aplomb and . . . clever use of details which S.W. must have heard or picked up from somewhere."[6]

There are hints in Jung's dissertation that while he was pondering these matters he was beginning to formulate in his own mind the concept of a many-faceted unconscious which, when activated, could yield up a wealth of material which is not to be accounted for solely by a theory of repression. But something had occurred which inhibited Jung's tendency to speculate further at that time. After the productions of S.W. had reached their climax with the description of "Ivenes" and her retinue of relatives and reincarnations, a gradual decline became noticeable. The ecstasies grew more and more vacuous and the phenomena became shallower, with the characters who had formerly been well differentiated becoming now confused and amorphous. In short order the communications became uncertain and cautious, and the rather prosaic adolescent began to come through the disguises.

It had become noticeable to Jung that she now began visibly to force her "spirits" to act, and the performances soon took on the character of a fraud. At this point Jung lost interest and withdrew, much to his subsequent regret.

Jung conjectured that the various personalities which had emerged, specifically the ones which were clearly defined and appeared with regularity and continuity, were possibly representations of unconscious aspects which had become disassociated from the subject's conscious personality. During the séance, the subject in the process of verbalizing is accessible to suggestion which acts hypnotically to isolate the speech center. For example, the question to the medium, "Who is speaking?" can act as a suggestion for synthesizing the unconscious personality. He was able to demonstrate how the unconscious personality gradually builds itself up through suggestion, and how the very formation of unconscious personalities has enormous suggestive power on the development of further unconscious personalities. He conjectured that when the split-off unconscious personality emerged in a séance, the emotion connected with it had to be transformed into something not seeming to be a part of the subject's own feelings. Could it, therefore, be finding symbolic expression in the guise of clairvoyants and other remarkable figures long dead? Now for the first time in his writings Jung mentions Freud: "Whether this offers a parallel to the results of Freud's dream investigations must remain unanswered, for we have no means of judging how far the emotion in question may be considered 'repressed.' "[7]

As to the visual hallucinations, Jung looked for a possible basis for S.W.'s visions just as she was dropping off to sleep. Where silence favors auditory hallucinations, darkness favors visual images. The expectation that one *could* see a spirit causes an excitation of the visual sphere. Then appear the "entoptic phenomena," slight amounts of light in apparent darkness which seem to assume shapes, especially in the presence of a vivid imagination.

What is especially important about this initial published work at the beginning of Jung's career is his assumption that the receptivity of the unconscious for strange and mysterious experiences far exceeds that of the conscious mind. Jung achieved this insight in a day when the concept of the unconscious was only beginning to be talked about in the field of psychology (although it had been well known to artists and poets and playwrights and certainly to the romantics of all ages).

Naturally Jung discussed the progress of his dissertation from time to time with his chief. Eugen Bleuler must have had mixed feelings as he examined the work of the young doctor who seemed drawn to deal with material which was highly questionable in terms of its suitability for a scientific treatise. No doubt he was fully aware of the balance that was needed when he steered Carl Jung into working on the studies in word association at the very time that S.W. and "Ivenes," and the revelations of mystic sciences were consuming a large portion of his attention.

The work on the Association Experiment occupied an enormous amount of Jung's energy while he was at the Burghölzli Clinic. It was as though he were willing to put all the fury of his creative energy into proving that the responses could be measured and evaluated. Perhaps he was weary of pondering the questions that had been raised for him by S.W., and still more by the mysterious "Ivenes," who arose out of somewhere, certainly not out of the past experiences of the simple-minded, poorly educated fifteen-year-old girl.

The Word Association Experiment was one of the first psychological projective tests ever devised, if not the very first. The term "projective test" was not yet in use at the time, and the word "experiment" was used instead of "test" with reference to this work, for the reason that "test" suggests that there can be only one correct answer to the question or problem posed, while "experiment" suggests that there is no specific answer expected but that the subject is free to respond spontaneously to what is asked of him. Furthermore, an experiment must be open-ended since it is conducted for the purpose of discovering something that was not known before, while the purpose of a test is to find out how close the person being tested can come to giving the response desired by the tester.

In the Association Experiment, the clinic patient was told first of all that this was not a test, there were no right answers or wrong answers, and there was to be no competitive evaluation. The patient was given one hundred words—one by one—and he was to respond to each word as quickly as possible with the first word that came into his mind. He was told that his responses would be noted and the response time would be clocked. After this was done, the list of words was given to the patient a second time, and this time he was asked to reply using the same word he gave the first time if possible. The purpose of the experiment was to discover the role of word associations in establishing diagnoses for mental patients.

Professor Bleuler had stated, "Every psychical activity rests upon the interchange of the material derived from sensation and from memory traces, upon *associations*." He was convinced that apart from the somewhat questionable capacity to perceive pain and pleasure, which is perhaps inherent in the smallest organism, any psychic activity without association was unthinkable. He had expressed his amazement that "the proposition that our laws of thought are but rules of association is strangely enough still contested." He asserted that the laws of thought and the laws of association must seem almost identical, once it is realized that the laws of association are not so simple as to be exhausted by placing them in a few well-ordered categories (association by similarity, contrast, simultaneity, and so on). He was sure that every association in the thinking process is accompanied by an almost endless number of more or less distinct presentations. Among the associations that might present themselves could come those related to events from the past experiences of the individual. These might include specific events in his life or fantasy experiences which had occupied him at one time or another. Another rich source of associations might be the purposes or intentions of the individual which were too rudimentary to be recognized as thought. The mood of the subject could inhibit or else supply adequate associations. Bleuler concluded:

"On the activity of association there is mirrored the whole psychical essence of the past and of the present, with all their experiences and desires. It thus becomes an index of all the psychical processes which we have to decipher in order to understand the complete man."[8]

When questioned by his colleagues as to the possibility that he may have been overemphasizing the importance of the "small matter" of what association a certain word might evoke, Bleuler strained his proposition even further. He went on record as saying that in a certain sense "*every* psychical event, *every* movement, is only possible to that particular man with his particular past, in one definite way. Each single action represents the whole man: the endeavor to deduce the whole man from his handwriting, physiognomy, shape of his hand, his style, even the way he wears his shoes, is not altogether folly."[9]

As far as verifying Bleuler's hypotheses upon which the experiments were based, the work Jung and his associates carried on over a period of several years was a spectacular failure. Types of associations did not correlate in any significant way with various disease entities. There were a few exceptions, but on the whole the various types of associations as defined were spread throughout the normal and the patient population. As to reaction times, when these were averaged, it was found that, in general, men tended to respond slightly more quickly than women, and that educated people tended to respond slightly more quickly than the uneducated. But it was not possible to establish that patients' diseases could be diagnosed on the basis of the categories of their associations.

Pondering the disappointing results of his work, it occurred to Jung that he had failed to focus on one factor which had shown up in the experiments, namely, the great variation in response time from one word to another in individual patients. He found this to be true in normal subjects as well. While most stimulus words given would call forth responses in something between one and two-and-a-half seconds, certain words would produce a prolonged interval before the response, and some words would draw even a complete blank from the sub-

ject. Jung's question, "What does this mean?" proved to be
the seed for future development. And so, what had been a
descriptive theory of association now suddenly became a dynamic theory of association; the problem was no longer "What
sort of association is this?"—it was now, "How does the process
of association work, what promotes it, what interferes with
it, and why?"

The keys to the process of association, as Jung understood
them, were *intention* and *attention*. The conscious attitude
of most of the people most of the time is an intention to
associate one bit of information with another. This is what
thinking is in its simplest form, putting two and two together,
and also it is what thinking is in its more complicated forms.
While we intend to relate facts or concepts or ideas one to
another, we find that in order to do this successfully we have
to direct our attention. To the degree that we are attentive
to what we are hearing or reading or seeing, we are able to
think about it and draw meaningful inferences from it. In
the Association Experiment when the attention was focused
in on the word, the intention to respond promptly could be
carried out. There were words, however, which when pro-
nounced by the experimenter, brought about an unusual reaction, an interruption of attention. Such unusual reactions,
Jung thought, pointed to complexes. In addition to prolonged reaction time, there were other complex indicators.
These were first noted by Jung and later became some of
the classical diagnostic clues to be used thereafter in the practice of psychotherapy in practically all schools of thought.

Some of the complex indicators were: 1) reaction with more
than one word; 2) reaction against the instructions (this could
be related to distractions or could indicate limited intelligence); 3) mistakes in reproduction (these could suggest
avoidance or memory failure); 4) reaction expressed by a
change in facial expression (being caught unaware like a child
with his hand in the cookie jar); 5) reaction expressed by
laughing (there might be a displacement of affect as in attempting to cover up a painful association); 6) movement
of feet, body, or hands (suggestive of uneasiness, discomfort);

7) coughing or stammering (playing for time in order to find a secondary association in lieu of the first which came to mind); 8) insufficient reactions like "yes" or "no" (these could point to blocks making a genuine association impossible); 9) not reacting to the real meaning of the stimulus word (this would be a defense of the individual's image of himself); 10) habitual use of the same word (this too would point to avoidance, and possibly to stereotypical response to pressures); 11) response in a foreign language (here it would be important to find out what part the language played in the life of the individual); and lastly, 12) a total lack of reaction (for this is also a reaction, and a meaningful one; in psychotherapy "no-thing" is something).

So Jung was off on a whole new track, that of discovering how the presence of complexes in the mental patients subjected to the experiment interfered with the process of their associating words to one another. The same difficulty was experienced by other people who were not mental patients; and while the results were less dramatic than with the patients, they nevertheless supported the findings that disturbances of association come from interruptions of attention, which in turn result from collision with the complex. The pattern of associations and their interruptions points to the complex.

In the analytic process the trend of the patient's association is followed very closely by the analyst. By stimulating the process of associations through the asking of well-placed and open-ended questions, the associations can lead back to the complex and the complex can be unraveled to disclose its nuclear elements. But the patient does not speak in terms of complexes to his analyst; he is more likely to disclose his private demons, because that is frequently the way in which complexes appear. Let us take for an example the case of Paul.

Paul was the operator of an independent realty firm. He had several people working for him, but he was clearly in charge, and he handled most of the important transactions. He had made a great deal of money at various times in his life, often through questionable dealings. In the process he had lost friends and made important enemies. Now things were going badly for him, and he began therapy hoping to find an alternate way of viewing his life. His presenting complaint was severe depression and an absence of the energy and enthusiasm that had fired him previously. The analysis had been characterized by a series of "true confessions" about all his wrongdoing in the past, and punctuated by his expression of a desire to change, and of remorse for the sins and errors committed in making his outrageous fortune. With all the ventilation, there was no relief of the depression. I thought that there had to be a great deal more to come before we would begin to see daylight, so I waited for a clue. At last it came, in the form of the following dream: *I am sitting in the living room with my wife, talking about some problems I am trying to work out in my business. A small object is on the table in front of me, near the edge of the table. I think to myself—if this object falls off the table I'll have financial disaster, but if it stays on I'll be successful. If I don't touch it, it will be safe. But if the object were to get to the center of the table, I think, then it will be absolutely foolproof, secure. So I begin to move it gently toward the center of the table, but my thumb catches it and it falls off. Now I am sure that my unconscious controls my conscious mind through this device of making me move the object.*

I asked Paul if he ever had feelings in waking life similar to those that he had in the dream. He replied that he very often had the feeling that certain happenings in his life were omens, that they showed him how things were going to work out, and when they made their predictions there just never was any way out of what they predicted, they always seemed to work out in the way that he had known of beforehand. I asked him if he could recall any other instances, could he perhaps trace back to the first time when something of this nature happened to him?

He thought awhile and then said he thought he knew what might have been the first of this kind of experience. It had happened on a golf course. He had managed to play his way into a tournament by a combination of cheating when he thought he could get away with it, and a run of very good luck. Now he was in for the big money, but this time there was no chance to cheat, and although he was a good player, he was really outclassed. It would have to be a very lucky day if he were to have a chance of winning. And he wanted very much to win. He was in excellent physical shape and his competitive nature was honed up to its sharpest. He played well. He was, in fact, playing for all he was worth. Tension mounted. He had managed to tie his contender for the game, on the second to the last hole. His opponent teed off and set the ball well down on the fairway. Paul took careful aim, his ball landed near the other. The opponent had another good shot and landed on the green. Now Paul swung a little off, his ball dropped in the rough, and Paul began to pray. He told himself, now I'm really getting it. This is happening to me because of what I've been doing lately in my business. If I get out of the rough and win this hole and the match, I'll straighten out for once and for all, and stop this dirty business I've been involved in. By the time he had gotten to where his ball was, the bargain had been struck. The opponent made a long putt that wavered on the edge of the cup and stayed out. Paul was feeling relaxed and easy. He blasted off and came up onto the edge of the green. He knew now he could do no wrong. Then his opponent nudged his ball into the hole. Paul made a perfect putt and sank his own. The score was tied. The last hole was the best and smoothest Paul had ever played. He won the match by a single point.

But the next day, of course, at business, Paul was back to his old tricks. The game was far from his thoughts. After that, though, he was never very good at golf. Whenever the going got tough, he would mess it up. He would know ahead of time that he was going to do it, and it always worked out that way. He knew it was because he had not kept his bargain.

There were quite a few more instances where Paul was plagued. He unraveled a series of events in which there was always some irrational factor that was managing his life for him in ways that he could not control. Always there was the punitive element coming from a source outside himself.

He was reminded of a time when he was playing poker. Once he had gotten into a game which was really too big for him. He did not have the courage to admit it to the other men, and so he played with them time and time again, often losing more than he could afford. On one particular day he dropped his hand down on the table, and when he picked it up he found that he had accidentally picked up six cards instead of five. He quickly discarded the one least likely to succeed. Quicker still were the eyes of the men playing with him, and he was thrown out of the game as a cheater. But he "knew" that "something" was forcing him out of a game he didn't belong in, and that he couldn't have stepped out by himself.

Paul had been born and raised a devout Catholic. As a child he had been taught that if he would pray, God would hear his prayers and answer them. But in order to get what he wanted from God he had to obey the rules that were set out by Mother and by the Church; if not, he would surely be punished. Though Mother was a faithful churchgoer, Father preferred to sleep on Sunday morning. Father didn't seem to be too concerned about the rules, he did just about as he pleased. That included staying out late quite often and coming home drunk, and paying very little attention to the needs of Paul and his brothers and sisters. If Paul wanted something he had to find his own ways of getting it. When he wanted money he would take it without asking from his parents' dressing table. When a dime was given to him for the collection plate he would pocket it and later spend it on himself at the candy store. But always with the uneasy feeling that something bad would happen to him for his misdeeds—and when on occasion something bad did happen, he "knew" that it had to happen. He could not escape the all-seeing eye of God. In later life, when he drifted away from the Church, the "eye" lost whatever benevolence it might once have had for him. It became the eye of the demon, with whom he might sometimes bargain but who would always exact his due. The demon would drive him, the demon would get in his way, the demon would watch him.

Jung had described the acute effects of the complex in one of his very early essays, "The Psychology of Dementia Praecox," written while he was still at Burghölzli. Recognizing that his concept of the complex was as yet in a very rudimentary phase, it is nevertheless interesting to see how he has caught the sensation associated with it, and how it comes across with much the same emotional tone as that expressed by Paul in the grip of his obsessional ideas.

Jung wrote:

Reality sees to it that the peaceful cycle of egocentric ideas is constantly interrupted by ideas with a strong feeling-tone, that is, by affects. A situation threatening danger pushes aside the tranquil play of ideas and puts in their place a complex of other ideas with a very strong feeling-tone. The new complex then crowds everything else into the background. For the time being it is the most distinct because it totally inhibits all other ideas; it permits only those egocentric ideas to exist which fit *its* situation, and under certain conditions it can suppress to the point of complete (momentary) unconsciousness all ideas that run counter to it, however strong they may be. It now possesses the strongest attention-tone.[10]

Over the years Jung made many advances in his complex theory. He developed a concept of psychic energy which he thought of as being analogous to the concept of physical energy in physics. "Modern psychology," he wrote in 1934, "has one thing in common with modern physics, that its method enjoys greater recognition than its subject. Its subject, the psyche, is so infinitely diverse in its manifestations, so indefinite and so unbounded, that the definitions given of it are difficult if not impossible to interpret . . ."[11] He goes on to say that the definitions which result from the methods of observation are much easier to derive. Out of his empirical research, observing many clinical cases, Jung recognized that a certain psychic condition interpolates itself between the subject (that is, the psyche) and the experiment, which one could call the "experimental situation." This "situation" could then jeopardize the whole experiment by *assimilating* not only the experimental procedure but also its purpose. By *assimilation*, Jung meant "an attitude on the part of the subject, who misinterprets the experiment because he has at first an insuperable tendency to assume that it is, shall we say, an intelligence test or an attempt to take an indiscreet look behind the scenes."[12] Such an attitude on the part of the subject brings him to attempt to disguise the very process which the experimenter is trying to observe.

It was, therefore, of utmost importance that Jung's discovery of the complex came not as a result of looking directly for proof of a hypothesis that such a mechanism as the complex did indeed exist. Rather, the complex was discovered inadvertently, as the method of the association experiments was disturbed by the autonomous behavior of the psyche, that is, by assimilation of the apparent purpose of the experiment. Then it was that Jung discovered the *complex*, which had been registered before as a *failure to react*.

The discovery of how the complexes interweave in their nuclei the archetypal roots of the personality and the environmental stimuli, and then draw to themselves associated contents, made it evident to Jung on how weak a footing the old view stood—that it was possible to investigate *isolated* psychic processes. He asserted that there are no isolated psychic processes, just as there are no isolated life processes. "Only with the help of specially trained attention and concentration can the subject isolate a process so that it appears to meet the requirements of the experiment. But this is yet another 'experimental situation,' which differs from the one previously described only because this time the role of the assimilating complex is taken over by the conscious mind, whereas before this was done by more or less unconscious . . . complexes."[13]

Anyone who has become aware of the existence of a complex, and particularly of his own complex, cannot hold to the naïve assumption of the unity of the consciousness. For that would mean that there would be no barrier between the will and the act, and that an individual would be able, invariably, to accomplish what he sets out to do, unless purely external circumstances intervene. But who has not set forth in the morning with a task to do and nothing in the world, apparently, to stop him and returned at the end of the day with the task still undone? The unity of consciousness is disturbed by intruders from the unconscious—they impede the intentions of the will, they disturb the memory, and they play all kinds of tricks, as we have seen.

Jung offers this definition of the feeling-toned complex:

> It is the *image* of a certain psychic situation which is strongly accentuated emotionally and is, moreover, incompatible with the habitual attitude of consciousness. This image has a powerful inner coherence, it has its own wholeness and, in addition, a relatively high degree of autonomy, so that it is subject to the control of the conscious mind to only a limited extent, and therefore behaves like an animated foreign body in the sphere of consciousness. The complex can usually be suppressed with an effort of will, but not argued out of existence, and at the first suitable opportunity it reappears in all its original strength.[14]

I would like to show how the autonomous complex operates, and how the victim of it attempts by all possible means to avoid it. Leroy was a corporation executive who had the responsibility of administering his company so that he would get the maximum possible amount of productivity out of his employees. Leroy was known to his associates as an extremely firm and determined man in his dealings, but still open to advice and counsel from the men in the company to whom he was directly responsible. He was an eminently successful businessman, clearly on his way to becoming the next president of his company. He was, however, constantly in a state of dissatisfaction with his work. He spent most of his spare time reading trade journals, calculating his investments in the stock market, conferring with subordinates, and in general attempting to improve his own abilities to handle his work. In the meantime his wife and family had the leavings of his wearying days. The estrangement between himself and his wife, which was hardly noticeable to him, was suddenly brought into sharp focus when she told him that she was tired of being disregarded and used as a menial to grease the wheels of his smoothly functioning machine, and that she wanted out of the marriage.

He hardly knew what had happened to him—after all he had done to provide her with material things, and status, and the opportunities to follow her own interests. At the same time, he was vaguely aware that no matter how hard he worked there was always more to be done and no matter how much he studied there was more to be learned. He was running on an ever-faster-moving treadmill, and he was desperately tired. He knew that he needed help, and so he consulted an analyst.

In the first session Leroy told me that he had been extremely upset lately, that he was sleeping poorly and that his nights were full of dreams, and images that he could not be sure were dreams—maybe they were waking visions. He was especially disturbed about the latter. I reassured him that the visions were hypnagogic, which means that they come in the drowsiness that precedes sleep when the conscious defenses against the unconscious are down, and that they are quite usual. Leroy had never discussed such matters with anyone, and consequently he was anxious and did not know what to make of them. I suggested that it might be worthwhile for us to talk about these experiences together, and that if he were to have such a vision before the next session, perhaps he would like to make a sketch of it and bring it in. He demurred, saying that he was no good at drawing, and I replied that I was not an art critic, but that his drawing might provide a good way to let me participate in those visions. It could be helpful in the process that we were undertaking, and also, he might discover some things about himself that would be surprising. The last remark caught his fancy, and when he arrived for the next session he had a picture with him.

Leroy was not sure whether it had been a dream or a vision, but he had sketched the picture. It showed a man high up and clinging to a poorly constructed tower made of loose stones fitted together. It looked as though he were trying to get away from something. But his foot slipped and knocked one of the stones out and it was falling. A woman was sitting at the base of the tower. More than likely the rock would fall on her head.

Since this was only the second session, we did not go into the dream too much, except that I asked him how he could imagine that the dream represented his life situation. It came out that he was really very worried about his business, and his whole life for that matter, because his business was his major concern. There were many unreliable people working for him; he had not been able to trust some of them. He suspected that many weaknesses and failures had been covered up for his benefit in order to show a promising balance sheet at the end of each year. He definitely felt that he was in a shaky position, and that the picture depicted what he had been unable to admit to himself. And he saw his wife as a potential victim of his instability.

At this point, I reflected, it might have been possible to have gone into the exploration of the tower as an image of himself and his own development, characterized by uncompleted tasks and haphazard habits. The woman at the bottom may have represented something of the not-yet-conscious other side of himself which was in jeopardy. But I did not know the analysand well enough yet to jump to any such conclusions, so we left the picture as something that we could ponder further, and that would, in the course of the analysis, probably take on deeper shades of meaning. I recognized that the motif of climbing, the one of the shaky foundation, and that of the damsel in distress were all archetypal themes well known in myth and legend, and that any one of them might point to the nucleus of a complex.

The next session with Leroy continued to set the stage for the drama which the analytic process would bring to light. It centered about a significant dream which I will report here with some of Leroy's comments.

The dream begins: *I am made a king. Everyone seems to be quite nice and accepting about it. It is connected with a church.*

Here he broke in to tell me, "I've never wanted to admit

it, because it is a bit ugly, but this has always been a key word. My name is Leroy, which comes from *le roi*, which is French for 'king.' Although I was named after my grandfather, I always thought there was something fateful about it. I remember when I was quite young thinking I was going to be something special. It seems my mother determined that her son was going to grow up to be a 'great man' of some kind. The extreme limit of this, I remember, came one day when I wondered if *I* was the next messiah.

"Maybe the church has something to do with the fact that in trying to be very much my father's son, in trying to be just exactly what he wanted me to be, I went to church with him (my mother was not religious in this sense) and became exceedingly religious at a very early age. I remember one birthday I was given money which I took and went, with my father of course, to a 'religious store' and spent the whole amount on religious items such as a big leather-bound Bible, pictures of Jesus, crosses, and such things. I was going to be a minister in those days."

I asked him if he ever has any feelings today that resemble those early memories he was speaking about.

"This feeling of being 'king' I still get," he replied. "I will be sitting with a group of people, usually strange people, perhaps in a business conference. I am not at ease with them, and I will suddenly notice that all of my attention is focused on myself. It is as if I am too big, or too *there*, as if I expect everybody else in the room to feel as I do, that I am the center of attention. Somehow I connect this feeling, which I find very uncomfortable, with earlier feelings of being the favorite child, destined for great things, admired by all my parents' friends. My parents would always make a big point of telling me when somebody said what an admirable, outstanding boy I was—and when I heard this I couldn't have been more pleased. It seems this was my major goal in life at that time, impressing upon everybody what a good boy I was: I mean good in every sense of the word—good-looking, moral, hard-working, devoted to my parents, and so on. Even now, very often, I find myself expecting to be better than other people." He hesitated, and I waited. Then he continued, "Even now that I've admitted I need help from you, I catch myself saying to myself, 'Well, in the end, you *will* turn out just as you always expected. You will learn about yourself, get straightened out, and still be a great man.'"

He went on, "I mentioned the problem I have getting all my work done the way I want it. When I am going at it too hard I sometimes get a strange feeling in the pit of my stomach that says, 'You'd better stop right now if you know what's good for you.' Maybe my work is the ladder by which I try to climb to the top of the tower to be king."

I thought of the young woman sitting at the bottom of his tower; and of him, oblivious to the fact that he has kicked loose the stone that will fall on her head.

The dream continues: *I learn that Jack has secretly conceived a plot to kill me. He seemed nice like the rest but he was plotting to kill me. He was only prevented from this by being killed.* Jack is the head of a division in Leroy's business. He had been rising rapidly. But he was doomed at the start, Leroy told me, because he, Leroy, was not going to let anybody get ahead of him, so he had handled this by giving Jack impossible tasks in which he was bound to fall short. Then Leroy would miss no opportunity to point out these failures in the company meetings.

I am king of a little principality at Waterford Road. [This is the street where he grew up.] *It reminds me of a little French court. I have my subjects and they dress up and have nice parties. I reign for some time and then the time comes for choosing a successor. My subjects are playing a game whereby they are trying to shoot me with a bow and arrow. I am trying to escape from them. I am afraid of them and I am trying to fly away from them, running behind the house, trying to fly up in the trees, but I am hard pressed.*

I asked him about the flying, and he told me: "Ever since I can remember, this 'flying' has been an important part in my dreams. It always takes the same form. I flap my arms up and down as hard as I can, exerting the greatest possible effort, and am always barely able to rise in this fashion. I

always make agonizingly slow progress, and I always know
that if I stop flapping my arms just as hard as I can, I will
fall to earth. Very often when I am doing this with all my
effort, I don't move at all. These are the worst moments."
He continued relating the dream: *Three of my subjects come
after me from different directions. I have to flap my arms
like crazy to make any progress. I am having a very hard time
keeping clear of them. Finally I realize that the only way
to avoid being caught or wounded by them is to disarm them.
So taking a risk, I manage to get close enough to them, without getting hit, to disarm them. But others may be coming.
I continue trying to fly around in this manner. I am above
the front lawn, working at it like crazy, flapping my arms,
barely able to keep in the air, only with great effort making
any progress. Mitchell* [another executive in the firm] *comes
along and I tell him he can be king. It seems there is an
end to my confusion about who will be king. Then it seems
as if the problem is not really solved. A lot of people want
to be king and I haven't yet found anyone who would be
really appropriate.*

Until now Leroy has tried to solve his problem in four
ways. First he depended on his right of kingship, his authority,
to maintain his regal position. Second, threatened, he tried
to escape, using whatever resources he had readily at hand.
Third, finding progress too slow, he decided to demolish the
threatening agency. And fourth, knowing that he could not
depend on destroying all opposition everywhere, he decided
to maintain his authority by designating his successor. But
this, also, did not seem to solve the problem.

The dream is not finished yet. *I fly up in the air with
great effort as usual, to the top of the house. I land on it
and use it as a resting place and push off on it on my trip
to another section of the house. There is much less effort
to this mode of travel through the air than trying to go wholly
under my own power.* Leroy now begins to make use of an
existing structure, and he gains some support and impetus
from it, as he could not do when he was isolating himself
in mid-air and depending upon his will alone.

Then I see some trees in front of me and I decide to pull them back and allow them to propel me through the air. I will pull back a few of these locust trees. But their trunks have thorns on them and as I reach them I am pricked in the right hand by two thorns. They go into my fingers, through the gloves I am wearing. For the moment I am chiefly concerned with finding out if the thorns broke off in my fingers (it seems they did not) and if I am bleeding (not too much, it seems).

At this point I realize that there is only five minutes left in a TV show before the end of which a new king must be chosen. In a way I am desperate because no appropriate king has turned up and I have assumed that it was up to me to pick him. The way the deal works is that he walks up the road, or appears in some other manner, and my subjects, all of whose attention is directed to awaiting him and looking for him, would pounce on him and choose him king.

Suddenly there is a big commotion in the yard. Someone has come in at the last moment and been chosen king. I go down and, lo and behold, he is quite appropriate though not whom I had expected. In fact it seems I barely know him. But he will make a good king.

When Leroy turns to the trees for help he is actively reaching out beyond the limits of his own capacity, that is, his ego functioning. No longer has he to find his deliverance all on his own from "the pursuing demons who threaten his 'superiority'"; there is help from another source. Trees may be understood symbolically, and there is a whole literature on this. But for our purpose here it is enough to say that the tree, with its roots underground and its branches rising toward the sky, symbolizes an upward trend and is therefore related to other symbols, such as the ladder and the tower, which stand for the general relationship between the "three worlds" (the lower world: the underworld, hell; the middle world: earth; the upper world: heaven). The three worlds of tree symbolism reflect the three main portions of the structure of the tree: roots, trunk and foliage. In its most general sense, the symbolism of the tree denotes the life of the cosmos: its consistency, growth, proliferation, generative and regenerative processes. All this, and especially the "three world" symbolism, must have been in the unconscious knowledge of the dreamer, given his religious background and the archetypal basis underlying it.[15]

But the particular tree selected by the dream itself, the locust tree, is significant on several counts. To be sure, the locust tree has spines, which could conceivably wound a person in the way that the dream suggests. The prick of the thorn awakens one to consciousness in many a fairy tale. Locusts have very hard wood, resistant to injury and lasting a long time. They grow rapidly. They spread by means of suckers that spring from the roots, as well as by scattered seeds. So, like the rhizome that stays alive through the seasons while the blossoms perish, which seemed to Jung to be a metaphor for the continuity of unconscious processes in contrast to the transience of the conscious ones, locusts spread and grow from the activity under the surface. All of this leads to the thought that the locust may be an agent of transformation, and this seems to be suggested in this dream. The idea is not new; it can be found in the Bible. When Moses was leading the children of Israel through the wilderness of Shur they were three days without water. And when they came to Marah they could not drink the waters of Marah for they were bitter, and people murmured against Moses. "And he cried to the Lord and the Lord showed him a tree, *a locust tree*, and he threw it into the waters, and the waters became sweet."[16]

As the dreamer, Leroy, was considering his wound, as he was trying to assess the results of getting help from something beyond his own ego, namely the locust tree, he suddenly realized that his time was nearly up. He was brought with a rush back toward the world of everyday consciousness—the TV show would soon be over, and that was all the time that was allowed. The dreamer was desperate, but only "in a way"—and that meant that his desperation was based on his assumption that he had to be the one man in control, and that nothing good could happen if he did not manage it. Suddenly he found out that this was not the way it was going to work but that destiny had its own way of determining who shall rule and who shall lay down the scepter.

When the time was right, the appropriate person arrived and was chosen king. It was not that Leroy did it, and it was not whom he expected. In fact Leroy hardly knew him. But he did know that he would make a good king.

The complex which had Leroy was clearly delineated by the dream. It was a power-complex, pressing on him the feeling that by reason of his birth—and his name was his birthright —he was entitled to be and expected to be in a controlling position. This nucleus, "the king idea," had conditioned much of his behavior from early childhood. As the years went by, in his religious fantasies with their messianic flavor, in his successes in social situations and at school and later in his business, one incident after another supported his tendency to dominate every situation, to relate to others sometimes benevolently, sometimes tyrannically, but inevitably to support his image of himself as the superior man. And all the time, on the unconscious side, he was haunted by the fear that he must be sorely inferior to the expectations he had for himself, and to those he evoked in those who knew him. How difficult life must have become for this man who felt required to support such heavy burdens!

If the dream points the way to the origin of the complex, it also offers an attitude which could be helpful in coming to terms with the complex. In fact, the dream suggests much that will be worked through in the course of the analysis, for it is one thing to see what needs to be done and quite another to shift lifelong attitudes and alter ways of thinking and consequently ways of behaving. The purposive aspect of the dream is the indication that too often the dreamer attempts to function out of his ego, by his will alone. He must learn that when his ego, his will, is out of harmony with the demands of nature or destiny or biology in the broad sense or, if you will, the cosmic rhythm that some call God; if he is out of harmony with that, he cannot prevail. So, when the feeling comes that what he is doing at tremendous cost

and effort is getting him nowhere, then he must respect the
nature of things outside his own will and control, and allow
them to help him. And finally, when all else fails, he must
be willing simply to "let it happen," and then the end which
he had formerly pursued in the most energetic and hopeless
way now is easily and simply achieved. *I barely know him.
But he will make a good king.* This dream helped to show
the way for Leroy to trust and pay attention to the wisdom
of the unconscious. It was possible, then, for the analysis to
move on.

The unconscious contains the human potential which needs
to be actualized in order for an individual to move toward
individuation, that is, toward becoming whatever he is innately
capable of being. As such it is the *Urgrund* of our being,
the *original basis* from which everything valuable may develop.
At the same time, its mysterious depths hold strange shapes,
which emerge at times to frighten us, as they have done since
the dawn of man's consciousness. The world of the unconscious, as seen in its collective and mythological dimensions,
has long been a theme of Mircea Eliade, historian of religion,
and friend of Jung. Eliade explains the mystique so often associated with the unconscious, the unknown, as follows:

> In archaic and traditional societies, the surrounding world is
> conceived as a microcosm. At the limits of this closed world be-
> gins the domain of the unknown, of the formless. On this side
> there is ordered—because inhabited and organised—space; on the
> other, outside this familiar space, there is the unknown and dan-
> gerous region of the demons, the ghosts, the dead and of for-
> eigners—in a word, chaos or death or night. This image of an
> inhabited microcosm, surrounded by desert regions regarded as
> a chaos or a kingdom of the dead, has survived even in highly
> evolved civilisations such as those of China, Mesopotamia and
> Egypt.[17]

Jung would insist that the images of archaic man are much
closer to the European and American psyche of the twentieth
century even than Eliade had admitted in the preceding para-
graph. He tells us in his essay on "Archaic Man"[18] that
"it is not only primitive man whose psychology is archaic.

It is the psychology also of modern, civilised man. . . . Every civilised human being, however high his conscious development, is still an archaic man at the deeper levels of his psyche."[19] He describes various customs practiced by natives in their rituals and ceremonies, as he observed them in his travels to the interior of the African continent. The aborigines he met disclaimed any awareness of particular significance of their acts, including their intercourse with ghosts, ancestral spirits, and the like. Jung was unwilling to allow that their ways of thinking, their taking for granted what seems so strange to us, are really as foreign as we would like to believe. He illustrates his contention with a hypothetical case:

> Now let us suppose that I am a total stranger in Zurich and have come to this city to explore the customs of the place. First I settle down on the outskirts near some suburban homes, and come into neighbourly contact with their owners. I then say to Messrs. Müller and Meyer: "Please tell me something about your religious customs." Both gentlemen are taken aback. They never go to church, know nothing about it, and emphatically deny that they practise any such customs. It is spring, and Easter is approaching. One morning I surprise Mr. Müller at a curious occupation. He is busily running about the garden, hiding coloured eggs and setting up peculiar rabbit idols. I have caught him *in flagrante*. "Why did you conceal this highly interesting ceremony from me?" I ask him. "What ceremony?" he retorts. "This is nothing. Everybody does it at Eastertime." "But what is the meaning of these idols and eggs, and why do you hide them?" Mr. Müller is stunned. He does not know, any more than he knows the meaning of the Christmas-tree. And yet he does these things, just like a primitive. Did the distant ancestors of the Elgonyi know any better what they were doing? It is highly improbable. Archaic man everywhere does what he does, and only civilized man knows what he does.[20]

It must be added that archaic man exists within every living person today, just as does civilized man. To the degree that the non-rational motivates behavior, man's functioning is characterized as archaic, and to the degree that the rational functions predominate, man is said to be functioning in a civilized way. I hasten to add that I have no intention of placing a

value judgment either on archaism, or on civilization with
its material and technological progress. Rather, I am attempting to differentiate between these two strands in the organization of the human psyche, which co-exist irrespective of time
or place.

Since the psychotherapist is aware of hidden individual differences which may be at the base of psychological disturbances, it is necessary for him to approach the patient in terms
of his own way of being, if the two are to meet on any
common ground at all. The psychotherapist must gently encourage and go along with the patient to seek out the complexes, fully prepared to find in the place of the expected
complexes apparitions resembling demons and other strange
spirits. This attitude made it possible for me to share some
strange experiences with a young widow, Matilda.

The first few analytic sessions did not disclose the real nature of the underlying complexes. Matilda was severely depressed but she was not suicidal; she appeared much too passive for that. Rather, her mood was more one of utter disgust
with the world in general. It was a vague, diffuse feeling; she
lacked interest in nearly everything she was doing. Matilda
was only twenty-three years old. Her husband had been killed
in an automobile accident a year previous, after they had been
married only four months. She was now about twenty pounds
overweight, careless of her appearance, apathetic in manner,
presenting a generally unattractive impression, although her
features were basically good. She had suffered a great deal
and was still suffering over her husband's death. She told me
that she regarded it as a completely senseless and horrible
accident of fate. She said that there was no way of understanding it or accepting it; that the whole thing was pointless, and
it proved to her that life, itself, was utterly pointless.

No, there could not possibly be any sense to it. She could
not look to God for help, as some well-meaning friends had
advised her to do. She could not believe in God. She could
not believe there was anybody up there pulling the strings,
determining what would happen to a person. She could not
believe that there was any such thing as destiny. Things hap-

pened by mere chance. Everything was a kind of random accident. There was no use trying to exert effort or will; you had no control anyhow. Life was a series of aimless events. Such was Matilda's conscious attitude when she came to me.

I let her know that I accepted her attitude as being a logical one in the face of what had recently happened to her, also because of earlier events in her life which had led her to reject various forms of authority, including that of the fundamentalist Protestant religion in which she had been reared as a young child. But I asked her if she could see that her attitude must be unconstructive, because it is impossible to build any structure, psychic or otherwise, unless there is purpose, plan and wider view. I suggested that purpose depended on finding some meaning in life, and I suggested, in this connection, that she read a little book by Viktor Frankl titled *Man's Search for Meaning*. In this book Frankl had written of his experiences as a Jew imprisoned in a Nazi concentration camp. He had observed that some of the internees submitted to their fate and were led without a fight to the gas chambers. Others, however, used every wily device and trick imaginable, and stretched their endurance to the utmost, so that in one amazing way or another a considerable number of these latter managed to survive. Those who lived through the darkness of the abyss were the ones, Frankl observed, who had been able to find some meaning or mission in their lives, some purpose for which they felt they were intended to live. They were impelled by a sense of destiny, and with that sense they would not or could not break faith.

In the particular session that enabled her to bring forth secrets from her hidden depths, Matilda began talking about Frankl's book. It was clear that her feelings were ambivalent. She began by saying that there were some things about the book that she liked very much, but then she quickly switched to a critical attitude toward the author's "faith" in something "supernatural." She said that she could not go along with his attributing the internee's ability to survive to a notion of something moving him outside of his own energies, that is to say, outside of his personal courage and determination. The idea

of something being "arranged" ahead of time collided with
her "rational" views, namely that all events depended on prior
cause. She could not see that there were times when an anticipation of the future could affect events or behavior in the
present. She seemed so centered in her pragmatic attitude
that I felt the need to ask her whether she had ever had
a dream that took her beyond her world of palpable reality.
Oh yes, she announced almost with embarrassment, there had
been this dream that had recurred several times: *I dream that
I am standing in among the trees. There is nothing in sight
except fields and trees. I walk up to the top of a hill and
as I stand there I look up at the sky and all of a sudden
the universe starts parading in front of me. All the planets
come within touching distance. The sound of the wind is
like choral music.*

It was clear to me that this had been a particularly moving
dream for her, for she brightened in the telling of it. I asked
her if she had experienced anything like a sense of awe when
the planets had come "within touching distance." She replied
that she had had a feeling that it was glorious, but not awe.
The gloriousness came from seeing that Saturn was so luminous that she could see it with all the rings around it, and
all the other planets, just this tremendous sense of nearness.
But *awe*, that was an expression reserved for a fear of God,
but she didn't see God in this—she felt that this was nature,
that the entire experience was wholly natural and she had
felt very good about it, but insisted that any sense of awe
was lacking.

There was little more to be said about the dream, and we
fell into a period of silence. I sensed that the recollection
of this dream had led her thoughts onto something else. She
seemed hesitant to speak, she almost began once or twice,
and finally, "There was another dream. I dreamed it over a
year ago."

The dream occurred shortly after her marriage. At this time
she was a child care worker in a home for delinquent children,
a job which necessitated her staying overnight at the home
once or twice a week. It was on one of those nights at her

place of work, she dreamed: *I receive a phone call one night about 10:30. It is a Michigan State policeman. He tells me that Bill has been in an automobile accident, and is dying. He is in a Grand Rapids hospital. The rest of the dream concerns my attempts to get transportation to Grand Rapids in time. There are no commercial planes going, a cab can't take me, and none of the staff that are on duty have cars. I am attempting to rent a private plane when I wake up.*

The dream had upset her so much that she had told her mother about it at the time. The mother could verify what she said.

About two months after this dream, the patient's husband was indeed killed in an automobile accident. She was called by the state police and told that he was dying. She was sleeping in the children's home at the time, and she had great difficulty in getting transportation to the hospital where he had been taken. There were no commercial planes. There were no private cars available where she worked. She had to argue with someone from a taxi company and finally was able to get a driver to take her to the place. The only difference between dream and reality was the location of the accident; the direction was the same but the distance was closer.

Matilda told me that this apparently precognitive dream had weighed heavily on her and that she couldn't get it out of her mind. And since then, whenever she had a dream in which a tragedy took place, she got uncontrollably anxious. It was her recurrent anxiety that had led her to seek psychiatric help a short time before she came to me. It hadn't worked out and she had terminated the therapeutic relationship.

I asked her whether any particular event or circumstance had precipitated her getting to the psychiatrist at that time. She answered, "Yes."

"A couple of months after Bill's death," she told me, "I was in the hospital giving blood to replace some of what Bill had needed. While the blood was being taken I realized that something was going wrong. I felt that there had been some kind of interruption, I had the feeling that the blood was co-agulating, that a blood clot was forming, and that it was moving toward my heart. I felt that I was going to die, and it seemed very easy just to give up and let go. But I called the nurse and she quickly removed the needle. I felt very faint and shaky. After some black coffee I felt better physically, but the feeling of letting go of life stayed with me. It preyed on my mind so much that I thought I had better see a psychiatrist, and a couple of weeks later I did just that.

"Naturally I told him the dream which had so accurately predicted Bill's death. He questioned me about my relationship with Bill and discovered that, like any marriage, it had had its imperfections. He announced his conclusion, which was that unconsciously I had really wanted to see Bill dead. The dream, according to him, was a manifestation of a death wish. I couldn't accept that," she said most emphatically, "because the dream was too close to what actually happened. His typical Freudian explanation just didn't seem to fit."

"If that doesn't explain it, then what do *you* think may have been behind your experience?" I asked Matilda.

"I allow very much for the possibility of precognition, or ESP." Now it all began to come out. "I don't understand it, but I have studied the experiments of Dr. Rhine at Duke University and I have been forced to recognize that I've had those kinds of experiences too. Ghosts? I don't know if I believe in ghosts, but . . . let me tell you this . . . a week after Bill died, when I was very, very upset, some friends came to visit. As I was talking with them I began to get really involved emotionally. All of a sudden a stack of dishes rattled loudly. There was no physical reason for the rattling. The stack had been sitting in the sink all evening, but at this particular moment they rattled. I don't know what to make of it."

Getting all wound up now in her narrative, Matilda continued. She talked about an old lady who had been a neighbor of hers, who had been sickly, and whom she had visited from time to time in her home. A few months before the incident, this old lady had been taken to a nursing home, which was on the road that Matilda took each day as she drove to work. For several days she had been thinking that she ought to stop

by and see the woman, but she was always in a hurry, or
had errands to do, and so kept putting it off. Suddenly one
morning as she passed the nursing home she felt the strongest
impulse pulling at her and saying, "I must go and see her,
I have to go and see her." She had already gone by the nursing
home, but now she backed up, stopped the car, went up and
knocked on the door. There she was told, when she asked
for her friend, that she was too late, the old lady had died
that very night.

Then she recounted another experience—Bill had once said
to her, out of the blue, "You know, Cartwright is dead." Cartwright had been a good friend in another city whom they
had not seen or heard from in several months. A few days
after that they learned that Cartwright had suffered a fatal
heart attack, and at almost exactly the time Bill had felt like
saying, "Cartwright is dead."

I have not yet found any explanation for these kinds of
experiences that satisfies me, and therefore I had no easy answers for Matilda. I found it particularly interesting that all
of this came out after she had firmly declared herself against
any explanations of behavior or experience that could not be
tested and validated biologically or physically. She had, in
reading Frankl's book, attributed to him a belief in "supernatural forces," although the book had not actually made any
such assertion. I had to understand her "disbelief" as being
her way of avoiding dealing with something that she knew
was of a certain kind of reality, even though she did not know
the nature of that reality. I could see that she had left her
Freudian therapist very much as Jung had left Freud long
ago, when Jung had brought his "mystical speculations" to
Freud and Freud had refused to take them seriously, in fact,
had gone to great lengths to explain them away.

Jung did not feel that everything had either to be explained
or else left outside the boundaries of scientific investigation.
He preferred to deal with the mysteries in whatever way he
could, and often his way was to speak in metaphors, to take
psychic experiences as though they were palpable realities, and
speak of them "as though." He was able "to image" concepts,

and if this is imagination then it is out of imagination that reality emerges. William Blake tells us in one of his Proverbs: "What is now true was once only imagin'd."

The imagination, the ability to form an image of something one has not yet seen, appears to be a universal quality which may be enjoyed by all men. Unwilling to recognize the possibility of perceiving what does not stem directly from the senses, Matilda had become a victim of a complex centered around a deification of rationality and the conscious will. She could not go beyond the limit of sense perception; she could not risk the belief that some things were not only beyond her understanding, but even beyond the possibility of understanding. In her effort to sustain her faith in faithlessness, she had constantly repressed the awareness of the non-rational in her life. And so the denial-of-the-mystical complex had grown, drawing to itself more and more inexplicable contents with which she refused to deal. Far from being forgotten, they acted as magnets, attracting her energies and keeping them from more productive channels. Hence the deepening depression, the sensation of loss of energy, the absence of any enthusiasm for life. All this was expressed by her statement, "It's not that I want to die, it's just that I see no reason to go on living."

For me, Jung's explication of the complex makes the cases of Matilda and the others more comprehensible. He also clarified the correspondence between complexes and demons:

> The personal unconscious . . . contains complexes that belong to the individual and form an intrinsic part of his psychic life. When any complex which ought to be associated with the ego becomes unconscious, either by being repressed or by sinking below the threshold, the individual experiences a sense of loss. Conversely, when a lost complex is made conscious again, for instance through psychotherapeutic treatment, he experiences an increase of power. Many neuroses are cured in this way.[21]

So far, Jung and Freud were in agreement in their view of the complex. But here is where Jung entered unfamiliar territory:

. . . when, on the other hand, a complex of the collective unconscious becomes associated with the ego, i.e., becomes conscious, it is felt as strange, uncanny, and at the same time fascinating. At all events the conscious mind falls under its spell, either feeling it as something pathological, or else being alienated by it from normal life. The association of a collective content with the ego always produces a state of alienation, because something is added to the individual's consciousness which ought really to remain unconscious, that is, separated from the ego. . . . The irruption of these alien contents is a characteristic symptom marking the onset of many mental illnesses. The patients are seized by weird and monstrous thoughts, the whole world seems changed, people have horrible, distorted faces, and so on.[22]

To this Jung added the following qualifying footnote:

Those who are familiar with this material will object that my description is one-sided, because they know that the archetype, the autonomous collective content, does not have only the negative aspect described here. I have merely restricted myself to the common symptomatology that can be found in every text-book of psychiatry, and to the equally common defensive attitude toward anything extraordinary. Naturally the archetype also has a positive numinosity . . .

He went on to say:

While the contents of the personal unconscious are felt as belonging to one's own psyche, the contents of the collective unconscious seem alien, as if they came from outside. The reintegration of a personal complex has the effect of release and often of healing, whereas the invasion of a complex from the collective unconscious is a very disagreeable and even dangerous phenomenon. The parallel with the primitive belief in souls and spirits is obvious: souls correspond to the autonomous complexes of the personal unconscious, and spirits to those of the collective unconscious. We, from the scientific standpoint, prosaically call the awful beings that dwell in the shadows of the primeval forests "psychic complexes." Yet if we consider the extraordinary role played by the belief in souls and spirits in the history of mankind, we cannot be content with merely establishing the existence of such complexes, but must go rather more deeply into their nature.[23]

The cases I have used as examples of complexes and their effects on behavior illustrate the contemporary importance of going more deeply into the ramifications of Jung's complex theory. These examples show how the complex works in the life of the individual. The complexes of the collective unconscious have far-reaching effects which go beyond the experience of the individual, affecting groups of all kinds within a given society. All social movements could probably be understood from the standpoint of the factor which Jung has called "the autonomous complex arising out of the collective unconscious."

3

FROM
ASSOCIATIONS
TO ARCHETYPES

When Jung explored the implications of his discoveries about the complex, he often was able to trace its origin to some experience in the life of the patient which made a deep and shocking impression, so painful that it could not be endured for long in consciousness. The mechanism of repression helped to insulate the wounded psyche from the source of the pain so that it could continue functioning. Sometimes a loss of feeling occurred, for repression is a kind of psychological anaesthetic, but when there is great suffering an anaesthetic serves a purpose. It leaves the wound untouched, but the patient is able to tolerate it.

Jung's work on the Association Experiment led him to reread Freud's *Interpretation of Dreams*, a book which he had put aside a year or two before. Now it was suddenly a revelation to him, for he recognized that in his work on dreams the father of psychoanalysis had come upon the concept of repression from an entirely different direction, but that his understanding of the mechanism was almost identical with his own. Much of what was new to Jung, and had derived from his work with schizophrenic patients at Burghölzli, had already been formulated by the older man.

This discovery led Jung to follow Freud's work avidly, and to introduce the study of psychoanalysis to the clinic where he worked, even beginning a study group on Freud among his professional colleagues. Bleuler followed this trend in Jung's work with interest, if with some reservations. In time a correspondence began between Jung and Freud, which culminated in an invitation for Jung to visit Freud, and eventually full participation by Jung in the Vienna circle of psychoanalysts. Even before the first personal meeting between the two men had occurred, Jung was writing articles supporting the new psychoanalytical findings.

In 1905, Jung had become lecturer in psychiatry at the University of Zurich; the same year he became senior physician at the psychiatry clinic. His published works on association and dementia praecox (as schizophrenia was then called) were beginning to advance his status at the University. At this time Freud was definitely *persona non grata* in academic circles, and any connection with him would have been damaging in scientific circles.

I find it ironic, in looking back from the perspective of all that followed, to realize that at the very beginning of their association, Jung was an up-and-coming member of the psychiatric establishment, firmly based in respectable scientific research, while Freud was considered a man of highly speculative theories which were mentioned surreptitiously if at all by "important people." Jung could easily have published his own work without mention of Freud. But in 1906, at a congress in Munich where a lecturer discussed obsessional neuroses but carefully avoided mention of Freud's work in this area, Jung decided to take a stand. In connection with the incident he wrote a paper for the *Münchener Medizinische Wochenschrift* on Freud's theory of the neuroses, which had contributed greatly to the understanding of obsessional neuroses.[1] Two German professors wrote in response to the article that if Jung continued to defend Freud he would be endangering his academic career. The learned professors' threats did not deter Jung, once he had taken his stand.

A decade later, when the Freud-Jung friendship had reached its apogee, then deteriorated, and finally disintegrated with Jung's withdrawal from the psychoanalytic movement, Freud was in his full maturity and recognized as a giant in the world of psychology. At this time Jung was routinely being dismissed as a speculative philosopher who was incapable of loyalty to the psychoanalytic establishment. He was roundly criticized from that time on for "lack of scientific objectivity," and the Freudians studiously ignored him.

But we anticipate. The early relations between Freud and Jung were extremely cordial. It is reported that on the day of their first meeting, in Vienna in 1907, the two men who had been following each other's work so closely held a conversation which extended for thirteen hours!

One of the effects of this mutual conversation, as Jung reviewed in his writings many years later, was his realization that sexuality had for Freud an emotional commitment that made it a central principle with the quality nearly of a religion for him. With respect to this subject, Jung found that Freud's normal skepticism and critical manner were not applied. This was the keystone upon which his whole theory was balanced; it must be upheld at any cost. With respect to the elaborations on the various aspects of his theory, Freud was able to elucidate each point with great clarity and precision. His logical structure was highly credible, and especially for the neophyte in the field it was nearly impervious to challenge. Once certain basic premises were established, they could be extended indefinitely to cover almost all psychological phenomena. His conclusions were definite and technical, that is, they led to a method of treatment with specific techniques through which it could be carried out.

Jung's approach, in contrast to Freud's, was relatively vague, yet this permitted him to be more comprehensive in his view of the nature of man. Perhaps Freud put this down to the fact that Jung was still in the early stages of his psychological development, his ideas not anywhere near to being fully formed. The passage of time was to show that Jung's focus of interest would tend to be in the direction of symbolization and through the symbol toward the essence of meaning. He was not to be nearly so bound by concrete data and material facts as was Freud, but was to lean more heavily on intangible factors in his search for meaning. Furthermore Jung was essentially a man of religion, although he had left far behind the rather narrow fundamentalistic approach of his parson father, as he, the son, immersed himself in the discipline of scientific and medical education. His early childhood, lived under the shadow of the church steeple, with all its mysteries attending the transformative experiences of life—birth, confirmation, marriage and death—had not failed to establish certain patterns in his thinking. His world was full of unseen forces, which could only be known through their manifestations.

For Jung, questions of the spirit were of highest importance. By "spirit" he did not mean the supernatural, but rather those higher aspirations which are so much a part of man's striving, whether they are expressed in works of art, in service to one's fellow man, or in attempting to understand the workings of nature and her order. He derived the feeling that Freud was resistant to some of these impulses in himself, as he heard Freud saying that expressions of spirituality were to be suspected as stemming from repressed sexuality. "Anything that could not be directly interpreted as sexuality, he referred to as 'psychosexuality,'" Jung said of Freud. And Jung had protested that such an attitude, if carried to its logical conclusion, would place a dubious value on the achievements of human culture—a statement to which Freud unhesitatingly assented. Jung asked, "Could culture be construed as the morbid consequence of repressed sexuality?" Freud had replied, "Yes, so it is, and that is just a curse of fate against which we are powerless to contend."[2] Jung was not altogether impressed with Freud's pansexualism but at the same time he did recognize the enormous importance of opening up the sexual area as a possible way of approaching the sources of the patient's neurosis.

In the main, Jung was fully in agreement with Freud's basic principles, despite his questions about Freud's emphasis. Jung's own strong feeling was that there existed a whole tremendous area of psychic functioning which Freud recognized but did not fully accommodate into his psychological theory.

Both men affirmed that the unconscious was a hypothetical entity which could be inferred from material that came to consciousness in an incomplete form, leaving a trail of ideas and experiences which could not easily be explained or understood. This material could arise in the form of dreams or slips of speech, bungled actions, or in superstition or errors, as Freud had pointed out in *The Psychopathology of Everyday Life*. They could also be seen in disturbances of association and in complex behavior, as Jung had shown in his *Studies in Word Association*.

Freud's chief, though not exclusive, interest in the unconscious came from his observance of its manifestations in his analytical work with patients. His investigations into the unconscious were methodical. Starting from the symptoms of his neurotic patients in their daily life situations, and also from their dreams, he inferred the unconscious as an unknown and hidden area where reality was cleverly concealed by an elaborate system of defense mechanisms. Freud had conceptualized the unconscious as being composed of two basic kinds of contents. The first part of that unconscious reality, which Freud called the *id*, is associated with the instinctual drives which are innate or *in potentia* at birth. Freud's sexual theory gave primacy to those drives which stem from the infantile need for gratification—a need which, he thought, is essentially sexual in its nature.

Posed against the *id* is the second aspect of unconscious reality, and this Freud called the *superego*. This refers to that part of the unconscious which arises not from within the human organism itself, but derives rather from the environment. It has its origin in the standards of behavior and attitudes of thought which are imposed from earliest infancy by the parents and later by the agents of the culture in which the child is raised—namely his friends and relatives, his church and school, and then the traditions of his community and the culture at large. Insofar as the assimilation of these directives is conscious they fall under the category of learning, and are dealt with in the process of ordinary rational thinking. But much of what the environment imposes upon the indi-

vidual is subliminally perceived and assimilated to the unconscious, so that the individual finds himself possessed of a value
system and of certain kinds of expectations, hopes, beliefs,
and prejudices, with very little idea of how they were arrived
at. Indeed, the unconscious value system with its consequent
expectations form a structure which then appears to the individual as part of his very being—as stemming from within
himself. This psychic structure is the *superego*. Its unspoken
rules come into play to exercise a restricting and controlling
effect on the instinctive side, the *id*, thus giving rise to conflicts which are carried on in the unconscious and become
apparent only as they interfere with the natural, relaxed, and
productive functioning of the individual.

These two elements of the unconscious come into active
confrontation very early in the life of the infant, perhaps as
early as the beginnings of the emergence of the *ego*, the sense
of being a separate entity, something different and discrete
from the mother, set adrift in an alien world when the warm
arms and nourishing breast are taken away. The various cries
of infancy demand that the child express its instinctive needs
in one way or another. These instinctive needs are accepted
in the beginning by the parents as natural, but there comes
a time when the rules of the household and the expectations
of the parents begin to be felt as inhibitory controls of the
instinctual component. These rules and expectations are transmitted much more through unconscious channels than
through active directives. There is an unconscious learning
process going on constantly, in which the child learns much
more by tone of voice, manner of touching or not touching,
the subtle quality of the attention he receives, the general
atmosphere between family members, than he ever does by
what he is actually told.

The central problem of infancy, as Freud had identified it,
stemmed from the attachment of the young child to the parent of the opposite sex, with all of the sexual overtones, since
gratification was to Freud essentially sexual in nature. This
attachment, countered as it was with the fear of reprisal from
the parent of the child's own sex, placed the child in a bind

where to feel close was to invite punishment, but not to feel close was to invite alienation, which was also something to be dreaded. This resulted, of course, in the well-known oedipal dilemma.

Jung did not disagree with any of this, in fact he wrote several articles discussing the theory of infantile sexuality as it related to Freud's theory of dream interpretation. He even decided to follow Freud's methods explicitly in his own practice, for it was his opinion that only another analyst could properly study and evaluate the hypotheses put forth by the founder of psychoanalysis.

When Jung began to concern himself with child development, he started from the Freudian point of view by examining the so-called "incest wish" which occupies so central a place in psychoanalysis. He wrote to Freud in 1912, "I started out expecting that I would be able to confirm the established concept of incest, and had to see that it is different from what I thought."[3] Far from being blind to the "superhuman struggles of the child to effect a compromise between the compelling force of his primitive instincts and the growing harshness of reality," Jung's background in archaeology and anthropology had led him to an awareness of those primitive forces, and to a recognition that they are not purely individual drives or isolated propensities, but are rather collective in nature, shared aspects of the general human condition. Thus the neuroses and psychoses of childhood were regarded by him as universal phenomena, and seen in a different perspective from that of Freud.

In exploring how the hypothesis of the unconscious could be enlarged to include Freud's discoveries as well as phenomena that seemed to be outside of their scope, Jung began his own investigation of psychic images and ideas. He carefully observed his own dreams and those of his patients, paying particular attention to those features which did not appear to refer to actual experiences in the life of the dreamer. He also analyzed the fantasies and delusions of the insane, and he engrossed himself in the study of comparative religion and mythology. Noting that similar images and myth motifs could

be found in widely separated places all over the earth, and at
different periods throughout the history of mankind, he came
to a decisive insight: that *the unconscious is at its basis collective in character*, that is, it is composed of contents that
are universal in their nature. He wrote: "From the unconscious there emanate determining influences . . . which, independently of tradition, guarantee in every single individual
a similarity and even a sameness of experience, and also of the
way it is represented imaginatively. One of the main proofs
of this is the almost universal parallelism between mythological motifs . . ."[4] The unconscious, therefore, contained a
wealth of potentialities for image formation, and this could
lead to the creation of new ideas and positive personality
development.

Jung pointed out how Freud had shown in a little essay on
Leonardo da Vinci[5] that Leonardo was influenced in later life
by the fact that he had two mothers. This was real enough in
Leonardo's life, but the idea of double descent has played
an important role in the lives of other artists as well. But
beyond this, double descent is a mythological motif, occurring
over and over again in the lives of legendary heroes. Sometimes it is two mothers, sometimes two fathers, and sometimes
two sets of parents. Otto Rank, a colleague of Jung and Freud
in the Vienna circle, had developed this idea in his book
The Myth of the Birth of the Hero[6] published in 1909. In
brief: the hero is the son of parents of the highest station,
his conception takes place under difficulties, and there is a
portent in a dream or oracle connected with the child's birth.
The child is then sent away or exposed to extreme danger.
He is rescued by people of humble station, or by helpful
animals, and reared by them. When grown he rediscovers
his noble parentage after many adventures and, overcoming
all obstacles in his path, becomes at last recognized as the
hero and attains fame and greatness. The best known, as mentioned in this series, are Sargon of Agade, Moses, Cyrus, and
Romulus; and Rank has enumerated many others to whom
the same story applies either as a whole or in part: Oedipus,
Karna, Paris, Telephos, Perseus, Heracles, Gilgamesh and

others. To the list we would surely add Sri Krishna and Christ.

Freud had contended that the inner source of the myth was the so-called "family romance" of the child, in which the son reacts to the change in his inner relationship to his parents, and especially to his father. He theorized that the child's first years are governed by a grandiose estimate of the father, and that later on, under the influence of the disappointments and rivalry within the family, the child becomes more critical of his parents. He then concluded that the two families in the myth, the noble one and the humble one, represent images of the parents as they appear to the child at successive periods in his development.[7]

Jung could not accept as complete this view of the unconscious sources of universal mythological motifs, or *mythologems*, as the core elements of myth are called. He had, after all, subjected the hypothesis of the unconscious as put forth by Freud, to exacting tests by using the psychoanalytic method on his own patients. And, in the process, from many separate investigations it became increasingly clear to Jung that *the psychopathology of the neuroses and of many psychoses could not dispense with the hypothesis of the collective unconscious.* It was the same with dreams. In dreams, in neurotic fantasies, and in the hallucinations of psychoses, Jung saw numerous linked ideas to which he could find parallels only in mythological associations of ideas, that is, in mythologems. If his thorough investigations had shown that in the majority of such cases it was merely forgotten or repressed material, he would not have gone to the trouble of making extensive researches into individual and collective parallels in legend and comparative religions. But, he wrote, "typical mythologems were observed among individuals to whom all knowledge of this kind absolutely was out of the question, and where indirect derivation from religious ideas that might have been known to them, or from popular figures of speech was impossible."[8] Jung asserted that such conclusions forced him to assume that he must be dealing with "myth-forming" structural elements in the unconscious psyche which produced out of themselves revivals of these mythologems, independent of all tradition.

These products were ". . . myths with a definite form, but rather mythological components which, because of their typical nature, we can call 'motifs,' 'primordial images,' types, or —as I have named them—*archetypes*."[9]

These archetypes represented certain regularities, consistently recurring types of *situations* and types of *figures*. Jung categorized them in such terms as "the hero's quest," "the battle for deliverance from the mother," "the night-sea journey," and called them archetypal situations. He suggested designations for archetypal figures also, for example, the divine child, the trickster, the double, the old wise man, the primordial mother. Of archetypal situations and figures Jung makes his meaning clear in a footnote to his discussion: "To the best of my knowledge, no other suggestions [for archetypes] have been made so far. Critics have contented themselves with asserting that no such archetypes exist. Certainly they do not exist, any more than a botanical system exists in nature! But will anyone deny the existence of natural plant-families on that account? Or will anyone deny the occurrence and continual repetition of certain morphological and functional similarities? It is much the same thing in principle with the typical figures of the unconscious. They are forms existing *a priori*, or biological norms of psychic activity."[10]

The great primordial images, as Jacob Burckhardt once aptly called them, give evidence of the inherited powers of human imagination as it was from time immemorial. Jung believed that this inheritance accounts for the phenomenon that certain motifs from myths and legends repeat themselves the world over in identical forms. He also found in it an explanation of why his mental patients were able to reproduce exactly the same images and associations that could be discovered in ancient texts. He has given innumerable examples of these textual parallels with the fantasy life of modern patients in *Symbols of Transformation*, and in other places.[11]

It was Jung's understanding that *the archetypes, as structural forming elements in the unconscious, gave rise both to the fantasy lives of individual children and to the mythologies of a people*. Unlike Freud, who had early asserted that the fantasies of children stemmed entirely from their personal experiences in confrontations with their own parents, and the conflicts between instinct and the controls imposed by the parents, Jung formulated the concept of the archetypes as preformed patterns of thinking into which the child's actual experiences fell, and through which the resulting childhood fantasies were given their shape. Freud had asserted that the myth forms were reflections of children's experiences somehow transferred to an entire people, along with their attending fantasies. But Jung, in what appears to be a more parsimonious explanation, saw the myth as a collective version of the emergence of the archetypal expression into a society, just as he saw fantasy as the emergence of the archetypal configuration in the individual.

The archetype, according to Jung, is a dominant of the collective unconscious. In order to comprehend the role of the archetype, therefore, it will be necessary to see how Jung conceived the collective unconscious. This is an extremely important issue, in which Jung has gone beyond Freud in viewing the scope of the unconscious—an issue which is crucial in its application in the therapeutic process.

We now need to consider briefly the difference in the views of Freud and Jung on the matter of the *structure* of the unconscious. I find these differences comparable in their therapeutic consequences to the divergence between the two men with respect to the role of the infantile trauma in the formation of neuroses; there Jung had accepted the Freudian concept of the *contents* of the unconscious, as far as it went, but he did not regard the early Freudian view of the contents as sufficiently inclusive.

As outlined by psychoanalyst Edward Glover, Freud had postulated an *unconscious system* of the mind on the basis of his having demonstrated that ideas and potential affects (an individual's subjective experience of his emotions) exist apart from consciousness and yet can be made conscious by the use of a technique which overcomes certain "resistances." These resistances indicated the existence of a barrier of repression, a kind of psychic frontier. *Consciousness* was henceforward regarded as another system of the mind, having the functions of perception to perform. Between these two systems was a borderline area, the content of which could be described as generally unconscious, although with appropriate stimulation it could be more or less recalled at will. He called this the *pre-conscious* system, thereby avoiding the term "subconscious" which would have confused the vital distinction between consciousness and the true (dynamic) unconscious. "This tripartite division constituted Freud's first outline of the *mental apparatus*, an organization whose function was to receive the incoming charges of (internal) instinct and stimulation coming from the external world, to master these charges and stimulations and to procure them satisfactory discharge (adaptation)."[12]

It is not to be questioned that Freud created the foundations of modern depth psychology through his epochal discovery of the unconscious as a dynamic entity which makes a profound impact upon human awareness, which is consciousness. The unconscious realm, according to Freud, manifests itself in dreams and in everyday conscious life through neurotic symptoms as well as in faulty actions. Freud's concept of the unconscious has greatly enlarged and deepened man's potentiality for self-knowledge and for understanding of the needs and motivations of his fellow man. The basic concept as enunciated by Freud, which met with such a storm of indignant rejection when it was first published, is commonly accepted in depth psychology and in psychiatry today. The question is no longer whether the concept is false or true, but whether it does indeed encompass all that needs to be said about the unconscious and its structure.

Jung's formulation of the concept of the archetype led him to what he called "another step forward" in his understanding of the unconscious. This was his differentiation of two layers of the unconscious. These are, in Jungian terms, the *personal unconscious* and the *collective unconscious*. Jung's description of the personal unconscious follows:

The personal unconscious contains lost memories, painful ideas that are repressed (i.e., forgotten on purpose), subliminal perceptions, by which are meant sense-perceptions that were not strong enough to reach consciousness, and finally, contents that are not yet ripe for consciousness.[13]

The collective unconscious may be thought of as an impersonal or transpersonal unconscious because, as Jung says, "It is detached from anything personal and is entirely universal, and because its contents can be found everywhere, which is naturally not the case with personal contents."[14]

The difficulty experienced by many people in grasping Jung's concept of the unconscious may be the result of taking him too literally. They assume that there must be a clear demarcation between the personal and the collective unconscious, and that the personal unconscious refers to everything that Freud said the unconscious was, while the collective unconscious is some peculiar construct of Jung's that no one else had ever thought of. As we read Jung's works we become gradually aware that in the psychological material brought up by individuals, the personal material shows the effects of its collective background and often is as a personal voice giving expression to an age-old liturgy. The personal unconscious is not really an exact parallel of the Freudian concept of the unconscious (including the pre-conscious), because it does not include specifically those instinctual elements common to all men, which were for Freud an important aspect of the unconscious. These Jung considers to be "transpersonal," i.e., universal. Also, Jung stresses that the personal unconscious contains contents that are "not yet ripe for consciousness," these contents evidently never having been in consciousness in the first place, are thus not a result of repression. It is important to note that the "not yet ripe" is part of the personal unconscious and it is suggestive of the thrust toward becoming conscious of *new material*, which defines the individual's potential.

The collective unconscious is better conceived as an extension of the personal unconscious to its wider and broader base, encompassing contents which are held in common by the family, by the social group, by tribe and nation, by race, and eventually by all of humanity. Each succeeding level of the unconscious may be thought of as going deeper and becoming more collective in its nature. The wonder of the collective unconscious is that it is all there, all the legend and history of the human race, with its unexorcised demons and its gentle saints, its mysteries and its wisdom, all within each one of us —a microcosm within the macrocosm. The exploration of this world is more challenging than the exploration of the solar system; and the journey to inner space is not necessarily an easy or a safe trip.

4

ARE ARCHETYPES
NECESSARY?

Are archetypes necessary? Most academic psychologists, if they have addressed themselves to the question at all, have answered *no*. It is difficult for me to imagine that there can be those who have failed to recognize that man is often moved by strange, mostly inexplicable forces; yet those very people who profess expertise in dealing with the human psyche have hesitated to name the mysterious pattern-forming elements which play so fundamental a role in the experience of man. Consciousness consists primarily of what we know, and what we know we know. As far from conscious experience are the archetypes as the center of the earth is from its crust. That the archetype defies the scientific mind is clear enough when we read one of the leading interpreters of Jung's thought: "It is impossible to give an exact definition of the archetype, and the best we can hope to do is to suggest its general implications by 'talking around' it. For the archetype represents a profound riddle surpassing our rational comprehension. . . . [It] expresses itself first and foremost in metaphors; there is some part of its meaning that always remains unknown and defies formulation."[1] Since archetypes cannot fully be grasped by man's mind—their being, in a sense, the very source of his thought processes and, consequently, of his attitudes and behavior—the concept of the archetype is bound to raise more questions than it can possibly answer.

It is understandable that most psychologists might consider archetypes beyond the area of their competence. They work painstakingly to try to remove vagueness and mystery from mental functioning. I, for one, have no wish to plunge the infant science of psychology back into the realm of metaphysical speculation from which it has only in this century emerged. But I do not believe we can avoid questions about the ultimate ground of human thought and behavior simply because answers do not present themselves with clarity and precision.

Nor can I, as a Jungian, be satisfied with reducing these primordial forming elements to a few well-known instincts such as hunger, self-preservation, sexuality, power drive. These are important, to be sure, but they do not account for the richness and productivity of the human mind when it is rooted in its ancient ground.

Are archetypes necessary? Are typical patterns of behavior-potential present in the young at birth? Perhaps the experimental psychologist will be the last to know. But the great playwrights and artists have always known, and the poet has asked the right questions:

> With what sense is it that the chicken shuns the
>   rav'nous hawk?
> With what sense does the tame pigeon measure out the
>   expanse?
> With what sense does the bee form cells? have not
>   the mouse and frog
> Eyes and ears and sense of touch? yet are their
>   habitations
> And their pursuits as different as their forms and
>   as their joys.
> Ask the wild ass why he refuses burdens, and the
>   meek camel
> Why he loves man: is it because of eye, ear, mouth
>   or skin,
> Or breathing nostrils? No, for these the
>   wolf and tyger have.

> Ask the blind worm the secrets of the grave, and why
>   her spires
> Love to curl round the bones of death; and ask the
>   rav'nous snake
> Where she gets poison, & the wing'd eagle why he
>   loves the sun;
> And then tell me the thoughts of man, that have been
>   hid of old.[2]

Psychologists have turned away from the *whys* of behavior, even while they have attempted to manipulate the *hows* of behavior. Even the great pioneer of depth psychology has hesitated at the portals of the darkest level of the collective psyche. It may be that Freud's bent toward speculative abstraction was so powerful that he was afraid of being mastered by it, and so he felt it necessary to counter this tendency by studying concrete scientific data. Ernest Jones reports in the biography that he had once asked Freud how much philosophy he had read. The answer was, "Very little. As a young man I felt a strong attraction toward speculation and ruthlessly checked it."[3]

It was Jung's belief that Freud had repressed the archetype of *spirit* in his own nature, with his insistence on his sexual theory. David Bakan develops this idea more fully in his book *Sigmund Freud and the Jewish Mystical Tradition,* the thesis of which is that in the background of Freud's development the Kabbalistic mysteries which had occupied his rabbi-grandfather had been transmitted to him—not directly, but via the negativistic attitude toward those ideas on the part of his father, who told him in effect: "We don't any longer subscribe to these antiquated superstitions." Yet Jung knew that the two problems which most occupied Freud were sexuality and archaic vestiges in modern man.

Jung said that he alone of all Freud's followers logically pursued these two problems which most interested Freud. He recognized the large part that sexuality plays as an essential—though not the sole—expression of psychic wholeness. But Jung's main concern, he said, was to ". . . investigate over and above the personal significance and biological function [of sexuality] its spiritual aspect and its numinous meaning, and thus to explain what Freud was so fascinated by but unable to grasp."[4]

The record of Jung's divergence from Freud and the discovery of his unique position vis-à-vis the unconscious is to be found in the autobiography of his own soul's wanderings. There, in a chapter titled "Confrontation with the Unconscious," he tells how he observed the formation of various sub-personalities which appeared as personifications of aspects of the unconscious. Gradually over the years these images fell into categories, as though they were formed on specific patterns. Jung came to know the forming elements out of which these patterns emerged as *archetypes*. The dynamic symbols, based on the interaction between the archetype and a particular culture, he called *archetypal images*.

Are archetypes necessary? That Jung found the concept of the archetype fundamental to the understanding of the psyche would be merely a metaphysical assertion if the archetypal elements did not manifest themselves in human experience, and particularly in that experience of the deeper levels of the psyche that are exposed in psychological analysis. The collected works of Jung are, of course, filled with examples of archetypal phenomena. The archetype always seems to lie behind and beyond the personal experience. The poet perceives that the child is born out of the primordial past of humanity. A few lines from Tennyson's *De Profundis*[5] expresses the human condition—consciousness emerging from the great mystery:

> Out of the deep, my child, out of the deep,
> Where all that was to be, in all that was,
> Whirl'd for a million aeons thro' the vast
> Waste dawn of multitudinous-eddying light—
> Out of the deep, my child, out of the deep,
> Thro' all this changing world of changeless law,
> And every phase of ever-heightening life,
> And nine long months of antenatal gloom
> With this last moon, this crescent—her dark orb
> Touch'd with earth's light—thou comest . . .

· · ·

> Out of the deep, my child, out of the deep,
> From that true world within the world we see,
> Whereof our world is but the bounding shore—

The recognition of the two worlds which are really one, that of consciousness and the unconscious, is necessary if we are to make the concept of the archetype meaningful in our own lives. But were it only in theory or poetry that the archetype occurred, it would be of little significance. Therefore, I want to indicate, through the use of some examples from my own analytic practice, how the archetype takes on meaning for people in our own day, indeed, how the archetype concept may deliver the suffering individual from a sense of personal disaster.

Sara is a woman of about forty. She is a business executive, well respected by her peers and subordinates. To the public she looks like a successful career woman, and the fact that she is not married is accepted as probably a matter of her preference. But this is far from the truth. Sara has never been able to establish a close love relationship with a man. In college she had dated some, but whenever it came to the possibility of physical intimacy, she would find some pretext for breaking off. Sara had always been very close to her widowed mother, and though the mother now lived in another city, she would spend many weekends with her mother and most vacations. She was frequently on the phone with her mother. "We kept in touch and looked out for each other," as she put it. She felt responsible for her mother's happiness and sense of security. Gradually, in the course of her analysis, Sara was able to recognize the domineering element in the old woman's "protectiveness." She brought into consciousness her resentment for the mother's having kept her in a very restricted life-style, making her remain close to home, criticizing all friends of her own age until she gave up inviting them to her house. There had been always the ominous, inexplicit warnings about "keeping away from boys." As well as about modesty and humility and going to church. And being good to maiden aunts.

As the analysis progressed, Sara reviewed the events of her

childhood, adolescence and young womanhood, and she began to express the anger she felt against her mother. She arrived at the point where she could verbally release her hostility to her mother, but still there was much bitterness. She relived traumatic episodes. She cursed. Although she understood the personal bases of her mother problem, it was by no means resolved. She was as tense as ever in relationships, even while she was trying to free herself from the sense of being watched over, controlled. The hypothesis that repressed affect is at the root of the neurotic development did not seem to be useful here. Repressions had been lifted. There was insight into the "cause" of the problem, but the insight did not bring relief.

Affect is the way in which feelings and emotions are experienced. In the psychologically healthy person the affects are freely expressed; feelings surrounding pleasant or unpleasant experiences are accompanied by appropriate facial expression and body postures and movements. These same affects can be noted when the person is merely talking about the experiences. The observation of affects is one of the most important diagnostic tools of the therapist. When the affect is inappropriate, when the patient laughs in recounting a sad event or becomes anxious totally out of any anxiety producing context, it may be assumed that the real affect has been repressed. This then becomes a clue to investigate in attempting to uncover the workings of the defenses—to try to discover what kind of material is being covered up.

It was more difficult in the case of Sara to determine the basis of her difficulty. If liberating the repressed affect was not the key, then it might be possible that the root of the neurosis did not stem from some personal experience entirely. I had, after all, dealt quite thoroughly with the personal history of the patient.

Then suddenly one day everything was different. Although in the past several sessions she had been vituperative in her anger against her mother, I had had the feeling that there was still more there, and that perhaps the still more did not really center on her mother at all. I did not intend to tell this to the patient because I thought she would have accepted it intellectually, as she had accepted other ideas I had presented in the past, and she would have continued as before, confident that she had achieved another bit of insight. So I waited, expecting that what I knew and what I was attempting to stimulate by keeping her as close to her affects as possible, would erupt in its own time. I was not surprised therefore when one morning she came to our session deeply shaken. I could see she had not slept much that night, that whatever had occurred had been a deeply moving experience. I listened as she told me about it:

"A few days ago I awoke in the morning before daybreak in a sweat, aware of a 'presence' within me; so intensely aware that I can recall exactly how it had felt:

"In the middle of the marrow of the bone in me, as far in as you can go without coming out, there was a mist in me that condensed into this shadowy form. . . . I felt it in every portion of my being . . ."

Then she went on to talk about the maternal image which she recognized not *as her mother*, but as existing *in herself* and *in her mother* as well, and also in her grandmother, and through the maternal line throughout generations. Each generation had carried that possessive and devouring style of behavior from the generation before—as a wraith, permeating the body and the soul. The image was so impressive that Sara was able to confront it, to speak to it. She did this in her fantasy, and it was so vivid that she was able to write down the words afterward:

"You have controlled me, stunted my growth, kept me from fulfilling mature sexual function. You frightened me with a story of men who have a big organ they stick into you—I thought it was a stick. You said not to disagree in public, you cut off my expression. You told me to 'come on in'—to see your friends—I wasn't ready to, I was angry, you forced me. You threw a murky shade over me, undermined my own expression, my own confidence. I was not me. You controlled my brothers—usurped their lives, decimated the identity of my father.

"Why have you done these things? Why do you live in me now? You *are* in me, specter-form. My mother is not my enemy—*You* are. You hold her captive too. You are not even my mother's image in me—separate spirit—Thing that has lived in her to capture me—I should slay you!

"I refuse to keep the peace—which is on your terms. I will awaken, arouse you—confront you. You may wrap me in indifference but I shall needle you enough to engage you. You shall answer why—maybe, even, I can forgive you—but it may be dangerous to think thus."

What more striking example could there be of the emergence into consciousness of an archetypal image, the Great Mother? She is the terrible female whose awesome power looms over the child—boy or girl—she knows all there is to know and from her everything must be learned—she metes out punishment or affection according to her own unfathomable laws, she has control over life and death through giving nourishment or withholding it, through inflicting pain or offering comfort and healing. Each mother-child pair acts out the archetypal drama in the nursery—of power standing over weakness, wisdom looming over ignorance. And if, in the confrontation with the Great Mother—a symbol arising from unconscious depths—the enemy can be seen in its archetypal rather than its personal form, then there is a chance that the personal aspect of the problem can be separated from its archetypal core. Through such a separation, the profound effect of the archetype upon the individual can be markedly depotentiated.

The archetype of the Great Mother can also present itself in a positive way, unlocking the strength and power of the individual. The Mother image appeared under strange circumstances to my analysand Margaret in an hour of very great stress, providing her with an experience of heightened consciousness.

Margaret is a mature woman who had been recently widowed when she came to me. She was working with the problem of discovering inner resources within herself which would help her to compensate for the loss of a strong and competent life partner. She insisted that she had no religious faith, and that she did not believe that there could be any possible help outside of herself. And, since she felt quite inadequate to the demands of readjusting her life, she had come to me to help her find new ways of thinking about her problems. When I probed the question of whether she had ever been open to the possibility that some of the helpful character she associated with her husband or with her relationship with her husband might still be accessible to her, she brushed off my remark as unrealistic. However what I said must have struck a responsive chord below the level of her awareness, for shortly after that in the course of her analysis she revealed the following incident:

"Some years ago I was spending a few days with a friend of mine in a remote area of the country. Her husband had to be away on a business trip, and since she was well advanced in pregnancy she had been reluctant to stay alone. One night a tremendous storm came up and there was a power failure so that the lights went out and even the telephone service was interrupted. We both became anxious, though I tried to hide my feelings as much as possible and to reassure my friend. At this time it happened that she went into labor, and there was no hope of getting any help to deliver the child. I felt absolutely lost, not having the faintest idea of what to do, except that I busied myself making sure that there were candles around and heating on the gas stove the water we had thoughtfully drawn while the storm was approaching.

"I guess you might say it was the classic situation of being 'beside myself' with fear of what might happen and with no one to turn to. And at the same time the feeling grew within me that help would come. It arose at first, I think, as a wordless sureness, and then I felt myself relaxing, growing nearly numb, but no longer anxious. I sensed the formation of words in my head, something like, 'I will do it' or 'I know how to do it,' and then the words became distinctly audible and seemed to come from a certain direction. I turned my head from my friend who was breathing heavily between her pains, lying there sweating on her bed, and saw in the gloom in the

far corner of the room up near the ceiling a faint glow of
light. As I stared at it, the light took the form of a woman,
my mother, who had been dead some fifteen years. In the
same moment I knew that the voice I had heard was her voice.
Then the scene shifted, and I could see my mother standing
by the bed, next to my friend, and it was as though I was
off in the corner of the room observing. And yet I was also
with my mother. As her hands moved to soothe the woman
in labor, to help her bear down, as her voice gently encouraged
my friend, I felt a great relief that it was going all right. I saw,
to my great wonder, the baby slowly emerge from between
the thighs of his mother, saw as though I were right there
that this was a strong active little boy, heard him cry, and
yet the cry was heard still from the distance of the corner
of the room. Soon my mother was holding him, wrapping him
in a tiny blanket, placing him beside his mother.

"What occurred then is vague in my mind, but it seemed
that I swam out of that dark corner and entered into the place
of my mother, or I came there and she entered into me, and
then departed. A shimmer of dim light in the far corner of
the room was there for an instant, then disappeared, and I
found myself fully present and fresh as though just awakened
from a good night's sleep, sitting at my friend's bedside. There
was blood on my hands and on my apron. Her child was
cradled in her arms and sucking at her breast, and she smiled
up at me and said, 'Margaret, I felt so calm, so secure—however did you manage?' I never told her, and in fact did not
allow myself to think about it, and soon the memory of those
uncanny moments faded. I have never spoken of them until
this day."

Margaret is an upper-middle-class, well-educated woman
who has always been well adapted to her life as a suburban
matron with family and community responsibilities. She is
not a person whom one would ever suspect of seeing spirits,
nor has she ever shown an interest in the lore of the occult,
quite the contrary. I have chosen her experience to indicate
that she represents a very great number of people who have
had one or more experiences with archetypal phenomena. In

this case the mother-archetype was embodied in the familiar image of Margaret's own mother. The experience is not explainable by the rules of ordinary sense perception, the ways in which we come to know the external world. It rather belongs to those intuitive phenomena by which we apprehend directly the inner experience, without the intervention of rational thought or inference.

The experience of the archetype in the parent-child relationship requires an explanation that goes beyond the theory of infantile sexuality as propounded by Freud. This experience was the subject of research which occupied Jung's major attention during the period from 1911 to 1913 when he was most active in the Vienna circle. At this time he had become so valuable to the psychoanalytic movement that Freud had designated him as "crown prince" in the hope that he would some day assume its leadership. However, Jung's independent spirit demanded that he follow where it led, and at this time it was leading him far from orthodox psychoanalytic doctrine. He had for a long time struggled with Freud's theory of infantile sexuality as delimited with respect to the personal experience of the individual, and now he began to investigate the archetypal roots of the oedipal situation.

This was a difficult and painful period for Jung. As he was clarifying his own ideas he was drawing further and further away from Freud, for whom he had all the ambivalent feelings of an aspiring son for a brilliant father.

For one thing, Jung felt that he had been overpowered to some degree by his older colleague, who had advanced his sexual theories with all his usual vigor for which he was well known. In the main Jung was highly interested and agreed in principle, but he did hold certain doubts and hesitations. When he tried to advance these reservations he was met with Freud's suggestion that his questions were due to his lack of experience. Here the "patient father" figure exercised a gentle control over the ebullient Jung. And Jung, for his part, may have expected to be joined in a discussion as an equal, even though he recognized that he did not, indeed, have enough experience to support his objections.

In his autobiography Jung referred to the crucial essay "The Sacrifice," saying that while he was working on it he knew it was the statement which would cost him his friendship with Freud.[6] Here Jung presented his own conception of the meaning of incest, which had been the cornerstone of Freud's sexual theory. Jung felt that the incest problem was to be understood symbolically and not literally. Thus libido had become for him more than the force behind sexuality; it had become the divine creative force of nature. The problem of incest was seen no longer as a purely individual dilemma, but as a phase in the collective experience of man as he develops toward a higher form of consciousness.

The problem of the sacrifice, the dissolution of the oedipal tie, had been treated by Freud as an individual problem. Each child had to work it out with his own mother or mother-surrogate in the process of moving toward maturity.

Jung saw the child's sacrifice of the paradise of the early and rewarding unity with the mother in a far wider context. He turned to a series of myths, which he regarded as the language of the collective unconscious, to Greek and Norse mythology, to Goethe's *Faust*, and to the Gilgamesh Epic of the Babylonians, finding everywhere the eternal and ubiquitous theme of sacrifice—of slaying the primal being in order that the world may be born. Perhaps this theme was most beautifully expressed in the Rig Veda:

Purusha (Man, Anthropos) was the primal being who

> Encompassed the world on all sides
> And ruled over the ten-finger place
> The highest point of heaven.

Jung wrote:

As the all-encompassing world-soul, Purusha had a maternal character, for he represented the original "dawn state" of the psyche: he was the encompasser and the encompassed, mother and unborn child, an undifferentiated, unconscious state of primal being. As such a condition must be terminated, and as it is at the same time an object of regressive longing, it must be sacrificed in order that discriminated entities—i.e., conscious contents—may come into being.[7]

Then came the sacrifice of this primal being by gods and men and it was said:

> The moon was born from his mind;
> From his eye was born the sun;
> From his mouth Indra and Agni;
> From his breath Vayu was born.
> From his navel grew the atmosphere;
> From his head the sky; from his feet the earth;
> From his ear the directions.
> Thus the worlds are made.[8]

Jung declares it is evident that "by this is meant not a physical, but a psychological cosmogony. The world comes into being when man discovers it. But he only discovers it when he sacrifices his containment in the primal mother, the original state of unconsciousness. What drives him toward this discovery is conceived by Freud as the 'incest barrier.' The incest prohibition blocks the infantile longing for the mother and forces the libido [Freud's term for sexual energy] along the path of life's biological aim. The libido, driven back from the mother by the incest prohibition, seeks a sexual object in place of the forbidden mother. Here the terms 'incest prohibition' and 'mother' etc. are used metaphorically, and it is in this sense that we would have to interpret Freud's paradoxical dictum: 'To begin with we knew none but sexual objects.' "[9] Jung insisted that the fact that the infant takes pleasure from sucking does not prove that it is sexual pleasure, for pleasure can have many different sources. That the archetypal experience appears in the young child by no means implies that it is limited to the young child. Archaism is a dynamic factor in the psychic life of adult civilized men as well, according to Jung, and the evidence is all about us if we will but notice it. One place where it may appear is in our dreams.

An example of an archetypal dream in a young adult will show how a Jungian analyst looks at a dream which contains material which the patient cannot connect with his early life or indeed, with any personal experience. David, a patient of mine, began his university career studying physics. Behind this

choice of a field of concentration, he told me, lay his desire
to find out how the world works. But as he gathered more
and more knowledge he found himself becoming increasingly
dissatisfied. It seemed to him that there was more that he
needed to know, or a different *kind* of knowledge, from what
he was being taught. Seeking an understanding of the logical
structures behind the processes observable in the material universe, he turned to philosophy. This too, failed to provide
him with answers; it only gave him neater ways to deal with
the questions. Finally, he had taken up theology. Here he
sought a wider meaning behind the apparent order of nature,
one that would go beyond the logical processes which could
be contained and controlled by his own intellect. But even
theology disappointed him—"Who can say what God is, and
how much less, what He wants?"

David came into therapy in despair; everything he had tried
to study had led him to *culs-de-sac* in the labyrinth that was
his world. He felt that life was pointless. He had learned so
much and he had discarded so much that he found it difficult
to communicate with anyone who had not achieved a very
high level of education. Even many of his professors, he found,
saw only one view. "You can't talk to them." He felt isolated,
and he derived little joy from anything except possibly his
compulsion to add more and more books to the library that
overflowed his shelves.

One night he had the following dream: *I am watching a
rocket take off. Suddenly it curves around and becomes a ship.
I am aboard—there is a tempest. The rocket-ship pitches me
about on a stormy sea until finally it overturns. I manage
to escape drowning by getting into a small lifeboat. Then
a dragon rises out of the water and swims rapidly toward me.
I am terribly afraid. For a moment I try to hide in the bottom
of the boat, but I know it will be of no use. He has come
up to the edge of my boat. Nearly paralyzed with fright, I
do the only thing I can do. I reach my hand overboard and
into the water and grab the fearsome dragon by its leg. In
this moment he turns into a small horse, a toy made of wax
about ten inches tall.*

David commented on the dream: "In thinking about this the morning after I awoke, I was amazed at how the dragon became small and harmless after I reached out and grabbed its leg. Also, I think of it in a positive way ever since. It seems like a psychological victory for me. I felt in a festive, jovial mood as I held up the small horse as if to say 'this is the great giant that I feared; he is really small and harmless.' "

The etymology of the word "jovial" was not overlooked. David had broken out of the boundaries of a constricted intellect by making an immediate and direct contact with the fantastic dragon, which symbolized the irrational element within himself. Victorious in bridging the gap between his own limited powers and the mysterious power he ascribed to a totally exterior supernatural force, he was able to assimilate to himself some of the energy that had been until then inaccessible to him. The psychic energy that had previously been contained in the unconscious, "bound up in the dragon," or in his fear of the non-rational, now became accessible to the conscious part of him, his ego. No wonder that he felt suddenly strong, like the immortal Jove, ruler of Olympus. No longer would the student have to live off the frothy scum of knowledge on the sea of the unknown and unknowable. Now he understood that he could reach into the depths, and bring up contents of the unconscious, rational or irrational—no matter how they might appear—and take hold of them and see what they might look like.

The archetype may be manifested in archaic form and so be terrifying when one faces it as a helpless individual. But when we know that our own experience of fear or disillusion or futility is more than a matter of personal dismay, that it is an experience that shares a common core with all mankind, then we become aware that there must always have been ways of dealing with the archetypal problems. Mythology provides us with classic solutions—sometimes we can become aware of them through a diligent search, but more often we bump into them somehow, without ever having been told how to apply them.

Another patient of mine was introduced to his personal myth in a peculiar way. Murray was an artist who lived in a shabby apartment with his girl. He loved her very much, but he was not entirely sure of her affections. She had told him that she wanted to go on a trip for a couple of weeks to visit her parents in another city. While she was gone he wanted to do something for her which would show her how deeply he loved her. He thought about what to do, and then he hit upon an idea. He found a few planks of wood around his studio and he built a bedstead of his own design, to surprise his girl when she returned. I asked him why, of all things, he had done *just that*. He told me that the idea just occurred to him one day as a very strong impulse; he knew it was the right thing to do to express his feelings, so he did just that.

I asked Murray if he had ever heard the story of Ulysses' return after the long years of wandering on his way home from the Trojan War. I told him how the traveler had returned incognito to the palace of his wife so that he could look over the situation without being recognized by the suitors who had taken control of his lands and were contending over who should have the hand of his beloved Penelope. A contest was suggested, in which it was agreed that the strongest among the suitors should win the lady. Ulysses, in rags, displayed his strength by stringing the great bow which he had left behind him, and which none of the suitors could even begin to bend. But Penelope, fearing some trick, or that some god was attempting to seduce her, demanded still further proof from her professed husband that he really was who he said he was. Thereupon he told her what no one knew but the two of them and the single maid who took care of the bed-chamber, the guarded secret of how he had built with his own hands from a living olive tree the bed that they shared when their love was young. No one else could have known that he had constructed their bedchamber around a sturdy tree, that he had cut down the branches, and had used the stump for the centerpost of their bed.

My lovesick analysand may or may not have known the

myth of the *Odyssey*; he did not recall it. Yet he had somehow known that the act of fashioning the bed had a symbolic meaning to him which he had not understood, but truly felt.

The mythologem reappears and reappears.

The archetype, as we have seen in the case of Sara, manifested itself by a sudden awareness in the course of the analytic process. In the case of David, it became apparent in a dream. Murray came to it through the work of his hands. Still another way in which the archetype emerges in the psychic life of man is through language. As a matter of fact, only recently have scientists begun to recognize the "innate symbolic machinery, common to all men, [which] may have been used before the beginnings of formal language to communicate about such basic concerns as birth, life, death, love, combat and fear of the elements, which are common to both animals and men."[10]

According to a report headed "Language study indicates collective unconscious exists," Joseph Jaffe, M.D., is willing to admit that "the existence of a collective unconscious common to all men is quite believable when translated into terms of recent studies on the foundation of language." He notes that babies all over the world begin to exhibit language behavior at the same time and in the same way. This behavior, he says, is not taught but is innate and preprogrammed and coincides with certain stages of brain maturation and the ability to form concepts. "The specific language being spoken in the environment serves only as a model for selection of a set of rules and distinctions which are automatically abstracted by the child" as his powers of conceptualization grow. . . . "That which is innate and common to the world's babies in learning a language, then, is a schema or catalogue of concept categories [this is exactly what Jung has understood as the archetypes of the collective unconscious] that are related by the brain to the subject matter of the environmental language by means of transformations (i.e., sentence X fits into category Y in such and such a way)." Dr. Jaffe concludes, "The fact that there is no natural language which does not contain a comparable catalogue of directions, assertions, negations, etc., is evidence for the existence of a universal grammar and semantics in all races."[11]

The evidence produced by research like that referred to above is often supported in surprising ways by the unconscious itself, which produces its own proofs for its existence and its nature. A dream brought to me by Ben, a schoolteacher in his first year of teaching elementary-school children and only beginning to perceive the manifold ways in which learning takes place, is a case in point: *I am in some kind of underground laboratory, teaching animals to speak. I'm trying to teach them to say words with a long "e." A man comes in, some kindly caretaker, and asks me if I've lost my mind. He says that animals have their own language. They don't care about my goddam phonics.*

The kindly caretaker, the man who knows animals because he has watched them day after day, is intuitively aware of what the teacher often does not know, and the scientist strains to discover. What the caretaker has known for a long time, and what he has to teach the teacher, is not so very different from what Noam Chomsky, one of the outstanding linguistics scholars in our time, had to say on television recently. I cannot reproduce what he said verbatim, but based on the notes I took as I was listening, the sense of his remarks was that the major properties of language structure are inherent in the human mind. The child is born possessing these qualities, and he has only to learn the particularities of the specific language of his own culture. Chomsky cautioned: Do not underestimate the originality and initiative of the human mind to develop language.

How very different is this point of view from that of the behaviorists who look upon the human organism as born possessed of a more or less inert and vacant machine called the brain which is programmed by the effects of the environment (television, parents, teachers, etc.) as input. If the organism-machine has been inadvertently fed the wrong data, been programmed badly by exposure to the wrong stimuli, well, then, let's get busy and pull the switches to extinguish the objectionable concepts, and then reprogram man in our own way. In the dream, is not the unconscious (personified by the old caretaker) telling the dream ego (Ben's schoolteacher aspect) that he is not to overlook the innate potential for development that expresses itself spontaneously in children as in all forms of life?

Two ways of thinking must be considered in connection with archetypal experience: *convergent* and *divergent* thinking.

A *convergent* way of thinking is to try to reduce psychic experience down to its "causes"—which may be found in the early experiences which established behavioral patterns, and which in their turn set the stage upon which future episodes of his life's drama would be enacted. The residues of the past must be examined, of course, for they contaminate the present with their content, and I cannot imagine that any depth psychologist would deny that. But we must not forget that the archetypal core, too, is present in all human experience. Its importance is that it not only helps to explain the past, but that it also provides a basis for anticipating possibilities in attitude and behavior for the future. Of course it is possible to change behavior without resorting to an understanding of archetypal processes. Men and women and children can be trained and retrained much as animals can be domesticated. People can become useful citizens, adapted to their world, willing to accept its glories and defeats, to fly the flag of their country, even to march off to senseless wars—for the glory of those who sit back and pull the strings or push the buttons and smile as they regard their profit-and-loss sheets. People can be changed, they can be made more productive, they can be pacified, they can learn to live in our world—all this without ever a reference to the concept that each man carries within him the potentiality for initiative, for independent thinking, for becoming what he is meant to be.

Convergent thinking conceives of life processes as being susceptible to being broken down into "problems" which then have to be solved. For every problem there is only one answer, or there is a "best" answer, and the objective is to find that answer. Sometimes problem-solving takes the form of a search for the cause of the trouble, the single traumatic event. Sometimes problem-solving consists in attempting to resolve difficulties by shifting behavior from a less acceptable kind to a more acceptable kind. Invariably the idea that there is a right way which has only to be found and instituted permeates convergent thinking. If you can figure out what the teacher wants, you get an "A." Pick the right answer from the multiple choices offered.

Problem-solving is not the primary aim or goal of archetypal psychology. If anything, the ability to handle problems may be a by-product. If we are ever to effect constructive and lasting changes in our own lives, we must strive for a *transformation* (note: I did not say a "cure") of the potentially disturbing or disrupting problems, by reaching toward their archetypal cores. Such a transformation cannot take place before one has gone beyond the personal to the universal dimension. In this process man, becoming more and more conscious, will not be satisfied by being told what his place in society is. The modern man needs to rescue himself from his cultural provincialism. No one can do it for him. To accomplish this, the convergent way of thinking is often just the wrong approach. The view that directs man's thinking reductively, always and again backward toward his childhood, infancy, and birth, soon reaches the limits of consciousness.

Divergent thinking is a more creative approach. It is an approach whereby many avenues fan out from the central core —which is the situation in which man finds himself in a given moment. The roads may indeed lead backward, but they may just as well lead forward, and there are ways that lead in other directions: neither backward nor forward. The divergent-thinking man regards his situation as being a "given" simply because he is there at the moment in which he contemplates it. It does not matter that he could have avoided it, nor that he should be somewhere else right now; the fact is that he is there, and that is what he must deal with. Recognizing this, it is not difficult to see that the situation in which he finds himself is similar in certain fundamental respects to experiences other people have had before. There are, he finds, fundamental life experiences, which become apparent when he begins to observe the nature of human experience. He will see the importance of discerning in which ways men are alike or similar—and where their experiences are primarily collective in nature. For only by knowing what we have in common with other men does it become possible to understand how we stand away from the mass, as free individuals. The study of mythology and fairy tales, and of literary forms and comparative religions, helps us to understand and recognize the power of the archetypal elements within all people, and then to put our personal experiences into the larger perspective. The archetypal idea, as Jung has said, "is essentially an unconscious content that is altered by becoming conscious and being perceived, and it takes its colour from the individual consciousness in which it happens to appear."[12]

At this point one might be tempted to ask how the world managed to get on so long without Jung's concept of the archetype. It did not. Jung did not lay claim to having discovered the concept—it is a very ancient one. In his essay, "Archetypes of the Collective Unconscious,"[13] Jung traces the history of the concept back to antiquity. He informs us: "the term archetype occurs as early as Philo Judaeus, with reference to the *Imago Dei* (God-image) in man. It can also be found in Irenaeus, who says: 'The creator of the world did not fashion these things directly from himself but copied them from archetypes outside himself.' In the *Corpus Hermeticum*, God is called . . . 'archetypal light.' The term occurs several times in Dionysius the Areopagite, as for instance . . . 'immaterial Archetypes' and . . . 'Archetypal stone.'

"The term 'archetype' is not found in St. Augustine, but the idea of it is. . . . He speaks of '*ideae principales*, which are themselves not formed, but are contained in the divine understanding.' 'Archetype' is an explanatory paraphrase of the Platonic *eidos*." And Jung concludes, "so far as the collective unconscious contents are concerned, we are dealing with archaic or—I would say—primordial types, that is, with universal images that have existed since the remotest times."[14] In the literature of the late nineteenth century, which Jung read during his student years, the concept of the archetype was implicit if not mentioned by name. In the field of comparative religion, scholars Hubert and Mauss referred to "categories of the imagination." The anthropologist Adolf Bastian, a hundred years ago, predicated "elementary" or "Primordial" thoughts (*Elementargedanken*). And Immanuel Kant stated that all human cognition possesses a priori sources of cognition, which seem to transcend the limits of all experience. Jung wrote that from these references it should be clear that his idea of the archetypes, literally a pre-existent form—does not stand alone but is something that is recognized and named in other fields of knowledge.

Students of animal behavior have coined the term "innate releasing mechanism" (IRM) to designate the inherited structure in the nervous system that enables an animal to respond in a predetermined way to a circumstance never experienced before. Chicks with their eggshells still adhering to their tails dart for cover when a hawk flies overhead, but not when the bird is a gull, duck, heron or pigeon. Furthermore, if the wooden model of a hawk is drawn over their coop on a wire they react as though it were alive—unless it is drawn backward, when there is no response.[15]

Tinbergen, who has given particular attention to the problem of animal learning, has shown that not only do differing species have different dispositions to learn, but that such innate dispositions come to maturity only in certain critical periods of the animal's growth. He writes about the Eskimo dogs of east Greenland, living in packs of five to ten individuals. The members of a pack defend their group territory against all other dogs. All dogs of an Eskimo settlement have an exact knowledge of the limits of their territories and where attacks from other packs may be feared. Immature dogs, however, do not defend the territory. They often roam through the whole settlement, sometimes trespassing into other territories from which they are promptly chased away. In spite of frequent attacks during which they may be severely hurt, they do not learn their territorial boundaries, and in this respect they seem amazingly stupid to the observer. When the young dogs are growing sexually mature, however, they begin to learn the extent of the other territories and within a week their trespassing forays are over. In two male dogs the first copulation, the first defense of territory, and the first avoidance of strange territory, all occurred within one week.[16]

A number of popular motion pictures have shown the phenomenon of the laying and hatching of eggs of the sea turtle. The female comes out of the water, and finds a point on the beach safely above the tide lines. There she digs a hole and deposits hundreds of eggs, covers the nest, and returns to the sea. Eighteen days later a small army of tiny turtles comes flipping through the sand and unerringly makes for the waves as fast as possible before the gulls overhead can dip low enough to pick the little ones off. Campbell, in describing this scene, observes that no more vivid representation could be desired of the spontaneity of the quest for the not-yet-seen. There is no opportunity here for trial and error, nor is there a question of fear. The tiny turtles know that they must hurry, and they know how to do it. Evidently they know where they are going, too, and that when they get there they must swim; and they know how to do that immediately as they reach the water.[17]

What does it all mean, the awakening to the functioning of the archetype all about us, and especially in our own lives? How shall we utilize this recognition? Is it a way of synchronizing the beating of our own hearts in time with the cosmic rhythms? Is it a way of sensing that we are not only the products of our history, we are also the makers of history, and moreover that we are living history itself?

That which is now known as myth and legend was once the core of belief. Today, because another age has created another language, the ways in which the archetypes manifest themselves are strange to us. We may recognize the archetypal image in the cathedral, but it is not so easy to be aware of it when it beams upon us from the television tube. The contents of the archetypes have changed, as they change with every age. But the forms of the archetypes are the same—there is still the encompassing Great Mother, the awe-inspiring

Father-God, the Divine Child, the Hero, the Trickster, the Old Wise Man, the Mana personality, and all the rest. Only they appear in new shapes. There is a new format. Dialogues have a new twist, but themes recur and recur.

Are archetypes necessary? It is not the task of the investigator, it seems to me, to determine whether what he discovers is necessary or not. (Is a walk on the moon necessary?) The investigator's task is to make his observations and report on them, on "what is." Whether the investigator is an experimental psychologist studying animal behavior in the laboratory, or a clinical psychologist interpreting test results, or a psychotherapist analyzing a patient's dreams—certain conditions inherent in the subject become evident to him. He formulates them in concepts. These concepts, when traced back to their roots, lead eventually to the archetypes. It is not that the *archetypes are necessary*—that would be the kind of value judgment the scientist is often reluctant to make. It is simply that the *archetypes* exist as categories for thinking and that they become manifest in images which point toward their ultimate meaning.

5

ANALYSIS
AND THE
COUNTER-CULTURE

I am concerned about the university students who speak so freely to me about what is bothering them. They tell me that they are unhappy within the halls of academia where the goddess is sweet rationalism, her handmaidens logic and order and objectivity. Of course I recognize that the students whom I see professionally are the unhappy ones. The others do not seek psychotherapy. On the other hand the students say that at some of our "best" universities, the "shrink" is at least as important to the progress of the student as is the professor. Some say the first makes it possible to endure the second.

A bright young woman undergraduate studying in the humanities told me not long ago: "The academic role drops like an albatross around my neck when I step into a university building. My posture changes, I get constricted, I feel that I am expected to fit into a pattern as outmoded as the fake gothic architecture of the quadrangle. It all reminds me of when we were kids—there were things that we were graded on:

How does she perform?
Is she cheerful?
Does she do as she is told?
Is she prompt?
Is she neat?

Is she clean?

Does she get along with the other children?"

She said that depression is frowned upon. "You are not supposed to be uneasy, that is all wrong. Anxiety? 'Here, try some tranquilizers,' they tell you at Student Health.

"There is, and there needs to be, a deadening of sensations. Just plain messing around is discouraged. It's like when they used to tell us to be sure to color within the lines."

A woman graduate student reaching toward the Ph.D. has an especially hard time, especially if she is not in one of the traditional women's fields (education, social service, child development, etc.). I was told this by Nora, who is in the anthropology program. She had been married just a few weeks previously. Nora came to her session one day with sparks shooting from her eyes, and just about ready to explode. This woman had been talking to her faculty adviser about her dissertation proposal. Although she had always been an excellent student, she had gotten out of her former rhythm now that she was trying to prepare some fairly decent meals, keep her apartment in order, and get to bed a little earlier with Tim. She told me frankly that she had not been burning much midnight oil. But she had been putting in a normal day's work on her studies. Here is the way she sputtered it out when she at last got to her analytic hour, and could let fly:

"The prof was telling me that my ideas are good, but that I have to be more of a craftsman. Being a creative person is all right, but the technical precision of the research technique is most important. In fact he said, 'Most of the time we turn out good craftsmen.' Then he praised a certain graduate student, one he admires above all the others. 'This man had stayed up all night with his wife until she had her baby at four in the morning, and the same morning at ten-thirty he was in the library stacks researching out his dissertation.' When the prof told me that I could only think of one thing to say, and I told him—'You must be out of your fucking mind!' "

Unbelievable? Not when entering students are initiated by

a university president's remarks like these which are supposed to set the tone of their college life for their next four years.

> The university's primary goal is intellectual. Its purpose is to expand the intellectual powers of the human community. Its basic dedication is to the powers of reason, and commitment to reason is not an easy one to make. It insists upon intellectual rigor, humility, honesty and an abundance of energy. And it demands that we examine so-called "fashionable doctrines" held by our peer groups, as well as those irrational inspirations or flashes of insight which come to us in the middle of the night. Mere faith is not enough; innocence offers no guarantee. One must constantly seek new methods to cut through to truth. It is excellence that is required; there can be no compromises. Our goals, then, are to comprehend our intellectual heritage to be able to reach the limits of knowledge and, ultimately, to guide others on the path of reason.

It may be more than a meaningful coincidence that many of the eighteen-year-olds who listened to the lecture were on pep pills or tranquilizers before the first quarter of their academic year was over. The goals set forth are undeniably valid for those who are able to devote themselves unswervingly to the pursuit of knowledge and reason, and I have no criticism of them per se. But I wonder whether they are enough to capture the minds and hearts of the best students today? It seems to me that the great urban university of the late twentieth century, set as it often is in the midst of a ghetto full of crowded tenements running over with ragged children and sullen teen-agers, cries out that more is needed than to bury one's self in books.

Many students find the life of the campus tantalizing but frustrating. The stimulation of great books is there all right, but they tell me that often reading lists are so long that it is possible only to skim over those works which, so many of them, represent the distillation of one man's entire creative lifetime. The undergraduate may only touch and taste; there is no time to savor before he must move onto something else. Always and always the sense of incompleteness, of hurrying like a child dragged by a harried mother through a fabulous toy store in the last days before Christmas.

To excel—is exceedingly demanding. It is clear by the very definition of the word, that not all students are going to be able to *excel.* For to excel is to be distinguished by superiority, to surpass others. And what of those others who are surpassed? Where do they find their approval, their sense of fulfillment, the consonance of their lives with the goals set forth by the university hierarchy? Whatever they do in the world of classroom achievements cannot come up to the ideals set forth by the collective. For each student who "succeeds" in the sense of excellence, there must be several who are disappointed, who are frustrated, who need to find a way to block themselves off against the smell of defeat and the embarrassment of facing their friends and their parents and most of all themselves, with the fact that they have not met the standards that have been set for them.

It may be said that this situation is no different than it ever was, that there were always academic pressures, and there were always those who were unable to meet them, who had to be content or at least make their peace with being second best or worse, or scarcely in the race. I have been thinking about that, because subjectively I know there is a difference. I did my undergraduate work at the end of the thirties when the Second World War was brewing. I attended Ohio State University, a large school even then by the standards of the day, and it seemed to me then as it does to students now, that most of the teaching was uninspiring, while images of two or three professors still glow like beams of light through the fog of memory. But I don't think I was untypical of the earnest student. I concluded that a structure was there in which the educative process could take place, and that as long as there were libraries and laboratories and twenty-four hours a day to conjure with, that I could manage to wrest for myself as good an education as my energy and motivation would permit—and the professors be damned.

In the late 1950s when I returned to school to work on my master's degree it was not too different. You could do what you wanted to do within limits, and it was uncrowded. The students mostly were those who had been born in the depression and early war years, they were reared in difficult times and nurtured more on the milk of concern than on the honey of affluence.

But when I returned for my doctorate in the sixties it was all different. To begin with, I had been away from the United States for several years, studying in Switzerland. I had left a prosperous country, one which I had regarded as safe and secure. We had sold our house in the suburbs to get the money to study at the Jung Institute, but consciously our mind-style life-style was in many ways still in that house. We had left behind us the "good life," maybe even the American Dream.

The New Era burst upon us with astonishing suddenness one November evening in 1963 as we were sitting in our shabbily furnished hundred-year-old apartment in Zurich, quietly reading or studying. Suddenly there was a loud knock on our door. I answered and Fräulein Ekstein, our upstairs neighbor rushed in. Breathless from running down the steps, she blurted out, "Have you heard, have you heard, your President's been shot!"

In that instant I knew my country now was not the same country that I had left, that it would never be the same. I knew that the place, which in my mind had always meant internal peace and security, had been torn open by a barrage of bullets, that its bloody guts were exposed and spattered on the streets, that the wound if not fatal was grievous. All in that instant I saw my fantasy, that revolution-in-the-street was something that happened only in countries inhabited by hot-blooded Latins, was truly a fantasy; for it could happen to anyone anywhere, and indeed had happened to President Kennedy, and to the country he had served, my country.

There came into my mind a recollection of reading about Jung's vision in October of 1913 when he was suffering a sense of oppression which he felt "no longer sprang exclusively from a psychic situation, but from concrete reality." The vision: "I saw a monstrous flood covering all the northern and low-lying lands between the North Sea and the Alps. When it came up to Switzerland I saw that the mountains grew higher and higher to protect our country. I realized that a frightful catastrophe was in progress. I saw the mighty yellow waves, the floating rubble of civilization, and the drowned bodies of uncounted thousands. Then the whole sea turned to blood." An inner voice spoke to him. "Look at it well; it is wholly real and it will be so. You cannot doubt it."[1]

Fräulein Ekstein flopped into a big armchair, and we turned on the Telefonrundfunk to hear the news. As it came across in staccato reports I saw the rivers of blood spilling over my own country, while I remained safe and secure in the fortress that was Switzerland. It seemed clear to me that the fair country I had left, expecting to return to her in all her remembered beauty, now lay like a young woman raped and battered, left exposed at the side of the road.

Today's university students were impressionable youngsters when the death of John F. Kennedy had begun the process of toughening their minds to the necessity of accepting the fact of sudden brutality. That process was to move through many stages, finding later expressions in such fantastic aberrations of the American Way as the Manson family's ritual slaughter of Sharon Tate and her friends, and the "massacre" at My Lai. For the latter, Calley's defense was that he was only doing what the Army taught him to do:

> We learned one thing at O.C.S. that we had been taught through childhood was bad: killing. We came to believe that we would go to Vietnam and be Audie Murphys. . . . We would get a big kill ratio there—get a big kill count. In today's society everything is, "How many thousands?" "How many millions?" Which is a farce but it's the same at O.C.S.: it's numbers. The one thing wrong with O.C.S. was, we never learned that in Vietnam there will be friendly civilians all around us. Sure: in Saigon there will. In the secure areas the Vietnamese may be clapping and cheering like the French in the 1944 newsreels do, "Yay for America!" But we would be somewhere else: we would be where the V.C. are. It was drummed into us, "Be sharp! Be on your guard! . . . In combat you haven't any friends! You have

all enemies!" Over and over in O.C.S. we heard this. I told myself, *I'll act as if I'm never secure. As if everyone in Vietnam's going to do me in. As if everyone's bad* . . . One thing about my court martial is, I'll be learning things. What is a massacre? An atom bomb on Hiroshima isn't a massacre, but a hundred people's a massacre: I don't understand.[2]

Today's students don't understand either. Some are in college not because they want to be there but because it is that, or an education like Lieutenant Calley's. Either hand in your term papers and give the professors what they want on the exams, or tell it to the draft board. Either you make it with your intellect or you don't make it at all. The women get pulled into it too; if they want to stay in college they have to compete with men. In graduate school they have to do a little better than the men.

Jennifer will serve as an example of the disenchanted university woman, and Jennifer is by no means extraordinary. In fact, I selected her case because it is so typical. She had been one of the best students in her high school class in a medium-sized southern city. With hope and enthusiasm she had entered the freshman class of a top-ranking midwestern university. That was in September. By February she was in psychotherapy for the first time in her life. She was deeply depressed, getting stoned on grass every weekend and once in a while during the week.

She had told me that her closest girl friend is contemplating suicide, that in a girl's dormitory there had been fourteen suicide attempts in one year.

I asked her why she smoked grass. This was her reply:

"Thirty per cent of my entering class is now gone. It takes all I can do to get up and get going in the morning. When I first came here, I could study into the night—like—it was fun. But pretty soon the personal involvement was gone—they said —we demand this from you—it's got to be handed in on time— no excuses—then I got the flu—getting sick was a relief. The pressure they put on me would coincide with the pressure I'd put on myself. It was too much."

I asked her what happened then.

"When I felt well again I put in more and more time on my studies. I thought I'd gone a long way with my independent study of the philosophy of Whitman. Professor F said I had a square mind, and what could you expect from a little girl from Birmingham. He said, 'Your ideas are a dime a dozen.' I told him that rationality was only a means to an end. He was totally denying anything that wasn't altogether rational. You have to struggle to keep your humanity. He said, 'How can you work with anything where there aren't answers?' You could work twenty-four hours a day and they still wouldn't be satisfied. If I go to the Art Institute on Saturday morning, I feel guilty about it, and then have to stay up until three in the morning at my desk to make up for it. They are never satisfied with the work—you have to work harder. Everybody I know is solving it in another way—drop out, transfer, stick it out if you're near graduation, these incredible relationships, drugs, it helps you escape. I never thought about suicide till I came here.

"I have no trust, no optimism, two things I had when I came here. I feel like if the world came to an end it wouldn't really matter. There used to be more ups than downs. Now there are more downs than ups. Despair, despair, despair.

"It's like my mind saying, 'You're not going to study.' At one time I enjoyed it. If you've got your choice of realities—I find it very difficult to live with that reality; I don't even know if it is reality—

"It's a chunk of reality—so much that is real is left out of it—my emotions are just incredibly strong—I don't give it up. The people I know who have succeeded intellectually have been extremely immature emotionally. I've grown tremendously since I've been here in all sorts of ways. But have *they*, the intellectual ones? They have really sharp minds, but have they grown emotionally?

"In fact when I play my flute, or when I read what I really want to read, I feel guilty. I started to read a book on Jung. I keep my Jung book to the side. I say, okay, when I finish my History of Western Civilization, and my French and my

Biology, then, if I can still keep my eyes open I get to read the Jung book. It's like a lollipop.

"The only reason people stay in, or come back after they've dropped out, is that you can't let them feel that they've beaten you. I think about suicide. I'd commit suicide, but then *they* would have won, so I can't."

Mixed up? Disturbed? Not seeing reality clearly? Perhaps. But a few months ago Jennifer was a cheerful, well-adjusted, fun-loving girl who was also a good student and deeply involved in getting an education. Now she is listless, tired, and growing despondent.

One who managed to make it through college and get her bachelor's degree was Lynn. She wasn't quite as bright as Jennifer but more cynical. She gave the professors what they seemed to want, and managed to keep quiet about how she hated college. She squeaked through on passing grades, had a hard time getting a job when she finished, and reluctantly settled for a position as a welfare worker for public aid. The pay was better than what she could get elsewhere. I had seen her in therapy for several sessions when she was having trouble deciding whether to stay in school or drop out, and had given her the support she needed to continue. A few days ago I met her on the street and asked her how she was doing, and whether she was still working for public aid. "Oh yes," she told me, "but I'm going to quit in June, take the money I can save, and go spend the summer in Europe. Then when I come back I'll go on welfare until they get me a job. I don't suppose they'll keep a college graduate on welfare too long."

Madness in Academia. It is not the madness of a few "emotionally disturbed" who were bound to be misfits anyway. It is something far more serious, rather like a sinister plague that spreads over a healthy community, gradually weakening the inhabitants in ways that they hardly recognize until they have all but lost the ability to resist it.

And still, there are ways of resisting. There have always been ways of resisting the attitudes of the establishments, the "collective consciousness." People have not had to look far to find them. In a milieu where the intellectual values are overstressed, the non-rational elements of the human personality are forcibly repressed. Still active in the unconscious, they offer up ideas which become separated and unacceptable to the ruling elements of the society. Then it is that dissident groups develop, or dissident individuals, whose interests and behavior bring to light the formerly unaccepted and hidden aspects of the group's or the individual's nature. These are the people who form the counter-culture.

Jung invested a great deal of his energy and interest in exploring the counter-culture of his day, and not only that, he was interested in all counter-cultures of days past. Since he had been reared as the son of a small-town pastor, the culture in which he grew up and which formed his early attitudes toward what was considered "correct thinking" was that of traditional Protestant Christianity. Yet during the early period of his confrontation with the unconscious, he was forced by irruptions of material from the collective unconscious into his own life to look at some of the phenomena which grew out of that side of Christianity which had little relationship with what was preached in the churches—that is the mystical sects, the gnostics, and particularly the alchemists. He explained his interest in this way:

> Whereas in the Church the increasing differentiation of ritual and dogma alienated consciousness from its natural roots in the unconscious, alchemy and astrology were ceaselessly engaged in preserving the bridge to nature, i.e., to the unconscious psyche, from decay. Astrology led consciousness back again and again to the knowledge of . . . the dependence of character and destiny on certain moments in time; and alchemy offered numerous "hooks" for the projection of those archetypes which could not be fitted smoothly into the Christian process. It is true that alchemy always stood on the verge of heresy and that certain decrees leave no doubt as to the Church's attitude toward it, but on the other hand it was effectively protected by the obscurity of its symbolism, which could always be explained as harmless allegory. For many alchemists the allegorical aspects undoubtedly occupied the foreground to such an extent that they were firmly convinced that their sole concern was with chemical substances. But there were always a few for whom lab-

oratory work was primarily a matter of symbols and their psychic effect.[3]

No wonder the present-day "alchemists" have come into prominence on the college campus. And, like the medieval adepts and their feminine partners, called "sorors," who proclaimed *Aurum nostrum non est aurum vulgi* (our gold is not the common gold), the turned-on generation in speaking of its magical elixir similarly announces that "our panacea is not the common (medicinal) drug." The priest-sociologist, Andrew M. Greeley, in an article titled, "There's a New Time Religion on Campus"[4] described various groups which combine "the put-on and the serious, the deliberately comic and the profoundly agonized, . . . the bizarre and the holy," as manifestations of a neo-sacred movement now observable around the country. He quoted Professor Huston Smith of MIT, himself deeply interested in Asian studies. Smith had taken this trend into account and offered an unstructured seminar for some of his best students. Professor Smith wrote:

> I cannot recall the exact progression of topics, but it went something like this: Beginning with Asian philosophy, it moved on to meditation, then yoga, then Zen, then Tibet, then successively to the "Bardo Thödol," tantra, the kundalini, the chakras, the *I Ching* [a book presenting an ancient Chinese divination device which enables one to make decisions—a sort of pre-I.B.M. computer], karate and aikido, the yang-yin macrobiotic (brown rice) diet, Gurdjieff, Maher Baba, astrology, astral bodies, auras, parapsychology, witchcraft, magic. And underlying everything, of course, the psychedelic drugs. Nor were these students dallying with these subjects. They were *on* the drugs; they were eating brown rice; they were meditating hours on end; they were making their decisions by *I Ching* divination, which one student designated as the most important discovery of his life; they were constructing complicated electronic experiments to prove that their thoughts, via psychokinesis, could affect matter directly.
>
> And they weren't plebeians. Intellectually they were aristocrats with the highest average math scores in the land, Ivy League verbal scores, and two to three years of saturation in M.I.T. science.[5]

It was reported that the student body in a Canadian university was given a chance to have a voice in the selection of courses in their curriculum. The majority of the courses chosen had to do with astrology, Zen, sorcery and witchcraft.[6] Nor are the seekers interested in having their subjects technologized. For several months a big-city newspaper ran a horoscope column prepared by a computer. The paper reported, "That was a mistake. Readers neither liked nor trusted the machine." It announced that next Sunday it would correct its error. "Man replaces the machine, after months of searching for the right man."[7] We may hopefully assume the search was carried on by someone from the personnel department, and not by the computer.

Isaac Bonewitz is an enterprising young man who evidently believes in magic and convinced his advisers that the subject was a legitimate area of study. He concocted a magic course with ingredients from psychology, sociology, anthropology, religion, folklore and mythology, and received his B.A. in magic from the University of California at Berkeley. He considers magic "one step beyond parapsychology which painted itself into a corner years ago and is still there." The problem, he says, is that parapsychological research is limited to spontaneously reported cases or laboratory experiments. It doesn't take account of the past and all the reports of unexplained phenomena in primitive cultures.[8]

It is one thing for a university to sanction the investigations of a student *about* magic, especially if the faculty advisers can be assured that the "research" will be carried out primarily in the library. It is quite another matter when the curious try to find out about magic through their own experience. Some universities, a very few to be sure, are taking what they consider to be a progressive attitude toward the appearance of strange campus cults. One discovered that it had a coven of warlocks (male witches) on campus. The dean said, "A couple of hundred years ago we would have burned them at the stake. Twenty-five years ago I would have expelled them. Now we simply send them all to psychiatrists."[9]

The fact that Jung wrote a doctoral dissertation with the

title *On the Psychology and Pathology of So-Called Occult Phenomena* has attracted many people who have an interest in, or are fascinated by, the kinds of experiences that are generally grouped under the heading of "occult." For this reason there frequently come to the Jungian analyst people who have had some experiences with faith healing, extrasensory perception, precognition, the *I Ching*, Tarot cards, reincarnation doctrine and astrology. Such people often begin playing around with what they perceive to be unusual powers within themselves to influence others. Suddenly they feel that they have loosed a demon who has more power than they have, and they become frightened. They need guidance, and they believe that any psychologist other than a Jungian will refuse to take their experiences seriously. They seem to want support for what they are doing, that is, they want to see it in relation to the natural world. The very idea of supernatural powers can become terrifying to anyone who has been taught that demons do not exist. In my own practice I have been called upon often by such people, and I am sometimes shocked and surprised at what some of these people are involved in. Perhaps the most shocking part of it is who these people are, for they are not necessarily the kind of people you would expect to find dabbling in black magic.

Not too long ago I was asked by a man who was suffering from acute anxiety to see him in therapy. He was a graduate student in a theological school well known for its highly rational faculty and its disciplined demands for theoretical knowledge. In the course of his training in pastoral psychology, he had been assigned to visit and counsel with patients in a mental hospital. One woman patient interested him especially because of her suggestibility and the dramatic content of her hallucinations. She would see people and hear voices from the other side of death. After a time she was well enough to be discharged. The student took it upon himself to continue seeing her, now at her home, ostensibly to help her, but without the knowledge of his supervisor. He began practicing hypnosis on her and found it easy and fascinating to get her to go into a trance, during which she could become highly emotional and relate her visionary experiences of a "spiritual" nature. He came to me feeling that the material she brought up was of great consequence, but he did not quite know what to do with it.

I could see from the content of the discharged hospital patient's material that the divinity school student was provoking a psychosis that lay very close to the surface. Also, it was clear that he was becoming drawn into it, invaded, as it were, by the "psychic infection." I could see that he was unable to put any distance between himself and the material. Therefore I warned him to withdraw from that problematic relationship, and to refer the patient so that she could receive competent professional help should the manifestations continue.

This kind of advice was not what the young man was seeking from me, as soon became obvious. What he wanted was someone to share the responsibility with him for what he was doing, on one hand, and on the other, some help in controlling potent forces with which he did not feel prepared to deal. Soon after I suggested that he might need to consider his own motivations in pursuing the quasi-therapeutic relationship with the woman, he stopped coming to me. At termination he expressed the opinion that as a therapist I was much too rationally oriented.

My own unconscious has suggested that he may have been right. A few months after the incident mentioned above I was asked to lecture at the college this young man had been attending. My subject was "Jungian Psychotherapy." I tried to present Jung in a way that would make him somewhat acceptable to academicians whom I regarded as overintellectual. My presentation was scholarly and dull. I was unhappy about it. The night following my lecture I had the following dream: *I am in a hospital ward where I am to visit psychotic patients. I am in a very dark corner and I overhear a spirit-healer talking to a patient. He is accompanied by a female assistant. His words are, "There are people praying for you—do not worry—you are in good hands." All of this is said over and over again in a kind of hypnotic chant. I stand in the gloom just out of their view, perhaps behind a curtain or partition, but close enough so that I can watch and listen. All the time I am telling myself that if they are so "in touch" they will prove it by sensing my presence. At this moment they ("they" are the theology student who was my former patient and his fiancée), appearing as a warlock and a witch, reach out to where I am standing and grab me. They try to force a confession out of me by holding me down and massaging my inner thigh, which has at one time an exciting and a calming effect on me. Then there is a struggle for dominance between them and me. I was not sure how it came out.*

The dream brought out into clear focus my own ambivalence concerning the matter of psychic forces about which so little is known and their ways of affecting sense impressions, thought and behavior. I have tried to keep an open mind to the phenomena brought to me by my patients, for I know that there is a thin line between intuition and vision, and between vision and hallucination. And I also know that the difference between madness and creativity lies not so much in the nature of the inner experience of seeing something in a new way, but rather in what is done by the individual with that inner experience. The forces which push their way out of the unknown into consciousness are not always comprehensible. We can test them, as apparently I was portrayed as doing in the dream, or we can deny them and make an end to the matter. In testing them, I took a certain risk, to be drawn into the power system which I could not control. The dream showed me an attitude I could have taken vis-à-vis the man—a more open attitude, which would then have put us into a hand to hand combat to see which were stronger—the powers of reason or the strength of the irrational. I could not help drawing an association to my dream from the Biblical story of Jacob, who in the darkness of night in the desert wilderness is called upon to wrestle with the stranger. In the combat the stranger touches Jacob on the inner thigh, and Jacob will not let him loose until he has extracted a blessing from him. In that moment Jacob is transformed, that is, he

is given a new name. The name is Israel, meaning "he who
has striven with God and with men and has prevailed."

The messenger from beyond, sometimes called a "medium,"
is a character who has appeared historically in an endless
variety of different forms in every land and in every generation. From the most primitive times there have been those
who have "spoken with the spirits," the ghost seers, the ones
who could call up the voices of the dead. A firm belief in reincarnation or in the possibility of resurrection from the dead
continues to be held by millions of people, even in this last
third of the twentieth century. Even among many who do not
profess such beliefs, there is a sometime queasy attitude—
when they hear a tale of spirit apparitions which is supposed
to have actually happened, their response is often something
like: "Of course I don't believe it, but then it *is* rather
uncanny."

One cannot help but wonder what happens to the warlocks
and witches and dabblers in black magic when they come
face to face with the typical psychiatrist. I can, however, report that as a Jungian analyst I have had my share of students
and others who selected me as their psychotherapist or analyst because they already had some information about Jung's
openness to the weird world of archaic thinking, where magic
as an explanation for remarkable events is self-understood.

Jung's essay "Archaic Man"[10] calls to mind the stereotypical views of primitive people who live close to nature and hold
ideas which seem quite alien to the "civilized" contemporary
adult. Jung uses the word "archaic" to mean primal, original.
He has suggested that it might be possible to survey the world
of archaic man and the meaning that it had for him from a
superior standpoint, since our mental equipment is more differentiated than his and we are so far removed from him in
time as to be able to avoid the prejudices which flower in
propinquity. Indeed, this was the attitude of "an authority
in the field of primitive psychology [who] never wearies of
emphasizing the striking difference between the 'prelogical'
state of mind and our own conscious outlook."[11] This famous
armchair anthropologist Lévy-Bruhl was fond of referring to

"collective representations," those "widely current ideas whose truth is held to be self-evident from the start, such as the primitive ideas concerning spirits, witchcraft, the power of medicines, and so forth." He makes the distinction that "while it is perfectly understandable to us that people die of advanced age or as the result of diseases that are recognized to be fatal, this is not the case with primitive man. When old persons die, he does not believe it to be the result of age. He argues that there are persons who have lived to be much older. Likewise, no one dies as the result of disease, for there have been other people who recovered from the same disease, or never contracted it. To him, the real explanation is always magic. Either a spirit has killed the man, or it was sorcery. Many primitive tribes recognize death in battle as the only natural death. Still others regard even death in battle as unnatural, holding that the enemy who caused it must either have been a sorcerer or have used a charmed weapon."[12]

Jung reviews the many ways in which the thinking of "primitive man" is reported to be of a distinctly different nature from that of the modern cultivated European or American. He then comes through with his ironic little joke, which is that "it is not only primitive man whose psychology is archaic. It is the psychology also of modern civilized man, and not merely of individual 'throw-backs' in modern society. On the contrary, every civilized human being, however high his conscious development, is still an archaic man at the deeper levels of his psyche. Just as the human body . . . displays numerous vestiges of earlier evolutionary stages so the human psyche is a product of evolution which, when followed back to its origins, shows countless archaic traits."[13]

What is it then, that gives us the feeling that the world in which magic is an everyday occurrence is a world that is prodigiously strange? Is it an affront to the establishment, whose rational presupposition it is that every effect has a natural and perceptible cause? For to the establishment, specifically the academic establishment, causality is one of the most sacred dogmas. "There is no legitimate place," says Jung, "for invisible, arbitrary, and so-called supernatural powers—

unless, indeed, we descend with the modern physicist into the obscure, microcosmic world inside the atom, where, it appears, some very curious things happen. But that lies far from the beaten track. We distinctly resent the idea of invisible and arbitrary forces, for it is not so long ago that we made our escape from that frightening world of dreams and superstitions, and constructe⁷ for ourselves a picture of the cosmos worthy of our rational consciousness—that latest and greatest achievement of man."[14]

Shades of the university president's keynote address! Is it any wonder that the archaism in the mind of civilized man, forcibly isolated from the realm of intellectual development, finds its expression in its own curious ways, seeking to experience mysterious happenings which cannot be brought under the control of the academic hierarchy? I believe that it is a protest against a one-sided educational system in which the intellect is finely tuned at the expense of the whole person, including his passions and his tenderest sensibilities. These latter, then, remain inferior in the sense of being undeveloped, and so in a relatively archaic state. The original idea behind magic is again being accepted, the idea that certain people are capable of employing a power by which they can exercise *control over nature* so as to make nature obey their laws rather than her own. This is, of course, quite the opposite of those feats of technology which reverse the courses of rivers or harness the energy of the atom in order to demolish a city. Our scientists have *discovered the secrets of nature* and are applying them in a natural way to bring the anticipated effect out of the predictable cause.

Magic is and has always been an element of the counterculture in the area of religion, as Jung has shown. In speaking of religion here, he means "a careful and scrupulous observation of what Rudolph Otto[15] aptly termed the *numinosum*, that is, a dynamic agency or effect not caused by an arbitrary act of will."[16] The *numinosum*, then, refers to a sense of that "quality belonging to a visible object or the influence of an invisible presence that causes a peculiar alteration of consciousness." Since the influence of this dynamic agency is not subject to control by the human will, the experience of it is said to come to a man by virtue of a (divine) grace. Jung offers the example of the administering of the sacraments in the Catholic Church for the purpose of bestowing their blessings on the believer. To avoid the suggestion that this might imply in the slightest way enforcing the presence of divine grace, "it is logically argued that nobody can compel divine grace to be present in the sacramental act, but that it is nevertheless inevitably present . . ."[17]

Still, many religious practices and performances seem to be carried out for the sole purpose of calling forth the power of the *numinosum* at will by invocation, incantation, sacrifice, meditation and other yoga practices, self-inflicted tortures and other devices of a magical nature. Looked at another way, the magical demonstrations may in fact be an expression of man's frustration at *not* being able to control his own destiny, and hence his need to find ways of creating the illusion that his small ego can somehow counteract the inexorable power of the "wholly other." In this way the "witches and warlocks" may be shown that their magical games are evidence of a sense of impotence in the face of an overwhelming authority. That authority may appear as a transcendent god, or a human figure, or as a vaguely malignant "system"; in any case the god must be propitiated.

On one level the fascination with and use of magic may be seen as a degenerated form of religion, in which man acts out his need to feel less impotent in the face of powers beyond his control. Reducing this, bringing it down in the analytic process to the infantile problem of rebelling against parental authority in the attempt to assert one's self as an individual in his own right, removes from the experience the energy charge with which it is filled. The whole quality of the experience, with its mystery and suspense, would be destroyed; and the tremendous investment of energy would be withdrawn.

As a Jungian analyst I would reject the reductive approach, for I recognize in the use of magical devices and practices a symbolic way of dealing with a very real problem: man's impotence in the face of what he experiences as divine omnipotence. To face this ultimate reality does not dispose of the matter, as reduction to the simplistic issue of parental authority might seem to do. The symbolic approach, instead, opens up a whole new area for exploration, and consequently for enlarging the scope of psychological understanding.

The symbol had a special meaning for Jung. It was not merely a representation in an analogous or abbreviated expression of something already known. Such an interpretation, in the Jungian view, is merely a sign, capable of telling the individual what may lie behind it, as in the case of a roadside danger signal, a policeman's badge, or, one step removed, a phallus-shaped tower appearing in a dream. Jung has written that such views are *semiotic*, meaning that one image is used to stand as a sign in the place of another image or an idea. For Jung, the symbolic expression is something quite different. It is the best possible formulation of a relatively unknown thing, an archetype which cannot conceivably be more clearly or characteristically represented. To Jung, the semiotic interpretation of the symbol was dead, since it merely served as a conventional sign for associations which are more completely and better known elsewhere. Thus Jung found it quite impossible to make a living symbol, that is, one which is pregnant with meaning, from known associations. "What is thus manufactured can never contain more than what was put into it." The living symbol, on the other hand, was for him an expression that designated something that was "only divined and not yet clearly conscious."[18]

The symbolic approach offers the analyst a way of taking seriously the process which leads intelligent and searching people into the half-humorous, half-serious questing after the magical. It provides insight into their quest for ultimate truths and ultimate values which lies behind their accessibility to seduction into a fascinating world of illusion—the world of the magician and the sorcerer. The symbolic approach provides also a way to deal with the phantasmagoria that arises out of the drug scene, another and a more serious distraction than magic for some young people. Nearly all psychotherapists these days are called upon to treat patients who have found themselves unable to continue to study effectively or to do their work effectively or who have suffered psychological or even physiological damage after taking certain drugs. A specific type of person tends to look to a Jungian analyst for help, I have observed. He has been experimenting with hallucinogens such as marijuana, LSD or mescaline, with some awareness of what it is he is seeking. He calls it a search for expanding consciousness or some more colorful phrase. He does not consider himself "sick," but rather a well person who has temporarily lost his balance. He has glimpsed an intensely vibrant world of sights and sounds which have all but overwhelmed him, and needs help in making some sort of sense out of it. He may rationalize that his reason for his trying out the drugs in the first place was a need for relaxing tensions, for getting out of the bind he felt himself to be in, for breaking through inhibitions in his work or productivity.

Recounting this sounds so dry in the cold light of a spring morning. It would be better to feel into it through the description of this kind of experience just as it occurred, in the words of Carol. She was a graduate student, immersed in study and research in a Ph.D. program which tested her intellectual capacities to the utmost and left her strained and exhausted until she was nearly ready to give up. She realized that she would never make it if she continued in the direction in which she was going; then she had an opportunity to try mescaline and she took it—not as a lark, but with a receptive attitude to accept whatever she might find out about herself. Since the experience was not to be undergone for its own sake primarily, but rather for the purpose of increasing her awareness, she kept careful notes. These she offered to me to read after the first few analytic sessions.

The sheet of paper describing the feelings that remained after Carol's first mescaline trip was titled "Boundaries: having the center move." She wrote: "This intensity is new, without death. Did I feel as if I were dying not so long ago? Now a terribly intense feeling that I don't want to die; things are too full. No compulsivity; free energy. Without this intensity there is death. How could I be in this bad place before? Before this, came up-tight stuffing experience—an equivalent compulsion. No reason not to be at peace, to leave things calm and clear. The beginning of a new epoch for me."

Soon after this initiatory experience, Carol's interest in her studies began to slide rapidly. There were more mescaline trips. During one of them she had written: "Amazing how a compulsion can spread through life, killing everything. And the attempts to cure are the same as the disease. Dis-ease. Ease a little, let things go. Cease striving; then there will be self-fulfillment."

Here seemed to be the key to the door Carol was opening, "self-fulfillment." The goal became infinitely more meaningful to Carol at this point than any sense of urgency to fulfill the requirements of others or the demands of the academic program in which she was enrolled. How could a professor's approval, a grade on an exam, even the future prospect of a diploma, compete against sensations she could experience whenever she wanted to, sensations like the following:

"The Earth Mother: in me, a source, a spring, a watering, a calm powerful peace. The force of that peace is fantastic. And to see the world as if for the first time, clear and sharpened perceptions. A dynamism, generating energy."

Here the archetypal nature of her own being as a woman was revealed to her. What was timeless became for her the vessel of her experiencing; no longer could she or would she be bound by the restrictions of time and other conventional forms that had deviled her life until now. She was feeling fully the energy that had been locked up in the archetype awaiting her discovery of it. The discovery freed her, but she had no control as yet over the freedom. She experienced it in the symbolic form of "spinning," the word which titled the next passage in her notes:

"Spinning forms, all the forms dropping away, dropping away, with the swift, slippery, sliding-off of a newborn baby's caul, or a snake's skin, leaving a beautiful new form underneath, the same as the old, but fresh and clean. O shallow water sliding off a smooth sheet of rock. All of the forms, all the structures of reality, the appearances which were somehow not attached to something real—all of that slipped away, dissolved as a sheet of invisible maintaining energy between us— and the energy of the forms, the energy in keeping up or keeping together the hollow structures, the rigid impermeable sheet; the appearances—they too went, leaving only force against force, each deriving power and succulence from the other, a circular broken exchange, enervated and innervated. An underground spring surging into open space, created by returning to itself. Watertight means death; no dissolution of forms without a dissolver, and room to do it in."

Mescaline, for Carol, was the dissolving substance. Through mescaline she came to that fullness of vision which William Blake had promised when he wrote, "If the doors of perception were cleansed, everything would appear as it is, infinite." Carol, not knowing fully what the "infinite" was, could only identify it with herself and with her own sexuality. She wrote:

"My own power. My breast is a mountain, a volcano, spinning fire, not to destroy but to inflame, to fling the intensity of my body outward, focused into my love's mouth and body.

"Spinning: spinning wheel, spinning forms, geometric forms in open space. Spinning, weaving the space between us. A fabric, but also a sound in dimensions, a spatial vibration. Echoes of meaning, all implicitly there. Fleeting, must catch. The computer board, all the flashing lights getting tangled with one another without a stop—endless combinations with nothing to hold one down, to stop it for a moment, to make it a base with endless equivalences. Endless interconnections, building on building, never letting one be exposed long enough to stop the explosions, the fragmentation into infinity. Let one go—let them all go—they will be back. Speed . . . destruction. When differentiation and association get out of hand. So much to integrate. To have so strongly the sense of all of those, at once."

She was in a process that carried her. The excitement pitched higher and higher and she rose with it. It had to fly its own rhythm until it came to its place. She wrote on:

"Consummation. The relationship is consumed, each part

consuming the other and both feeding into the super-natural. Life above and surrounding us, created by our combination. The act of combination—life, creation, death."

Then into the experience of the sublime came fear. The fear of death, which was the fear that there was nothing, nothing beyond what she had already experienced. And still there was hope that along with the fear was the possibility of finding a way through it, a recognition that death meant the sacrifice of one kind of reality. Some strand of the past remained in the fabric of the immediate experience, and notic-ing this kept her from leaving school, although she was not really in it either. In coming down from one of the last trips before going into analysis, she had written these words:

"Fear, clarity, power, death. The progression of experience of a new part of the self. Fear of making something clear, fear of *not* making something clear, fear of the diffuse, confus-ing, amorphous thing which experience can become . . . clar-ity must come, or death returns, a pulling down, stuck, stopped, never going forward . . .

"Have I lived? So much more . . .

"Never going forward, confusion, feelings of being attacked by my own body, possessed by a hard knot in my throat which refuses to go away. Desperate state; requires solution. Then, the feeling of things pushing out, crowding to be seen and understood . . . I must force them out, feel them as strongly as I can and then, bit by bit, comes clarity, a stable way of making meaning for the feelings, and the release and satis-faction which comes from that. But with more or less clarity, comes power from the release of all the former burdens, but also from the certainty of knowing that I figured something out. The power is doomed to a horrible pulling-down kind of death if the clear things are allowed to remain static. But then, then next to clarity is the feeling that there is always a process through the cycle, that the power which comes from clarity must be a kind of faith that the cycle can continue, that death is not the end of a just defined part of the self, but that the cycle can and must go on. So it is also that clarity must be, to keep the death away, but so must death follow power—it must be touched upon again and again, but never allowed to catch and mire.

"The only reason I can think of to stay alive is because I am. And because I don't want to choose when I die."

Through the confusion and the clarity alternating, symbolic death pursues Carol as the one who waits to capture her in the very moment she rests from her frenzied seeking after the answer to a question she does not know. Sometimes there is a calm in the center of the disorientation, like the eye of a hurricane. It was at such a time, in anticipation of being caught up again in the wild and terrifying spinning, that she sought psychological help.

Carol does not need to return in therapy to her infancy, for hers is no classical neurosis in the psychoanalytic sense. Nor does she need to be urged to adapt to her chosen role in society, to return to her study cubicle which once held her snug and tense. She has already grown far beyond that, and can neither be what she was nor what she expected to be. As it was not for Western man when Columbus had discovered the West Indies, the world will never be the same for Carol. Her experiences and her writings about them are pure symbolic expressions of the mysteries of the unconscious, which she was able to glimpse when the inhibitions of her conscious perceptions and preconceptions were swept away by the hallucinogens.

Carol needed first to learn that the conscious mind establishes boundaries for its own reasons, knowing that the waters of the unconscious are to be tasted in sips and swallowed, and are not to be allowed to inundate or overwhelm. Carol had experienced many symbols, among them—Mother, spinning forms, snake's skin shedding, energy of forms hollow and rigid, merging into sexuality, exploding, fragmenting. Not to analyze these away by saying that this means this and that means that, but by expanding the feelings and ideas that the symbols evoke—this is the way to break the endless cycle of vision and response, and response eliciting vision. Into all of this I had to bring myself in the person of the analyst, and not necessarily as a person only, perhaps more as a place, a way-station where Carol, the traveler, would rest and gather herself together, and make sense of what has happened along the route and look ahead toward that end which is, in Robert Browning's words, "the last, for which the first was made."

It is true that Carol's case was not typical of the usual psychedelic experience, yet the usual psychedelic experience may and frequently does include some flashes of the kind of vision that Carol was able to report. The search for the pharmacological panacea, which began as an effort to transcend the difficulties and the disciplines which are imposed upon young people as they approach the brink of maturity, ends up by distracting many of them from all that is most valuable in their rebellion. Also, as Theodore Roszak pointed out in *The Making of a Counter-Culture*,[19] it threatens to destroy their most promising sensibilities. Roszak wrote: "If we accept the proposition that the counter-culture is, essentially, an exploration of the politics of consciousness, then psychedelic experience falls into place as one, but only one, possible method of mounting that exploration. It becomes a limited chemical means to a greater psychic end, namely, the reformulation of the personality, upon which social ideology and culture generally are ultimately based."[20]

In the end, psychedelic chemistry at best becomes less than the means for exploring what Aldous Huxley called the "perennial wisdom." It tends to become an end in itself, a source of boundless lore and contemplation, of conversational elaboration; in short, it is the whole show. The way back to that wisdom which persists through the seasons and returns year by year is not an easy or a quick way. It requires the individual to look at himself with the clearest and most critical eye, and not only at that which appears on the surface, but at whatever can be exposed of the hidden aspects within.

Analysis offers one way back, and of all the analytic schools, that of Jung is particularly receptive to the implications of the symbols which appear during altered states of consciousness. The work of Jung in the study of comparative religion and mythology provides a model for the Jungian analyst, a model which teaches him to regard the terrors of the uncon-

scious as a part of the archetypal heritage that is common
to all men in all ages, and which erupts into consciousness
in the presence of a state of mind when ordinary consciousness is put away and the person opens himself to the translucence of reality. This translucence means that the apparent
solidity of things, which gives them their boundaries, is actually not solid but permeable, and permeated with the quality
of infinity that connects everything to everything else. To see
this is to see the spaceless world, which is also timeless; that
is, the continuum of space or time which stretches like a ribbon before us and behind us with never any end. Our lives,
then, become a short stretch, a tiny segment on that endless
ribbon, separated from it only by our state of consciousness
in which we become aware of ourselves as individuals. This
awareness seems to require us constantly to be wresting
more and more consciousness from the unknown and unlimited. And, paradoxically, in order to become more conscious, many people attempt to "let go" of their customary
conscious attitudes and enter into a state which is more open
to direct perception of what we may call the "archetypal
world." In this case, "less is more."

Unhampered by the conventional attitudes of their parents,
young people today move freely into a society of rapidly changing mores. With many choices to make in those important
years between eighteen and twenty-five, choices of whether
or not to seek a higher education and if so what kind, choices
of career, and of marriage, and of life-style, the individual
is often bewildered. Now, in the early seventies, the dominant
age group in this country is coming to be the eighteen- to
twenty-five-year-olds, who were born in the baby boom that
followed World War II. Within the few short years between
1948 and 1953 the number of babies born in the United
States rose by an unprecedented 50 per cent, the biggest birth
increase ever recorded in this or any other country. Is it any
wonder then, that these young people, feeling their strength
within a group, as a freshet on the parched land of their parents, are also frightened to stand alone, as individuals, to formulate new ways—but rather seek refuge and comfort, and

possibly (although they would be the last to admit it) surrogate parenting from the group?

Witness, then, the popularity of "the human potential movement" which has swept the country during the last few years. Growing out of the concept within certain churches of "koinonia," an intimate spiritual communion and participative sharing in common religious commitments and in a spiritual community, the group left the church behind, and found new bases for their communality. Drugs were, of course, one of the first of the sacraments of the new community to be mutually shared, and not so much for the sake of the drugs themselves, although the protection of the group was a factor here, but more than that the sharing of the *experience* of seeing the world in an excitingly new way. True, the vision was frequently distorted, but it broke through the bind of conventionally superficial appearances and offered the possibility of *seeing into*, rather than just *looking at*. The groups took shape, and each group was part of a group of groups, each doing its own thing. The movements' supporters make the claim that the individual's self-awareness and sense of well-being is expanded within the group, and that a new feeling of community develops which strengthens both the individual and the group.

Each group, as might be expected, has a *creed* of its own. A creed in this context is something apart from a religious matter, and hence departs from the original "koinonia" sense of a group. Jung makes an important distinction:

A creed gives expression to a definite collective belief, whereas the word *religion* expresses a subjective relationship to certain metaphysical, extramundane factors. A creed is a confession of faith intended chiefly for the world at large and is thus an intramundane affair, while the meaning and purpose of religion lie in the relationship of the individual to God or to the path of salvation and liberation. From this basic fact all ethics is derived, which without the individual's responsibility before God can be called nothing more than conventional morality.[21]

He goes on to say:

Since they are compromises with mundane reality, the creeds have accordingly seen themselves obliged to undertake a progressive codification of their views, doctrines, and customs, and in so doing have externalized themselves to such an extent that the authentic religious element in them—the living relationship to and direct confrontation with their extramundane point of reference—has been thrust into the background . . . To be the adherent of a creed, therefore, is not always a religious matter but more often a social one and, as such, it does nothing to give the individual any foundation. For this he has to depend exclusively on his relation to an authority which is not of this world.[22]

I believe that Jung is here using the phrase "this world" to mean "limited to this world," or rather limited to that segment of the ribbon of infinite length of which we can have conscious awareness. The emphasis of the group movements on the here and now, and on the emergence of the individual through the support of the group, amounts to a creed—a valuable creed in some cases, when it serves to widen the individual's sense of himself through seeing himself not only subjectively but also through the eyes of others who give him feedback with candor. But too often the support of the group is limited to the duration of the group experience, and is effective only within the context of this particular group setting. Thus the Monday-morning hangover from a "marathon weekend" is often more painful than the traditional alcoholic hangover, because the whole psyche is aching from a sense of being let down, of having to face the everyday world which has its own creeds but does not offer the loving supports of the group.

It seems to me that the spiritual experience of the individual within the group requires a taking in of the experience in a highly personal way, as Jung would have said in an expression he used often, *sub specie aeternitatis*, under the aspect of eternity. This view of experience is essentially what Jungian psychology is all about: the seeing of a single experience as an aspect of totality, and a seeing of one's self as a part of the whole, and the whole of one's self as the synthesis of

many parts. Thus all barriers are eventually removed, including
the delimitations of any group.

An experience in the analysis of an individual who was participating in a creative group experience, may serve to illustrate. It will show how the group, functioning in one of its
most positive forms, can serve as an adjunct to the wholly
individual process of looking within to discover the meaning
of the event in the group, in its wider context.

Eric is an art teacher in high school. Before he studied
in art school and at the university he was relatively free and
original in his drawing and painting. Competition and a desire
to gain approval influenced him to adopt a conventional slick
style. During the past few years he has been unable to break
out of this. Quite aside from his desire to free himself ar-
tistically, he joined an encounter group after the failure of
a love affair, seeking new relationships of a non-binding nature.
It was one of those groups where people stay together for
two weeks, without ever knowing each other's family names
or their professions. Eric had been in analysis for just a short
time, and he and I agreed that the introduction to more social
interaction would be desirable at this time.

After the extended marathon was over, Eric wanted to discuss in therapy something that had happened in the group.
One afternoon had been devoted to making abstract paintings
in which people were to attempt to portray graphically the
feelings that each one was then currently experiencing. Eric
was able, he said, to forget his learned techniques, and to
return to a spontaneous way of playing with colors on a huge
sheet of paper. In his painting he expressed the height and
majesty of high mountains, the airiness of sky, the verdure
of growing things, and all throughout a sense of pervading
sunlight. He was sure it was the most beautiful painting he
had ever done, even though there was no evidence of artistic
"method" in his work.

Late in the day, the paintings were tacked up on the wall
and the members of the group looked at each other's work
and spoke about what they saw in the various paintings. There
was one picture, painted by Jim, who had been working near

Eric throughout the day. Jim's style was exceedingly primitive, obviously disclosing the naïveté of one who had little confidence in himself—small constricted forms of people, shapes isolated on a blank field. And yet there was something in the pattern which was interesting. In the discussion it was obvious that Jim did not think much of his own work. But, like some other members of the community, he praised the painting done by Eric. At this point, and with complete spontaneity, Eric offered to exchange paintings with Jim, as souvenirs of the encounter. That done, Eric reported, he felt very happy.

The event might have passed from his mind, were it not that he had brought it up when, in the analytic hour, I had asked him what was the most memorable event of the group sessions. We then tried to understand why that particular episode had brought forth the sense of overwhelming joy—what was it about it that was so "right," that evoked a feeling of total well-being?

The first part of the answer came from the recognition that Eric had not really "tried" to make a beautiful painting. He had not had to rely on what he had been taught, he had not needed to perform, in a technical way, he had not even thought about what he was doing. He had simply opened himself up and the painting had come as if it had been given to him. He had the feeling that he had broken out of the boundaries of his own personality, and had become lost in the sense of all-encompassing space of which his sheet of paper was only a tiny fragment, but nevertheless a microcosmic element of the whole as a drop of water carries within it the whole of the ocean.

In the process of this realization, Eric had lost his sense of identification with the painting. The painting did not feel like a product of his own efforts, although certainly his efforts had contributed to its creation. Or had they? The sensation was that as he had begun painting he had felt energized, even the wherewithal of the effort, the energy behind it, had been "given," for he had been tired before he began, the result of several successive nights with little sleep. But he was not in the least tired when he finished.

Looking over at Jim's picture, Eric recalled his own earlier frustrations as a small boy, wanting to express himself but not knowing just how. The painting was crude, brightly colored, without perspective. We had uncovered, earlier in the analysis, some aberrant childhood behavior which had led Eric's parents to seek therapy for him when he was about five years old. The advice of the therapist had been to get him started in some activity in which he could express himself adequately but in a non-verbal way, and this had resulted in his having been given art lessons and encouraged to draw. Eric had "seen into" Jim's difficulties and his limitations, and had sensed an affinity with him. And, quite unconsciously, it came to him that Jim longed for the artistic quality of Eric's being through Eric's painting. That painting had represented to Jim what he desired above all else, freedom through an easy, spontaneous competence. Each had something of the other in his painting. Eric knew with an inner knowledge that the paintings had to be exchanged, and so they were.

But the second insight that came out of the analytic confrontation in which all this was discussed, was even more important. It involved something which Eric surely knew, but which had yet to be brought to consciousness, and the analytic interchange served to do so. Taking my lead from his assertion that his painting was "given" to him and therefore could be given away, I sensed a profound religious emotion in Eric that was struggling for expression. It was that of being overwhelmed with gratitude in the sudden knowledge that he *could* give the picture away, because the picture was not the important thing; the important thing was the capacity to create the picture. And whoever is given *that* is rich, he can give away the fruit of his craft over and over again, and never be impoverished. The ever-present stream of creative energy flows into him and through him. The second is important, it must flow *through*, for if it is held in, stopped, if the painting and all that it meant had been held onto, the flow would have been dammed up, the precious waters of creativity would have become stagnant. So Eric began to understand not only why he *could* give away his painting, but also that he *had* to give it away. And in doing so, he had not only broken through the dam in his own soul, but had started a reciprocal movement in Jim.

Eric came to know this partly as a result of his group experience, but the group experience was insufficient to bring out the total meaning. Always, when we depart from the conventional patterns (as the modes of the counter-culture demand that we do) our foundations are shaken. Unless we are willing to settle indefinitely for the artificial support of the group, it becomes necessary to find our own individual meaning in our experiences, and that comes through the lonely search.

There are many types of group experiences, just as there are many types of drug experiences, and it is clear that the cases I have discussed contain examples of what is most promising and most hopeful in these expressions of current new ways of combating the stasis which young people sense in the society devised by their elders. It is not necessary to speak of the dangers and degradations inherent in both kinds of experience, the popular media are sufficiently full of horror stories. It goes without saying that many of those who use drugs indiscriminately or those who fling themselves upon the gentle mercy of a group, do so seeking support from outside themselves to bolster a weak personality structure. Support, the analyst would contend, is a palliative at best—for some people it serves the purpose of tiding them over until the self-regulating function of the psyche reasserts itself and nature restores them to a more balanced state. At worst, the palliative masks the real disturbances in the personality, helps to build up defenses against the ugly realities, and teaches ways of coping through defending the fragile aspects of the individual by giving him a sort of group mask behind which to live.

Another area of activity which has been taken up by the counter-culture is that of organizing various movements to effect changes in society through mass pressure. It is, of course, necessary to differentiate between the joining of free individuals in a common task to improve some aspect of society, and being sold on the idea of marches and mass meetings conducted in the spirit of obstructing or destroying the current scapegoat in the name of social progress. Where efforts to reform are constructive, it seems to me, they have arisen out of the willingness of individuals to contribute their energy and skill to the common good, which good can ultimately be realized only through self-knowledge and through a study of the objective situation from the standpoint of the contribution that each individual is best able to give. With this individual commitment, people are able to achieve their highest potential and, in doing so, to make their greatest possible contribution. This attitude, which is so characteristic of Jung, has often been misunderstood as an "elitist concept," but what it seems to me to mean is that individuals are essentially different and that those who emphasize the development of these differences to their highest potential must necessarily become more differentiated than those who are satisfied to go along with everybody around. As Jung put it in his essay on "The Gifted Child": "The levelling down of humanity into a herd, by suppressing the natural aristocratic or hierarchic structure, must inevitably lead sooner or later to a catastrophe. For if all that is distinguished is levelled down, then all orientation is lost and the yearning to be led becomes inevitable."[23]

Patriotism is a case in point. As members of "the establishment," identified with our nation as we are with our own family, we feel that we must support our nation in whatever she does. Even when we view with sorrow a war in which we wish we had never gotten involved, some people insist that since we are in it, we must above all win it, or at the very least, find a way to pull out with honor. But, as participants in the "counter-culture," we dissociate ourselves from national policy and cry out with horror and outrage at the crimes committed in the name of country, all with protestations that what we do is really patriotism, for we love our country so much that we are torn to pieces when she acts immorally, as we would be over our own delinquent child. So we join forces with one side or the other, pay attention to the literature and public utterances from that side only, and see the other side as holding an untenable if not actually criminal position. We would do better to consider the words of Jung:

> We need not be ashamed of ourselves as a nation, nor can we change ourselves as such. Only those individuals can change or improve themselves who are able to develop spiritually beyond the national prejudices. The national character is an involuntary fate which is imposed upon the individual like a beautiful or an ugly body. It is not the will of the individual which conditions the rise and fall of a nation, but suprapersonal factors, the spirit and the earth, which work in mysterious ways and in unfathomable darkness. It is therefore illusory to praise or bless nations, since no one can alter them. Moreover the "nation" . . . is a personified concept that corresponds in reality only to a specific nuance of the individual psyche. The nation has no life of its own apart from the individual, and is therefore not an end in itself.[24]

It all comes down to the realization that if we would change society, if we would change our culture, we must begin by changing ourselves. Many ways have been tried throughout the generations of men to accomplish this, some crowned with notable success, some with quiet happiness, and many with disappointment and failure. There is no one way that provides salvation for all who would follow it, despite the claims of the new psychological fads that burst into print every few months.

There is a process in which all men are engaged, and which is a developmental process. It has been called by many names; Jung has called it the Way of Individuation. In his lifetime of absorption in matters of the psyche, he has come to some basic understandings. These have served me well in my work as a Jungian analyst. I have found much help in Jung's statement, "All life is individual life, in which alone the ultimate meaning is to be found."[25]

6

INDIVIDUATION:
THE PROCESS
OF BECOMING WHOLE

In Chicago, which depends for its existence largely on mechanics and electronics, there is a section called New Town. It is the successor to Old Town, which used to be the center of counter-culture activity until it started going downhill when the pushers of hard drugs moved in. People who had begun to fear for their lives in Old Town and who had outgrown their fascination with the psychedelic experience as an end-in-itself, have been opening up small shops and businesses in New Town, where they make, display and sell interesting and unusual products. You can walk down a busy street when suddenly the delicious odor of bread baking streams out from a little storefront bakery and wraps you in nostalgia. The "Clay People" make and sell ceramics and invite you to come in and learn their craft. Artists paint in shop-studios, and there is a shop where people sit around and do macramé and sell their ingenious belts and ties and wall hangings at a fair price.

These are children of the generation who grew up in the Great Depression, whose parents married during or just after World War II, settling down to work hard for the good life. Father was the Organization Man, with his home in the suburbs and his new car every two years. He had to pay a high price for his security—the loss of his individuality—and most of the time he never realized that it was gradually slipping away. But his children, unhampered by fear of hunger or the unavailability of education, have looked about them and have become disenchanted with the stereotypes of the affluent society. Many have withdrawn from an overorganized and overstandardized system, and are searching for alternatives that seem to offer a better opportunity to express their individual needs and talents.

While this expression seems related to a need which is especially congruent to the state of the world today, it is also in the spirit of what Jung was advocating as early as the First World War; in this as in other ways he was far ahead of his times. His advocacy of coming to selfhood through a distinctly individual and personal effort offered a way which is increasingly attracting the attention and then the commitment of those who feel the necessity of breaking out of the bonds imposed by the collectivity that characterizes our cities in the 1970s. That effort, as Jung conceived it, is the way of *individuation*.

The individuation process, in the Jungian sense, means the conscious realization and integration of all the possibilities immanent in the individual. It is opposed to any kind of conformity with the collective and, as a therapeutic factor in analytical work, it also demands the rejection of those prefabricated psychic matrices—the conventional attitudes—with which most people would like to live. It offers the possibility that everyone can have his own direction, his special purpose, and it can attach a sense of value to the lives of those who suffer from the feeling that they are unable to measure up to collective norms and collective ideals. To those who are not recognized by the collective, who are rejected and even despised, this process offers the potentiality of restoring faith in themselves. It may give them back their human dignity and assure them of their place in the world.

What is this "individuation process" in which people become free to realize themselves in a way which does not depend on the approval of any outside agency? In "The Relations between the Ego and the Unconscious," an essay in which Jung set forth the fundamentals of the individuation process, we find that "Individuation means becoming a single, homogeneous being, and, in so far as 'individuality' embraces our innermost, last, and incomparable uniqueness, it also implies becoming one's own self. We could therefore translate individuation as . . . 'self-realization.' "[1] It is an easy thing to say "be yourself" but quite another thing to know who you truly are. How can you be yourself if you do not know that self? Therefore, the process of individuation becomes a seeking after self-knowledge.

The criticism is often made that searching for self-knowledge is a very introverted, self-centered thing to do. I have had analysands confess to me that they are abashed at admitting that they are spending so much time and energy on their own inner processes. They find that it is hard to justify, when, as they correctly observe, there are so many problems out in the world crying for solution.

Is it not true with respect to social problems of our day that the nature of the person who deals with these problems and issues will affect the nature of the solution? I see it in psychotherapy all the time—a person studying to become a psychotherapist will master the basic subject matter in the field of psychology and he will learn certain rules, techniques, or methods of this or that discipline. But in the end, the person of the therapist more than anything else determines the progress of the case. Likewise in social issues, the *values* set by individuals upon different kinds of changes or improvements in the environment determine the courses of action that are eventually taken. Values stem from the viewpoint of the individual; they are the result of the collision between his essential nature and the impact upon that nature by the experiences of living.

The essential nature of the individual includes not only strength but weakness. Each of us has the potentiality for creativity and, equally present, the potentiality for destructiveness. The Hindu gods, Brahma, Vishnu, Shiva—Creator, Preserver, Destroyer—live in each of us; all must be reckoned with. It is as though we exist in a psychic system where an ecological balance must be maintained. One analysand of mine put it this way: "I was reading about how the government took all that highly dangerous nerve gas and sealed it in tons of concrete and took it out and dumped it in the Atlantic to 'dispose of it.' I realized how wrong that statement was, for we never really get rid of anything, there isn't any 'out there' to consign it to. Even in the Atlantic it is still with us, and even in the ocean the space is limited and what is there affects the land. And so in the psyche, we cannot 'dispose' of dangerous or destructive aspects of ourselves, we can only know of their presence and how they tend to function. If we work at it we may be able to transform these dark elements from something virulent to something manageable. That is part of the greatness of Jung's concept of the self-regulating nature of the psyche: he never supposed evil could be done away with, but sought to expose and understand the potentiality for evil in our own souls as well as that for good."

When my analysand understood that, she understood that individuation requires the discovery of what is operating in us and determining our determinations. What are our goals and how do we come to them? Jung noted in his Introduction to *The Secret of the Golden Flower*:[2] "An ancient adept has said: 'If the wrong man uses the right means, the right means work in the wrong way.'" This Chinese saying stands in sharp contrast to our typically Western product-oriented or success-oriented belief in the "right" *method* irrespective of who applies it. Jung wrote, "In reality, in such matters everything depends on the man and little or nothing on the method. For the method is merely the path, the direction taken by a man. The way he acts is the true expression of his nature. If it ceases to be this, then the method is nothing more than an affectation, something artificially added, rootless and sapless, serving only the illegitimate goal of self deception."[3] Perhaps the stress on method and the lack of stress on man's relatedness to his own deepest needs and commitments is one of the most serious problems in the practice of psychotherapy today.

Let me give you an example of how the right means fail

in the hands of the wrong man, from a case of my own practice. Dale came to me in a state of utter despair. His latest marriage was falling apart and he was on the verge of quitting his tenth job in the past seven years. Dale was no fool, nor did he lack for charm or self-confidence. Or perseverance. He had been reared in a succession of foster homes where he learned to get what he wanted by manipulating and flattering people until they would fulfill his demands. Then he would enjoy his little luxuries so craftily won, and not be particularly concerned about exerting himself for the benefit of anyone else. The game came to be "see how much you can get and at the same time how little you can manage to give." He was marvelous about courting a woman until he got her to bed, and after the first successful conquest he would concentrate upon getting his own satisfaction whenever and however he pleased. Woman after woman would tell Dale, "As soon as I began to feel committed to you, you suddenly turned off." His marriages all started with the usual charming approach, but before the honeymoon was over, the wives, each of them in succession, would complain that Dale had completely changed. He didn't see it, he never could understand what went wrong.

This man had joined the Army, where he got into trouble in one relationship after another. He became involved in fist fights, was called down for insubordination, until at last it got so bad that he was given a psychiatric discharge. The Army recommended psychotherapy, and was willing to pay for it. In addition he was awarded disability benefits, so he did not have to go to work.

Therapy promised to be rather long-term and, having nothing else to do, Dale decided that he might as well while away the time between the sessions by going back to school under the G.I. Bill. He happened to be intelligent enough so that he managed to get an advanced degree in engineering. He became engaged in research on waste and sewage treatment, and soon was an authority on the subject. At the time not much study had been done in the field, so that when Dale graduated he was very much in demand for employment. In fact he laughingly stated that he was one of the most sought-after garbage men in the nation. He felt powerful enough then, and whenever he took a new job he would make sure that his duties were clearly outlined so that he could do exactly what was expected of him, "not a bit more and not a bit less," he would say dogmatically. Taking any criticism was out of the question, or doing any bit of work that could possibly be done by a subordinate was not even a matter for discussion. He asserted that he wouldn't take any shit from anyone, but ironically the nature of his work was such that he was taking shit from everyone.

Despite his acknowledged expertise, he was continually either quitting or getting fired. Then he would get a new job for more money and the whole thing would start all over again.

His lack of stability made him anxious, and at length he sought analysis. I asked him about his work; he had little to say except that "it's a living." Or he would add that he wouldn't hang around past 4:45 in the afternoon. He would leave a boring job to go home to a boring wife, and be in a hurry to do it, but none of it meant anything to him. It was difficult to draw him out about the nature of the work he was doing, and only with a great deal of prodding did I learn that he had written several important papers and had given one or two at meetings on ecology; also that he had been invited to take positions in teaching or in research, but that in contemplating the material rewards he had turned them down—although not without some second thoughts.

It was only when we began to explore his unconscious feelings underlying the choice of his vocation that we began to understand what inner processes had brought him to this work. He had an unshakable feeling of rottenness about himself, through and through, as if to say, a child who has been rejected from the moment of his birth must be disgusting indeed. And ever after he had had to face a hostile environment, and somehow manage to make it endurable. The world, plainly speaking, was a pile of shit, and the best he could do was to clean it up a little. And so he learned to do this in a highly sophisticated way. The method was all right, yes, he was an expert in the method, but it didn't help much, either in the impact he was able to have on the world, or in his own feeling about himself.

Only in the analysis, when he began to confront the unconscious, could he learn that it was his own feeling of being garbage, worthless, that he was projecting upon the world. Then something began to happen. He first had to face the dark side of himself, to find out who the eminent scientist really was. And he was not a pleasant subject for self-knowledge. He could not clean up what he saw by getting an easy job that paid a lot of money; he could not redeem his self-image even if he fulfilled the explicit requirements of the job. He began to see that he had externalized his need to develop a thorough rebalancing of his psychic functioning by differentiating the positive and potentially constructive aspects of his individuality from the negative and potentially destructive aspects.

We talked a great deal about his "inner ecology," without much mentioning his work. Gradually he began to think of himself less as a discard from the human race, and more as a member of it, whose survival and productivity depended very much upon his making himself and his knowledge useful to the world, with its people and their needs. Gradually, he began to give a little, instead of only taking. And one day it dawned on him that the analytical work in which he was engaged could be understood as "psychological ecology." He had known it all along, in his *head*, but suddenly one day he accepted it fully as a fact of his total being. He knew that he was a microcosm of the whole world, and that in his inner life he could work to convert his own filth into clear life-giving waters and fertilizer, just as in his professional vocation he could act to convert filth and pollution in the environment into breathable air and drinkable water. A change of attitude appeared quite suddenly, but the potential for it had been in him all along. It had been the inner urge for redemption from his own filth that had arranged the neurotic behavior which got him out of the Army and into a place which could prepare him to fulfill his inner necessity.

Once, at the start of our work together, he said that he had just drifted into this particular branch of engineering because it was a wide-open field—not many people were interested in spending their working days examining the decomposing wastes from the city sewers—and the pay was good. Some time later he admitted he had experienced the strong feeling of an inner voice that had guided him to choose the courses that he did, unpopular as these courses were in the university at the time. For some reason which he was unable to fathom, the field of work appealed to him, and so he followed his feelings there and applied himself to his studies. Recently Dale has come to see purpose in what he is doing, and I am guardedly hopeful that if his potentialities now unfold, that he will make an outstanding contribution to society. He is beginning to know who he is. Today there exists the possibility that the right man will begin to work in the right way.

The analysand who has gone through the current problems of his life and attempted with the analyst's help, to see what the meaning may be behind the symbolic forms of behavior, and who has been willing to trace back the current behavior to whatever earlier stages hold the key for unlocking the patterns that now operate, has come to a crucial point in the analysis. It may be that now that the crisis is passed, the urgency for psychotherapy is no longer present. It may be that some symptoms are no longer visible, or that if they are, the analysand begins to learn to live with them and to exert enough control on them so that they do not interfere overmuch with his functioning. He is better, the most obvious damage seems to have been repaired. It is at this point that a decision will be made, and that decision is whether to go on in the analysis, to take the dark journey which reveals what it is that has been hidden—not only that it was something unmentionable and unacceptable, but just what is its composition and how does it function.

The process of individuation, as it is experienced in analysis, requires a long and laborious process of pulling together

all those fragmented and chaotic bits and pieces of unconscious personalities, into an integrated whole which is conscious of itself and the way in which it works. Referring back
to one of our initial dreams, the question put was simply—is
it sufficient that you have learned to drive the car, or shall we
look and see what is under the hood? Most people go through
life without ever knowing what is under the hood, and that
is perhaps good enough on a city street where every few blocks
there is a mechanic who can help you if you get into trouble.
But, if you want to be self-sufficient on the longer journeys,
and if you want to possess the freedom to take whatever road
you will, then for you it is a necessity to see what is "under
the hood."

How is the decision made whether to continue therapy past
the point of the relief of symptoms, and toward the further
end? There is no single answer for this, as one sees it in practice, and yet it is my belief that there is one answer under
which all answers which are given by the analysand or by the
analyst may be subsumed. Many people come into Jungian
analysis after having been exposed to Jung through reading
his works, and have become deeply interested in the individuation process. They enter analysis knowing that no amount
of reading will give them any more than a superficial description, and that they must embark on that journey—reading
the guidebook is not an acceptable substitute. So the desire
for individuation is expressed as an inclination from the very
start. Even so, not all of the people who seek this way are
able to do what they say they wish to do. An attempt at analysis simply may not yield up the symbolic material that evokes
the archetypal substratum of the personality.

On the other hand, sometimes the analysis yields up too
much. One woman had come into treatment after she had
been having a great many impressive and moving dreams for
several years. She had become interested in reading Jung and
finding in Jung the symbolism which, she felt, could help
her to interpret her own dreams. We began analysis. As time
went on she found herself waking often in drenching sweats
or panic, or feeling exhausted, as though she had been pur-

sued all night. The more she read and tried to understand, the more she would get the bizarre and disturbing dreams. In analysis she brought several dreams each time she came to a session, and they were so fantastic in their plots and so luminous in their imagery that to my chagrin I sometimes found myself looking forward to her hour like an art student anticipating a day at the Uffizi. The following dream which she brought made clear the potential danger for some people in stirring up the unconscious in the process of individuation: *I was standing on a high balcony leaning out into the night. Out of the sky a star glowed brighter and brighter in the east, and came rolling toward me. As it approached it grew larger and glowed a deep sapphire blue. A silver halo surrounded it, and it came closer and closer, shining ever more brightly. I knew that all the air in the universe was bound up in it and that it would come close enough for me to step out onto it and be as light as air. It came as I expected, as huge as a moon and I could nearly reach out and touch it. I felt light enough to leap onto it, but then there in the distance I saw another star growing large and sailing toward me from the south. It was a huge glowing ruby, and as it neared I could see the fires raging within it. It came very close and hung in all its glory just a few yards beyond where I was standing, and I knew I could be warm forever if I let myself go out to it. Then out of the western sky a ball of purest white came flying in my direction, and I could see that it bubbled and foamed as though a million whitecaps were tumbling over each other in brilliant sparkles. As I leaned forward it occurred to me to look back, and suddenly I saw that the balcony on which I stood had detached itself from the building, and that the whole earth was a brown ball receding from me in astonishing swiftness.*

Without going into the symbolism of the dream, it was clear enough to me that the analysand needed *not* to go forward into the mysteries of the collective unconscious, but rather that she should be protected from the fascination of the archetype. Standing on the brink of the abyss, the analysand needed more than anything the support which would help her regain her hold on the material world. The stress of the individuation process was surely contraindicated for her at this time.

But the following dream presents quite a different message. It was brought by a woman whose life situation was progressing adequately, and who was reasonably successful in her job, although it did not offer her opportunity commensurate with her ability. She felt that she could grow beyond that job were she able to loosen up and express her ideas in a more forceful way. But she lacked courage. She dreamed: *I was in a house that looked like the house in which I grew up, and I was standing before the door to my father's workshop. That was a room which I had been told not to enter; now I know that it was where father kept certain electrical tools which could have been dangerous. But, as a child, I had been warned that terrible things would happen to me if I went in there, and I imagined that it was full of monsters and bogeymen who would get me if I ever opened the door. As I stand before this door I see that it is of enormous size. In the center of it there is a square brass plate with a great brass handle on it, and underneath the handle a keyhole. I am standing there wondering what to do, and you (the analyst) come up behind me. You place a key in my hand and then I am alone again. I walk up to the door and place the key in the keyhole. It turns as of itself. I step back and the door slowly opens. I look inside, but all that I can see is blackness. I am trembling. I then hear a voice which says, "Why not go in?" I feel that it must be all right to do so, and I walk into the darkness. That black space stretches as far as I can see. Nevertheless I take a few steps inward. Soon in the uttermost distance I can distinguish the faintest shade of deep gray and I know that beyond my vision there must be light somewhere. I take another step and pause, and the darkness begins ever so gradually to pale.*

This woman was prepared to begin the exploration of the unknown depths, and we went ahead.

One more dream, this one from a young man who had difficulties relating to people in a feeling way. He tended to

recognize only his own needs and to be unable to sense the
more subtle responses of other people, especially those who
were reticent in expressing themselves. He was afraid to be
open with the people who were close to him. Therefore he
felt unable to carry on any intense relationship. This is his
dream:

*I am in a new house. I find a bird stiff and dead. Maybe I
make an effort to warm him. But he is dead.*

*Later I come back to move into this house. I am going to
throw him out. Somehow I find that he is alive. Immediately
I begin to try to revive him. It is very cold in the house. The
coldness is what killed him. I begin trying to warm him. I
bring him near a source of heat. The room is drafty. I cup
my hands behind him so that the heat will be shielded in and
the draft kept away. I do this for a long time.*

*Then he is awake. The windows in this room are open. I
hold the little bird in my cupped hands so he won't get away
and maybe fly out of doors by mistake. He would never live
out there. Then I walk around the room closing the windows
with my elbows.*

*Then I am standing near the source of heat again. I am
cupping my hands behind him, trying to capture as much of
the heat as I can for him. His feathers begin to soften. He
fills out and softens. I think he is a white bird, with full soft
feathers and a long tale* (sic). [N.B. This is not a typographi-
cal error, but rather a slip which carries its specific meaning.]

*Then he is nipping at my finger or hand. Why is he doing
this? Is he trying to bite me? For a minute I am afraid. But
that passes. He doesn't.*

*My parents come in or are there. I tell them about the
bird, that he is alive. I am very moved in telling them. They
don't seem to notice.*

*Then the bird climbs onto the source of heat, the radiator,
and sits down. I am afraid that it might be too hot for him.
I feel it and it seems fine. He gathers his legs under him,
and sits up there looking out, collected and warm.*

*My mother and father open the window. I tell them not to
do that. I go around and close the wide-open window and*

*some others that were a little open. Now it will be really
warm in here. No chills.*

*Then I look to the radiator. There is the bird, sitting as
before, looking out, collected, all there, himself.*

*Then I am worried about food. At one point I thought he
looked hungry. I look around and find a set of bird things on
the table there, with water, a place for him to go to the bathroom and so on. I feel that he must know what he is doing
around this place. I decide to leave these things where they
are. Then I look and find a bag of bird seed.*

*The next thing I know, I look up and see the bird winding
up a toy doll on the mantel. I am absolutely amazed. I point
this out to my parents. They ask me if my brother didn't pick
this place out well with the fireplace and all.*

*Then the bird is skiing on little skis. He skis down the cur-
tain, then he skis down my shirt. He has little ski poles which
I saw first, and little silver skis.*

*I notice that somebody was skiing outside the window and
that the bird saw this and got the idea himself. I am amazed
that the bird is so intelligent. He is so amazing.*

Then I say:

"This is the spirit of a reincarnated holy man.

"This is the spirit of a human being of former times."

The young man's dream is rich with symbolism that could
be discussed and amplified to bring light upon his orientation to his life, his difficulties and his potentialities. I have
not reproduced it in detail for that purpose, but rather to
give the reader the flavor of the dream as it was reported, the
very slow and gradual development of the relationship between the dreamer and his bird. The bird, being a creature
of earth yet not entirely of earth, since he can fly, is a symbol
for that incomprehensible part of man that is sometimes
called "spirit." It evokes the feeling of relatedness on a plane
which is not strictly material—there is a non-corporeality
about the man-bird connection. In our discussion of the dream
we understood the bird as the expression of that unconscious
aspect of the dreamer that is most responsive to the tender
feelings of being cherished and cared for. It is this quality

in the dreamer that is portrayed as dormant, and all but dead. He nearly gives up on it, but then as he returns to make sure that there is no hope, he discovers that perhaps after all, there is still a breath of life there and it is worthwhile to try to revive him. Then comes the long and difficult period in which he bends all his efforts toward counteracting the coldness that killed or nearly killed the bird. The care and effort expended corresponds to the analytic process and the devotion manifested there; the close watch on the feelings and responses is what makes it possible to bring warmth and life to where there was before only coldness and immobility.

As the feelings became more active, the analysand was able to experience his emotional life more fully. The white bird with the long feathers and the white "tale" evoked the image and legend of the holy ghost. For the dreamer, this referred to a mystical aspect of relationship which required accepting another on faith—something that had always been difficult for him. The acceptance had first to take place as an inner experience, growing out of his receptivity to that threatened, hardly living, sensitive aspect of his own being. As if to test him, the bird nips at him; this suggests that his own openness makes him more vulnerable to being hurt, an idea which he resisted at first but then accepted as a necessary part of the process. It was even something to rejoice about—in the dream it was a sign of life and strength in the bird, in the psyche it referred to an increasing ability to deal with the possibility of rejection from others if he would reach out to them.

The appearance of the parents and their activity symbolized a regressive trend in the dreamer, for his parents in the dream, as in reality, tended to treat him as a child whose feelings were not worth noticing. He had wanted, even when very young, to express himself and to get back some reaction in depth, but he was usually merely brushed off—his parents were more concerned with other matters. The rejecting attitude, despised as it was, had been unconsciously adopted in childhood by the dreamer. In his efforts to win approval first from parents and then elsewhere, he had rejected his own sensitive spiritual side, his "white bird."

The dream showed him liberating the power of feelings inherent in the bird by not allowing the presumed death to take over. He considered the slightest sign of life as worthy of his full devotion. Gradually the dreamer was able to become mature enough to oppose his parents, who corresponded to his inner tendency to resist his feelings. Closing the windows meant that he needed to keep this newly revived capacity of his within bounds, and by all means avoid letting the parental "critical" attitude endanger the new development. When he decided to take a firm stand, to care for the bird regardless of what the parents might think, he found that everything he needed to carry through had already been provided for him—thus the bird's food and water and other things which appeared when the dreamer looked for him.

With the marvelous humor that dreams sometimes provide, the bird suddenly became an independent creature, and was winding up the little toy doll, much to the dreamer's amazement. How much like life: when we finally learn to do something in a new way, that knowledge takes over and begins to have an existence of its own, introducing us to possibilities of which we have never dreamed. The skiing is a case in point —it is sheer exuberance! The dreamer was utterly amazed that what he thought was a small creature who could at best be a pet, turned out to have imagination and flair. The dreamer associated the skis with the special meaning that mountains have for him—the pristine heights where spiritual values are the primary values. The dreamer had been interested in reading about mountain religions, and the symbolism from these religions often colored his dreams. In this particular dream, however, two opposing and disjointed aspects of the dreamer came together: one was the rarified intellectual interest in religion as a discipline acquired through reading and study, and the other was the capacity to extend the abstract concept of the unity of all things to a sense of relatedness with actual living things. That the bird was seen as the spirit of a reincarnated holy man, a human being of former times, seemed to convey a sense of the connection between "former times" and "this moment," a binding of the remote old wise man with the tenderly present fluttering creature in the hand of the dreamer.

I cannot say much more about this dream, except that in dealing with it both the dreamer and I were deeply touched. It was an important individuation dream in that it enabled him to move along in the process with a sense of having come through a period of being constrained and fearful, and in that he was entering upon another phase in which he would be careful and responsive, but no longer fearful in the same blindly anxious way. Concern would begin to replace anxiety. This dream, and others which came along, proved to be guideposts which could provide orientation for a newly emerging personality as yet unsure of its direction.

The question was raised: how is the decision made as to whether to proceed from therapy into analysis on the way of individuation, or whether to conclude therapy when the symptoms which precipitated the call for help have been more or less satisfactorily resolved? Perhaps, in the course of reviewing these few dreams which clearly refer to the individuation process, the decisive factor has become apparent. That factor is, of course, the unconscious itself. The unconscious, through dreams and through its manifestations in everyday life, provides all the information we need to know. The unconscious, with its ingenious way of symbolizing, sets the picture before us: this is how it is, there are these and these obstacles, but there is a chance of breaking through to a new position with a wider perspective. Or the unconscious may place violent objections in the path, warning of disaster if the stirring up of archetypal material is encouraged to continue. Such a warning was clearly present in the balcony dream of the prepsychotic woman. It is the responsibility of the analyst to "read" with utmost care the unconscious material that is brought up, and to allow himself to be guided by it.

This is not to say that the process is dependent entirely on the unconscious and its manifestations. Jung laid great stress on the decisive role played by consciousness and its capacity for insight, though he rejected the "dictatorship of consciousness" and insisted that attention be paid to the contents which emerge from the unconscious. It is a two-pronged effort in which unconscious material is given the attention which is due to it, while at the same time a continuing effort is made to strengthen consciousness so that it may become equal to the demands made on it in its encounter with the contents of the unconscious.[4]

Each person will, in the process of his analysis, find his own methods and ways of confronting the unconscious. The possibilities are varied, and throughout the course of this book I will continue to give examples. What is essential to all of these ways is that the individual commit himself or herself fully to the unconscious process, and, at the same time, determine to maintain a strong hold on the mundane realities and responsibilities that his life imposes. I, for my part as analyst, make it clear to the analysand that our work together will not provide for him an easy out by which he can excuse himself from difficult relationships with people, or demand extra time off from his work because of emotional disturbances, or expect his wife to tolerate his bad temper or lack of attention. I recognize, of course, that the analytic effort may at times put the analysand under a great deal of emotional strain—and I let him know this at the beginning. If it appears that he is not able or willing to sustain the additional burdens of increasing consciousness, he ought not to subject himself to the rigors of the individuation process in analysis. That discipline is a personal discipline, and those who undertake it must do so on their own responsibility, and not expect to be made whole at the expense of their friends or wives or lovers.

Another question arises, perhaps more in my own mind than in the analysand's. Should the analysand, entering on the deeper levels of exploration, expect the analyst to carry him along and to be an ever-present support and protector? Has he a right, by virtue of the mutual commitment of analyst and analysand, to expect the analyst to be available to him whenever he gets into unusual difficulty? The answer is not easy—my first impulse is to say that he should be guided by the analyst not to proceed too rapidly, and to make sure that on each step along the way the new discoveries and insights can be thoroughly assimilated so that they become usable as the analysand prepares to move forward. Furthermore, it could be said that the analyst should encourage the analysand to utilize his own critical judgment in regarding his dream and fantasy material, by allowing him ample opportunity to participate in the interpreting of it during the analytical hour.

But the fact of the matter is, all this is purely theoretical; it simply does not work out this way in practice. The Jungian analysis, unlike most kinds of therapy that I know anything about, does not take place primarily in the consulting room. This is especially true at the more advanced stages of analysis. The consulting room is, in large measure, a sort of staging area, where the experiences and the insights stemming from them are assembled, and the analytic discussion takes place, a discussion which is aimed at finding meaning in what has been brought for consideration. Then the analysand is sent forth again into the battle with the world, armed with whatever understanding has emerged as he and the analyst have together dealt with the material at hand. Often, after an illuminating session, I have had to say to the analysand, "What is really important is what you do with all this now, now as you walk out of here, and between now and the time you return again. That is what will prove whether what we have done is valuable or not."

As it happens, there is nothing I can do to assure the analysand or myself that he will be able to cope with unseen or unanticipated dangers. There is no guarantee that he will not get into a panic, or that he will not be seized with a depression that he cannot manage. If I sense this as a possibility, I may let him know that he is to deal with it as well as he can, and there are specific suggestions which I may make, depending on his needs as an individual. If, even so, he feels in urgent need of help, he may call me and I will try to be available to him. In my experience there have been very few people who have abused the knowledge that I could be accessible to them when necessary; there have been occasions when even talking together on the phone for a few minutes has brought about a calmer view, but more often the knowledge that I would be there, if it came to that urgency, was sufficient to tide the person over a difficult hour.

There is, too, the matter of the limitations of the analyst as a human being. I believe it is a mistake for an analyst to make himself unreachable by telephone except during certain brief and specified hours. On the other hand I believe it is an even greater mistake for an analyst to behave as though he were omnipresent and omnipotent. The analyst who does not reserve time for his own relaxation and recreation and reading and enjoyment will not sleep very well at night. The crown of thorns will become most uncomfortable.

In short, the tool with which an analyst works is himself. It is his responsibility to his patient to keep this tool, himself, in good physical and psychological condition, and he has to discover what is the best way for him to do this, so that he may keep functioning at the highest level he is capable of. There will be times when he will sit with a colleague and submit himself to the analytic process, to help restore his own objectivity and to re-engage with his unconscious life. Whatever else he does, he will need to set aside time each day to reflect on his work and evaluate it, to consider where he gained understanding, where he overlooked something important, and where he needs to reconsider what was done and find additional meaning in it. He must be aware of the feelings of his own that were stirred during the course of his day's work, and why. I usually review each session at the end of the day while it is still fresh, and note down any ideas that may come up in me as to how I may want to approach the next session. I need to do this in order to bring a degree of perspective to my work, but there is still another reason. I expect the analysand to reflect on the substance of the session and to integrate what he can of it into his awareness and possibly even into his behavior—have I the right to expect him to do more than I am willing to do myself?

The between-session work that is carried on by analysands is so varied that it might be said that each person's work is unique to himself. The one characteristic that binds all this work together is that all of it, in one way or another, is a confrontation of unconscious contents by the ego. Not all of it is verbal. The technique of the confrontation will be discussed in chapter twelve, *Dreaming the Dream Onward: Active Imagination,* but here it may be helpful to offer a sample of that private and individual work which is done by the analysand alone, and which contributes so much in the long run to the transformation of the personality.

The example was brought to me in the form of a meditative poem. In the process of writing it a man was working his way through a depression. He had a boring job, and sometimes in his frustrations arising from work he tended to be unpleasant to his wife, who then reacted negatively. It became then just a matter of time until he began to feel that none of his efforts was appreciated, that he must be just a worthless person, and he sank into the morass of self-pity. In the past he had countered this tendency with a few drinks or an argument with his wife. He gradually learned in the course of his analysis not to try to escape his depressions, but to allow himself to go into them and experience them fully—to see what they were made of. To do this, he would retire to his room and write out his feelings just as they came to him. He gave the name "A Man's Individuation Hymn" to this example of his efforts to work his way through a depression. Here is the text as he gave it to me:

When I am low, when all my magic is scattered,
a little bit placed on each of my friends.
that's when my loving wife soothes my soul with
"For God's sake, the world doesn't revolve around you, you Know."
That's when she becomes oh so panicky for it's rejection that she feels,
and she is right as she can be.
i do reject her and all she stands for.

there are times when a man needs space,
when he craves to be alone
to let his mind wander and play with all sorts of notions

about himself and those with whom he has been in contact.
sometimes a good husband must entertain the idea of his
wife's death with joy.

but of course it is not she who is the problem
that is plain to me.
rather the demon who lives within and not without.
to remember that at the same time it is being projected
onto your wife is the key to a golden marital relationship.
that is no easy trick, you know;
it requires what i like to call
the delicate inversion of the butterfly.

i could explain this as i have been known to have done
so many philosophical times before,
but now let it stand as it is,
and let those who understand be quiet
lest this too be scattered in the wind.

i will go soon, again to try to cause to take place
all that is in my heart,
but in order to clear the air with my wife
and with myself, let me issue this final phrase,
"I reject myself, not my loving wife, and I will not run
away to some accepting image of the past. I will stay put
in my rejection of this sloppy, good-for-nothing
irresponsible, wormy day that is about to close, and already
I sense that by staying put
and keeping my wife out of my network
there is something like the dogged determination
being born within
that will be needed to get back on my path on the morrow."

There is no need to explain this, for he has said it well
when he wrote "let those who understand be quiet." I only
want to note one interesting detail of which the writer was
not aware when he brought the piece into analysis. That was
the capitalization of the word "I" at the very beginning, then
the use of the lower case "i" all through until the very last
lines, when again the capital letter is used. It is nearly as
if the ego were in charge at the beginning, but then gave
over the process to the unconscious throughout, until the end,

when the ego returned with its big "I" to reassert itself as an individual who goes out to meet the world.

This movement is characteristic of the individuation process, especially as it proceeds during the first half of life.

7

PSYCHOLOGICAL TYPES:
KEY TO
COMMUNICATIONS

A well-known actor was being interviewed recently on the subject of actors in politics. The interview made reference to several actors or former actors who had gained important elective offices.

And then the interviewer asked, "Do you think actors should enter politics?"

The actor thought about this for a moment, and then replied, "I think that an actor, like any other man, should take an interest in government. But as far as running for office, I don't think that is a good idea, because actors are essentially introverts, while politicians are essentially extraverts."

He was then asked how he could consider a man who continually faces an audience to be an introvert. To this he answered, "In acting, a man's greatest concern is placing himself into the role of the character; that means he has to let the feeling of that character affect him, he has to live it in a very personal way from his own insides. This requires knowing yourself, for unless you know yourself you cannot really know another person. Actually the audience is a relatively unimportant consideration to the actor as he masters his role. But with politicians it is all different. There the game is to conquer the crowd. Playing the part is incidental."

I was interested to hear the words "introvert" and "extravert" used as household words, and to realize that they were understood by everyone, though perhaps few in the audience were aware that Jung had coined these words fifty years ago. He had identified two basically different attitudes which characterize people, and called these attitude types extraversion and introversion.

In his essay, "The Psychology of the Unconscious," the first of his *Two Essays in Analytical Psychology,* Jung described the development in his thinking that led him to his theory of psychological types. His book *Psychological Types* was published in 1920. Jung stated that it was the fruit of twenty years of consideration of the problem of individual differences. This consideration was brought into sharp focus between 1907 and 1913 when he was working closely with Freud and the members of Freud's early circle. Among these was the brilliant analyst Alfred Adler, who was one of the first to leave Freud after a series of violent disagreements with the master. Adler founded his own psychological school, which he called Individual Psychology. This proceeded from quite different premises than did Freudian psychoanalysis, despite the fact that both Freud and Adler had been working with the same kinds of cases, the same general body of data.

Jung had observed the dissension and bitterness, and also the great variance of position between the two men in their understanding of the causal aspects of neuroses. He saw that for Freud the basic assumption was that the growth of culture consists in a progressive subjugation of the animal in man. Culture is "a process of domestication which cannot be accomplished without rebellion on the part of the animal nature that thirsts for freedom."[1] Jung traced this point of view back historically, all the way to the Dionysian orgies that surged into the Greek world from the East and became a characteristic ingredient of classical culture. He described how the spirit of those orgies had contributed toward the development of the stoic ideal of asceticism in the innumerable sects and philosophical schools of the last century before Christ, and had produced from the polytheistic chaos of that period the ascetic religion of Christianity. Later, during the Renaissance, and afterward, successive waves of Dionysian licentiousness swept over the West, each bringing in its wake another variety of repressiveness, as in the puritanism at the time of Freud. The Freudian reformation was based mainly on the sexual question, which had come up as a major issue in European society during the last half of the nineteenth century.

Freud confronted directly the fundamental fact that man's instinctual nature is always coming up against the checks imposed by civilization. He recognized that the neurotic participates in the dominant currents of his age and reflects them in his own conflict. For Freud the major areas in which repressions were imposed were those which created the "erotic conflict." As Jung capsulized it in discussing the Freudian system of dream interpretation: "The Freudian mode of investigation sought to prove that an overwhelming importance attaches to the erotic or sexual factor as regards the origin of the pathogenic conflict. According to this theory there is a collision between the trend of the conscious mind and the unmoral, incompatible, unconscious wish."[2] He went on to say, "The Freudian school is so convinced of the fundamental, indeed exclusive, importance of sexuality in neurosis that it has drawn the logical conclusion and valiantly attacked the sexual morality of our day . . ."[3] Jung objected to the narrow view which he read into Freud's concept of "the Eros principle" and, for himself, insisted that Eros belongs on one side to man's animal nature and on the other is related to the highest forms of the spirit. "But he only thrives when spirit and instinct are in right harmony."[4]

Leaving his concerns about the Freudian approach, crediting it fully for its breakthrough on the side of freeing sexuality from the repressiveness that had held it crippled, while at the same time noting the limitations of the "Eros theory," Jung moved on to consideration of another point of view. This was Adler's "Individual Psychology," which Jung characterized by the descriptive phrase, "the will to power." The phrase is Nietzsche's, and refers to the philosopher who taught a "yea-saying" to instinct which, carried to its extreme, resulted in his establishing for himself his own morality, which was characterized as "beyond good and evil." Nietzsche believed and wrote that he lived his instinctual life in the highest sense. But Jung saw this as an impossible contradiction. For living the instinctual life suggests a simple naïveté, expressing directly and without a lot of intellectualization the feeling and desires that arise in one. Nietzsche was a philosopher, and as such he did more philosophizing than he did living out his instincts. Jung asks the pertinent question, "How is it possible . . . for man's instinctual nature to drive him into separation from his kind, into absolute isolation from humanity, into an aloofness from the herd upheld by loathing? We think of instinct as uniting man, causing him to mate, to beget, to seek pleasure and good living, the satisfaction of all sensuous desires."[5] He then comes to the issue where Nietzsche's attitude struck a respondent note in Alfred Adler. He noted that sexuality and, more broadly speaking, the desire for a harmonious human relationship, is only one of the possible directions of instinct. "There exists not only the instinct for preservation of the species, but also the instinct for *self-preservation*."[6]

According to Jung, Adler saw the instinct for self-preservation as being expressed in a power instinct which wants the ego to be in a controlling position under all circumstances and by whatever means. The "integrity of the personality" must be preserved at all costs. Adler stressed the great need of the individual to meet every attempt or apparent attempt of the environment to obtain dominancy over him. Adler formulated his view of neurosis based as exclusively on the power principle, as Freud's was based on the sexual question. Their views contrasted in a whole series of principles. As Jung explained: "With Freud everything follows from antecedent circumstances according to a rigorous causality, with Adler everything is a teleological 'arrangement.' . . . The Freudian method at once begins burrowing into the inner causality of the sickness and its symptoms . . . If, however, we look at the same clinical picture from the point of view of the 'other' instinct, the will to power, it assumes quite a different aspect."[7] Then it becomes a situation in the environment which affords the patient an excellent opportunity to exert a childish urge to power.

Jung imagined the dilemma of a judge called upon to decide between two views and he says: "One simply cannot lay the two explanations side by side, for they contradict each other absolutely. In one, the chief and decisive factor is Eros and its destiny; in the other, it is the power of the ego. In the first case, the ego is merely a sort of appendage to Eros; in the second, love is just a means to the end, which is ascendancy. Those who have the power of the ego most at heart will revolt against the first conception, but those who care most for love will never be reconciled to the second."[8]

Jung advanced the theory that the greatly varying views espoused by Freud and Adler, and the tenacity with which each insisted on his own position, corroborates the differences in the attitudinal sets of the two men. Regarding these incompatible views, Jung felt the need of a position superordinate to both in which it would be possible for the opposing views to come together in unison. In examining both theories without prejudice it became apparent to him that both views were attractively simple, both possessed significant truths, and that though these were contradictory they should not be regarded as mutually exclusive. From this Jung concluded that these two theories of neurosis must represent opposite aspects of the phenomena being observed, and that each theorist had grasped only one aspect. "But how comes it that each investigator sees only one side, and why does each maintain that he has the only valid view? It must come from the fact that, owing to his psychological peculiarity, each investigator most readily sees that factor in the neurosis which corresponds to his peculiarity."[9]

This realization had far-flung implications for Jung's entire point of view. He carefully compared all aspects of Freud's and Adler's theories. I do not wish to go into the theoretical aspects here[10] because my interest is in indicating how these concepts actually work, both in psychotherapy and in their wider implications. For one thing, differences in attitude type seem to be deeply rooted in the personality formation of the individual. It does not seem to me to be particularly important whether these differences are inherent and present at birth or are derived from relationships and experiences at a very early age.

Jung seemed to believe that these differences may be present at birth as a part of the "psychological constitution" of the infant, at least in the sense of predispositions toward certain types of attitudes and consequently of behaviors stemming from those attitudes. My own experience has given me a basis for supporting his argument, at least with reference to some cases. I recall my work with a couple who were receiving psychotherapy for help in dealing with a pair of difficult four-year-old girl twins. The father told me that just after the twins were born he had spent many hours watching them from the outside of the glass window-wall of the hospital nursery. From the first moment he saw Colette, she was wriggling about in her crib, flailing her little arms and legs. Often she would be squalling, until a nurse would come and attend to her. Meanwhile Colleen lay peacefully in her crib; if she moved, she moved rather slowly and tentatively. Colette seemed usually to be red-faced, Colleen was pale. When the girls were taken home it was clear from the first day that Colette was the one who drew the most attention, and as time went on she became clearly more responsive to other people than Colleen. By the time they were two or three, Colette was generally pushing her sister around, taking away her sister's toys, and not infrequently bashing them over her sister's head. Colleen was relatively placid and indifferent, only the greatest indignities would cause her to cry, and then it was a soft, mournful sobbing. In nursery school Colette was the one who would pick a fight with the other children, and when the fray was heaviest, Colleen would be found shrinking away in a corner.

It was thought that Colleen's tendency to withdraw was a reaction to Colette's way of coming on so strong, so the teachers decided to place them in separate rooms, with different teachers. Here the same kind of personality development went on, with the exception that Colette developed into a manager and an arranger in the classroom, and unless she were interfered with she would soon have the class pretty well organized to carry out whatever she wanted to do. Colleen, freed from her necessity to come to terms with Colette, became closely attached to her teacher, and became a little "do-gooder" in order to win the teacher's approval and affection. And who could not warm up to Colleen, with her shy, winsome ways, Colleen who, if you didn't take care to bring her into the group, would become lost in her own daydreams?

At home there was a constant struggle between the twins. Whatever Colette wanted to do was opposed by Colleen. Colette would scream and demand, and Colleen would cry and cajole. Colette used the power approach and Colleen appealed to love. Neither could make her peace with the other, and the parents were at a loss to understand what was happening in their household. The whole matter was complicated by the fact that the parents, because of their own differences in attitude types, did not see eye to eye on any aspect of how the children should be handled. The necessity of recognizing broad typological categories which account for striking individual differences had to be made clear to this family before there would be any hope of a successful outcome to the psychotherapeutic efforts.

Theories of types are not new with Jung, but he was one of the first to utilize typology as a therapeutic tool. Differences in typology can be traced back to antiquity, as Heinrich Heine has done when he wrote in *Deutschland*:

> Plato and Aristotle! These are not merely two systems; they are also types of two distinct natures, which from immemorial time, under every sort of cloak, stand more or less inimically opposed. But pre-eminently the whole medieval period was riven by this conflict, persisting even to the present day; moreover, this battle is the most essential content of the history of the Christian Church. Though under different names, always and essentially it is of Plato and Aristotle that we speak. Enthusiastic, mystical, Platonic natures reveal Christian ideas and their corresponding symbols from the bottomless depths of their souls. Practical, ordering, Aristotelian natures build up from these ideas and symbols a solid system, a dogma and a cult. The

Church eventually embraces both natures—one of them shelter-
ing among the clergy, while the other finds refuge in monas-
ticism.[11]

Jung, in his work *Psychological Types*,[12] traces the many
approaches to the problems of typology through philosophical
and poetic writings from ancient times through the German
philosophic schools. The study of typology has occupied the
interest of many investigators up to the present day, and especially in the field of psychology. Most of those who were
interested have directed their efforts primarily toward research,
and have devised tests for the purpose of vocational guidance
and career selection. For this pragmatically oriented guidance,
the most popular tests develop a series of "occupational pro-
files" based on a statistical summary of answers to certain questions from people in various lines of work. The counselee is
then tested to see to what typological pattern his answers to
test questions most nearly correspond. The idea is that if your
"type" resembles the type of the average or typical person
in a certain line of work, then that line is indicated for your
consideration. There are other tests which are purported to
indicate the nature of the value system held by the individual—
based on the assumption that people with similar values will
be able to work together more congenially than those with
dissimilar values. Then, too, there are those people who assume that personality characteristics correlate with the shape
and structure of the body, while others, just as adamant, relate
the personality traits and tendencies to the position of the
celestial constellations at the moment of birth.

Whatever its basis, the typological question comes up with
every one of us the moment we find ourself in an "uncongenial
area," that is, when we are forced to come to terms with
people whose typology is radically different from our own.
The typical symptom of that is a cry of exasperation on one
side or the other, "I just can't seem to understand you," or
"You haven't the faintest idea of what I'm talking about,"
or, as Mary Magdalene said of Jesus Christ Superstar, "I don't
know how to love him." On an international level, nations

can spend months deciding on the shape of a table at which they are to sit down to discuss peace negotiations, and then, years later and millions of words later, it appears that they have moved no closer to accord than when the question was whether the table should be round or square. Different types, individually or collectively, operate from different premises.

Ordinarily when we as individuals find ourselves in uncongenial discussions, we are forced to come to terms with people whose typology is quite different from our own. They will see things one way and be quite convinced that they are correct, while we will see things in another way and be just as convinced. There can never be any reconciliation between opposing views unless there is first a recognition that matters may be seen in other terms than that of correctness or error. To realize that they are simply seen from varying viewpoints may be the beginning of understanding. This recognition is useful in all areas of life, from intimate personal relationships to campus disputes, national controversies, and international conflagrations. For always there is one set of facts which is regarded by different people in different ways.

The personality differences within the psychoanalytic circle which led Jung to conceive of his typology theory were at first seen by him in a rudimentary form. Later Jung elaborated on his original theory so as to make it cohesive and inclusive of every kind of behavior which he was able to observe, both among his colleagues and in his analytical practice. His system of types consists of two fundamental "attitudes" and four functional types, or, as he calls them, "the four functions." It may be helpful to compare the two attitudes, introversion and extraversion, as to their essentials.

The introverted nature is Platonic in that it is mystical, spiritualized, and perceives in symbolic forms, while the extraverted nature is Aristotelian in that it is practical, a builder of a solid system from the Platonic ideal. The introvert is directed primarily toward an understanding of what he perceives, while the extravert naturally seeks means of expression and communication. In the introvert, the subject, his own being, is the center of every interest and the importance of the object lies in the way in which it affects the subject. In the extravert the object, the other in and of itself, to a large degree determines the focus of his interest. The introvert's interest in self-knowledge prevents him from being overpowered by the influence of his objective surroundings. The extravert has a tendency to abandon concern for himself to his interest in others. Hence the concern of the introvert is in the direction of development of his individual potential while that of the extravert is more socially oriented. The introvert tends to set himself and subjective psychic processes above achievement in the public domain, while the extravert seeks the recognition of others as a predominant value.

Biologically considered, the relation between subject and object is a relation of adaptation. The extravert spends and propagates himself in every way (fertility), while the introvert defends himself against external claims, consolidating his position (security).

Jung held the opinion that the innate disposition is the determining factor in the type the child will assume, under normal conditions. In an abnormal situation, for example when there is an extreme valuation of one attitude on the part of the mother, the child may be coerced into the opposite type. A neurosis will almost always occur in such a case. Then a cure can only result when what is sought is the development of the attitude that corresponds with the individual's natural way.

It must be made clear from the start that no one is altogether an extravert or altogether an introvert. If he were, he would not be able to cope with the ever-changing demands of life in the world, and would probably end up in a mental institution. If introverted to the absolute extreme he would be diagnosed as autistic or schizophrenic, for he would be living a life of his own construction, in many respects bearing little resemblance to the world of everyday reality. But if he were extraverted to the absolute extreme, his madness would take the form of hysterical or manic behavior, or psychosomatic illness; it would be characterized by an irrational attempt to bend his environment and the people in it to his wishes. The rest of us who call ourselves sane find ourselves somewhere on a continuum between the extremes, perhaps closer to one or the other of the poles, perhaps closer to the center.

There was a time, and it is still true in some circles, that introversion was thought to be rather odd. The child who would rather curl up with a good book than go out and play ball with his friends is often looked upon as a little disturbed, and his parents urge him to get out and join the other children. The introverted child invariably finds himself at a disadvantage in our educational system also, for his way is to take hold of things slowly, reflect upon them, and to be hesitant to display his knowledge or his understanding, since he is acutely aware of his limitations.

The extravert, on the other hand, has a relatively easy time of it. He is naturally able to see what the situation demands. His desire for approval from others leads him to behaving in a way that will secure this approval, whether it comes to helping people, or earning more money, or placing himself in a position where he will win favorable publicity. Indeed, there are plenty of rewards for extraversion as anyone can plainly see. Consider which professions are most highly paid: many are those which please the public. The comic entertainer, for instance, is richly rewarded in contrast to the character actor, who is more interested in portraying his own understanding of a role than he is in what others may think of him. Then there are those who function with an eye toward public acceptance: the advertising account executive, the politician, the businessman, the manufacturer of what the public wants, and the manufacturer's representative who sells it. How much less our society rewards the members of the more introverted professions: writing, teaching, scientific research, and the composition of serious music!

It is to Jung's credit that he pointed out that these two types exist and that he accorded them *equal value*. He recognized that although individuals tend to live out their conscious lives either on the side of introversion or of extraversion, there is a tendency in the unconscious to express the opposing side.

The unconscious, as we have seen in our discussion of dreams, operates in a compensatory fashion toward consciousness; this is also true in terms of the attitudes. A person who is in a group, and consciously concentrating on the needs and experiences of other members of the group, is nonetheless experiencing his own emotional reactions to what is happening—however he is unconscious of them. The unconscious carries the opposing attitude, in this case introversion, which often makes itself heard by coming out with a thoughtless or inappropriate remark, or by interrupting another person in order to put forth an idea which has suddenly burst upon him with unreasonable urgency.

The attitudes, as we have seen, are broad general categories. The typological system is further differentiated into four functions, or *functional types*. The functional types are: thinking, feeling, sensation, and intuition. To further complicate the picture, each functional type may be experienced in either one of the attitudes: as introverted thinking, introverted feeling, and so on, or as extraverted thinking, extraverted feeling, and so on. This results in eight potential types, one of which will be the typical mode of conscious functioning for any given individual. And since everything which is experienced in consciousness has its compensatory function in the unconscious, in addition to the eight possibilities for a conscious attitude type and function, there must be an additional eight possibilities for the attitude type and function in the unconscious. As one of my analysands put it to me: "Jung's system of types has expanded my categories for people from two (like me—and not like me) to sixteen, which provides a good basis from which to appreciate the rightness of, and relate constructively to, some of the differences between people. Also, my understanding of myself has been expanded by looking for all these various types and functions in their varying degrees within myself."

In order to understand in depth our own reactions to situations as well as those of other people, we need to realize that there are alternately possible ways to take in the situation. One way may be considered non-rational, when the situation is taken in directly, without the mediation which involves *responding* to it. Into this non-rational category belong the *sensation* function and the *intuitive* function. The sensation function simply sees things as they are—it takes in all details directly, seeing sizes, shapes, colors, hearing sounds, and employing all the other senses. The intuitive function also sees things as they are, but in a more general way, without being aware of perceiving specific details. Its tendency is to gain a total impression of a situation and also a sense for where it is leading, that is, for what may come of it. To the extent that an individual perceives in details and is tied to the specific realities of the moment, he tends not to see the whole general picture and its implications for the future. Thus sensation and intuition are mutually exclusive, and to the degree that intuition is the superior function (the one most commonly seized upon by an individual), sensation will be the inferior function (the least used function and consequently the most poorly developed).

The rational category comprises the functions of *thinking* and *feeling*. Thinking does not perceive the situation directly; it is rather one step removed, for thinking is *about* a situation, that is, it abstracts data from it and goes through a step by step process of understanding what it means. Feeling, one might expect, should not belong to a rational category, but in fact it does employ a process of reasoning which takes it, like thinking, one step away from the reality of the experience. Feeling means *coming to a point of view about* a situation—it is not only perceived, but a judgment is made about it; one feels that it is acceptable or not acceptable, agreeable or not agreeable, delightful or disgusting. To the extent that an individual thinks through a situation logically and comes to a sense of its meaning, his functioning has been neutral and non-judgmental. But to the extent that an individual allows himself to respond to the situation with his emotions and come to a feeling-loaded response, he has taken an evaluative position, and so cannot be neutral. Hence thinking and feeling are also to be seen as mutually exclusive functions.

When we speak of a person's belonging to a particular type,

we mean that one of the attitudes and one of the functions automatically tends to be used more frequently than the others in a given situation. This, then, would be that person's *superior function*. The opposite function, that less frequently employed, is called the *inferior function*. The superior function is identified with one's conscious attitude and mode of behavior, while the inferior function tends to be underdeveloped and relatively unconscious. A person whose superior function is, for example, *introverted thinking*, would be expected to have *extraverted feeling* as his least developed or inferior function.

If we now try to put the two attitudes, introversion and extraversion, together with the four functions, thinking and feeling, sensation and intuition, we will then have our eight types, and we may gain some idea of how they work. The types described below are extreme examples; in actual cases they would be considerably modified.

The *thinking type* is one whose every important action proceeds from intellectually considered motives, or at least there is a tendency to conform to such motives.

The *extraverted thinking type* is one whose constant aim is to bring his total life activities into relation with logically thought-out conclusions. These are related to what is happening in the world, whether objective facts or ideas are being talked about. He will be competent at planning and organizing. He will repress the activities that are dependent on feelings, such as participating in aesthetic activities or cultivating the art of friendship. Non-rational expressions such as religious experiences or sexual passions are obliterated to the point of nearly complete unconsciousness. Eventually the aspects of life repressed by the thinking function may become indirectly perceptible through a disturbance of the conscious conduct of life. The inferiority of the feeling function in this type may manifest itself by the individual's neglecting his health, his social position, his family—all in the service of a goal—which is the sort of achievement that will be recognized by the important people. Such a person could work tirelessly for great humanitarian causes, while concurrently behaving in a mean and petty manner toward people who work for him.

But if the thinking function is introverted, its orientation is inward rather than toward the world. Facts are collected as evidence for a theory or a prejudice, never for their own sake. The *introverted thinking type* is daring in the world of ideas, yet he becomes extremely anxious when he has to transplant his ideas by communicating them to others. He rarely goes out of his way to prove a point, and then he often does it badly. He permits himself to be mercilessly exploited if only he can be left alone to pursue his ideas. Because of his insecurity in social situations, he supplies himself with a good repertoire of defenses which prove to be protective obstacles to human relationships.

The *extraverted feeling type* depends for his evaluations of any given situation on the premise that it is fitting to do so. He will value objects or ideas as "good" or "beautiful" because doing so will create a pleasant atmosphere in his circle. He is the first to take up the new fads, he gathers his friends together in his jalopy and heads for the rock festival three states away, or, if he has made it in the establishment, takes a box at the opera and invites his friends. Jung was of the opinion that as men comprise most extraverted thinking types, so do women comprise most extraverted feeling types. He asserted that a woman's feeling tends to correspond with generally accepted values, that she loves a "suitable man" because he corresponds in standing, age and capacity with the requirements of society. Jung regarded her feeling as genuine, however, and not manufactured. It is natural to her to believe that everything which corresponds to accepted valuation is good.

As I reflect that Jung was propounding this notion about the relative tendencies in typology between men and women I recall that his book on types was written in Switzerland long ago, and I wonder if he would have made the same characterizations today, and especially with reference to men and women in the United States. I am convinced that the descriptions of the types are valid enough, but I believe that as women become better educated they begin to take advantage of opportunities for highly differentiated thinking by becoming active in the kinds of work for which their education prepares them. This forces them to develop whatever potential they may have for extraverted thinking and to be less willing to adopt the compliant posture which may go along with introverted feeling. Nor is it so common today to find women whose inferior extraverted thinking function (the unconscious concomitant of a superior introverted feeling function) exists as a slave to feeling. For if it did, then thinking would be repressed and, as a force of the unconscious, would become infantile, archaic and negative. Yet when a woman's thinking function is repressed we often find that she tends to form her opinions on a scant basis of facts, and to use her charm or else her aggressivity to enforce her opinions without bothering to establish their validity. Men are not immune from this pestilence either; however, because the world is still the way it is, the circumstances of most men's lives demand from them a better-adapted capacity to think—just to hold a better job—and therefore many men have little opportunity to relax their hold on their extraverted thinking function. But when a man finds himself in a kind of work that offers him no challenge as far as thinking is concerned, that function may for him, too, lapse into unconsciousness. As a consequence his inferior introverted thinking may lead him to become cold and calculating about his pettiest personal affairs.

When we meet the *introverted feeling type*, we face someone who is silent, inaccessible, hard to understand, and frequently depressed. Such people neither shine nor reveal themselves. Their outward demeanor is harmonious and inconspicuous; they would never rock the boat. People of this type when it is extreme, may appear neglectful, withdrawn and indifferent to others. What is seldom recognized is that these people may be deeply, privately religious, given to meditation and gentleness. They are capable of great tenderness where they recognize a need, but no one ever hears of their generous, even sacrificial, acts. On the negative side, sometimes as an effect of their inferior extraverted thinking, they may assume a benevolent neutrality tempered with a trace of superior and critical attitude.

We move now to a consideration of the non-rational types, sensation and intuition. The *sensation type* lives by the data of the senses. Whatever he sees or hears he accepts, whether it is compatible with reasoned judgment or not. He does not always stop to take a "thought-out" position on it, nor does he react strongly with his feelings. But he can describe a room he has been in with accurate detail and has no trouble finding his way when he has once traveled over the terrain.

The *extraverted sensation type* is that type idealized by the devotees of sensory-awareness. His life is an accumulation of actual experience with concrete facts. His sensed "experience" is used to serve as a guide for fresh sensation. His aim is to enjoy the fullness of life, concrete enjoyment in the here and now, and his morality is accordingly oriented. Also, he is the type who lives to eat, and this may take the form of excessive eating, or of being a gourmet or, as is very popular these days, to make a great project out of only eating certain types of foods prepared in certain ways, and spending long hours discussing the "reasons" for this intense preoccupation with the experience of filling the belly. Again, depending on his social identification, he will make much of dressing in the latest style with all accessories carefully selected to make a complete ensemble, or he will affect the most outlandish costume, designed to attract by the instant impression it gives the sort of people to whom he wants to appeal. His weaknesses appear when repressed intuitions assert themselves. Then his imagination will run away with him, and he will suffer from jealous fantasies in the case of a sexual object. When his extraverted sensation is developed in the extreme, the compensation tends to appear in the form of certain specific neuroses. Such a person may develop every sort of phobia, and especially compulsive symptoms. These compulsions represent the unconscious counterweight to the easy morality of the purely sensual attitude. When the extraverted sensation type becomes neurotic he is difficult to treat in a rational way. I find that often the best avenue is to rely heavily on the attachment of the patient to the analyst in a transference relationship, where emotional pressure can be brought to bear in order to help the patient come to a state of awareness of what is being neglected while the extraverted sensation function is being served.

The *introverted sensation type* struggles with the difficulty of being unable adequately to express what the senses convey to him despite his intense awareness of the world about him. Looking at him from the outside, we can never tell what will make an impression on this type of person; his reactions are unpredictable and appear irrational because he sees what is before him but is not really related to it. His unconscious intuition is of an extraverted and archaic character. It has an amazing flair for the ambiguous, gloomy and dangerous possibilities behind the realities he observes. The unconscious tendency to suspicion at best acts as a wholesome compensation for the overly credulous attitude of consciousness. At worst it is beset with compulsive ideas and paranoid fears, stemming from the unconscious doubt that the world may not be, after all, as it appears through the impressions of his senses. Often, therefore, the introverted sensation type creates an atmosphere of beauty in his surroundings, and is an artist or a connoisseur of the arts.

Jung has defined *intuition* as a process which extracts the perception unconsciously, at the same time producing an unconscious effect in the object. Sensation as an inferior function disturbs the intuitive's clear, naïve perception with sensory stimuli, which direct attention onto the superficial, beyond which intuition tries to peer. Therefore, sensation is to a large degree suppressed in order for intuition to become paramount. Just as extraverted sensation strives to reach the most accurate perception of actuality, so intuition tries to encompass the greatest possibilities.

The *extraverted intuitive type* has the capacity for recognizing situations pregnant with future promise. He becomes easily bored with stable, long-established conditions, for his eye is constantly ranging for new possibilities. He is likely, for instance, to be in the foreground of movements for brief, temporary marriages, that is, if he is for marriage at all. New ideas and new ways appeal to him; he seizes upon them with intensity, not waiting to see first how they will work out in practice. Yet in time, ideas and ways that were once new become a prison to him. Thinking and feeling may not be so highly developed in the intuitive type, yet they are desperately needed to provide him with the judging capacity which is lacking in his type. The intuitive extravert can be the successful promoter. Often he is able to inspire other men. The danger is that he will squander his energy animating others, running after some new possibility, leaving his newly started business for someone else to carry on and turn into a profitable enterprise. Often he goes away empty. He also has the unconscious against him since in his enthusiasm he often represses sensation of actual though painful realities. These then suddenly command his attention at the point where they have become destructive.

The *introverted intuitive type* may be the mystical dreamer or the seer, or he may be the fantastic crank or the artist. As a rule the introverted intuitive stops at his holistic perception. In the case of the artist, the goal is the shaping of the total view. If thinking and feeling are both to some degree cultivated by this type, there may develop a form of judgment which, together with the capacity for imagining what the future could be like, would offer the basis for useful contributions in the moral sphere. The moral problem comes into being for him when he tries to relate himself to his vision and ask, "What does it mean for me and for the world?" The unconscious compensation for this type would be an inferior extraverted sensation characterized by impulsiveness and unrestraint. Who has not seen the angry father demanding self-control and righteousness from his children, while he himself is in the grip of his emotions?

I have described briefly the eight basic types along with their unconscious compensatory types. Perhaps, as you read, each type in its turn seemed extreme and improbable. The descriptions do, in fact, bring out the most outstanding features of the types, and therefore give a distorted picture. All of the types are represented in each one of us. The type which is most representative, the superior function, dictates the way in which the ego most typically responds, but of course it is far from the only possible response an individual can make. Different situations make different demands, and most of us are well-rounded enough to be able to call on any of the functions that seem suitable for a given situation. Some ways of functioning, however, seem to be more successful than others, and we tend to repeat our successful performances, thus strengthening the function that is superior anyway. It then may happen that the conscious attitude becomes exaggerated and absolutized, and the unconscious attitude correspondingly loses its compensatory attitude and becomes destructive.

One might expect the therapist to dig into the problem at either end: expose the conscious distortion or dig into the unconscious. But Jung has suggested another avenue. He takes note of the two auxiliary functions that are present along with the superior and the inferior functions. His investigation of individual cases revealed that "in conjunction with the most differentiated function, another function of secondary importance, and therefore of inferior differentiation in consciousness, is constantly present, and is a relatively determining factor."[13] The secondary function is always one whose nature is different from, though not antagonistic to, the leading function; it remains relatively unconscious and it *serves* the leading function.

Jung's important insight was that therapy is most effective via the secondary function. In other words, rather than treat an exaggerated intellectual, for example, by trying to develop the feeling function directly out of the unconscious, Jung suggested that the therapist work via the irrational secondary function, which is only relatively unconscious. The advantage, Jung said, is that the therapist avoids violating the subject's conscious standpoint (without which he cannot hang together at all) by lending it such a "range and prospect over what is possible and imminent that consciousness gains an adequate protection against the destructive effect of the unconscious."[14]

If his conscious standpoint is left relatively intact, the subject is not forced into an almost never-to-be-corrected transference.

By positing both a conscious main function and a relatively unconscious auxiliary function, Jung seems to have recognized an important avenue for therapists—one that provides a gentle and simultaneous entrance into both conscious and unconscious functions; one that never loses touch with the one even as it aims to modify or stimulate the other.

In actual practice I have found that very few people fall into the distinct categories that we have outlined. Most rely primarily upon a main function, and to a lesser extent on a secondary function, but the two work well together; thus, an extraverted intuitive-thinking type would be an extravert whose intuition is primary, and is modified by his thinking. The truest thing that can be said about psychological types is that there are many of them and anyone who concerns himself with typology must ask the question, "Will one type ever truly understand another?"

The question is extremely pertinent in psychotherapy when one is dealing with couples who are experiencing marital difficulties. So often I see couples who seem, potentially, to have everything going for them, and yet they are so cruel and disagreeable with one another that I despair of getting them even to listen to each other, much less take each other's views into consideration. Or, at the opposite pole, there is a degree of indifference that exists which leaves no doubt of the fact that the two individuals may be living in the same world, but from the way they view it it might as well be two worlds. It becomes necessary, in therapy, to give each person an opportunity to express his feelings and thoughts, his sense perceptions and intuitions, in his own characteristic way. When each one can present his view in all clarity with respect to a certain issue, and it becomes clear that the views are radically different, the introduction of the theory of types may be extremely helpful. No longer can each party make the assumption that there are two ways to look at the problem, "my way and the wrong way." They are forced to recognize that different views are frequently the only possible outcome of different typologies. They may be led to see that if each one can recognize the validity of the views of the other, and see the other's views as necessary to round out a more whole approach to a set of circumstances, the two may begin to consult each other before making a decision rather than fighting about it afterward. Each may learn from the other and so increase his or her own ability to respond in a variety of ways. And, where an individual cannot alter his own makeup, he can at least recognize the right of his partner to have free expression for her own intrinsic nature.

Recently I held premarital counseling interviews with a young couple who had contemplated marriage but couldn't come to a decision. They had been close friends and lovers for a very long time, and were accustomed to spending a good deal of time in one another's apartment without actually living together. Because of frequent disagreements and heated arguments they were hesitant about committing themselves to a permanent arrangement. In the previous session I had remarked that possibly some of the difficulty and uncertainty between them was due to a difference in typology. At this interview I asked them how they had reacted to the last interview. Had they discussed it? Did they have any questions? The young woman said, "Yes, during the last interview you said something about our being of different types, and I wondered what you meant by this." I gave the couple a very brief overview of the problem of typology, how people basically can be classified into certain psychological types. I did not go into the details of each type specifically, except that I did mention the terms I knew they were familiar with, introversion and extraversion, and I reviewed the distinguishing characteristics of each type.

Then I described the young man. I said, "You are a person I believe, who is interested in the shape of things, the feel of things, the look of things."

He replied, "Yes, that's very true. I'm a sculptor."

I said, "So what is important to you has a very concrete form, you're interested in touching it; as you touch it, it becomes reality, and that is what has meaning for you. The important thing is not so much how the world views it, but how you view it yourself, what it does for you when you construct your own reality, and perceive it as you are constructing it." I didn't use the term "introverted sensation" but I described the characteristics of this type, and he recognized himself without any hesitancy whatever.

Then I turned to the young woman. "Are you happy in your work?" I asked her.

She replied, "Oh, yes, it's really very satisfying and I enjoy it very much, and I'm good at it, I'm the best one in my office."

Then I asked her to describe what she did. "My job is writing responses to the letters that come into the office of a well-known politician. He has a whole staff of us who answer these many, many letters that come in with all sorts of questions."

I suggested, "Evidently you like to deal with problem situations, you like to take a letter from someone whom you have never seen, and imagine what this person is like, what his hangups are, what his difficulties are, what kind of background he has, what kind of help he needs, what his self-interest demands, what kind of language will win his support. You are able to project what you write into the future and somehow to realize how what you say will affect that person, how it will determine his or her vote." I described her getting into this unknown quantity and being able to respond to it from within herself. She is not a trained psychologist, but she has a kind of inner way of putting together material for which she has only the barest clues and coming out with some kind of statement, and directing this statement to that object, a person whom she has never seen. She is, of course, very clearly the extraverted intuitive type.

When the extraverted intuitive type gets together with the introverted sensation type, there are bound to be some disagreements. I told these two that when people are of opposite types, they are foreordained to see the world differently. I illustrated it with the following example: "Supposing you two were looking at a house." I said to the young woman, "You are at the front of the house, and you're looking into the living-room window." And to the young man, "You're at the side of the house, and you are looking into the same room. Now you're both looking in at the house, which is our symbol for objective reality. Supposing you, young man, described what you see. You might say, 'I see a beautiful room with plush furniture, wood-paneled walls, and all done in blues and green with an expensive oriental rug on the floor.' And you, the young woman, you say, 'No, it's not like that at all! There's a fireplace, and a hearth, a perfect place for parties, and the mood of the place is friendly. It's a really really wonderful place, but not at all as you described it.'

"Well," I told the couple, "the two of you could very easily have a big argument about this—'you say it's like this and I say it's like this, and we'll never agree; I must be right and you must be wrong, and there's no reasonable conclusion.' On the other hand, you might say, 'I see this, and this is as much of the room as I can see, but you, with your different viewpoint, with your different orientation, see something completely different. I'll tell you what I see, and you tell me what you see, and we'll try to visualize what each other sees, and between the two of us we'll both have a much richer and deeper concept of this house that symbolizes reality than either one of us could have alone. But in order to have this, we have to trust each other, we have to respect each other, we have to give to each other the recognition that your point of view is every bit as valid as my point of view, that neither one of us has a corner on reality, and that we two can very well live together respecting and affirming each other, even when we disagree.'"

This couple was able to see that there are two possible ways to deal with the problem of typology. One is to allow it to become an insurmountable barrier and to become resigned to the feeling that one type can never understand the other. The second way is to recognize that each type provides the other with insights into the world which he would never have without that particular partner. Rather than standing up for one's own point of view and tearing down or depreciating the other's, it makes more sense to try to understand the other's point of view, to learn from the other, and in doing so to fill in the gaps in one's own personality. In the case of this particular couple, the sculptor really could not verbalize; he could not see a problem in his mind but had to work it out through his fingers, and he did not concern himself with the implications for the future of what he was doing. The writer, on the other hand, was always busy thinking about what could be and what might be. Very frequently she would get into anxiety states and she would be unable to deal with a present situation because she was paralyzed at the thought of what might come of it. The two could very well learn from each other, and become much more whole as human beings, and, gradually, through their relationship, enlarge their own capacities for functioning.

In my work as a psychotherapist, I rarely have the experience of seeing people who have worked out a typology problem naturally, without the need of psychotherapeutic assistance. Not long ago, when I was teaching a course on Jung, I was particularly pleased with a short paper written by a student of mine. The paper had been touched off by my lecture on Jung's typology, which had been followed by a lively class discussion on whether a person should marry someone of a similar or dissimilar type. I am indebted to this student, who in the remarks below offers insight into the way a relationship of husband and wife of differing types can work out in a life situation. The student wrote:

"My mother and father are very dissimilar, but appear to have a happy and fulfilling marriage relationship. Mother and father have been married forty years, have had hard times and better times financially and healthwise, and have worked hard all their lives so that their children could all have college educations—a 'necessity' which was impossible for either of them. I have never doubted that they loved each other deeply and they created a home and family atmosphere for their four children which was basically happy and free.

"Mother seems to be typed easily: she's the extraverted-thinking-sensation type. When she was sixteen years old she graduated from high school and left her extremely poor farm home to begin nurse's training. She lived those three years on the seven dollars a month that students were paid to work on the floors in the hospital. She was then, and is now, a 'doer.' She's always doing something for someone else, even when she's dead tired. She has lots of friends, loves her work, reads little, and is thought by other people to be a 'rock' of common sense. She's concerned with facts and reality. No matter what the catastrophe, others can always count on her to be calm and collected, showing little emotion, and able to grasp the concrete situation from several perspectives. Though she seems to show some creative ability, the general trend is towards conventional ways of thinking and acting. She 'needs' to be liked and accepted by others—and she is, among other reasons because she is over-considerate of others. She finds it extremely difficult to say 'no,' to anyone for anything that they might ask of her. Mother loves a good time, beautiful things, and cultural entertainment, though she has no talent herself, at least no developed talent for any of the finer arts.

"Father, on the other hand, is more difficult to 'typologize,' but he seems to be more the introverted-feeling-sensation type. He graduated from eighth grade first in his class; but he immediately had to find work to help support his family of ten children. He became a plumber's apprentice by day and read books or sang in light opera by night. The first thing he ever bought himself was a piano. Father is shy, so shy that he panics if he is forced to talk on the phone more than a minute or two before handing the phone to mother. He still loves to read, and he enjoys sharing quiet evenings with his few but intimate friends. Though he lacks confidence in himself, he has been a successful business man operating a conservative but active printing company with his brother. Though he shows little emotion on the outside, he's very sensitive and full of feelings on the inside. He's dangerously scrupulous about matters of religion and morality and carefully avoids any critical statements or negative judgments about anybody. He appears to be very accepting of others, but in reality I think is afraid to criticize or judge negatively, rather than positively accepting. Father likes quiet sessions at home with his family and is the beloved 'Grandpapa' of his eleven grandchildren.

"What seems to make this marriage so 'right' for both Mother and Father is that they admire and respect and cultivate the qualities dominant in the other. While Father thinks Mother's constant 'doing' for others is a quality of value and beauty and always tries to be helpful, Mother plans with an eye to making the situation pleasant for him. She encourages him to read and to be with his friends."

It is extremely heartening to see how the human personality and all its relationships may be enhanced with an understanding and respect for variety in typology. Unfortunately the opposite is also true, a great deal of misery can result from a failure to recognize one's own basic typology and to live in accordance with it. The result can be a great deal of neurotic suffering, which can only be set aright by uncovering the natural typology of the individual. Sometimes a dream, stemming from the deeper levels of the psyche, can lead the unhappy individual to an understanding of his real nature, and to the possibilities for realizing it in his life and work.

A young man in his second year of medical school suffered from periodic depressions. Often he would feel that he was exhausting himself in his studies and that it was all pointless; too much energy had to be expended and too little reward was forthcoming. In all, general feelings of apathy characterized the depressions. A little background will set the stage for relating a crucial dream which clarified the central problem for the student. James had wanted to become an architect when he was in high school and during his undergraduate years. He had enjoyed envisioning interesting structures in which form would follow function, and function would be the outcome of a philosophical approach to life. What stopped him in his plan to go into this field was the necessity of learning to handle the graphics—the extreme precision and attention to detail required in drawing went against something in him.

He shifted into a pre-med program, then medical school. Here was another way, he thought, of serving men's needs. At first he was delighted with the change, but his original enthusiasm soon began to wear thin as he found himself confronted with difficult course work—physiology and anatomy and much rote memorization. He was required to participate in discussions in seminars demonstrating his knowledge of great masses of detailed subject matter. Studying became more and more difficult for him; it was often boring. Concentration became hard to maintain. He would fall asleep over his books. All of this caused him much anxiety. He came into analysis and, as his life history unraveled and his feelings about what he was doing became clearer, I began to wonder if James might be a *turntype*, that is, someone who by force of circumstances was attempting to function in a type that was not his natural superior function, but rather the inferior function. His current dreams did not throw any light on the question, but he told me that he had had a dream just before he gave up architecture for medicine, and that the dream had haunted him ever since. It remained so vivid that at the retelling he could recapture the feeling tone with all the intensity that there had been when the dream occurred. It was altogether an auditory dream. There was no visual image whatsoever. This is the dream: *I was asleep. I heard vague music off in the background. It sounded like something that could only have been composed by Wagner. There were the deep sonorous tones, with really beautiful crescendos. The music grew louder and louder. At first I was fascinated, then I began to be afraid because the music was uncontrollable. It continued to increase in volume and depth, louder and louder. I got the shivers and the shakes and I had to force myself to wake, and I woke up in a sweat, in a real panic. As I became fully awake the music stopped, and I gradually began to calm down. As I started to drift back to sleep the music began again. It was more quiet now, but slowly swelling and becoming more imposing. As it grew I felt the great, spacious quality of the Wagnerian opera, the wild Teutonic strains, at once primitive and utterly refined. As it grew louder, the anxiety returned, and then the panic, and I forced myself awake again.*

After relating the dream, James commented, "I wish I had been a musician, for then I could have written down this music."

The dream expressed the fundamental personality type of the dreamer; he is an introverted intuitive-feeling type. The dream, coming as it did at a period in his life which offered an opportunity to change his vocation, sounded a clear call for the dreamer to pay attention to the "music" which would evoke his own personal harmony and life-style. In a sense he *had* paid attention to the chords from the unconscious; he had recognized that he needed to work in a profession that would allow him to use his intuitive ability to grasp the whole of a situation, along with his capacity for feeling with and responding to another person. He then told me that what he most wanted to do was to become a psychiatrist. Medicine was a means to that end, rather than an end in itself. Furthermore, the study of psychiatry, he now felt, would give him more insight into his own nature—that was the introverted aspect of his career choice. His remembering this dream at the particular time that he did was not without its significance. In order to become a psychiatrist he had first to complete the general medical training program, which involved mastery over an infinite amount of detail, and particularly at the pre-clinical stage of study. This meant that he had to face his inferior side and make use of his inferior function constantly. Sensation was his inferior function, and he was forced to concentrate on it. It involved learning to note carefully anything that might possibly have reference to diagnosis or treatment. He would be helped in this through his secondary function, thinking, through finding meaning and order in the relations of the details. And lastly, he would have to utilize forced extraversion in making oral reports and in participating in class discussions to establish the level of his knowledge. All this time, then, he had to suppress his introversion, his intuition and his feeling—qualities which would serve him well in the practice of psychiatry, but were not exactly the most helpful assets in medical school.

The kind of music that the dream suggested, the kind of music that beat upon his ear with such strength and fury that it had to be listened to before it overwhelmed, this was music on a grand scale, rooted in myth and mystery. It was music of a transpersonal nature, dealing with the elemental dramas of mankind. If the dreamer could sink into the meaning of the myth which is given voice in the music, he would find a way of experiencing his life as more than a mass of petty details. He would begin to envision the larger plan, the archetypal model of man, into which every detail may be seen to fit, like single notes in the score of a great opera.

The theme of the dream was amplified by exploring the symbolism of the mythology which the dreamer connected with the music, so that it became an ongoing experience for the dreamer. That music was to have its place, always, in the background of his life as an expression of his own myth. Its sonorous tones would provide a welcome accompaniment while he would be living in conscious awareness of the necessity of keeping in touch with his natural typology, even while exercising perforce the less differentiated functions. But the music would become loud and insistent and demanding, nearly deafening, when he would become too one-sided, and not let his real nature have the space it needed to stay alive. The dream of music became for him a sort of inner gyroscope; it would help him to measure his inclinations and it would serve as a guide for him on the path toward individuation.

The concept of the psyche as a self-regulating system is seen more clearly as we come to understand that the inferior function, like the dream, can lead the way to the unconscious and, with the co-operation of ego consciousness, can help to bring about a continuously growing synthesis between the conscious mind and the unconscious. Archetypal images like the music in James' dream, act as unconscious "regulators," springing into action whenever there is a psychic imbalance. It is only from this angle that Jung's theory of psychological types can be properly understood. "These types are not static positions, but a dynamic interaction of polaristic psychic patterns of behavior and adjustment, in which any one-sidedness is complemented by its opposite, thus forming the starting point for further assimilation of unconscious contents."[15]

8

PERSONA
AND SHADOW

A very proper young woman from a respectable conservative family was in analysis with me. She brought the following dream: *I came to your office in a beautiful gown of black velvet with a high neck and long sleeves, but when I turned around there was no dress at all in back, just bare skin from top to bottom.*

In becoming civilized, we compromise between our natural inclinations and the patterns of society. We assume a certain character or stance through which we can relate. Jung calls this stance a mask or a *persona*, the name given to the masks worn by the actors of antiquity to signify the roles they played. The persona is oriented toward society or, more precisely, toward the expectation of society that an individual may have. Seeking to find his place in the particular milieu in which he must function, he assumes the accoutrements of the milieu. The side which fronts society is geared to meet it, and on its terms. Often the one who goes out dressed to the teeth for the party is the only one who does not realize that his backside is showing.

The persona is a collective facet of the personality that is only adaptively unique to the individual, for its appearance and meaning are defined by the society. Jung wrote:

Only by reason of the fact that the persona is a more or less accidental or arbitrary segment of collective psyche can we make

the mistake of accepting it *in toto* as something "individual."
But, as its name shows, it is only a mask for the collective psyche,
a mask that *feigns individuality*, and tries to make others and
oneself believe that one is individual, whereas one is simply playing a part in which the collective psyche speaks.

When we analyse the persona we strip off the mask, and discover that what seemed to be individual is at bottom collective;
in other words, that the persona was only a mask for the collective psyche. Fundamentally the persona is nothing real: it is a
compromise between the individual and society as to what a
man should appear to be. He takes a name, earns a title, represents an office, he is this or that. In a certain sense all this
is real, yet in relation to the essential individuality of the person
concerned it is only a secondary reality, a product of compromise,
in making which others often have a greater share than he. The
persona is a semblance, a two-dimensional reality.[1]

The symbols for the persona are the cover-ups: they may
appear in dreams as dress, hats, armor, veils, shields; or they
may take on the characteristics of a profession or trade, as
tools, equipment of various sorts, certain specific books; or
they may be reflected in an automobile, or even in some instances a house or apartment. Or the persona may be expressed in awards, diplomas, or a variety of so-called "status
symbols." Persona problems are common in all parts of society,
for as people identify themselves as belonging to a certain
category they begin to adopt behavior appropriate to that category and to discard what does not fit. Thus the "identity crisis"
about which Erik Erikson has written so much, tends to find a
partial solution, at least, in the assumption of a persona. It
may not be the best solution but it often works, until something happens to break down the persona. While the persona
is functioning well, many people identify with it. "I am that,"
they tell themselves. "I am a doctor, or a schoolteacher, or a
radical socialist, or a rock musician, and I will let you know
this even before you have a chance to exchange a word with
me."

This was the case with my patient, a priest in a large
suburban church. He came to one analytic session carrying
a letter in his hand, and evidently quite upset about it. The

letter had come from a parishioner, an elderly lawyer who had recently retired and did not have very much to keep him busy. Church activities were the mainstay of his life, and he was a substantial contributor to the building fund. This man had attended church the previous Sunday, and had gone home and written a letter in a half-apologetic manner, stating that the priest's reading of the psalm from a newly published translation of the Bible had disturbed him greatly, he had missed the "glorious prose" of the King James Version. He had gone on to write that in another part of the service Father Leo had overlooked the customary rubric of reading a certain prayer himself and instead had asked the congregation to join with him. The lawyer was adamant about maintaining the traditional practices of the church. The letter ended, "I am sure that you are glad there aren't too many lawyers in the church to pressure you about these kinds of problems!"

Father Leo was furious. He felt himself under attack. "There's no possibility of pleasing everybody! If I listened to the conservatives like this attorney, I would lose all the young people in the congregation. If I make all the changes these young people want in their cries for 'relevance' I'll lose the ones who have been members for years and who are the financial support of the church. I always have to compromise, but no matter what I do there is always somebody who gets unhappy about it."

We talked about his being what he thought he had to be, that he *was* the priest, that role was or seemed to him to be his entire existence. He was able to recognize that everyone, in the course of pursuing a career, assumes a role, whether it be that of clergyman or butcher, schoolteacher or analyst. We learn as we grow into our "position" that certain practices are acceptable and that other practices are not acceptable. Sometimes these are subtle matters; the preacher's tone of voice, the analyst's pause, are like the mask held before the face: when you see the mask raised you know what to expect from the actor. We talked about how dress indicates to people even before they meet us what they may expect.

Father Leo, who sat in front of me, customarily wears a

black suit with a clerical collar. His persona makes it clear
to people that they shouldn't swear in front of him, that he
is to be treated with proper respect. Even the policeman who
stops him for speeding waves him on with a smile, when he
sees the garb, or lets him off, suggesting, "I'm sure you're
hurrying to see a sick parishioner." But when Father Leo
comes to see his analyst, he typically wears a sport shirt and
a pair of slacks. He gets across that he doesn't expect to be
treated with the deference here that he gets when he is wearing his preacher-persona; he wants a more direct confrontation,
so that is how he presents himself.

The persona problem that Father Leo has is that he identifies too much with his persona. He doesn't quite know where
the priest leaves off and the man begins.

The lawyer was not criticizing Leo the *man*, he was criticizing *his priest*, the one who appears in a black suit on Sundays
in the pulpit and who does not quite correspond to his, the
lawyer's, idea of how a priest customarily conducts a service.
When Leo assumes that he is criticizing Leo, the person, he
has identified with his persona. Ego and persona have become
indistinguishable.

Leo had to discover that his reality is that of an individual
who assumes a certain role for professional purposes. This is
not to say that he doffs his beliefs or his concern with matters
of the spirit when he takes off his collar, not by any means.
But that aspect of his profession which is required by society
must come to mean to him simply that "I have to do this
in order to convey to people that I am their spiritual leader,
but I remain my own person, with my own beliefs. I recognize
that I cannot be all things to all men, and I make my peace
with that."

But how to deal with the lawyer? Once Leo began to understand how the persona was functioning with him, he was then
prepared to take the next step, which was to put into the
life experience itself the insights that emerged in analysis. It
would have been an easy thing to pass off the letter from
the lawyer by telling him, "I'm sorry you were upset about
that, but we have to make changes in the church from time

to time," and then jolly him over a cup of coffee. But what if the lawyer was also identified with *his* persona? Could he be using his persona in an unconscious way as a means for getting attention from Father Leo? Here was an elderly man, retired, who had held positions of importance in the past, who now wanted some emotional support from his pastor, and who knew no other way to get it but to retreat into his traditional way of doing things, that is, into his own persona, that of a lawyer. So he made legalistic, nit-picking remarks about the church service.

When a person is in analysis with me, it is understood between us that he has the responsibility in his interpersonal relations to be conscious of what is going on below the level of appearances. If one does not gain the capacity to deepen his level of awareness, then of what need is analysis? So Leo was expected to be able to understand that the attorney was identified with his own persona, with his attorney role, and that he related to Leo's persona, which he mistook for Leo himself. It is with the persona that he took issue. Leo then had to understand that he was not personally being attacked but that it was his persona which got attacked. Once he recognized this he could step back and discuss the whole matter with his attorney-congregant without feeling personally threatened. It put a wholly different light on the confrontation. Instead of having to defend himself in an apologetic or self-deprecating way, he could meet it head-on. Leo could explain to his friend that, yes, he had considered the matter and he saw the validity of the other's viewpoint. However, a new generation and changing times necessitated his taking into account not only the very valuable contributions of the older people, but that he also had to maintain rapport with the younger people who wanted services in a language which they recognized as their own.

Father Leo could not expect his elderly parishioner to meet him halfway. It was his responsibility as an analyzed person to carry the burden of greater consciousness. That required him to meet his friend where he was, on his own ground, and to lead him along by presenting to him the dilemma in which he found himself; that was, the dilemma of maintaining the cohesiveness of the church by recognizing the needs of all the factions within it in such a way that no one would need to feel too far away from the central function of the church as a place of worship. But in order to do this, Leo could not allow himself to feel personally endangered every time his method of performing a service was attacked. He had to recognize that only the technique was being attacked, and not the individual who was acting in accordance with his own sense of what was valuable.

Ego functioning is always, to some extent, overlaid with a certain amount of persona. The ego is in a constant process of receiving stimuli from the environment and is also receiving impressions from the unconscious—which sometimes support the event that is going on and in which ego is participating, and sometimes in conflict with it. The ego needs always to mediate stimulus and response; what this means practically is that we are constantly having to make split-second decisions in the process of adapting or not adapting to the demands that are made upon us. Every decision means choosing one of the many possible attitudes and rejecting all the others. As we have seen, the individual's typology plays an important part in determining the nature of the ego and consequently the choices the ego will make. These decisions, supported by the underlying typology, act to build up a persona, a way of responding to a demand from some collective that is characteristic for its role. It would be wrong, according to Jung, "to leave the matter as it stands without at the same time recognizing that there is, after all, something individual in the peculiar choice and delineation of the persona, and that despite the exclusive identity of the ego-consciousness with the persona, the unconscious self, one's real individuality, is always present and makes itself felt indirectly if not directly. Although the ego-consciousness is at first identical with the persona—that compromise role in which we parade before the community—yet the unconscious self can never be repressed to the point of extinction. Its influence is chiefly manifest in the special nature of the contrasting and compensating contents of the unconscious."[2]

Besides the persona there is another, darker side to our personality which we do not consciously display in public: the *shadow*. It is what is inferior in our personality, that part of us which we will not allow ourselves to express. The stronger and more rigid the persona, and the more we identify with it, the more we must deny the other important aspects of our personality. These aspects are repressed to the unconscious, and they contribute to the formation of a more or less autonomous splinter-personality, the shadow. The shadow finds its own means of expression, though, particularly in projections. What we cannot admit in ourselves we often find in others. If, when an individual speaks of another person whom he hates with a vehemence that seems nearly irrational, he can be brought to describe that person's characteristics which he most dislikes, you will frequently have a picture of his own repressed aspects, which are unrecognized by him though obvious to others. The shadow is a dominant of the personal unconscious and consists of all those uncivilized desires and emotions that are incompatible with social standards and with the persona; it is all that we are ashamed of. It also has its collective aspects which are expressed mythologically, for example, as the devil or a witch. But the shadow also has a positive value, at least in its potential. There is no shadow without consciousness, no darkness without light. The shadow is a necessary aspect of man; he would be incomplete, utterly shallow without it. Jung writes:

> The shadow is a moral problem that challenges the whole ego-personality, for no one can become conscious of the shadow without considerable moral effort. To become conscious of it involves recognizing the dark aspect of the personality as present and real. This act is the essential condition for self-knowledge, and it therefore, as a rule, meets with considerable resistance. Indeed, self-knowledge as a psychotherapeutic measure frequently requires much painstaking work extending over a long period.[3]

An extreme example of what happens when the shadow goes completely unrecognized came out in the case of an elementary-school principal, whom we will call Brian B. On casual acquaintance he was the last person one would have expected would be in analysis, and indeed, he was careful not to let the fact be known. Obviously, it did not belong to his persona. Brian B. was a man in his late forties, handsome, clean-cut, a typical red-blooded American boy grown up. He described himself to me as "very lucky." "Things always go for me," he said. He let me know that he had a marvelous sense of timing, that he knew just when to promote a new program, when to hold off. He handled his faculty well, was popular with the students, put in long hours at his work, and frequently received commendation from the school board.

He came to me, he explained carefully, not because of himself but because of marital difficulties. (I have long ago learned to beware of the patient who comes into therapy to learn to live with somebody else's problems!) His wife, he said, was grouchy and irritable, and she constantly belittled him in public. She had a mania for neatness which he could not abide, and she was quite independent and controlling. He said that he would like to get out of his marriage, except that it would probably cost him his position which is very important to him, so much so that he could not turn it off. Often in the evenings he attended the sports events at school or meetings of various sorts, and many weekends were consumed with outings and camping trips with students. Hardly much to criticize here, especially from the community's point of view!

Brian B. came from a farm background and a family with rigid conventional moral standards. He was brought up to respect women and to believe that the place for all sexual activity was within the structure of marriage, and that the purpose of sex begins and ends with *procreation*. Evidently the idea of sex as *recreation* had never occurred to him.

Outside of sexual relations once with a prostitute while he was in the Army, he had no sexual experience whatever until he began to date a young woman who had "been around."

As he put it, he got carried away with his emotions one night, and as a result she became pregnant. He married her because "it was the gentlemanly thing to do." But there had been little sex in the marriage—he did not especially want it. His bored wife had had a brief extramarital affair. He scolded her as he would a naughty student, then promptly forgave her. The impression he gave me was, he just can't be that good! If he were, I asked myself, why would his wife have been so obviously unhappy with him? Why had she become pregnant by him in the first place? Surely she was not that naïve? What did she find out later that was not apparent when she decided to marry him?

Brian B. told me about a recurrent dream he had. It was a dream of being in a fight: *I meet someone I don't like. In fact I hate him and I'm furious with him. In the fight you throw the hardest punch you can but in the end it is like slow motion, it droops over and you can't do anything.* These were Brian's exact words. I could not help noticing that when he came to the implication of impotence he could not associate it with himself, and so he switched from narration in the first person to the second person. The obvious reductive interpretation is that he was unable to make it sexually with his wife, and that sexuality was for him an aggression which he had wanted and needed to express, but had denied to himself, until it had become completely incapable of expression. But there was more to it than that; it went beyond the explicitly sexual. As he moved through life repressing his hostilities whenever they arose—and who in a position of constant contact with students and their parents and a faculty and an administrative body would not be at times frustrated and angry?—so the hostility continued to gather energy in the unconscious. There was a need to discharge this energy in his waking life, to relieve the tension it produced. However he was afraid to do so, because it did not fit the role, the persona. The dream offered the fight, by way of compensation for his conscious attitude. The proper nice guy became the aggressive bad guy. Then came the fear that he would not be able to bring it off; it showed up in the impotence, he could not follow through. This unconscious fear crossed the aggressive drive, creating an insoluble conflict in the unconscious. The ego was identified with the persona, the side facing the world confidently, amiably, agreeably. He allowed himself to be overworked because if he didn't "they" might have found out that he was really inadequate. The shadow, the mean one carrying all the aggressive needs, would not deal with the hostility he felt.

As his analyst I listened to his recital of a series of superficial symptomatic problems. All the while I was wondering where the shadow might be finding its way to expression, and I thought that it must have been in some deeply unconscious aspect of his life. I had a sense of foreboding. I have seen apparently well-put-together people stumble into analysis just before the personality begins to blow up, as though they knew the catastrophe was about to happen and they wanted to be in a safe place when the moment came! I had this kind of feeling about Brian B.

All the same, for several sessions all I got from him was the-power-of-positive-thinking approach. "I can do anything I really want to do, all I have to do is try hard enough." I felt like replying, "Whom are you trying to convince, yourself or me?" Then one day he told me about a crisis that had arisen at school concerning some racial tensions among the students. His handling of the matter had not prevented a bloody confrontation on the playground, and he was called to account by the school board. He was deeply shaken. I felt he was a different man. He appeared utterly frustrated, deeply depressed, relatively uncommunicative. His easy, pleasant manner had vanished. His persona had failed to prove invincible.

A few days after he had recounted this incident he came to his analytic session with some scratches on his face. He told me about a drinking episode. It occurred following a fight with his wife, after which he had stormed out of his house and gone to a bar on the other side of town, there consuming quite a lot of whiskey. He had then phoned an old army buddy who lived in that neighborhood, and, though it was past midnight, the friend had invited him over for "a few drinks." He went to his friend's house, and drank a good deal, he had not the slightest idea how much. The friend, he recalled, invited him to stay the night, but he remembered he had to get to work the next morning. The next thing he remembered was a flash of awareness that he was speeding down the expressway at about ninety miles an hour. Things went blank again. Then he was in a parking lot opening the doors of unlocked cars, looking into glove compartments to see what he would find. He fell on his face, and didn't know any more until he woke up, and dawn was beginning to gray. He looked around, had no idea where he was, but somehow managed to find his car and get back onto the road. He found the street intersection where he was on the road map, and from there traced his way home. But for the scratches on his face, there was nothing to show that any of it had happened; but he was all changed. This time he was ready to face his shadow. In fact, he had no choice.

It came out in subsequent sessions that he had had periodic episodes of drinking combined with stealing. The stealing only occurred when the drinking had released him from certain inhibitions. He never stole anything he especially wanted, and his stealing always had a certain dramatic flair about it. There was the time he walked out of the bus station with someone else's briefcase. When he got home and sobered up and realized what he had done, he took it back to the station and surreptitiously placed it near where he had picked it up. Another time he had taken a picnic table and two benches from a public park, and carried them off in his station wagon. Whatever he did was risky and defiant. When I asked him if he ever took money, he replied, "No, that would make me a thief!" He regarded his "episodes" more as adventures, to show "them" that he didn't have to follow their silly standards "unless I damn well want to."

When one attempts to live out only one side of his personality, the conscious, adapted attitude, the opposite side remains in the unconscious, waiting for some situation which allows it to break through. The turn-of-the-century French psychologists called this state an *abaissement du niveau mental*, a lowering of the level of consciousness, a state which allows the contents of the unconscious to break through into awareness. The state of sleep is such a condition, and that is why we have dreams which show us sides of ourselves we would never have access to otherwise. When the ego identifies with the persona, when the major concern of the ego is to appear as the public image demands, then the repressed shadow will sooner or later find a way to collapse the out-of-balance persona.

Early in analysis it may be expected that there will be a considerable struggle in which the ego tries to maintain its position against rapidly emerging unconscious contents which seem so destructive as they tear away at the person's image of himself. The ego may clutch at the persona ever more frantically, as the persona begins to disintegrate in the face of pressure on it coming from the unconscious. Such a situation was dramatically portrayed in the dream of a man in this stage of analysis, and frightened at the prospect of having to revise his entire view of himself. This was the dream: *I spent the night building an electric netting around the house to protect it from tanks and infantry. We also had anti-tank guns. Someone in the group kept trying to tear down the netting. He lived in a house nearby, and when we saw him undoing our work and saw him going over to his house we blew it up with an anti-tank gun. Then the scene changes. I'm on the second floor looking out the window in the morning and I see two or three elephants busily tearing up the electric wiring and the camouflage. They are under the direction of several men. For some unknown reason there is no glass in the windows where there should be. I rush over and pull the switch. The elephants bellow and charge. Wire sticks to their trunks. They have quite a time, but finally they get the wire from their trunks with the help of their feet. One of the men tells the elephants to find the switch. Apparently their feet insulate them against the shock, or the current isn't strong enough to stop them. One elephant comes to the win-*

dow where I am and pokes his trunk in and around to find a switch. I felt sure he would see me, but he didn't. As soon as he leaves that window I run down the stairs.

The dream shows the ego forces trying to protect the psyche from the onslaught of the unconscious factors that were long repressed and had an untold amount of strength bound up in them. Electricity is the image provided by the dream to evoke the concept of the life energy which is, in this patient, all directed to protecting his house (his psychic structure) from destruction. There are also the anti-tank guns, instruments of attack which seek to destroy that shadow element of his personality, the one who is trying to undo the work of the defense. And even though the initial battle is won, it is of no avail, for in the moment he is asleep (unconscious) the electric-wiring-defense is again attacked, but this time by vast, inhuman forces. The elephants seem to belong more to the collective unconscious than to the personal unconscious, as they had no specific meaning for the life experience of the patient.

It was as Jung has written:

Once the personal repressions are lifted, the individuality and the collective psyche begin to emerge in a coalescent state, thus releasing hitherto repressed personal fantasies. The fantasies and dreams which now appear assume a somewhat different aspect. An infallible sign of collective images seems to be the appearance of the "cosmic" element, i.e., the images in the dream or fantasy are connected with cosmic qualities, such as temporal and spatial infinity, enormous speed and extension of movement, "astrological" associations, telluric, lunar and solar analogies, changes in the proportion of the body, etc. The obvious application of mythological and religious motifs in a dream also points to the activity of the collective unconscious . . .

The wealth of possibilities in the collective psyche has a confusing and blinding effect. With the disintegration of the persona there is a release of involuntary fantasy, which is apparently nothing else than the specific activity of the collective psyche. This activity brings up contents whose existence one had never dreamed of before. But as the influence of the collective unconscious increases, so the conscious mind loses its power of leadership. Imperceptibly it becomes led, while an unconscious and impersonal process gradually takes control.[4]

Now we can understand the overwhelming significance of the elephants. Huge, lumbering creatures of inestimable age, they represent powerful forces in the unconscious which, when they are stimulated, may overrun the conscious position. The very stimulation of these forces may be an effect of the overzealous attempts to keep them at bay. A hopeful element in the dream, though, is the selection of this particular image. For elephants can, with the proper treatment, become friends to man exerting their greater strength to help him accomplish what he cannot do by his frail powers alone. The question might logically be asked, Why stir up these dangerous forces? Might it not be better to leave them alone, and encourage the conscious attitude to strengthen its defenses against them? In this case that is exactly what the patient was trying to do, more or less consciously, but his deeper problems were of such magnitude that there was no way in which the confrontations could be avoided. Jung teaches that to plunge into this process may be unavoidable "whenever the necessity arises of overcoming an apparently insuperable difficulty." He tells us, "It goes without saying that this necessity does not occur in every case of neurosis, since perhaps in the majority the prime consideration is only the removal of temporary difficulties of adaptation. Certainly severe cases cannot be cured without a far-reaching change of character and attitude. In by far the greater number, adaptation to external reality demands so much work that inner adaptation to the collective unconscious cannot occur for a very long time. But where this inner adaptation becomes a problem, a strange, irresistible attraction proceeds from the unconscious and exerts a powerful influence on the conscious direction of life. The predominance of unconscious influences, together with the associated disintegration of the persona and the deposition of the conscious mind from power, constitute a state of psychic disequilibrium which, in analytic treatment, is artificially induced for the therapeutic purpose of resolving a difficulty that might block further development."[5]

Anyone who has experienced it knows that the collapse of the conscious attitude is no small matter. Previously ordered systems become chaotic, burdens become intolerable, the life situation seems to be completely out of control and there is absolutely nothing one can do about it. It is an anguish beyond comprehension. What has happened is that the ego has given way to the collective unconscious, which has now taken over leadership. There are times when, in such a crisis, a "'saving' thought, a vision, an 'inner voice,' came with an irresistible power of conviction and gave life a new direction."[6] But just as often, the collapse brings about a catastrophe which destroys the former life and fails to offer a new way in its place. How will the individual react to this? That is the crucial question.

Jung proposes that there are several possibilities. One is that the individual will be overpowered by the unconscious and will take flight into psychosis where he no longer has to deal realistically with the morbid ideas, or into a suicidal depression. When this tendency appears it takes all the energy of the therapist to assume the role of the conscious ego, utilizing the power of the transference attachment, until the damaged psyche regains the strength to assume again the responsibility for its own independent functioning.

A second possibility is that the individual may "accept credulously" the contents of the collective unconscious. Then he may become obsessed with certain strange or eccentric ideas, probably ideas of apparently cosmic significance: he comes to feel that he is miraculously the possessor of a marvelous truth that no one has ever realized before. He may become an eccentric with prophetic leanings, but nothing ever comes of it because it all seems as real to him as it seems phony to those who listen to him. As his friends turn cool toward him, he may then revert to a rather childish petulance and gradually cut himself off from contact with others, becoming a social isolate, a sad man with a mission in which nobody is interested.

224 BOUNDARIES OF THE SOUL

A third way is what Jung terms "regressive restoration of the persona." This tendency appears following some destructive turn of fate which destroys all that an individual has built up in terms of career, love relationships, hopes and plans for the future. Such a person, deeply wounded as he may be, laboriously tries to patch up his life with as much strength as he can muster in face of the fact that he is frightened that it will all go to pieces again. So he looks for a new position which will not be so demanding, or a new relationship in which the challenge is not so great. He restores his functioning but on a level which is far below his natural ability. As Jung says: "He will as a result of his fright have slipped back to an earlier phase of his personality; he will have demeaned himself, pretending that he is as he was *before* the crucial experience, though utterly unable ever to think of repeating such a risk. Formerly perhaps he wanted more than he would accomplish; now he does not even dare to attempt what he has it in him to do."[7]

Such a man will utilize most effectively the defensive measure of *projecting the shadow*. This means that he will not see his own weaknesses, but will find causes everywhere else for his inability to accomplish more of what he sets out to do. Always there will be an unfortunate combination of events which works against him, or there will be somebody who is out to get him. That somebody will inevitably be described with great vehemence as having just those despicable qualities which he fails to see in himself, but which dog his every step.

An Indian guru once told his disciple, "You have to gather your own manure and put it on your own plants. Some very foolish people carefully gather up their own manure and throw it away and then they go out and buy somebody else's manure to put on their plants."

The way which is sought for dealing with the shadow is a difficult one. It requires a continuing search for evidence of this dark force, and when it is found it must be brought to consciousness: this is what I am, this is what I am capable of doing. The dreams must be scrutinized for every occasion when the shadow asserts itself, in whatever disguise, and it

MAUREEN

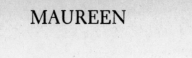

1

RUNNING WITH CRAYONS

2

3

WANTING FREE

Running to her friend, Gray Mouse

4

5

6

Sometimes the mind runs faster

7

CHARLES

DOLORES

1

2

3

4

A lonely God— enthroned in lonely space
Created us as we are—
As single as a tree— as separate as a star.

is necessary to face the meaning of that image as it relates to the life-style of the dreamer. Every situation in life which carries for an individual a charge of strong affect, which makes him excessively angry or anxious or even delighted, must be considered in terms of the possibility that the extra investment of energy may be coming from the unconscious in the form of a shadow projection. This is, moreover, not something one undertakes for a limited period in the course of the analysis, and then, when the shadow is laid to rest, can assume that he is able to go on to the finer and more glorious aspects of the analysis. The shadow is, in truth, a devilish form, and just when you think you know who he is, he changes his disguise and appears from another direction. So it is, in the Jungian analysis, that the analysand is initiated into a lifelong process, that of looking within, and being willing to reflect long and hard on what he sees there, in order to avoid being taken over by it.

Nor, I must add, is the analyst immune from the onslaught of the shadow. It is a quest which the analyst must continue as long as he is an analyst, and probably as long as he lives. In his work he must be able to differentiate his responses to the analysand so that he will know what actually is coming from the analysand to him, and what is a reflection of his own unconscious contents that he is projecting onto the analysand. Furthermore, he must know that the matter of shadow projection is a double-edged sword, for even while he looks out for what he may tend to project onto the analysand, he must also be noticing what the analysand may be projecting onto *him*, else he may fall into the trap of accepting the analysand's judgment of him, when at bottom the analysand is judging those hidden aspects of himself which he dare not face, or envying those potentialities which he fails to recognize in himself. Unless the analyst is able to sort out all of this, and utilize it in the analytic process to enlarge the area of awareness, first in himself and then in the analysand, he stands in danger of himself being unknowingly entrapped by the influence of the unconscious. Again, I must point to the importance of a long and thorough training analysis which is required to prepare the therapist to deal in depth with complexities of unconscious processes.

The shadow problem occurs not only within the individual as a conflict between the conscious mode of adaptation and the negative or repressed autonomous aspects of the unconscious. The social or societal aspect of the shadow problem is analogous to what is experienced in a personal way. We have seen how certain qualities which have been unknown to an individual are recognized as hostile and evil when they are brought to consciousness. Because the ego is not prepared to assimilate them as its own, they are projected onto other people and onto destructive events, which are sometimes termed "accidents." Most people feel no particular need to make these projections conscious, although by refusing to do so they place themselves in an extremely precarious state. If this is true for the individual as microcosm, it is surely true for the nation as macrocosm. "The psychology of war has clearly brought this condition to light: everything which our own nation does is good, everything which the other nations do is wicked. The centre of all that is mean and vile is always to be found several miles behind the enemy's lines."[8] This statement written by Jung in 1928 is as applicable today as it was when it was written. How tragically we watch as the inhumanities of war perpetrated by our own side are justified as being in the long run for the common good, while those of the enemy become a justification for the continuations of our own immorality. It is only when our own youth return from the war zones, wounded and drug-ridden and sick in their souls that those who stay at home and watch the war from a lounge chair propped up before a television set begin to get the message. Those who have been there have had the projections stripped from before their eyes; they have had to confront reality in the faces of the enemy, and also in the faces of this nation's friends.

We, as a nation, need to discover our own shadows. We can find them in the images we project, if we can only remember that they are *our* images. Such recognition can only begin with the *individual's* willingness to recognize his *own* shadow.

Before he does this he is ill-equipped to assign praise or blame
to other individuals, much less to nations. This is not to suggest that social concerns are incompatible with an analytical
approach. Quite the contrary. The person who will be most
effective in his strivings toward social justice is the one who
is most critical of himself, who takes care to differentiate his
own flaws and to take responsibility for them before he goes
out to correct his neighbor's. He will make his impact more
effective by setting an example, than by bludgeoning his opponent into submission. The person who commits himself to
a life of continuing confrontation with the unconscious within
himself, will also confront the unknown in the world at large
with an open mind, and what is more, with a heart of wisdom.
I am reminded of a phrase quoted to me by a friend which
was supposed to have been a remark of Jung's, although my
friend confessed he never could find the source of the quota-
tion and may even have dreamed it. In any case, I pass it
on to you—the old man is reputed to have said, *"Meine Her-
ren, vergessen Sie nicht das Unbewusste ist auch draussen*
[Gentlemen, do not forget that the unconscious is also on
the outside]!"

9

ANIMA AND ANIMUS: WILL ONE SEX EVER UNDERSTAND THE OTHER?

Of old, Heaven and Earth were not yet separated, and the In and Yo not yet divided. They formed a chaotic mass like an egg, which was of obscurely defined limits, and contained germs. The purer and clearer part was thinly diffused and formed Heaven, while the heavier and grosser element settled down and became Earth. The finer element easily became a united body, but the consolidation of the heavy and gross element was accomplished with difficulty. Heaven was therefore formed first, and Earth established subsequently. Thereafter divine beings were produced between them.

> Creation myth from the eighth-century A.D.
> *Nihongi* collection (Chronicles of Japan).[1]

The ancient myth relates that creation begins with a primordial wholeness which is in a state of chaos. It divides itself into two, and the two thus separated are able to come together in coitus; the earth conceives and brings forth. Through the power of this union, this *coniunctio*, everything that fills the world is brought into being. The two halves which are required for the creative act are each incomplete without the other. Their longing for each other brings them together. Their separation produces their longing.

There is an archetypal need, also, for a *conjunction of opposites* in our lives as human beings. This is experienced through the natural biological opposition between men and women, which generates the spring of all creativeness. The opposition between the sexes is also experienced as an opposition within the individual. Every man has a feminine side to his being, and every woman has a masculine side. The contrasexual sides are largely repressed as we develop our conscious adaptation in the process of growing up as a man or as a woman. The feminine aspect within the man remains or becomes largely unconscious, and likewise the masculine aspect within the woman.

To say, however, that these contrasexual aspects are *merely* the result of repressions would give an entirely wrong impression. It would suggest that the social structure into which we are born determines what is to be repressed, and that these repressions give form and shape to our unconscious image of the opposite sex. This is only partly true. Other factors play important roles in the formation of this unconscious figure that we carry in us.

We must go back to biology for a second factor and recognize that, as Jung has said, "the whole nature of man presupposes woman, both physically and spiritually. His system is tuned in to woman from the start, just as it is prepared for a quite definite world where there is water, light, air, salt, carbohydrates, etc."[2] Similarly, the nature of woman presupposes man; therefore she seeks union with man, whether or not she consciously wishes to do so.

Our early experiences with our parents are a third factor which contributes to the development of awareness of the differing qualities inherent in the nature of the two sexes. The young child not only experiences the parents as they are, but he derives his own subjective impressions of them. These impressions are highly charged with responses to hurt and jealousy and also to love and dependency needs. Later, in the process of development, as the child begins to gain distance from his parents and to make other associations, the parents' general attitudes become internalized as a part of the child's own value structure. They are accepted unconsciously by him as modes of functioning associated either with the masculine or with the feminine temperament. Father becomes the son's model for manhood, mother becomes the feminine ideal. Or, mother becomes the daughter's feminine model and father her masculine ideal.

In my work every day I hear adults recalling small incidents which were crucial to them as children, causing them to bury any desires they may have felt to function according to the traditional style of the opposite sex.

A little boy has watched his mother knitting. Alone in his room he manages to figure out how it is done, and he takes her needles and yarn and manages to knit a few inches together. Proudly he brings out his production when his mother's bridge club is there, expecting to be praised for his cleverness. The ladies laugh derisively at him.

A girl is asked by her grandmother what she wants to be when she grows up, and she answers "a doctor." Grandmother looks at her and with a smile of saccharine wisdom says, "You mean a nurse, don't you, darling?"

A five-year-old boy comes into the living-room, stumbling about in his mother's shoes and blouse. Mother and Father look at each other in a funny way, and Father says sternly, "You go into the bedroom and take those things off, and don't you ever put them on again." The child never quite understands, but the investment of emotion behind the prohibitions is not lost on him. There is something mysterious, something forbidden about things belonging to the other sex. Each person is expected to renounce that mystery, with all of its temptations.

Thus we can distinguish three sets of factors which contribute to the development of a contrasexual element within the psyche: the *archetypal*, the *biological*, and the *sociological*. Taken together, these factors constitute the basis of what Jung has called the *anima* in the *man*, and the *animus* in the *woman*. The man's anima and the woman's animus are potentially guides to the depths of the unconscious; they will so function if only man and woman can learn to relate to them within themselves in an open and constructive way. But this is not an easy matter, for animus and anima are unlikely to be experienced directly, since they present a point of view which is opposed to the dominant attitude of consciousness. Therefore animus and anima remain for the most part unconscious, and are experienced primarily in a projected form in relationships with people of the opposite sex. The anima and the animus endow relationships between the sexes with a special quality of strength that transcends nearly all other human feelings. The yearning for the beloved is a longing for all that one is not, consciously—but may be, unconsciously.

The longing is not all. There is also a sense of awe, a fear of the unknown and the incomprehensible. The ages have received the impress of these mixed feelings, and a man is a psychological heir to them just as he is a biological heir to the instincts. The crucial primordial image or archetype for the man is the Great Mother. This does not refer to "any concrete image existing in space and time, but to an inward image at work in the human psyche. The symbolic expression of this psychic phenomenon is to be found in the figures of the Great Goddess represented in the myths and artistic creations of mankind."[3] The whole of history bears witness to the effect of this archetype. Her workings are apparent in the rites, myths and symbols of early man, and through literature and art in every age. In our own day she may be seen in the dreams, fantasies and creative work of both the emotionally sound and the man who is sick or disturbed.[4]

The Great Mother archetype gives rise to many different kinds of feminine images in the psyche of men, as has been pointed out by Jung and others.[5] In my view, the images of the Great Mother archetype are equally present in the psychic formation of women, and they precondition women's attitudes and behaviors quite as much as they do those of men. Both sexes experience this archetype as the reality of an all-powerful, numinous woman upon whom they are dependent for all things. She precedes the awareness of the personal mother who, with her own distinct personality, emerges for the child as his ego develops and begins to interact with hers. Furthermore, throughout his life, the archetypal image

of The Mother continues to stand behind the conscious perception he calls "my mother."

A woman perceives the archetype of the feminine differently
than a man—it is accessible to her consciousness for the reason
that she is able personally to experience the incomparable feeling of being a woman, and this is something which will always
remain in some part a mystery to a man. As the depths
of the earth contain their mystery—the germinating seed in
the damp darkness—so it is within the body of the woman,
unseen, that transformation takes place. There are at least
four distinct transformations which women experience and
come to know intimately, and which in their essence elude
full awareness by men. The first menstruation brings about
an extremely important transformation, much more so (according to Erich Neumann)' than the first seminal emission
of the male which generally occurs during sleep and is quickly
over and done with. For the woman, menstruation is an ongoing process for several days, and because what is involved
is blood, with its strong association with the substance of life,
it is an experience which changes her whole being from that
of a child into a person who is now capable of bearing children
of her own. The event is celebrated with awareness of this
new capacity; the taboos and responsibilities associated with
it as well as the fears, do not fail to make their impression.
Woman's second transformation occurs with conception and
pregnancy, in which the unfathomable space within her body
becomes filled. The third transformation is the act of giving
birth; it entails sacrifice in her physical separation from the
infant—giving up to the world what once belonged alone and
fully to her as woman. The last transformation is the one
which causes milk to flow from her breasts and makes it possible for her to nurse her infant.

It seems to me that the essence of the difference in the
ways in which a man or a woman perceives these transformations is that woman experiences them over a protracted period
of time, during which something is going on *in her*, while
a man experiences these transformations indirectly, that is,
through her. Woman is there, and in her condition of being

a woman she is like the earth, waiting patiently for the rain, which comes when the clouds are filled to bursting and stops when they are emptied. All of this is well-known to women, for we have plenty of time to brood on it. Our cyclic life provides for periods of less and periods of more activity, a balance of introversion and extraversion of a sort which may escape a man because he is less at the mercy of his body. And even though, in our day, many of the biological restrictions which women have felt as impositions have been greatly lightened, the woman who elects to bear children must carry them just as long as did her prehistoric forebears, and she may feel responsible for them and their welfare even longer. Furthermore, the woman who chooses not to bear children must remain acutely conscious of her decision if she is not to become trapped in an unwanted pregnancy. A man's involvement in all this may also be intense, but rarely to the same degree as that of a woman. Society teaches a man responsibility for his family, for a woman it is instinctive.

William Blake has said, "The cistern contains: the fountain overflows." Women cannot ever fully understand man's profligacy. That he produces sperm by the million and casts them away only to produce more, is remarkable to a woman who brings forth only one ovum at a time, and whose whole bodily processes are designed to nurture and protect that one. I think it must have been the anima of Christ that urged him to seek out that one lost sheep, and during that time to disregard all the others.

The unconscious feminine side in man, the anima, leads him on a search to discover what is unknown and strange to him, to fill the interstices of his personality which exist because there is no part of his conscious adaptation that involves him fully as a whole man. He seeks his opposite in projected form, in a woman who will embody for him what he cannot be for himself.

Sometimes a man whose work demands a certain toughness and practicality and allows no room for sentiment or fuzzy thinking, finds appealing the warm-hearted, rather naïve, soft and pretty woman who makes him feel complete. She may not be the woman with whom he will choose to share his life, for the woman who receives the projection of the man's anima is not necessarily the one who is most suitable for him over the long term. She will exert her power over him for as long as he invests her with the mysterious excitement of the unconscious, the side which he cannot live out. She will create in him the illusion of well-being, even though everything about her may be at odds with the way he attempts to lead his life.

The woman who is well developed in the same areas in which a man is competent is not so likely to appeal to him in that special "magical" way. If he is secure in himself and well-rounded, he may find companionship and profound love with such a woman. But if he is too intellectual himself he may be off balance with her.

This has been perceived by college women, much to their unhappiness, as one of my students wrote in a paper recently: "On the wave of the last class discussion of the animus/anima, I found myself asking why, exactly, men are so inimical to educated women. It seems that men have assigned all the mysteries and luxuries to women—beauty, compassion, intuition, grace, concern with aesthetics, the right to decorate themselves, the right to be tender, to express gaiety, the right to express emotions, sensuality, closeness to nature and many other traits and properties. The only difficulty is that when women are deprived of a significant context within which these 'rights' can be exercised, they tend to feel trivial. For example, women are allowed to be emotional, but their emotions are seldom given full play in the political arena where they might bring about significant change. Women are allowed to cultivate and express aesthetic values in their clothes and appearance, but are discouraged from becoming fashion designers. Men grant that women are gifted in understanding the nuances of interpersonal relations, but do not encourage them to enter the helping professions. As a whole, it would seem that men insist that women confine their gifts and talents to the purely personal sphere, and that beneath this insistence is a fear that women are potentially superior. One can view human history as man's striving to find meaning as deep as the 'given' of woman's ability to bear life, and to project on to woman sensuality, earthiness, and closeness to nature. Given the capacity, motivation and opportunity, women can develop their intellect rather easily; certainly this is demonstrated in college classrooms every day. It seems to be more difficult to wrest men from their concern with power and to orient them positively towards the anima."

Orientation toward the anima would mean, of course, the man's becoming aware of the potentiality for those "feminine qualities" of warmth, receptivity, patience, and openness to the other within himself. If he could realize these elements and learn to exercise them without having to feel less of a man, he would find himself more sensitive to woman and to her need to exercise those qualities of her own which resemble his cherished "masculinity." These include activity, decisiveness, logical thinking and determination.

A man who in his personal relationships tends to see and to use women primarily for his own gratification may be utterly charming to them in the process. He may, as *Playboy* suggests, make elaborate preparations to stock his kitchen with the most elegant delicacies to support the seduction scene. The game is not only to get her to submit herself to him but to make her enjoy it in the process. Soft music from all four corners of the room alert her sensibilities, and gentle wines are there to blunt her inhibitions, so that she will allow herself to be taken, and I do mean "taken." He does not expose himself to her total self, but only to her sexual self, an area in which it is clearly understood that he will be the leader and she the follower. However enthusiastically she may respond, she must be aware that it is response primarily that this sort of man desires and seeks; and the brainwashed women who write for the popular women's magazines advise the girls to "fake it" if they cannot really respond fully in sexual intercourse. This is supposed to be the way to get along with men.

The need in this sort of man to dominate his woman arises out of his basic fear that he will not be able to control her if she ever realizes the power that she has within her. It is not alone her power to help a man find *sexual* fulfillment that concerns him, but his need of her in order to find *total* fulfillment. He needs her to provide him with what he has learned to expect from a woman ever since he nursed at his mother's breast. Nourishment, soothing when he is fretful, encouragement, a home within which he can be protected from the world, a place where he is accepted for what he is, expectations which he can fulfill and for which fulfillment he will be praised—all of this is firmly assimilated into the unconscious before he even enters kindergarten. All else that he learns about women after this is superimposed upon his essential image of Woman. She is as she was from the beginning, the powerful person on whom he depends for sustenance and comfort and who, when she withdraws her favors, brings about the most terrible psychic catastrophes. So he learns to court her favor while at the same time persuading her to forget the true nature of her power over him. He simultaneously represses his fear of her, and selects a type of woman for his relationships whom he thinks he can "handle."

A thirty-year-old analysand of mine who had a dominating and controlling mother, chose young girls for his sexual affairs who had far less education and social position than he did. He treated these girls very well as far as taking them to all the better places and telling them how beautiful they were and how they turned him on, but he structured the relationships primarily to suit his own sexual needs. This somehow made him feel more confident of himself. He was attractive, well-spoken, and his girls seemed to enjoy his company despite his cavalier approach. At any rate he regarded himself as "in charge," at least he felt that way on the conscious level. The unconscious had quite another picture of the situation, as this dream suggests: *I am on the east side of a wide, wide road or field, at least fifty or sixty yards wide. I start on the diagonal to the northwest, walking. There is only one person in sight on the same road. She is wearing a long dress, all the way to the ground. Her direction is northeast. It is obvious that if each of us travel in the same continued direction, we will cross somewhere in the middle of the road. I have the feeling that, as this is a woman, I will have no difficulty in winning. We are about equidistant from the point* of crossing. At that moment my mind makes a mental statement that if I am able to cross the path of this woman before she can cross mine, I will be very successful in something I am working on. So I pick up the pace of my walk a little, and view the relationship between myself, the point of the expected crossing, and the woman. It is apparent that I will have to pick up my pace if I am to cross before the woman. I do so. But as I pick up the pace, so does the woman, except a little faster. I try and try to be faster, but am losing ground and pace no matter how fast I move. I feel anxious and pressured from within. I fear defeat. Still the woman, showing little or no effort, keeps and sets the pace. She moves smoothly. Just a skirt gliding over the surface, no movement of the legs apparent. Finally, as I am hurrying with all the effort I can bring forward, the woman passes in front of me, defeating me.

Here is the unconscious image of the powerful anima who has the capacity to control the situation, no matter what the man may intend. The dream shows that she is undervalued by him. He bets that he can best her, but her endurance and swiftness is of an altogether different quality than his; it is of her nature and thus is effortless. Unconsciously, he feels helpless in competition with her and consequently in his conscious attitude, he has to depreciate this overpowering image by consorting with women whom he can use in his own way for his own satisfaction. The anima demands too much from him, or seems to. The nameless, faceless feminine image embodies what is terrifying and yet inescapable in woman. She is so deeply rooted in the man and so threatening to his image of himself as an independent person who can do what he wishes that she is kept as far away from consciousness as possible. The unconscious exposes only enough of the anima figure for this man to enable him to conceive of two possible ways of relating to her: either conquer her completely or else be conquered by her.

Every man in his relationships with women has present a participant in the form of his own feminine side, and most of the time this is unconscious in a man. She is the anima, and her effect on the relationship is to invest it with an extraordinary sense of depth and importance. Her terrifying aspect is only one of many ways in which she may manifest herself, and perhaps this way has to be stressed because one of the strongest primal feelings is that of utter dependence upon the mother, who is the source of life to the child, and whose withdrawal from him demands that he test himself to the utmost to see what he can do by himself, without her help. It begins on a wordless, conceptless level—not having what you want, not being able to walk to get it, seeing it just out of sight, straining every muscle to creep and crawl toward the desired object and, in doing so, beginning to overcome the dependence on the mother. It goes on as the child grows; it is all told in the hero myths of the ages. The battle for the deliverance from the mother is the story of the labors of Heracles to gain his manhood. The counterparts of Heracles live in every age and in every culture.

The strange thing is that the anima, for all her terrors, is also the one who inspires a man to strive for his greatest achievements. As she challenges him, she also encourages him; as she threatens him, she also teaches him. She is his taskmistress and also his muse. The anima is all his feminine feelings internalized and held as the part of him which is rarely exposed to the world. She is the soul of man, opening the way for him into his own depths and also she offers a way for him to come into touch with the unknown which is in the world outside. This is why she is all that his conscious attitude is not.

The animus lives in woman as the element of the unconscious which corresponds to man's anima. The animus represents for woman all that her conscious attitude is not. This means, quite naturally, that the animus is very different in its nature from the anima, having a different psychological basis. To understand something of what the animus is, it is first necessary to have in mind the most elementary concept of what the woman's conscious attitude toward herself is. By "elementary" I mean that we need to get behind the impress of our cultural and our individual experience into the primal experiences upon which everything else is an accretion, for it is here that the differences between men and women begin, and what happens here filters through and has its effects upon all the events which occur throughout the existence of the individual.

Woman's first experience of herself is as a girl-child who knows herself as a daughter to a mother, and a daughter who has the potentiality of growing up to be a mother herself. This, and the inevitability of death are the foreordained facts of life, even if nothing else is. The daughter's first experience of womanness is that a woman is the one who is there to nurture the child and to provide the surroundings in which the family grows and develops. Never mind if the mother is sometimes a surrogate mother, and if the surroundings are sometimes a nursery school or grade school later on; the image of the one who takes care of the child is still primarily a feminine image and the child's early surroundings are sheltered places designed for nurturing and growth under the aegis of the feminine. To the girl-child the father-world is outside of all this and, unlike the boy-child, she is not assured that it is just a matter of time until she becomes a fully participating member of father-world. She has only to look around her to find out what her life will be like when she grows up. It is *not taken for granted,* as it is with a boy, that she will be a full member of society with as much access to positions of authority and control as her brothers will have, or as her father has. It *is* taken for granted that her greatest source of fulfillment will be through her home and family and that, if she works, her career will be secondary to that of her husband; or that if her work becomes too important to her that she may have to forego marriage or may have to dissolve the marriage that she is in. Not that she lacks in energy or drive or intelligence as far as elementals are concerned. They are all part of the baby girl's psychological potential, just as the infant boy has within him the potentiality for tenderness and nurturing. This is just the problem. Girls have, in our society, opportunities for equality of education at least up to a certain point, and they do rather well at it. From kindergarten through the undergraduate years female students have been shown to achieve more academically than their male counterparts. They begin to develop all sorts of expectations and ambitions. Then somewhere along the way, more or less subtly they are told in effect, "You've come a long way, baby." Accent on the "baby," as if to add, "but you've got your limitations and don't ever forget it."

I, personally, am one of the lucky ones, who should have been able to forget it if anybody could. I am the daughter of a woman who successfully juggled a marriage, a family and a journalistic career and showed that it could be done. My father co-operated with her needs and ambitions in a way that was far in advance of the cultural patterns preceding the Second World War. Nevertheless, I observed carefully in my growing up years the stresses to which my mother was subjected in trying to rear a family and manage a home at the same time. I also saw the strains that showed up in her professional life where she had to compete against men who did not have the additional burdens she had. She had to do her job at least as well if not better than they, and for less pay, because she was a woman. I saw how my father was considered by friends to be "extremely indulgent," and how my mother steadfastly proclaimed her inability to balance a checkbook for as long as my father was alive. I also saw that while I was encouraged to enter a profession, it was a "woman's profession," that of teaching, while my desire to become a doctor was not taken seriously by my parents. Doing what you really wanted to do with your life always meant overcoming the disadvantages of being a woman, and I admit that for me these disadvantages have been less than for many women. The coup de grâce, speaking of disadvantages, came when I applied for a financial grant to proceed with my graduate studies after my husband had completed his, and during which process we had sold our home and possessions and gone considerably into debt. I was told by the admissions counselor, "You shouldn't need any help from us, after all, you have a husband who has his Ph.D.!"

Animus is for a woman that masculine drive which enables her to break through the limitations that being a woman has imposed for centuries on end. It is the vision of the psychological "other" who is able to think coolly while she follows her natural sympathetic pattern of nurturing. It is the vision of the one who goes out to take on the world even while her destiny seems to be to make use of the spoils of battle for furnishing her home, his "castle." Animus in a woman is the aspect which tends toward clarifying the facts, gaining the authority to make the decisions, and implementing decisions with logic and strength and determination. But the animus can also be negative. To the degree that the animus is repressed, he may become hostile and inimical to femininity. To the degree that the animus is undeveloped, the animus function may come off as "inferior," that is, clarifying facts becomes a voicing of unfounded opinions, authority becomes a domineering manner, decisiveness becomes impulsive whimsy, and determination becomes stubbornness. But to the degree that the animus is accepted and developed as a legitimate aspect of her true nature, this figure in the woman's psyche becomes helpful, supporting, and strength-giving. In every man-woman relationship, the animus, like the anima, is a silent partner, for better or for worse.

Thus every man-woman relationship is really a partnership of four: man and woman, anima and animus. Jung has called this combination of relationships within a single relationship the "marriage quaternio." He distinguishes between the following aspects of the marriage quaternio:

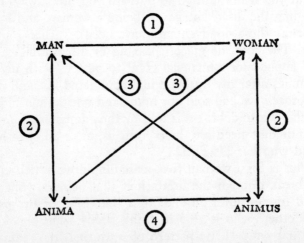

(1) An uncomplicated personal relationship.

(2) A relationship of the man to his anima and of the woman to her animus.

(3) A relationship of the feminine animus to the man and of the masculine anima to the woman.

(4) A relationship of anima and animus.

An uncomplicated personal relationship is a purely conscious relationship, that is, it occurs when one relates to what is evident and apparent in the other person. It is relatively uncontaminated by unconscious contents. Such relationships are generally of a superficial nature, or else they are based on some kind of service which one performs for the other and which provides the primary basis for the connection between them.

The relationship of the man to his anima or the woman to her animus nearly always has an influence on the "uncomplicated personal relationship," and this is what soon makes it complicated. Typically the man or the woman will have his or her idea of how the other ought to be or ought to react, and this expectation colors the feelings of each toward the other. To the degree that her image of the animus may play a part in determining her expectations of the man, and to the degree that his image of the anima may play a role in determining his expectations of the woman, the animus or anima image is projected onto the partner.

How does this work out in practical reality? A man has developed an unconscious image of an ideal woman, including her appearance and the way in which she will behave. When he meets a woman who seems to conform to this image, in part at least, he anticipates that she will conform to it in all particulars. She "should" understand his needs, conform to his schedule, make up for his deficiencies, and even, by some miracle of intuition, instinctively know what turns him on in bed without ever having to be guided or informed by him. In other words, she should be the living doll who is his incarnated anima. In the same way, a woman's unconscious designs the shape and function of her dream man and endows him with everything she needs and wants.

As long as the partner in the "uncomplicated personal relationship" corresponds to the image invoked by the anima or animus as the case may be, there tends to be a strongly emotional relationship, invested with unconscious factors as well as conscious ones. Nor are the expectations emanating from anima and animus necessarily helpful or pleasurable. Often they carry the negative implications of a controlling mother or an aggressive father, with the result that the expectations of the partner in a relationship may be correspondingly negative. Furthermore, the expectations, whether positive or negative, are rarely consonant with the actual person who is invested with them. This means that the expectations are bound to be unrealistic, with people expecting from their partners what the partners are often unable or unwilling to provide. The appearances that made one partner think that the other fitted his or her image were deceiving appearances, and so one partner feels deceived while the other feels put upon with demands. Is it any wonder that so often one sex fails to understand the other?

The third facet of relationship occurs when the traditional roles are breached and the woman positively relates to the man through her animus or the man relates positively to the woman through his anima. In this phase the woman may be able to put herself into his place and to understand his way of looking at her and, in a wider sense, his way of meeting the world. Because of her openness to his attitudes she is able to work with him, without expecting to be indulged for her own peculiarities. She is not ashamed or embarrassed to be forthright, to voice her views with conviction, to assert her values. The parallel development in man enables him to allow that side in him which has been repressed to re-emerge as a tender, nurturing quality, charged with sympathy and affectionate response. These welcome phases of contrasexual acceptance enlarge the personality by making the soul more conscious than it otherwise would be by reason of its own nature. The potentiality for greater consciousness of the contrasexual aspect comes through the projection which attracts a man to a certain woman or the woman to a certain man.

Each sees in the other what he or she loves, and each strives to adopt those qualities and so to integrate his or her own unconscious side. This is the happy or satisfying man-woman relationship.

Still, the opposite potential is also present in the aspect of relationship by which man's anima relates to woman, or woman's animus relates to man. The negative potential is that the traditional conscious attitudes toward the opposite sex cannot be overcome, because they are too powerful, or because the one who holds them is too rigid to allow for the penetration of the unconscious into consciousness. Then the anima of the man is set against the real woman, or the animus of the woman is set against the real man. If this happens, the inferior anima in man storms at the gates of his personality, and breaks through with all the unpleasant qualities he has unconsciously ascribed to women: nagging, stubbornness, moodiness, pettiness, gossip-mongering, and the like. Woman in a similar condition becomes animus-possessed, and she presents an image of the most unpleasant characteristics which she has unconsciously identified as masculine: she becomes shrill and demanding, positive of being in the right, superorganized and supercontrolling. Heaven help the man who is confronted by an animus-possessed woman, or the woman who is confronted by an anima-possessed man!

What usually happens in such a situation is sheer hell. This can occur in the fourth aspect of man-woman relationship, the relationship between animus and anima. It is a relationship on an unconscious level; men and women are controlled by it, and never know why or how it happens. Over and over again I see this in my practice, especially when I am dealing with couples who, on the surface at least, seem to have everything going for them. But for some unconscious reason they are desperately unhappy with each other. The woman's animus takes over the relationship, derides the man for all that he is not and cannot be and never was. At the same time his anima takes over from his side with petulance, complaining, sulking, or categorical statements "all women . . ." which indicate his utter despair. Or, the weak anima in the man breaks through his persona defenses and the woman's animus which has been lurking in the background waiting for an opening, jumps in for the kill.

An attractive career woman in the public relations field was in love with her client, an actor. They were engaged to marry. Fully unconsciously, with all the wary suspicion of a businessman about to be taken over in an exploitative merger, her animus was resenting the advantages her fiancé was about to acquire. Nevertheless, on the conscious level the romance went along marvelously well until the man became seriously ill. Suddenly he was shaken, insecure in himself, wanting sympathy. The woman asked herself, "Is this the man I was going to depend on?" But it was the woman's animus driving her to the conclusion that she didn't need him after all, and it was the animus that caused her to sever the relationship within a shockingly short time after the encounter with the man's dependent and demanding anima.

It is possible, however, for an anima-animus relationship—unconscious as it is and must be—to have a constructive effect on the total relationship between a man and a woman. It is not something that can be striven for directly, but rather emerges out of a situation in which the man is able to accept his feminine side as a helpful adjunct to his conscious mode of functioning, and likewise the woman her animus. This is the man who is secure enough in his strength to be tender, and the woman who prefers exercising her privileges to fighting for her rights. Such people, with the ever-widening consciousness their modes of functioning encourage, are able to meet the opposite sex, and indeed, the world, without antagonism. They are able to participate in unconscious communication with other people which takes place on a level so deep that only its effects are perceptible, and those not always. In close relationships their unconscious communication is responsible for the feeling of knowing what the other is thinking, for inexplicable awarenesses of danger to a person who may be very far away, for nameless anxieties and fears that often accompany love relationships, and for the sense of peace that may be experienced by two people as transcending all the problems and difficulties of the everyday world.

The unconscious relationship of anima and animus is, at best, the striving of the psyche toward that wholeness in which all its elements are harmonized into a well-functioning unity. Although this is an unconscious tendency which does not often achieve fulfillment, the efforts of this factor in the psyche are constantly being experienced as partial attempts to come to that state of equilibrium which is felt as being most desirable.

We have been speaking theoretically, but most interesting to me are the subjective experiences of animus and anima. I am particularly interested in the latter since, being a woman, I cannot experience the anima directly. Therefore I asked the students in my college class to write briefly about the ways in which they had experienced anima or animus. The anima as the "completely other" came to the fore in a paper of a shy, quiet, intellectual young man. His remarks showed his grasp of the complicated many-sided character of the anima and his own sensitive response to her appearance in his life:

> In the psyche, as in all the world, phenomena appear in pairs of opposites. The anima is no exception to this rule. The bright side of the anima is a lovely figure full of grace and healing— an enabler, perhaps best typified by the Lady of mediaeval romances or the Lady, Mater Dei of the same period. St. Bernard addresses the latter, "O Clemens, O Pia, O Dulcis," and so she is—on the face at least. But equally fascinating, quite probably more so in view of the relative difficulty in assimilating her into consciousness, is the dark anima whom we must expect to find right behind our Lady. She is Kali, the destroyer.
>
> The light and dark anima are inseparable like the two sides of a coin, and to accept only the light side is to bring on the consequences of the dark. Paris did not want war. He only wanted Helen, and war was the inevitable outcome of that desire.
>
> This dark side of the anima is well represented in a song from a rock opera by The Who, where she describes herself as being

the Gypsy Queen, high on acid and demanding full payment in
advance.

Simon Magus must have had his soul torn apart in much this
manner when he first ran across his Helen in a brothel. I think
I know what it's like. This Helen appears before me in flesh
and blood recurrently, and I am almost helpless before her.
Typically she is a tough but sad speed freak, and she's "guar-
anteed to break your little heart." (Ultimately, one comes back
to the Gypsy Queen's message: learn what she knows; free your
head and start to roam.)

The student who wrote this was involved with women in a
way which clearly showed that his anima was opposed to his
excessive concern with intellectual matters. She challenged
him to take up some non-rational ways and free himself from
the strict limitations of thought imposed upon him by his
rigorous academic program. The more he adhered to his rigid
and largely self-imposed discipline, the stronger would be the
pressure from within to throw it all away. Yet if he could
listen wisely to the anima and come to know that she served
him by offering a compensatory symbol which could bring
balance into his attitude, he would become more whole.

A quite different picture was presented to me by an analysand, Wayne, who had been immersed in a love affair with a
beautiful model who was extremely demanding of him in
every way, emotionally, financially and sexually. In return she
had devoted herself completely to him, always preparing for
his coming to visit her with all possible grace. She would be
beautifully dressed, the apartment which he provided for her
would be clean and shining; there would be candlelight and
wine and an elegantly prepared dinner and after that, delightful sex. He paid heavily for all of this, and he felt it was
worth it. But he never could do enough for his anima-woman.
Not that she insisted, but he could never come to her without
bringing an expensive gift. This necessity spurred him on in
his business to take advantage of every opportunity to make
additional money. He did not look too carefully to discover
whether his means of increasing his take were legal or moral.
They became less and less so. He noticed that he was begin-

ning to slip in his career, that people were losing confidence
in him. All the same he continued what he was doing because
he did not see any way out. I observed as he arrived for his
analytic sessions that he was becoming more tense and harried
week by week. Eventually the unconscious provided Wayne
with a new view of the situation in the form of an intensely
disturbing dream. Here it is: *I find myself hanging from a
trapeze bar by my hands, over a deep abyss, a bottomless
abyss. I am trying to pull myself up by my hands, and at the
same time I have to keep bouncing a ball against that bar,
keeping it from falling, as well as maintaining my own balance. The ball sometimes goes forward, sometimes backward,
and I have to maneuver the bar so that it will touch the ball
on its descent and bounce it up again. I feel myself getting
tired. I notice that attached to the ball is a string. The string
is not attached to anything other than the ball, in other words
it is free-floating. I could reach out and catch that string and
thereby secure the ball, but in doing so I would surely lose
my balance, for it is precarious enough to hang onto that bar
with both hands, let alone with one hand. I realize that sooner
or later I will probably have to let go of the ball. There is a
wide gyration of the ball, it is coming down quite a distance
in back of me. I will have to reach out quite a distance for it
or let it go. In that moment I realize that the ball will have to
go down into the abyss by itself, or that I will go down into
the abyss after it. I awaken in panic.*

Wayne's real situation was vividly represented by the scene.
He was hanging from a trapeze bar by his hands, it was all he
could do to maintain his position. It took every bit of his
energy and strength. His hands, his creative potential, were
employed merely in maintaining the status quo, and a very
precarious status quo at that. The deep abyss was the disaster
that was so close at hand threatening him, and which, until
the dream, he had refused to recognize. It was the collapse
of his whole conscious attitude, including his image of himself. His attention was on the ball, the plaything that had
become so important to him. It was the symbol of the anima
who was projected outward onto his mistress, the woman

whose loveliness on the surface covered a vampirish need for
more and more of his energy, his vitality. Yet the insidious
thing was that the relationship had in the beginning stimulated his creativity, but for unconscious reasons. He had come
to believe that it was only through her, only because of her,
that he could be successful in his efforts, so his self-confidence
became tied up with his unconscious need for fulfillment
through another person. That led him to believe that if anything were to happen to the other person, or to his relationship
with her, he would be destroyed. But, in his conscious life,
it was becoming apparent that if he continued to operate
the way he was doing, he would meet financial ruin. All this
conflict is characteristic of relationships which are based on
a dependency upon the projected anima.

The trapeze dream showed him that the anima projection
was endangering his entire psychic structure. The longer he
tried to maintain the relationship the more hopeless it would
become. In the end he would either have to let it go, or give
up his entire ego adaptation—that would mean to give up his
job and his family and throw himself on the mercy of a
woman, who might even leave him were he unable to go on
providing for her as he had been doing. The dream said simply, "Let her go, the only thing is to let her go." The ironic
twist was that the dream also warned that he might have to
follow her into the abyss anyway.

Events that followed proved that the unconscious was quite
accurate in portraying the dreamer's condition. He did break
off his relationship with the woman, but there continued to be
a strong pull on him from her direction. For quite a long
time he found it extremely difficult to stay away from her.
Her image would intrude itself upon his thoughts, often
when he least expected it. The image however, was clearly
something other than the discarded woman. That woman had
swiftly moved on to another relationship after the breakup.
But the anima still taunted him, she still needed to be served,
and she threw all sorts of obstacles in his path so that he
would not be able to turn his attention to rebuilding his
career. The disturbing events all seemed "accidental," yet

they were "striking coincidences," each one of which might
have been anticipated and with proper attention might have
been prevented had Wayne been more conscious.

We reconsidered the dream. It had proved so important;
perhaps there was still more in it that might help to point
the way out. Now the analysand drew a picture of his dream.
The trapeze was anchored to a bar, stretching across the abyss
but resting on the ground on either side. It appeared that it
would be possible for Wayne to climb back up the trapeze—
after all, he had gotten down there somehow—and he could
try to get off the dangerous place in the same way he had
gotten onto it. In the laborious process of climbing back he
would need the help of the anima, as he had needed her before; but this time he realized that the anima was not to be
projected outward. In the process of his painful experience
he had withdrawn his projection, and, still smarting, he did
not feel inclined to look for another woman to carry it. He
would have to understand *the anima—as the bearer of his
own latent capacities for relationship,* namely, the willingness
to hear the needs of other people, not merely his own needs
and, also, a receptivity to new ideas, whether they originated
within himself or were presented to him by other people.
The anima at her best has the capacity to further relationships
out in the world, as well as within the psyche.

It took a long time for Wayne to integrate these various
anima aspects and to make them a part of his own conscious
way of functioning. For one thing, these qualities belong to
the feeling-sensation type, and as such represented his inferior function. His superior function was intuition, but the
stimulation of sensation by the projected anima, in the form
of the mistress, had distracted him from following his natural
intuition. Also, blindly attending to her feelings undermined
his own thinking, or discriminating, function. It was necessary
for him to recognize that his secondary function, feeling, and,
to a lesser degree, his inferior function, sensation, could be
tutored to accompany his better developed functions. In this
way these aspects, formerly lived out through the anima, could

be integrated more into consciousness where they could serve him as aids to broaden his natural way of functioning.

Before, the unfamiliar functions of sensation and feeling had become so powerful and obsessive in nature that they had undermined the ego. Now the goal was to allow them to play a compensatory role to that of the ego. In order to come to this he needed to develop his own sensation and feeling functions, rather than to cling to the unconscious expectation that these functions could somehow be transmitted to him by a woman.

It is a necessary part of a man's development to meet the anima first in her projected form, that is, out in the world, and deal with her there. Concomitantly, the same thing needs to happen to the woman in connection with her animus. Otherwise, anima and animus remain locked in the unconscious and are not released to create the struggles that bring with them the potential for a widening of consciousness. Anima and animus cannot be experienced until they have first been projected onto the opposite sex. This has been true since the first man upon discovering his nakedness, put off his guilt with the explanation, "The woman whom thou gavest me to be with me, *she* offered me the fruit and I ate it." Meanwhile Eve promptly made her own projection, saying, "The serpent beguiled me and I ate." Projections are necessary; they serve the purpose of bringing the unconscious into view. However, it is altogether unsatisfying to attempt to live the anima or the animus as a *purely* psychological relationship. A real down-to-earth relationship is needed in order to achieve a sense of fulfillment.

And yet there are times in one's life when the purely psychological relationship becomes necessary, either temporarily or for an indeterminate span. It may occur within a marriage, when the marriage initially stemmed from an unrealistic view of what the other person was like. This may seem preposterous in these days when premarital sexual intimacy is more common than not. I do not think it is preposterous. As long as a relationship continues to exist without any legal bonds, it must be held together by ties of tenderness and feeling, or by the kind of mutual independence that demands from each a continual striving to increase the quality of the relationship. Illusions must be perpetuated, even increasingly introduced into the relationship, so that there is always something new to fascinate and to delight the partner. But with marriage there is a tendency to let the tension slacken a bit; there is not so much need, the partner will not so easily turn away. Then, too, there comes into life all the shared concerns of people who have committed themselves to one another. It is necessary for each partner to become more real in the relationship, and as the real nature of the other becomes more and more apparent the projections are gradually withdrawn.

If both parties can grow under this regime and become more fulfilled through developing new sides of themselves at a time when it is not necessary to pour so much into holding onto the relationship with the partner, there is a chance for a richer relationship to develop with a firmer base to it. But often this is not the case. Rather, the opposite frequently occurs. As the married couple get to know one another for what each really is, previously unnoticed areas of incompatibility come to the fore. This can happen any time in a marriage, but often a crisis occurs at special points in time; for example, when the wife takes a job outside the home, or when the children go off on their own, leaving the parents to regard each other as people for the first time in many years instead of, as before, partners in the joint enterprise of maintaining a home and family. Perhaps they discover that each has grown in a different way and that they are now very far apart.

This kind of situation has prompted much attention from writers on the subject of man-woman relationships. Marriage counselor Herbert A. Otto, in an article titled "Has Monogamy Failed?" has suggested several alternatives to the conventional, till-death-do-us-part marriages. One which seems to be rapidly gaining in acceptance is what he calls "serial monogamy," in which a marriage lasts until one or both of the partners outgrow it. Then there is a divorce and generally within a fairly short time the partners make remarriages to others more suited to their needs in their current stages of development.[6]

My own feeling is, in the light of Jung's anima-animus concept, that if more attention were paid to the *unconscious* components of the sexual and social commitment which individuals make to one another, they would be better able to find fulfillment in the marriages they have. Or, after a broken marriage, they would be better able to evaluate the causes for the breakup and to avoid the necessity of repeating the errors again and again. For one thing, a degree of forbearance toward the partner would become possible when the anima-animus expectations were relaxed. If a woman can realize that the capacity for creative work or for enjoyment of life which her beloved inspires in her comes not *from him*, but *through him*, then it becomes clear that what makes her feel happy is her own capacity for living a certain kind of life. Then she can fully enjoy what he offers her, but she is not utterly dependent upon him for it—she knows that it is possible for her to find stimulation from sources outside of their relationship, also that there are other people to whom she may offer the fruits of her productivity, so that there are many sources of meaning for her in her life. This then takes the pressure off a relationship, and enables one to let it live and grow on its own terms, with mutual respect of each partner for the other. And, if the relationship should come to an end, all is not lost, for the capacity to create and carry on a warm and loving enterprise between two people remains as the expression of the inward living of an awareness and relatedness to the anima or the animus.

I would like to show, through a pair of dreams, how a man who had just gone through a divorce became newly aware of the potentials for him in his new status. Long before his divorce, Brad had been involved in a deeply moving but platonic friendship with Andrea, who had been able to help him bring out his very best creative efforts. The friendship had ended when he moved away to another city. Only occasional correspondence kept it going for a time; then that ceased. He then began to think of seeking out new feminine relationships, not only for sexual gratification but for affirmation as a person, and for warmth and comfort. His friend James tried earnestly to draw him into his own circle, which consisted of a fast-moving group of men and women whose sexual pleasures were purely hedonistic, not really what Brad was looking for at this time of his life. The image of Andrea remained before him, as if to urge him to continue on the project that he had been working on for a long time, but which he had not touched during the last year of his unhappy marriage.

Brad's first dream: *I come into an old ruined house. It has been burnt out, only a shell is left and some charred remains. The light in the stairwell is still burning. Andrea is on the top floor but I cannot reach her, I can only get part way up the stairs, the rest is burnt out and there is this hiatus between us. However, on the level where I stand is my friend James, and I am able to go and meet him.*

A few days later a second dream followed: *There are many people, men and women, taking nude showers together. They ask me to join, but I hold back until all are finished and gone, and then I take my nude shower alone. Andrea appears and sees me taking the shower through a glass window. She comes into the room and embraces me.*

The first dream showed the ruins of his own psyche after the destruction of his marriage, the "burnt-out" relationship, which it really was with much damage to his image of himself. Yet the glowing light was hopeful, it suggested that there was still power available, and that the source from which it came was undisturbed despite the holocaust that had come and gone. But it was not possible to reach the anima figure within himself; first it was necessary to come to terms with James, who represented Brad's own shadow aspect. That dark side of himself had to be dealt with before he could devote himself to the creative effort which fell within the province to which he might be guided by the anima in the image of Andrea.

In the second dream, when the temptation to seek indiscriminate intimacy was put aside (the shower was taken separately), when he could stand himself naked and alone without looking for someone to serve as a buffer between him and his deep feelings of loneliness and void, then and only then did the relationship with the ideal feminine become possible. And then he did not have to go in search of her—she came to him.

I want to turn now to the psychology of the woman, her special way of viewing herself which then makes room in the unconscious for a complementary view of the animus. One of my students put her own ideas about a woman's self-concept into a logical framework in the following way: "One of the most universal notions about women—their receptiveness (which, if expanded, would include sympathy, understanding, compassion, softness, warmth—all enclosing and comforting characteristics)—comes from the sense of space within them. Receptiveness, if pushed further, could also come to imply negative qualities—possessiveness, the need to consume, and so on. These are universal assumptions about women; that they are found in all cultures is indicative of the *common perception of female space*, that they continue from generation to generation indicates a strong predisposition to these qualities in the unconscious as well as the strength of social instruction."

Jill, an analysand going through a passionate love relationship, became deeply aware of herself as internal female space as she experienced her sexuality not only as a personal transaction but also as a fragment of the eternal and ongoing cosmic interchange. Here is what she expressed of her exultation after a time of extraordinary intensity with her lover: *My body is an undulating hillside. He carries the moisture between my thighs to my breast, anointing me with the perfume of my fluid substance and his. Drinking of it, touching source with source, uniting the sensitive points of my body, uniting my body. Centering me, he is the force drawing the triangular ecstasy into another dimension. Like the eye at the point of a pyramid. Spinning into a cone, its rim the circle along which the experience of being touched from the outside changes into the feeling inside of being touched from the outside. Three dimensions only when he is there to make the form, to let*

*the feelings exist on more than one plane. Inside the cone
a whirlpool, eddying into the vortex at its point, where water
turns into fire. The swirling water opens, diaphragmlike to
reveal a core of orange-red throbbing heat. Beyond that everything is blackness until a thin spun glass shaft of silver glittering in the blackness with the sparkling colors of sunlight
in a tiny prism is flung like a spear through the blackness.
. . . The body points have their own energy but when
they are touched by another there is a flow, a movement.
When he touches me there is a flow, a movement, as my
skin is at the same time touched as though I were touching
myself . . . not a circle . . . you are me touching myself
. . . that's how I understand you . . . but my body feels
you as someone playing an instrument, releasing my harmonies, finding the right vibrations.*

This woman's way of feeling about herself was completely
non-personal, even though her experience seemed to her highly
individual. She seemed to have slipped into the collective unconscious, viewing herself as a personification of the age-old
image of the Great Mother in her most passive form, resting
in complete repose until the masculine principle touches her,
catalyzing her boundless matter into energy. The woman who
wrote this was a career woman with a responsible job in which
she was expected to deal tactfully and considerately with a
large number of people. She was extremely moody, and on
some days was able to carry on her work smoothly and effectively, but on other days she tended to be depressed, slow,
withdrawn. At those times when people approached her she
was apt to snap back with some thoughtless remark or impatient gesture. Active as she was in her work, her activity usually
came in response to someone else. She was as a rule very
much involved with one or another love relationship, and
when she was without one she felt desolate.

She felt that the quality of her functioning in all areas
from work to friendship to sports to reading, all of these depended on her being in a highly stimulating sexual relationship. She insisted that she needed this, otherwise she could
not accomplish anything. In her relationships she tended to

become so fiercely clinging that she frightened men away, and
then she would become relatively non-functional. In her writings she was able to move away from her purely subjective
experience and to relate to it as though she were a spectator.
She could see the masculine element in the relationship, as
well as the feminine. When I asked her how it was possible
to do that she was amazed to recognize how easily it had
come to her, without having strained to understand. It
was more nearly like an automatic sort of writing, as though
a channel had opened for her which was not ordinarily accessible to her. She had not only felt herself as the huge hill-
like mountain, immobile and heavy, she had also felt the
volatile sliver of sunlight finding its way swiftly into the dark
places. Could Jill have imagined that she had been able to
experience that, as an objective happening, only because it
had been already present in her, waiting to be actualized?
No, she was not yet prepared for this. Under the cloak of
the sexual relationship she was really seeking the warm and
supportive relationship she had had with her father when
she was a little girl, the tenderness which had been snatched
away when her father had left her and her mother to go off
on his own. The pattern of the passive little girl to whom
exciting things would happen if she would be still and be
good was never altogether broken. For her, the "good" depended on receiving it from a man. She saw herself as instrument, the harmonies and vibrations needed to be released by
someone else—though she had all the potentialities within herself, she was convinced that she could not use them without
help from a man.

In the analysis it was necessary for me to help Jill to get
unbound from her state of confusion with the animus—nearly
an undifferentiated chaotic state in which ego and animus
were mixed together, unable to be seen in their separate ways
of contributing to a total enterprise. We had a difficult time
in dealing with the transference in the analysis. Jill had always
seemed terribly afraid of me. I had been aware that although
she appeared open a good deal of the time, there would be
times when she would close up and look at me as though

I were about to put a gun at her head and pull the trigger. I realized there was something extremely irrational here, which needed to be brought out. Early in her therapy she had spoken about some sexual advances which her father had made to her when she was five or six. Her description did not make the incidents sound terribly traumatic, in fact I had the distinct impression that the fondling of her genitals had been pleasurable to her, and that she may even have solicited it some of the time. I had asked her where her mother was when this was going on—her mother had worked away from the home in the evenings, and this father-daughter sexual activity had occurred mostly while the father was putting his daughter to bed at night. If, as in our culture, we were not so thoroughly conditioned to erupt like a volcano whenever anything approaches the incest problem, we would not consider this the sort of psychological trauma that would necessarily have to damage a child for life. Yet, always, I had the feeling in talking with Jill that her explanations were too simple, that they seemed so innocuous that it was hard to believe there was not more to it. And her intense fear reaction to me seemed possibly to be the key.

I began to sense that there was a secret which she could not tell. She clearly could not verbalize it. It took months of analysis before she could trust me enough. I think that to some people who have not gone through the analytic process it must sound so painfully simple when people bring out things that have been long buried, that it is impossible for them to understand why it takes so much hard work. But like gold, these bits of information lie buried in the most inaccessible places, and all the ego's defenses are militated to guard against incursion. So it was with this woman, Jill, who at long last let me know what it was that had been so frightening about the experience with her father, that made it the keystone of her emotions then, and in all the years that followed. It was something her father had said to her during their sexual play, just one sentence: "Don't ever tell your mother about this, she'll kill you if she finds out!"

To tell me this was equated in her unconscious with facing

the risk of imminent death; consciously, it was felt as a terrific anxiety, the cause of which was unknown. Several times she had attempted to break off therapy as we had gotten close to it, but always the thrust toward the possibility of finding her own wholeness kept her in the process. At last she had done the one thing she had always wanted to do, but for which she had lacked the courage, and that was to tell "her mother." For, in the transference relationship, she had projected the mother image onto me, and all the fears associated with it. Attaching to all this was her dependency on the male element in her life, which had become internalized as an aspect of the animus. Just as she could only experience her mother in projection onto me, the image of her father was projected onto one or another of her lovers.

I was able to help her turn loose from her fear of the mother. That meant that the mother-in-her could be released from the bindings of unconsciousness—with her knowledge of what had occurred she could also stand vis-à-vis the father-in-her, who, until that time, had exerted absolute control over certain aspects of her psychological functioning. After this breakthrough she began to take a more active role with the men in her life. She learned to be a friend as well as a lover. She came to discover that not only the potentiality for dealing with the tasks and problems of her life lay within herself, but also the potentiality for actualizing them. Not that she no longer needed interaction with people, not at all. But Jill was able to see this interaction as a way of reflecting what she herself was, and of responding to the stimulation she herself offered, which in its turn maintained the dynamic of relationship by stimulating her creative-maternal side in return.

The question of man's relationship to his anima and woman's to her animus, are extremely important ones in view of their connection with two of the most important issues of our lives: sexuality and creativity. These two issues are perhaps essentially one, for they are different expressions of the archetype of *coniunctio*, the joining of two opposites so that out of them a third, something new, may emerge.

Even though sexuality is, in our times, frequently separated from its natural outcome, procreation, I cannot help but feel that the psyche as yet has not altogether made the separation. I recall a remark made by a woman at a party not too long ago, a remark which impressed me strongly. The woman was not an analysand of mine. She was a charming and literate woman in her late thirties, the mother of two very pleasant children, and the wife of a successful professional man. She was up on the latest books and the latest social movements, in other words she was the epitome of a conscious, well-adapted contemporary woman, fully in touch with the realities of her day. She said, "Ever since I have been taking the Pill, which is quite a few years now, sexual intercourse has lost something for me. Of course I enjoy it, but somehow it's not the same—it's as though the sport were taken out of it. By that I mean that when there is a chance, however small, that pregnancy will result, you are in a great, marvelous gambling game with the Lord God Almighty, and you submit yourself to Him and His judgment. Somehow you feel like a junior partner in the enterprise of Creation. I must say, I miss that."

I find in my work where people bare their most intimate thoughts the truth of the adage that the more things change the more they are the same. This is particularly applicable to the anima-animus problem. I see it most in dealing with youth who are in tune with changing times, and not at all stuck in the conventional morality of their parents. Even among these young people, and despite the efforts of the supporters of women's liberation among both sexes, it is still rather generally agreed, no question about it, it is still a man's world. Measured in terms of the important contributions to government, to science and the arts, to the economic development of our country, and to the military, everywhere men are in charge. Men are in all of the highest places and most of the secondary places. In higher education in the period from 1900 to 1968 the ratio of male college graduates to female ranged between three to one in 1900 to four to three in 1968, with the exception of the years of World War II when women graduates for a short period outnumbered men.

But in the graduate schools the drop-off of women completing degrees at the Ph.D. level was marked, with six times as many men receiving Ph.D.s as women.[7]

Whether it is a matter of innate intellectual ability, or whether it is a question of ability that is trained to perform is not the question. It is unlikely that in newborn infants, one sex or the other would show a distinctly greater aptitude for higher education if the aptitude could be tested at that time. Whether it be a matter of early training, or society's expectations, or the limitations imposed on women by the tasks and responsibilities of childbearing and child rearing, it is true that women do not, as a rule, develop their intellectual sides to the same degree of differentiation as do men. They furthermore do not, as a rule, develop those skills that demand highly differentiated thinking and decision making. It is impossible to know whether or not women could develop in these areas to a far greater degree than they have done because women concentrate instead on different areas of activity in their conscious lives from those of men.

What Jung stated in this connection nearly half a century ago is still basically true, although I believe that we are now standing on the brink of momentous change. He wrote:

> Just as a woman is often clearly conscious of things which a man is still groping for in the dark, so there are naturally fields of experience in a man which, for a woman, are still wrapped in the shadows of non-differentiation, chiefly things in which she has little interest. Personal relations are as a rule more important and interesting to her than objective facts and their interconnections. The wide fields of commerce, politics, technology, and science, the whole realm of the applied masculine mind, she relegates to the penumbra of consciousness; while, on the other hand, she develops a minute consciousness of personal relationships, the infinite nuances of which usually escape the man entirely.[8]

Jung asserted that the masculine consciousness was associated with matters of the world, with events and trends, with discrete knowledge, with information, with judgment of objective data. The feminine consciousness, he said, is associated with matters of relationship, caring for, nurturing, cultivating, keeping and preserving.

The Jungian concept of the conjunction of opposites leads us to expect the unconscious aspects of men and women to be correspondingly different. The specific characteristics of the anima and animus serve in many ways as compensations in the unconscious of the masculine and feminine conscious attitudes, respectively. For example, the anima is characterized by moods in the man which come from his unconscious and contrast strangely with his differentiated conscious attitude. In comparison with the moods of man's anima, woman's animus produces opinions. These come about in women as a result of their unconscious prior assumptions, often due to lack of objective information. While a woman is generally devoted to one man at a time, her animus gets projected in a number of different directions and many men concurrently may become the objects of her fantasy life. A man tends to have a larger number of significant relationships with women, but the compensating anima is usually directed toward one woman or toward a single kind of woman. A woman's animus often expresses itself in generalizations, "You're always doing that," to a man's eternal despair. When a woman gets into an argument, her animus generalizations tend to evoke the man's anima with a petulant, painstaking and patronizing step-by-step explanation of the "realities" of the situation. In a woman the animus tends toward accepting the collective values and urging her man to do what everybody expects of him—perhaps this comes from her lack of active and creative contact with society. He, on the other hand, functioning out of anima, may be deliberately quixotic and irresponsible about minor matters like dress, use of free time, and so on. Animus may come across as touching and childlike or downright help-less and stupid when it comes to practical matters, as in the clinging-vine type of women. A man, when his anima is in full charge, expresses childish feelings, such as irritability when he is sick or an oversentimentality on occasion. The animus has its critical side, which comes out in argumentative tones or would-be intellectualism that takes the form of harping on some small point while missing the main issue. The anima sometimes is present in the transference, when a man transfers the mother image to the wife. In such a case he would seek his wife's protection from household problems, from the children, as well as from making social decisions.

So there we have, in brief, examples of some ways in which anima and animus emerge from the unconscious to compensate a one-sided attitude in consciousness. These are, to be sure, less than comprehensive descriptions of anima-animus functioning but it is probably safe to say that they are generally as valid as they ever were in the large majority of people, or at least that this has been so until the current reconsideration of masculine and feminine roles has become an issue in our society.

Men and women need to come to terms with the very deep level of the unconscious represented by anima and animus. I believe that the times in which we live offer an opportunity for this in a way that has never been possible before. Always in the past small numbers of people have had the leisure and resources required for a life which included study and contemplation, enjoyment of the arts, and concern with matters of the spirit. But these days in which we live offer more exposure to more information, and more and different kinds of stimulation of thoughts and feelings and sensations than had ever been imagined before. Also, with increasing industrialization and consequent reduction in the hours of the typical work week, there is time for those who wish to use it to come closer to the unconscious dimensions of their beings.

It seems to me that the spirit of these times calls for a greater effort to be made by women in the direction of coming to terms with necessity for change, for breaking out of the centuries-old constriction that, once biologically based, became firmly entrenched in every aspect of our society. I believe that this is the impetus behind the women's liberation movement, and if so, there are many avenues of approach to the potentialities for woman's fulfillment.

At the bottom of woman's plight is that she has let much of it happen to her. She has not only been the victim of her biological vulnerability; she has also been the victim of her psychological vulnerability. She could not, for all the years until recently, prevent unwanted or ill-timed pregnancies, except by refusing sexual relations. In the past, many professional women with high levels of education were women who had never married. As late as 1963, a study showed that of about 25,000 women who held full-time teaching positions in universities and four-year colleges, more than half had never married, and 81 per cent had no children.[9] Unmarried or childless women were always considered to be "incomplete," while interestingly enough no one seemed to feel that a woman might be incomplete if she reared a family and kept an attractive home and slept with her husband regularly, even though she may have left her college without finishing, or quit a challenging job to marry. That is, no one has felt that this might be an incomplete life for a woman except perhaps the woman herself.

In my practice I am meeting more and more women who have realized that they have been expected to spend their lives taking care of other people, and providing an atmosphere in which husband and children are enabled to make the most of themselves. The woman has been expected to stand behind her family as the *femme inspiratrice*, the muse, infusing their spirits with the enthusiasm to create. All this is very well, and many women enjoy the role thoroughly. However, one woman recently remarked after attending a testimonial dinner for her husband, "I don't mind all this standing behind, but why can't *I* be out in front once in a while?"

One of today's realistic young women was deeply in love. Both she and her young man were in graduate school. She had just a few courses to complete, and was doing that in the late afternoon when she finished teaching school. He was in an M.A. program full time. He wanted to marry her, but she was not so eager. She preferred to share an apartment with him and wait until both of them finished their schooling before any decisions about marriage were made. If she married him now, and if he were offered a position in another city when he graduated, she would have had no choice but

to meekly follow along, no matter what career opportunities
might have been open to her elsewhere. But she figured that
if she waited, then when the two had both completed their
schooling and were considering the possibilities for employment, they would be on an equal basis. If he wanted to maintain his relationship with her, he would have to consider her
as a full equal and any decision would have to be made between the two of them and not unilaterally.

Another woman, married, had a two-year-old daughter. The
woman had been professionally trained, but had not worked
outside the home since she became pregnant. Her husband
was a schoolteacher. Dorothy did all the housework, took care
of the baby, and found little time or energy for doing anything else. She had compulsively thrown herself into maintaining a beautifully ordered household, and when her husband would come home in the evening she would quiz him
on his activities. He was not interested in discussing them
with her, but retreated into his study after dinner to read
or prepare for his classes the next day. At one point he took
to going out in the evenings to "meetings." Dorothy suspected
that he was having an affair with one of their friends, and
confronted him directly. He refused to reply to her
charges, and there developed tension between them which
grew with the passing days. Dorothy became increasingly nervous and critical of her husband. It seemed to her that there
was nothing she could do about the situation. She was at
a dead end. One day while she and her husband were out
driving they got into a bitter argument. She was at the wheel.
Distracted and upset, she ran the car off the road. It turned
over several times, but by a miracle they escaped injury. They
took it as a warning that they were in serious danger—the
next time could be worse. Dorothy decided to go into therapy
to begin dealing with the uncontrollable angers that had been
emerging in her.

It did not take very much analysis for Dorothy to recognize
that she had "let it happen." She had all too eagerly given
up her own interests in the world outside of the home and
indeed in herself as a worthwhile person. Her perfectionist

tendencies that had in the past stood her in good stead in her profession had become compulsive with respect to her home. She had become altogether one-sided and had lost her lively concern about what was happening outside. The animus which once took her into the world and kept her interested and interesting had now made a slave of her, and she unconsciously had been living out every one of its negative aspects.

In time and in the course of analysis, she became aware that this same animus could lead her back into the world, that he could support her in useful and challenging work. She would then not need to experience life vicariously through her husband. This time she drew her own conclusions. She did not ask her husband what she should do. Instead, she found a full-time job in her field of competence. Ironically, her salary was more than her husband's. At first this put her off—as she was concerned that this might injure the ego of her husband. Then she was able to realize that just as the monetary values of contemporary society had not proved her inferiority when she was earning nothing, neither did they establish her superiority now. What was important to her was to find her place, the place in which she would utilize the potential with which she was endowed, irrespective of the values placed on those accomplishments by the world's judgment.

She arranged for her child to be in a well-run day-care center near where she worked, and then told her husband that this was what she had done. She told him that she would need more help from him at home and that he would have to stay home with their child occasionally in the evening, so that she could do the grocery shopping and take care of some personal things. After some conflict, in which she held her ground, he agreed. As she began to find some of her satisfactions outside the home, the home which had seemed like a prison for her before, now became a sanctuary. The entire atmosphere changed. She no longer needed her husband as a hook on which to hang her frustrated animus; she now appreciated his sharing in what had previously been designated as "her" household responsibilities. He, in turn, became the recipient of her warmth and fullness. She was able to "let go" of him, and he no longer needed to run from her. The relationship began to regain the mutuality it had when they first met, before they had become dependent upon one another to fill the gaps in their own personality development.

Not every woman needs to go to work in order to find herself. But many women do need to explore the animus dimension of their lives with a view toward allowing this inner, fructifying element to emerge and to lead them into new growth. In the same way, men need to explore the anima dimension, which opens them to the thrust of "the other," and makes them receptive to new possibilities. A one-sided conscious attitude, which sees one's own role as the one prescribed by tradition and conventional expectations, becomes narrow and cramped. There are two tendencies: either accept the conventional role anyway—and repress all the anger and hostility that accompanies unreasonable sacrifices, or else rebel and demand the "rights and privileges" formerly accorded to the opposite sex only. Neither course can lead to inner harmony. What is needed is not the battle of the sexes, but an inner marriage, in which the lived-out side and the unrealized contrasexual side are bound together in a sacred union of mutual love and respect.

Without this inner marriage, each person feels enslaved in his singular sexual role. With it, the potentialities of the other, the lesser-known but deeply felt unconscious needs and desires, may surface and become visible. The truth seems to be that unless we are partners with that contrasexual side of our natures, the soul that leads us to our own depths, we cannot become full and independent partners with a beloved person in the world outside. Beyond and above this important consideration is the crux of the whole matter: even in the absence of a beloved person, or *especially* in the absence of a beloved person, the inner marriage is needed to give each one a sense of completion within himself or herself. The divine paradox is this—becoming complete, becoming whole as individuals, means that our completion is not limited to the bag of skin in which we live. Rather, it makes us open and porous, utterly permeable to the universal source of strength outside ourselves. This source is not really "outside" although it may in the beginning be so experienced. It is the greater Self, of which our own experiential self is a part, a participant, an integral part of the ultimate order. The human psyche is the microcosm which reflects in ways both known and unknown to us, the macrocosm that Jung has termed the Self.

10

CIRCUMAMBULATING
THE SELF

Infused with the energy that is liberated from the conflict of the ego with the animus or anima, and quickened by the assimilation of shadow contents once alienated by too much identification with the persona, the process of individuation now takes another twist in the spiral. The same problems which occupied us in the past may come into view again, but now they are regarded from a new level; they take on a different importance. The emphasis in analysis at this stage no longer needs to be placed on the development of patterns that led the analysand to just that situation in which he finds himself today. Irritation and pique and even loneliness and grief associated with one's personal problems are transcended, although the problems themselves remain in awareness and may not be avoided in the course of the wider quest. Events begin to be seen in terms of their intentionality. It is as though all events are manifestations of some purposive force, a force which has been appropriately termed "the goal-directedness of psychic energy."[1] It is this energy which provides the thrust for the individuation process. I cannot describe what it is, for I do not know, but I can tell how it feels. It feels as if one were being drawn inward toward a center of great luminosity, yet to fly straight into it would be like a moth darting into a flame or the earth hurtling itself into the center of the sun. So one moves around the center instead, close enough to see the brightness, to feel the warmth, but maintaining the orbital tension, a dynamic relationship of a small finite being to a source of light and energy that has no limits.

The small finite being is, of course, the "ego," the "I" of which each one of us is aware. The mysterious "non-ego" or, as M. Esther Harding has called it, the "not-I,"[2] is termed by Jung the "self." Jung's use of the word "self" is different from that of common usage, in which the self is synonymous with ego. "Self" as Jung uses it has a special meaning; it is that center of being which the ego circumambulates; at the same time it is the superordinate factor in a system in which the ego is subordinate. Self, as we use the term here, will refer to Jung's meaning, and the ego is defined as being subsumed under the broader concept of the self.

I have not wanted to get involved in abstruse philosophical constructs in this work, because my intention has been to write about the *experience* of analysis and not the philosophical justification for it. That something is justified and can be "proved" is no indication that it works. Jung arrived at his own rationales by observing and confronting the actual experiences of his patients, and then attempting to place them in the context of the experiences of mankind throughout the ages, namely, the mythologems. Likewise, we too, may talk about individual experience and draw parallels, as we regard the way in which individual experience recapitulates archetypal experience.

We come to know the self as it appears to the perceiving ego; we come to approach the mystery of it through the clues that become apparent to the searching eye. In religious terms one could say something analogous, that we come to know God as he manifests himself in man and through man. When the ego is barred from achieving the task it has set for itself, through the intervention of passion, impotence, pain or death, it must realize that it is not the supreme directing force in the human personality; it finds out that it is confronting a more powerful entity. When man bows before the awesome order of nature and realizes that he cannot subdue it, that the best he can hope for is to discover ways of learning its laws and functioning in accordance with them, then he knows that he is facing a greater entity.

One way to confront the self is through analysis. One way to approach God is through prayerful contemplation. I am not so sure that in their essentials these two ways are so fundamentally different. At the beginning of analysis the patient brings his symptoms and places them in the lap of the analyst, very much like the child who brings his small problems before his picture of Jesus, making bargains with the Lord. As time passes, each relationship, the analytic and the religious, goes through several transformations. Gradually, in either case, one grows out of the egocentric position and into an awareness of the true nature of the relationship between that which is finite and temporal, and that which is infinite and eternal. In my own experience, and in that of certain of my analysands, as analysis progressed beyond the elementary stages, the common thread of the two apparently different kinds of goal-directed movement gradually became visible. The variation comes mostly in the language of metaphor, which is demanded when we speak of the unknowable.

In the beginnings of human experience on this planet earth, all was primordial chaos. This was the undifferentiated self. Its primary characteristic was wholeness: everything was in it and nothing was separate from it. The discerning eye of man began to make separations—were they really separations or did they only seem so to man? As man's consciousness developed he began to be aware of a tension of opposites: wholeness and separateness, the one and the many, totality and otherness. The problem can be stated in an endless number of ways; it has fascinated man from his earliest beginnings. It was a problem which preoccupied the medieval alchemists who projected it onto "matter" and then went on to project "spiritual content" onto the material with which they were dealing. In those days science had not yet been differentiated from religion, for men did not see any need to isolate the study of the ways of God from the study of the ways in which nature functions. So their researches were at once "chemical" and "religious."

Jung believed that while men have been drawing the boundaries between science and religion ever since the Enlightenment and to some degree even before, that nevertheless in the deeper layers of the collective unconscious the analogies are merged into something like the identity that was apparent in the writings of the strange and mystical alchemists. For this reason he was interested in studying the old alchemical texts. Here he could see how man projected his own psyche into his work. The alchemical "opus" was at once an attempt to transform base matter into something of great value and an attempt to transform the animalistic aspect of man into the spiritual aspect. Needless to say, neither opus was then, nor has yet been, entirely successful. The point to be made here is that the opus corresponds to the work of the individuation process, and both may be best expressed in symbolic terms. The symbol is the best way to speak of that which is in large part unknown, since it evokes the feelings and associations which make it possible for us to be in a relationship with a mystery which cannot be touched.

The self, then, is most aptly expressed through the language of the symbol. The study of alchemy, as Jung has shown, begins with the *prima materia,* the original matter which we have referred to as "primordial chaos." It is the same as the undifferentiated self. Of it Jung has written,

> It was of course impossible to specify such a substance, because the projection emanates from the individual and is consequently different in each case. For this reason it is incorrect to maintain that the alchemists never said what the *prima materia* was; on the contrary, they gave all too many indications and so were everlastingly contradicting themselves. For one alchemist the *prima materia* was quicksilver, for others it was ore, iron, gold, lead, salt, sulphur, vinegar, water, air, fire, earth, blood, water of life, *lapis* [stone], poison, spirit, cloud, sky, dew, shadow, sea, mother, moon, dragon, Venus, chaos, or microcosm . . . Besides these half-chemical, half-mythological definitions there are also some "philosophical" ones which have a deeper

meaning. . . . "Hades" . . . "the animal of the earth and sea,"
or "man," or a "part of man."[8]

The self embraces all there is, whether known or unknown.
Where is the end of it? In asking the question the human
mind soon finds its limits, for the self is "greater than great."
The thoughts turn inward, seeking the essence of the self and
there it is found to be "smaller than small." How this can
be is related by Aldous Huxley in a story which he takes from
the Chandogya Upanishad, in which a father is educating his
son in these matters:

When Svetaketu was twelve years old he was sent to a teacher,
with whom he studied until he was twenty-four. After learning
all the Vedas, he returned home full of conceit in the belief that
he was consummately well educated, and very censorious.

His father said to him, "Svetaketu, my child, you who are so
full of your learning and so censorious, have you asked for that
knowledge by which we hear the unhearable, by which we perceive what cannot be perceived and know what cannot be
known?"

"What is that knowledge, sir?" asked Svetaketu.

His father replied, "As by knowing one lump of clay all that
is made of clay is known, the difference being only in name,
but the truth being that all is clay—so, my child, is that knowledge, knowing which we know all."

"But surely these venerable teachers of mine are ignorant of
this knowledge; for if they possessed it they would have imparted
it to me. Do you, sir, therefore give me that knowledge."

"So be it," said the father. . . . And he said, "Bring me a
fruit of the nyagrodha tree."

"Here is one, sir."

"Break it."

"It is broken, sir."

"What do you see there?"

"Some seeds, sir, exceedingly small."

"Break open one of these."

"It is broken, sir."

"What do you see there?"

"Nothing at all."

The father said, "My son, that subtle essence which you do
not perceive there—in that very essence stands the being of the

huge nyagrodha tree. In that which is the subtle essence all that
exists has its self. That is the True, that is the Self, and thou,
Svetaketu, art That."

"Pray, sir," said the son, "tell me more."

"Be it so, my child," the father replied; and he said, "Place
this salt in water, and come to me tomorrow morning."

The son did as he was told.

Next morning the father said, "Bring me the salt which you
put in the water."

The son looked for it, but could not find it; for the salt, of
course, had dissolved.

The father said, "Taste some of the water from the surface
of the vessel. How is it?"

"Salty."

"Taste some from the middle. How is it?"

"Salty."

"Taste some from the bottom. How is it?"

"Salty."

The father said, "Throw the water away and then come back
to me again."

The son did so; but the salt was not lost, for salt exists forever.

Then the father said, "Here likewise in this body of yours,
my son, you do not perceive the True; but there in fact it is.
In that which is the subtle essence, all that exists has its self.
That is the True, that is the Self, and thou, Svetaketu, art
That."[4]

The primary, all-encompassing archetype is the archetype
of the self. The archetype in this sense is the element in
the human psyche which makes it possible to conceive of such
an entity as the self. And immediately as the self is conceived
of there has to be that which conceives of it, the organ of
awareness, which has been named the ego. Does this mean
that the ego, which is somehow related to the self, is outside
the self? I do not think so, any more than the brain, which
is capable of conceiving of the body of which it is a part,
is separate from that body. Nor are the hands separate from
the body, although they are agents of the authority which
resides in the body and directs their movements. The separation of the ego from the self is a separation that is made

conceptually, for the purpose of thinking about ego/non-ego relations. When we say that the development of the ego is a process of becoming aware of one's own being as a separate unit of humanity, at first someone other than one's mother and later separate from all the elements in one's environment, we are speaking "as if." We strive to attain our individuality, yet at the same time we struggle to establish our unity with the whole. As I sit across from my analysand I raise the question: "This space that is between you and me—is it a space which separates us one from the other, or is it a space that unites us one to the other?" The answer, clearly, is that it is both, depending upon the way we choose to look at it. A child fights for his independence as a human being. At the same time he wants to be accepted as a member of his family.

Looking inward we see that the process of relating the ego to the environment is not unlike the intrapsychic process of relating the ego to the unconscious, and to its dominant archetype, the self. In analysis one aim is to differentiate the ego, which should direct the conscious modes of functioning, from all the unconscious aspects of the psyche which affect the conscious ego and guide it in ways not subject to the dominance of the will alone. The task in the early stages of analysis is to recognize the non-ego forces operating in us. These include, as we have seen, the persona and shadow, and the anima and animus, in all their many forms and guises. Other archetypes emerge in the analytic process, and some of them will be seen as we explore more dreams and other approaches to the unconscious. The ego's confrontation with figures of the unconscious is a counterpart in man's inner experience of the ego's confrontation with people and situations in the environment.

The first half of life is spent mainly in finding out who we are, through seeing ourselves in our interaction with others. We establish our own position vis-à-vis these others; we develop an attitude toward them; there are struggles for dominance in which our strength is tested and also that of our adversaries. If it works well, we find our place in the world—

our own level, so to speak. In the world, one hallmark of maturation is the realization of what we can do by ourselves, what we can do with the help of others, and what we cannot do at all. The mature man or woman has discovered himself or herself as a differentiated personality spending his days and nights doing what he is fitted for by his own nature, without frittering away his energies in pointless strivings or useless regrets.

If the aims of the first half of life or the early stages of analysis are reasonably well fulfilled, different aims will emerge during the second half or the later stages. While the first part is directed toward achievement, the second part is directed toward integration. Where the first part is directed toward emergence as an individual, the second part is directed toward harmony with the totality of being. In the beginning, the ego arises out of the depths of the unconscious. In the end, the ego surrenders to those depths. That is why the ancient Hebrews were told to rejoice when death comes to a friend, and to mourn at a birth—for it is a fearsome thing to send a ship forth on a voyage to an unknown destination, but a glad welcome is due when the ship returns at last to its home port.

Long before the ultimate union with the self can be achieved, the goal is shown to man, if he will but see it. The initial glimpse of what it would be like to achieve a seemingly impossible goal is often sufficient inspiration to carry the seeker through the laborious process of self-discovery. That glimpse may come through the image of the anima or animus, the guide to the depths of the unconscious. It may occur during the analysis itself. Or, it may occur outside of analysis as a mystical experience or a striking insight that may become the foundation stone for a lifetime of endeavor. Or, it may simply become the stone that the builders rejected.

Such a glimpse came to Vincent during his undergraduate years. Reared in a home that was strictly religious by conventional standards, he had been indoctrinated with a strong belief in a personal God who meted out rewards and punishment in accord with his moral laws. As Vincent studied sci-

ence and philosophy and was exposed to iconoclastic students
and teachers, he lost his traditional faith and the support it
provided him. After a time of struggle, he consciously put all
religious ideas out of his mind and concentrated instead on
all the usual things that undergraduates concentrate upon.
During this period he was struck by a dream so vivid that he
was unable to forget it, indeed, he found himself strangely
preoccupied with it. Eventually, circumstances brought Vincent to analysis. In his initial session he related the dream:
*I am walking with a woman slightly older than myself along
a mountain path. It is a glacial idyllic scene by moonlight.
I am also somehow watching myself. We come to some huge
gray boulders. They are blocking our path. We stop, and she
turns to me and looks at me. We are engaged in pleasant
conversation. Suddenly she turns extremely ugly. Her face
takes on a greenish color and she gets very old. I realize there
is only one way to help the situation and that is to have intercourse with her. My penis enters her vagina then goes through
her body and into the rock behind her. Then she disappears
and I am alone, having intercourse with the rock.*

Sometime later, with the dream still on his mind, Vincent
was sitting on a bench in front of the university library. These
words began going through his mind insistently. "By this rock
I will heal you, through this rock I will save you." Over and
over again. He told me what he had then thought about all
this. "I thought the woman was part of myself—I thought
something was wrong inside myself—that the unconscious was
extremely ugly. I started reading psychology and I stumbled
upon Jung's small book *Modern Man in Search of a Soul*.
After that I began reading more and more of Jung. He had
taken on a deep religious significance for me." Then Vincent
told me about how he had quit his church during his junior
year at college, and had started reading Mahayana Buddhism,
yoga and Zen. He had lost his sense of communication with
his own past and he was not at home in the Eastern religions
altogether, although he sensed that there was something there
that might have meaning for him.

This young man, who had not known anything about Jung

at the time of the dream, had experienced an archetypal configuration. Then some event in his life had led him to discover
what the experience was all about, if not to understand it.
Through his analysis Vincent was able to accept that the
woman in his dream was a representation of the anima, who
leads man to his unconscious depths if he will but dare to
approach her in all her beauty and sometimes terror. The
rock symbolized the basis, the solid, unchangeable impenetrable reality which in some mysterious way a man must penetrate with his creative potential. The self challenges man to
this task, and when it does there is no turning away from the
challenge without serious consequences.

The self is the instigator of the process of individuation.
This is true whether the process is undertaken consciously,
as in analysis, or in the dedication of oneself to a life of contemplative searching, or unconsciously, as in a commitment
to any goal which goes beyond the merely personal. The self
is the whole of psychic totality, incorporating both consciousness and the unconscious; it is also the center of this totality.
The ego belongs to it and is part of it, the ego being the
whole of consciousness at any given moment and also the
organ that is capable of becoming conscious.

From the point of view of the ego, growth and development
depend on integrating into the sphere of the ego as much as
possible of that which was formerly unknown. This unconscious content comprises two categories. The first is *knowledge*
of the world and the way it works; basically this is a function
of education of both the formal kind (schooling) and the
informal kind (empirical experience). The second category
is *wisdom*; this is essentially the understanding of human
nature including one's own nature as an individual. Thus the
goal of the individuation process as seen from the standpoint
of the ego, is the expansion of awareness.

From the point of view of the self, however, the goal of
individuation is quite different. *Where the ego was oriented
toward its own emergence from the unconscious, the self is
oriented toward union of consciousness with the unconscious.*
It may be said that life begins with the ego in the ascendency,

as the infant begins to wrest knowledge from the vast realms
of the unknown and thus to increase its competence in coping
with the ways of the world. Our whole lives are more or less
engaged in the confrontations between the ego and the unconscious, whether consciously undertaken or not. Each day
we begin with conscious intentions, and all day long we are
involved in interacting with forces within and forces without,
whose aims seem different from those we recognize as our own.
So follow the days and the years; and the ego, if one is fortunate, acquires more and more of those skills which enable
it to fulfill its needs and desires in the face of whatever opposition it incurs. But ultimately each life ends with the defeat
of the ego, however many victories it may have won during
its time. No matter how long or short the individual life
may be, the "identity" so bravely achieved by the ego gives
way to the anonymity of the unconscious. The victor of the
final battle is the self.

What then, it may be asked, is the point of all the struggle
for awareness? Why undertake the wearying and often fearsome journey? Why strain and strive and seek to know more,
when knowing more is only to open the gates to deeper mysteries? I have often pondered this question myself, and especially in my writing, as I ask myself what possesses me to sit
behind my typewriter on a beautiful summer's day when the
sky is a singing blue and the sailboats are bright in the harbor.
And you, the reader, may also be asking why you engage yourself in your own search for understanding, rather than satisfying yourself only with pleasures of the senses. I did take
time out from writing to watch the landing of the Apollo 15
mission on the moon, and to hear Astronaut Dave Scott proclaim as he set foot on the lunar surface: "As I stand out here
on the wonders of the unknown at Hadley, I sort of realize
there is a fundamental truth to our nature. Man must explore.
And this is exploration at its greatest." I do not think it is
fame, or fortune, or the need to sublimate a neurosis, that
leads people to undertake perilous journeys either outward
into space or inward into the depths of the psyche. That
"man must explore" is reason enough for the archetypal

journey. It has been sung of old as the hero's quest and though
all who undertake it are not heroes, there is a touch of the
heroic in all of us, else we could not live in this dangerous and
desperate world.

In the archetypal journey the ego winds its way between
the snares of the persona and the traps of the shadow. The
persona develops as a compromise between the intentions of
the ego along with the entire personality structure that supports it on the one hand, and the demands of society on the
other. The result is the taking on of the mask which is "a
segment of the collective psyche." Often, the ego becomes
identified with this persona. As in every compromise something is sacrificed, certain natural and spontaneous qualities
of personality fall into the unconscious, where they become
part of the shadow aspect. One of the first tasks of analysis
is to strip off the mask of persona; next, is to recognize the
shadow in its many and varied aspects. As the process continues, deeper realms of the unconscious become more and
more accessible to the ego. Each insight leads to the capacity
for further insight. Anima and animus begin to appear, and
they lead the seeker closer to the center.

I do not mean to suggest that this is all a methodical
process that advances step by step. The Jungian analysis does
not follow a set format that supposedly exists in the mind
of the analyst. The unconscious material determines the
process, and it is the analyst's task to follow where it leads,
along with the analysand who produces it. Because the persona is on the surface, it is the logical place to begin. Whatever the presenting problem which the analysand brings into
the initial session, the persona usually is a part of it. Most of
the time it can be readily recognized by the analysand; he
will generally admit quite easily that while it is a part of him
which he freely displays, it is not entirely what he envisions
as his personality in its totality. As soon as the persona is
tampered with, defenses arise to protect what lies behind it.
As the defenses are dealt with in analysis, the unconscious
aspects of the personality begin to emerge.

These unconscious aspects may appear as dream figures who

resemble people we know in our everyday lives, or dream figures who are strangers to us; they may be characters in fantasies or they may be the fantasies which we apply to real people. They may come to us out of forgotten myths and legends, or they may strike a responsive note when we meet them for the first time in literature or on the stage or screen. Or they may be brought up from our own depths through specific techniques which are used in analysis to probe the unconscious. While the figures appear to be individual, they reflect the archetypal background of the unconscious which gives rise to their formation. In this sense they may be thought of as archetypal figures.

These archetypal figures came to be crystallized by Jung as a result of his empirical observations of the vast amounts of unconscious material presented to him by his patients. They were augmented by his own inner search, a search which led him from his own dreams and fantasies to research into their parallels in myth and folklore and the history of religion. The images seemed to him to coalesce around certain themes. Jung used symbolic terms to express the themes of persona, ego, shadow, animus, anima, and so on, because the symbolic approach was the most effective way he knew to approach the area of the unknown. Anything else would have tied down and concretized something which is not to be concretized. By being too explicit we constrict the flow of thought and imagination. When we feel that we have the answer to a problem there is little reason for further exploration.

The struggle with the anima and the animus, sometimes leading us deeper into the unconscious, sometimes blocking the path, brings us into contact with other archetypal figures along the way. Each plays a role in the archetypal drama which has as its theme the fall of man from his original state of oneness with the primordial unity, to separation and loss of integrity and despair, and then at last to regeneration in a new unity that is marked by awareness of all the component parts and by harmonious functioning between them. The drama of transformation is played on many stages. The characters appear in all varieties of make-up and costume, but they are cast into certain definable types, who act in somewhat predictable ways.

The archetype of the *divine child* tends to appear in advance of a transformation in the psyche. His appearance recalls the marking of aeons in the history of the world which were heralded by the appearance of an infant who overthrows an old order and, with passion and inspiration, begins a new one. I know of no place where the power of this archetype is better expressed than in William Blake's poem, A *Song of Liberty*. The Eternal Female, the anima, gives birth to the divine child, a sun god with flaming hair. This evokes the jealous rage of the old king, the "starry king" of night and darkness and all the decadence that has come upon the world. Though the king flings the divine child into the western sea, the child will not be drowned. A night sea journey will take place and when it is finished the son of morning will rise in the east to bring his light to the world:

The Eternal Female groan'd! it was heard all over the Earth!
. . . In her trembling hands she took the new born terror, howling:
On those infinite mountains of light, now barr'd out by the atlantic
    sea, the new born fire stood before the starry king!
Flag'd with grey brow'd snows and thunderous visages, the jealous
    wings wav'd over the deep.
The speary hand burned aloft, unbuckled was the shield; forth went
    the hand of jealousy among the flaming hair, and hurl'd the
    new born wonder thro' the starry night.
The fire, the fire is falling! . . .

The fiery limbs, the flaming hair, shot like the sinking sun into
    the western sea. . . .
With thunder and fire, leading his starry hosts thro' the waste wilder-
    ness, [the gloomy king] promulgates his ten commands, glanc-
    ing his beamy eyelids over the deep in dark dismay,
Where the son of fire in his eastern cloud, while the morning plumes
    her golden breast,
Spurning the clouds written with curses, stamps the stony law to
    dust, loosing the eternal horses from the dens of night, crying:
Empire is no more! And now the Lion & Wolf shall cease.[5]

In analysis, the motif of the child frequently appears in the

course of the individuation process. At first the analysand
tends to identify this with his own infantilism, and this may
be appropriate to a degree. Wherever the appearance of the
child in dreams or other kinds of imagery bears a resemblance
to the dreamer himself, or to a form of the dreamer's behavior, the image may be helpful in understanding the personal aspects of the material itself. It may be helpful in tracing back neurotic elements to an earlier stage of development
in the individual. However, just as fantasy material may, in
part, be identifiable with the history of the one who produces
it, in part, the image of the divine child may also be new,
bearing no resemblance whatever to the previous experience
of the individual. It is this latter element that encourages the
imagination to dwell on the futurity of the archetype—that is,
to ask what this image may suggest about developments which
are still embryonic in the psyche but which have the potentiality for growth and change.

As our own children are, to a certain extent, extensions of
our own egos, so the "divine child" may be thought of as an
extension of the collective consciousness. As we pin our hopes
and dreams on our children, wishing for them the fulfillment
of our unfinished tasks, the realization of what we were never
able to realize—so the "divine child" represents the ideals of
a culture which it is not able, in reality, to fulfill. Often the
"savior" becomes the scapegoat for the sins of his society, and
by reason of his suffering and his sacrifice the society is enabled to continue, to have another chance.

The divine child is unusual from the very circumstances of
his birth, or even of his conception. Perhaps he is taken from
his mother in order to prevent some dire fate to the family
or the community. Moses, Oedipus and Krishna were taken
from their mothers and reared by strangers; Romulus and
Remus were abandoned to the wilderness; all of these children were saved for a special mission. Some miraculous design
kept them safe until the time was ripe for their task to be
fulfilled. In the intervening years the child would overcome
many difficulties, and develop his own sense of meaning and
a style of living which expresses that meaning. At the appro-

priate time hc manifests himself and brings into reality that dynamic change for which he was appointed. Shortly thereafter he dies, having accomplished that for which he came.[6]

In our own dreams the appearance of the special child often carries with it a profound meaning. In my practice I have found that it is common for a child who is maimed or ill or dying to appear in a dream. This may have no correspondence to the life of the individual, and so I find myself wondering— in what way is the dreamer's innate potential being distorted or cut off? The analysis of the specific details in the unconscious material, and some comparison with similar details as they appear in the archetypal situations in the literature of myth and comparative religion may enable the individual to get beyond his immediate concern and to see where he is going in terms of his life task. As Viktor Frankl pointed out in *Man's Search for Meaning*, his report on his concentration camp experiences, those who regarded their lives in the camp as "provisional" and lived only from day to day quickly lost their strength. The few who were able to find through their suffering in a place where their physical bodies were imprisoned, the challenge to free their spirits, these few tended to survive against nearly impossible odds. The divine child within us gives meaning to our immature strivings; he shows us the unconscious side of the limitations which we experience, and that is a vision of potentiality coming into flower.

Another archetype which we are likely to meet along the way of individuation has been called by Jung the *puer aeternus*, after the child god Iachhus in the Eleusinian mysteries.[7] He is described by Ovid in *Metamorphoses* as a divine youth, born into the mother-cult mysteries. A god of vegetation and resurrection, he has some of the qualities of the redeemer. The man who is identified with the archetype of the puer aeternus, with eternal youth, is one who has remained too long in adolescent psychology. In him, characteristics which are normal in a youth in his teens are continued into later life.[8] Perhaps the expression "high living" best describes what this archetype is about: the young man indulges his high-flying fantasies, living out experiences for their sheer excitement, picking up friends when he wants amusement and dropping them when they become in any sense a responsibility. Some of the heroes of the youth culture fall into this category, and again, for some "getting high" is the objective in and of itself. The aimless traveling, moving in and out of various groups, is characteristic of the puer. Homosexuality is an expression of this archetype, especially when homosexuality takes the form of casual and promiscuous relationships, compulsively arrived at. If he is heterosexually inclined, he forms one liaison after another, only to drop each one at the first suggestion that some commitment may be required of him.

Von Franz, in her study of the puer aeternus archetype[9] suggests that the man who is identified with this archetype often seeks a career in flying, but that he is usually rejected on application for the reason that psychological tests show up his instability and the neurotic reasons for his interest in this profession.

The dreams of an individual who is established in his life in a secure position, who may be already middle-aged, may disclose the operation of the puer aeternus archetype. The motifs of flying (sometimes without any plane, just by flapping the arms) high-speed driving, deep-sea diving, climbing precarious mountain cliffs, are all typical of one whose unconscious is dominated by this archetype. They may be taken as a warning signal to be aware of the ways in which the unconscious may be preparing to intrude its autonomous will in the way of consciously determined functioning.

There is, of course, a feminine counterpart to the puer and that is the *puella aeterna*, the woman who is afraid to grow old, although she will never admit it. Still, the fear dominates much of her existence. She is the one who never tells her age, who falls for every diet fad and for every new make-up with the fantastic promise of rejuvenation written into the advertisements. She is a "pal" to her children, and an everlasting coquette where men are concerned. In her dreams she is often on a pedestal, inspiring the adoration of men, or she is a siren or a whore or a nymphet. In life she generally is reckless and impulsive. When it comes to making an important decision, however, she vacillates a good deal and asks many people for advice. She then acts with surprising suddenness, and she regrets her actions almost before they are completed.

Living the archetype of "eternal youth" is not altogether negative, as may be inferred from some of the ways we see it manifest itself. Some aspects of the puer aeternus or the puella aeterna which are most helpful are youthful enthusiasm and the boundless energy to carry it along, spontaneity of thinking, production of new ideas and new ways to solve problems, willingness to strike out in a different direction without being held in by a desire to conserve the past and its values.

The puer puella as unconscious factors provide the needed impetus to start out on new paths. They do not necessarily offer the wisdom to discern whether the endeavor is worth the struggle, and they often do not provide the steadying and staying power to carry it through if, indeed, it is worth while. When this archetype is active great dreams and schemes will be hatched. If they are to succeed, even in the smallest part, a compensatory archetype must come into play. This is the "senex" archetype.[10]

Senex means old or aged, and, as archetype, it stands behind the forces that would preserve the traditional values, that hold out for keeping things the way they are, for applying sober judgment and consideration to the schemes of the eternal youth. At best this factor in the unconscious is expressed in mature wisdom born of experience, and, at worst, it represents a hidebound orthodoxy that tolerates no interference from those who would break with established patterns.

A variant of the figure of the puer aeternus, sometimes even incorporating aspects of the senex, is the enchanting archetypal figure who is known as *the trickster*. Of him, Jung says:

> Anyone who belongs to a sphere of culture that seeks the perfect state somewhere in the past must feel very queerly indeed when confronted by the figure of the trickster. He is a forerunner of the saviour, and, like him, God, man, and animal

at once. He is both subhuman and superhuman, a bestial and divine being, whose chief and most alarming characteristic is his unconsciousness. Because of it he is deserted by his (evidently human) companions, which seems to indicate that he has fallen below their level of consciousness. He is so unconscious of himself that his body is not a unity, and his two hands fight each other. He takes his anus off and entrusts it with a special task. Even his sex is optional despite its phallic qualities: he can turn himself into a woman and bear children. From his penis he makes all kinds of useful plants. This is in reference to his original nature as a Creator, for the world is made from the body of a god.[11]

The contradictory figure of the trickster has been associated with the carnival in the medieval Church, and today is present at such affairs as the Mardi Gras and the celebration of Fastnacht in Switzerland—festivals which precede the somber holy days and which are marked with merriment and partying and jokes of all kinds—when the natural, simple nature of people can be given full expression. He fits the medieval description of the devil as "the ape of God," and in folklore as the simpleton of whom everyone takes advantage.

We experience the trickster in our individual lives just when we are most unsuspecting. We meet him when we find ourselves at the mercy of the most annoying "accidents." A woman recently received an award for unusual distinction. She did not feel she had properly earned it, indeed, it was something of a fluke and all the more embarrassing because there was newspaper publicity about it. She received many letters of congratulation which she felt obliged to answer personally. However she had no more than just begun to write when she got up for a glass of water, stumbled over her own doorstep, and broke her right arm.

In dreams the trickster is the one who sets obstacles in our path for his own reasons; he is the one who keeps changing shape and appearing and disappearing at the oddest moments. He symbolizes that aspect of our own nature which is always nearby, ready to bring us down when we get inflated, or to humanize us when we become pompous. He is the satirist par excellence, whose trenchant wit points out the flaws in our haughty ambitions, and makes us laugh though we feel like crying. In society we find him as critic or gadfly, and he even pops up in the highest offices of our land.

The major psychological function of the trickster figure is to make it possible for us to gain a sense of proportion about ourselves. This he does by testing and trying us, so that we discover what we are made of. His motto might well be, "If the fool would persist in his folly, he would become wise."[12]

The figures of the divine child who becomes a hero or savior, the puer aeternus and his feminine counterpart, senex and the trickster, are only some of the aspects under which the archetypal forming-elements of the psyche may appear. There is no need to go into all the possibilities here, except to say that in principle they are unlimited, but that each individual encounters those archetypes which are relevant to his particular individual myth. Incorporating these various unconscious aspects into the sphere of consciousness divests them of their uncanny power to influence the individual unaware. They can be seen instead in both their positive and negative aspects, and the individual is then free to make his own choice from the various possibilities they offer. It is not an easy matter to integrate these contents of the unconscious. It is a long, hard task that is never completed because the unconscious is too vast to be brought into the domain of the ego. It is possible, however, to become well-enough acquainted with the forces at work in us below the level of consciousness so that we become familiar with their tricks and devices, and are able to recognize them through illusion and disguise.

The anima and the animus are probably the most difficult to integrate of all the unconscious contents. This may be because anima and animus are tied up with our sexual drives on one hand, and the utter mystery of their otherness on the other. We are both desirous and frightened of these mighty figures, yet the anima or animus, as the case may be, must become a part of our conscious experience if we are ever to approximate the ultimate goal of wholeness.

An aim of analysis is to reach a state where enough of the

unconscious contents become conscious so that they no longer need to express themselves as those anima and animus functions which interfere with relationships, inhibit productivity and undermine the possibility of inner peace. This means that the animus and anima are capable of being rescued from their roles as autonomous complexes. When this occurs, they lose their negative charge and become partners with the ego in what has been described as the inner marriage. The man is no longer anima-possessed, nor the woman animus-possessed. Each sees the function of the contrasexual part as a guide to those further mysteries of the unconscious which will arise out of the necessity of human curiosity.

The conquest of the anima or the animus and its integration into our own lives as a consciously experienced guide to the unconscious releases us from the kinds of conflicts brought about by the projections of these inner figures onto women and men whom we know. As the projections are withdrawn, the complex of energy that was bound up in the projection is also withdrawn. What this means practically is that a woman stops blaming her "lack of opportunity" on the construction of her genitalia, or on the prejudices of society, and begins to consider her own self-image as a possible basis for the inadequacy she feels. Instead of trying to be what she thinks will "succeed" in the world, or "what the world wants," she resolves to turn her attention to becoming more fully what it is her authentic nature to be. Jung describes the comparable situation as it applies to the man who has reached this stage of development with respect to "the conquest of the anima as an autonomous complex, and her transformation into a function of relationship between the conscious and the unconscious." He says: "With the attainment of this goal it becomes possible to disengage the ego from all its entanglements with the collectivity and the collective unconscious. Through this process the anima forfeits the daemonic power of an autonomous complex; she can no longer exercise the power of possession, since she is depotentiated."[13]

The process of individuation can then move on in its spiraling path, circumambulating the center, which is the self. As, one by one, complexes arising from the archetypal configurations lose their power over the individual, one would expect the ego to experience a new freedom, a relatively complex-free state. It is true that much energy is released and the individual feels expanded, uninhibited, open to the storms of the world and able to withstand them. The new sense of power that he experiences will very often endow the individual with a sense of his own very great importance. He is now "enlightened," no longer subject to the moods and tensions or the neurotic defenses that had previously been a load on his personality. Now he feels he can do just about whatever he sets out to accomplish, and, most particularly, that he is well qualified to advise anyone who comes to him with any problem. He is at once a "man of action" and a "sage."

The feeling of being able to subjugate nature through the use of this special power is, of course, not always what it seems to be to the person who experiences it. If one is able to resolve a conflict that had been absorbing his attention and consequently his energy, he may claim the mana—the power—that formerly was caught in the conflict, as his own. He may hold the conviction that he is able to exert his unusual power upon others. At the same time he may appear ridiculous to others who recognize the limitations to which he, the individual, is momentarily blinded. The truth is that the individual does not possess the mana himself, but rather is possessed by it, in the sense of demonic possession.

Mana is a Polynesian term having to do with power. The meaning can best be expressed by the concept of the "virtue" that resides in a man, or the "grace" that descends upon him. He who holds it is someone particularly blessed. In the beliefs of many primitive tribes [the Malays, the Malagasy, various African people, and some American Indians] disembodied souls (ghosts) and spirits (which were incorporeal) possess mana. Psychologically speaking, mana appears as a sense of unusual psychic energy. It may be experienced as a result of dealing successfully with archetypal phenomena. Or, after an experience in which a difficult problem is solved, mana may be felt as a tremendous sense of vigor.

The danger comes with identification with the mana-personality. Folk heroes from television dramas, Hell's Angels and the like, provide plenty of models of "mana" for young people today just at the age when they are breaking away from parental controls. Following the promise of mana, the young are willing to take unbelievable risks, in everything from drag racing, to hitchhiking in distant countries, to ingesting dangerous drugs without any notion of their source, strength or potential effect. The attitude may be something like this: I can do it, I can make it doing the forbidden thing, for the power to control myself is in me. I know that to gain knowledge demands experience, and that involves risk. But I have the power to overcome the dangers involved.

The situation is classical. It goes back at least as far as Phaëthon, the Greek teen-ager who had boasted to his friends that his father was Helios, the sun god, and had to prove it. Old Helios had warned him that he would never make it, for though his father was a god, he was a mortal on his mother's side. Disregarding the well-meant advice, Phaëthon waited around until the gates of morning were opened, sprang into the sun-chariot and was off on a mad, ecstatic ride through the heavens that ended with hero, chariot and horses falling headlong into the sea.

Reference was made to this myth at the time of the assassination of John Kennedy, who, people said, behaved as if he had a feeling of invincibility. The many risks he had taken throughout his life were climaxed by the last risk, that of refusing to accept the bulletproof covering for his limousine on that fateful day in Dallas. He and others appear to have been acting on the premise that they were endowed with the magic power—mana—which would save them from harm.

So, too, with Icarus, son of the architect of Crete who was imprisoned with his father in the labyrinth he had designed, with all exits barred. Daedalus carefully collected feathers of birds, and with these and the wax from candles, he fashioned wings. Then he and Icarus took flight. Daedalus warned his son to fly low over the sea but Icarus, possessed by this new and wonderful sense of power, soared delightedly up and up, paying no heed to his father's anguished commands. The heat of the sun melted the wax, and the youth fell to his death.

There are those who feel that the power is their own, and who believe it to be entirely under the control of the ego. Forgetting to reckon with the unconscious dimension of their natures, with the important forces within them which they are able to understand to a degree, but not to control completely, they are overcome by the real power. The problem is that they really do not know where the mana lies.

An analysand of mine had reached an important turning point in his analysis. Ever since Walter could remember he had been repressing his emotions in any situation where expressing them might have involved taking the risk of being rejected. He ascribed his tense, inhibited manner of functioning to the pattern established in childhood of pleasing his mother, whose rigid rules and requirements allowed no room for the spontaneity of youth. "If I ever said anything wrong, she would let me know how worthless I was, so I hardly ever said anything to her." Whatever emotions there were could be invested in religious fervor, since the family belonged to a church which preached man's complete submission to the will of an authoritarian God who would look out for his own, provided that they adhered closely to his requirements. There was no mercy anywhere. A torturous process was required in order to uncover complexes that had built up over the years and had blocked off normal feelings and responses to people and situations. It seemed for a long time that it would be impossible for Walter to ever gain a sense of personal value. Every time he would make a step in that direction, he would set up a situation in which he would be rejected, and rejected he was, in nearly every area except in his analysis. It was difficult for me to withstand his constant criticism and attacks on me without becoming personally aroused, and the only thing that saved me was the awareness that it was not the man himself who was deliberately trying to wreck the analysis, but the demonic element in him, from which he suffered far more than I did.

The anima problem was foremost, since the face which the

anima had shown him in the past was that of the all-powerful Great Mother in her terrible aspect. Walter kept projecting that image onto me in every way the unconscious could devise. I continued to behave in a manner contrary to his image until, little by little he had to expand the concept of the feminine so as to include his experience with me. I had to walk the fine line between putting him under the same kind of pressure he had felt coming from his mother, and encouraging him in any way. The difficulties extended into the most minute matters. An example of the first instance occurred when one day he brought a raincoat and placed it in my closet. As he was leaving I noticed that he was forgetting to take it on his way out. I immediately knew that if I reminded him of it, I would be for him the mother who scolded him for his forgetfulness, and that if I did not remind him he would have to come back for it, and in doing so would run the risk of interrupting my next session and incurring my "maternal anger." There was no way to win; the only possibility was to openly discuss the problem that presented itself so that he, too, could participate in the process of dealing with it. In the second instance, when he had one day come to some important insights, I was caught between deemphasizing them by an attitude of neutrality, in which case he would feel himself again as undervalued, or commending him. I did the latter, and he seemed pleased and relieved at the end of the session. Later on that night he got into a panic, having concluded that I would be expecting similar insights from him every time he came for analysis, and that he would be incapable of gaining them, so that inevitably his sham would be out in the open. Again, I had to confront him directly with the problem.

After dealing with innumerable problems arising from consideration of the autonomous elements of the psyche, Walter began to get better. He loosened up, became able to speak more freely and openly. In his work, his relationships with his coworkers improved considerably. His marriage was the only area that failed to improve. Among other problems, he was impotent with his wife, which was not surprising. He had

married a younger edition of his mother, a woman who took
no interest in his development and who took every opportunity to depreciate his analytic work. The only weapon he
had against her (and of course this was at first totally unconscious) was to deprive her of sexual satisfaction. On the
rare occasions that he felt sexually aroused, he would overcome the feeling with alcohol or sedatives.

After many a battle, the slaying of the dragon finally took
place when he had become free enough in his emotional life
to establish a warm relationship with another woman. Also
in his professional contacts with women he became more relaxed. He rejoiced, feeling that at last he had overcome the
negative anima. He was a changed man, enjoying life as never
before, pouring new energy into his work and into his relationship with women. He even managed to be more engaging
and pleasant to his family at home than he had been in years.

At this point Walter had a short but extremely important
dream. It was characterized, as such dreams often are, by the
recollection of every nuance of the strong emotion that accompanied it. Here is the dream: *I dreamed that I was Christ
and was doing the things he did for people. When I awoke
I found the dream made me quite uncomfortable, so I kind
of tended to change it into seeing colored slides of Christ
in different situations.*

For a man who has formerly thought of himself as worthless, to dream of himself as Christ is evidence that he has
identified himself with the mana of the Christ figure. In light
of the circumstances of the man's life, the evidence was confirmed. The unconscious had presented the problem in symbolic terms, and with its uncanny wisdom had also offered
the possibility of correcting the abnormal condition of possession by the archetype of the mana-personality.

To be Christ means, according to the dream, not just holding the power to accomplish whatever he wants to do. It requires that the one who has the mana be the one who actually
does the things that the Christ figure was able to do, and
to do them "for people." This does not mean saving one's
own soul, for this was the least of Christ's concerns, and the

dreamer readily admitted that. The dream had pointed out that it was necessary to bring matters down to size, for the dreamer to disentangle himself from the archetype and to see himself with his own human limitations, while at the same time holding before himself the image of a savior whose power derives from that "otherness" which is beyond the capacity of the ego to assume.

The mana-personality appears in many forms, but what they all have in common is a superior ability to subjugate nature which is not available to ordinary man. The mana-personality is a godlike person. Sometimes the priest assumes this role and sometimes it is associated with him. But the mana-personality is also the wizard, the sorcerer, or the medicine man. In our time the archetype is projected onto the magnetic men and women who capture the imagination and the loyalty of their admirers and all the more if they can die a violent death or by their own hands: Marilyn Monroe, Jimi Hendrix, Janis Joplin, even Charles Manson. Frequently, the mana is associated with the heads of state, the doctor, the analyst, or the great spiritual leader.

One of my analysands dreamed: *I come home from work early because my boss had sent me away due to some misunderstanding. I am in my apartment and I know that Dr. Jung is down the hall. I get up the courage and knock on his door. It is still early evening, but he is getting ready for bed, in pajamas. I ask him over for a drink. He comes over. I can find nothing to say. He finally says, why did you ask me over? I still say nothing. Then I tell him I am in analysis. He gets up to go, but motions for me to come over to his room. When we get there he takes two small liqueur glasses and pours a black liqueur into them. Handing me one, he says, "You must drink this cup with me."*

The dream suggests that the power comes through the agency of the revered teacher figure, but it must be sought, accepted, and assimilated by the dreamer. In the phase of analysis in which the mana-personality is constellated, the marriage quaternio, which we discussed previously in relation to the emergence into awareness of anima and animus, now un-

dergoes a change. By this time the shadow has already been
integrated for the most part; and this is what has made it
possible to devote the major attention to the contrasexual
aspect of the psyche. The relationship is again fourfold. In
the man it looks like this: the man, as ego, faces a real woman
with whom he is in a relationship. The third element is
the transcendent anima. The missing fourth element that
would make the triad a quaternity is the archetype of the
mana-personality, an Old Wise Man whose power is born of
understanding the timeless life processes which are never fully
comprehended consciously. A corresponding configuration appears in the psyche of the woman in this phase. She has a
conscious relationship with a man, and this is transcended
or underlaid, if you will, by her relationship to the animus
within. The missing fourth element is the deeply intuitive
feminine wisdom, the Primordial Mother. This is the new

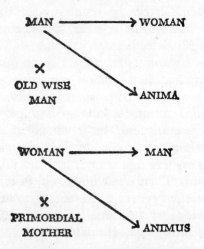

marriage quaternio. It has been called an inner experience,
although no experience is entirely "inner" in my view. Everything which is seen subjectively or from an "inner" viewpoint has its impact in the way the one who experiences it
behaves in the world as a result of the experience. Conversely,
whatever happens in the world touches the "inner" experience

and shapes and refines it in some way so that an impact is made on the unconscious.

The attainment of this second marriage quaternio is a precondition for the realization of the self. A marriage quaternio is, in Jung's words, "half immanent and half transcendent."[14] That which is immanent in it is the aspect through which the self is related to human understanding, even within the limitations of its finitude. That which is transcendent in it is the aspect through which the self is related to the unconscious, to the impenetrable, to the infinite and the unreachable. This is why Jung has said of the self, "The self . . . is a God image, or at least cannot be distinguished from one. Of this the early Christian spirit was not ignorant, otherwise Clement of Alexandria could never have said that he who knows himself knows God."[15]

The major work of the analytic process is the uncovering of unconscious contents and their assimilation into the ego. Jung makes this clear when he says that "the more numerous and the more significant the unconscious contents which are assimilated to the ego, the closer the approximation of the ego to the self, even though this approximation must be a never-ending process."[16] We have seen how this tends to produce an inflation of the ego, an unwarranted sense of its own capacity and potentiality. The only help for this is the clear differentiation of the ego from the unconscious contents: "I am not that, although that represents an element in my total nature. The better I know it, the less it will exert control over me." Jung warns against the attempt to psychologize the unconscious components of the personality out of existence. By our very nature we are in part conscious and in part unconscious, and we rest on the threshold between the two. As well try to escape this as to escape the necessity for sleep at the end of each day. The more we try to escape, the more it overcomes us, but the more willingly we accept it, the fresher and stronger we will be for it.

In our discussions of the shadow, the anima and animus, and other figures of the unconscious, we have seen that the symbols which infuse these archetypal forms are limitless.

Each man draws from the residue of human experience those palpable symbols which for him best evoke the images of the invisible and mysterious archetypal elements which are, in themselves, forming tendencies without specific content.

The self is also expressed symbolically, in images of many kinds. It is beyond the scope of this work to attempt to describe or even to name the basic symbols. Jung has made the exploration of these symbols the subject of several of his major works.[17] Of all the symbolic expressions of the self, the circle or sphere seems best to give shape to the ideas of the self's centrality, its extensity and its encompassing character. The circle as center and circumference is a symbol that is, of course, not exclusively Jung's, but one which has appeared as a motif in every sphere of man's endeavor, and in every corner of the world he knows. It is a motif in art and design, and, since the invention of the wheel, is an important element of technology. The circle is a synonym for a social group; a model for a city, a wedding ring or a royal diadem. Its path may be traced over and over again for it has no beginning and no end. As such it carries the meaning of everlasting life, for it is birth and life, death and resurrection, in an unceasing chain. Likewise, it is the journey of the sun hero crossing the sky in an arc from east to west by day and, from dusk's descent, returning under the night sea to dawn's arising. As such the circular path is the analogue for the way of individuation.

Mandala is the Sanskrit word for circle; it means more especially a magic circle. The circular design with the virtue of power attached to it is found in the East, where it is frequently seen in a *yantra*, an object used to focus the attention in meditative practice. It is also prominent in our own culture; the rose-window of the medieval Church structure provides an excellent example of the mandala. So, also, do certain of the sand paintings of the Navajo Indians. Jerusalem, the City of God, as described in the Book of Revelation is a mandala city. The gates on every side lead into the center, and in the center is the image of God in the mind of man.[18]

A suffering human being comes into analysis. He has lost

the sense of primordial wholeness that represents the paradise of innocence. He is troubled, feels separated from the world or from the mystery which he intuitively knows as his real self. His equilibrium is shaken. He needs to be made whole again. He needs to be reunited with that from which he has departed. I must tell you that in my experience I have seen many who have approached this task, but only a few who have fulfilled its arduous demands. Most people give up somewhere along the way, often very much helped by their participation in the process even though they have not seen it through as far as it can go. For many, the disappearance of nagging, annoying or blocking symptoms is sufficient, and when this is accomplished they can return to their everyday concerns. For some, and this refers especially to younger people, some psychological problem interferes with their ongoing lives, and it has only to be removed or overcome for the individual to terminate in therapy and get on with the business of living. Others go further and take into themselves as much of unconscious contents as they can comfortably deal with, and let the rest go awhile, perhaps forever, perhaps until another situation arises which demands returning to the confrontation with the unconscious. Any of these people may be changed to a greater or lesser degree through their experience of analysis, limited though it may be.

The journey into self takes as long as it takes, and when it has been long enough, both the analyst and the analysand know it. I cannot tell you how we know it, but it is clear. Not that the questing is ever truly over, for it lasts as long as life itself; but there comes a time when the individual is able to carry on the search by himself and this becomes evident to him through changes in his life and confirmed by his dreams.

For a long time Mark and I knew that his analysis was drawing to a close. It had gone through many phases and his whole personality had greatly changed in the process. He had developed from a frightened, inadequate young man to one who was moving toward recognized goals, with sureness and confidence and absolute humility. Toward the end we had spaced the sessions wider and wider apart as he acquired the independence successfully to interpret his own unconscious material. There was an affectionate tie between us, for we had joined hands in a complicated and trying mutual endeavor. Still, the analysis was not ended, although we were both aware that soon it must end.

To the last session he brought two dreams, which had come to him just a week apart. These are the dreams.

The first: *I am in an airplane which is flying over the mountains. It is a stormy day, and the passengers are upset as the plane rises and falls upon hitting air pockets. I go about the cabin reassuring people, calming them, making sure that everyone is securely fastened in his seat. I look to see where the exits are and I plan in my head how I will handle an evacuation if we should make a forced landing. I am not afraid, and I am prepared for whatever might happen. But we do not have to land there in the mountains after all.*

The second dream: *Again I am in an airplane, but this is a small one, a two-seater. I am beside the pilot. We find ourselves in difficulty. This time we are over a deep forest. We are not far from the treetops, and the pilot is trying very hard to handle the controls. I say, I think I can manage it, I'd like to try. I take over the controls as the pilot exchanges places with me. The wheel is very hard to handle. It takes all my strength, but I am determined to hold through. I look around and notice that the pilot is perfectly relaxed. The wheel now becomes more responsive to my direction. It is still difficult, but now I know that I am going to make it.*

There was not much to say after this. Both Mark and I knew that he was ready to take charge of his own life. He had learned as much as I could help him with, and now it was time for him to go away. At the door, we embraced as he was leaving. He looked back at me and smiled as he went down the hall. I smiled back at him. Only after the door had closed did I realize that my eyes were wet. In good times as well as in bad, it is a hard thing to be an analyst.

11

UNDERSTANDING
OUR DREAMS

I believe that the experience of dreaming is the clearest proof
we have that the unconscious exists. The inner life of an individual unfolds through dreams, and whoever carefully observes his dreams may gain access to dimensions of his nature
that would otherwise remain impenetrable. The way we approach our dreams depends very much upon our own attitude
toward the unconscious.

Long before they met, both Freud and Jung were committed to the importance of interpreting dreams as a means
of gaining access to unconscious processes. Freud's monumen-
tal study, *The Interpretation of Dreams*, provided a basis for
experimentation by the members of the Vienna psychoanalytic
circle. This group collected a great deal of dream material
from their patients to provide the basis for their scientific
research. They discussed methods of treating mental disorders
and advanced new theories about the way hidden processes
of the mind affected attitudes and behavior. A controversial
aspect of psychoanalysis was its insistence that dreams not
only contained important clues to the unknown, but that they
were also a means to healing. Freud showed that the conscious mind resists the pressure of uncomfortable ideas. Non-
psychoanalytically oriented doctors and psychologists objected
that the psychoanalysts were exposing aspects of the human

personality that they would have preferred to ignore. No one likes to have his secret wishes revealed, or to be told that beneath apparently respectable adult behavior there lurk unresolved sexual conflicts, or even infantile, incestuous aspirations. Under the most virulent kind of criticism, Freud steadfastly maintained his theoretical position.

During their early years together Jung supported this position publicly, against the advice of his elder professional colleagues in Zurich, and knowing that by doing so he was risking his promising career in academic medicine. In 1909 Jung published a paper entitled "The Analysis of Dreams,"[1] which is a straight explication of Freud's theory of dream interpretation. At that time he agreed fully with Freud's contention that dreaming, like everything else we do, has a meaning that does not arise out of bodily sensations felt during sleep, or even out of the events of the day. These merely furnish the elements upon which the psychological processes do their work. He explained how Freud saw the manifest content of the dream as a cover story for the real situation of the dreamer, which had to be a state of conflict between a repressed wish seeking expression and the need to keep the wish unconscious. In this essay, Jung made a passing reference to the possibility of getting to the latent content of the dream—the story hidden behind the dream events—through the use of the association experiment. Then he went on to explain how Freud would use the entirely different method of "free association" to lead back to the real basis of the dream.

Emerging differences in approach to dream material became explicit in 1909, during a lecture trip to the United States which Jung and Freud made together. They saw each other daily on board ship and spent a good deal of time analyzing one another's dreams. In the very uncomfortable process, each must have withdrawn from the other in terms of revealing his own inner life. Jung described the whole affair in his autobiography. From his point of view this encounter foreshadowed the dissolution of the relationship. Freud had presented a dream of his own, and Jung had indicated that he could do much better in interpreting it if he knew some more details

about Freud's private life. Freud is said to have regarded Jung
in that moment with a look of "utmost suspicion" and to
have replied, "But I cannot risk my authority!" For Jung, in
that moment he had already lost it.[2]

Jung also related a dream to Freud at that time, a dream
which Jung regarded as extremely important. It showed him
descending through several levels of a house, each level representing an earlier period of history, until at last he was in
a low cave cut into a rock, with thick dust on the floor and
in the dust scattered bones and broken pottery and a couple
of human skulls, all like remains of a primitive culture. For
Jung the dream was a gripping experience; it seemed to him
as a ritual of passage from the personal unconscious into the
collective unconscious, where the remnants of his archaic heritage rested.

Freud had paid relatively little attention as Jung related
the succession of downward transitions which brought the
dreamer from a cheerful room such as might have been inhabited by his grandparents, to older and more ancient dwell-
ing places, the deepest of which contained only the two skulls
as evidence that it had ever been a human habitation. Out
of all this wealth of dream material, what Freud had focused
upon was the two skulls. He hinted that these must be some
manifestations of a death wish, for were not all dreams insti-
gated by an unfulfilled wish in the unconscious? He demanded
that Jung say whose the skulls were.

Jung knew perfectly well what Freud was driving at, but
he could not see the dream in purely personal terms. Yet
he was still somewhat sensitive about challenging the older
man, or at least about doing so openly. Jung found his own
way to the significance of the dream, after he rejected Freud's
interpretation. He was unable to agree with Freud that a
dream is a façade behind which the meaning lies hidden—"a
meaning already known but maliciously, so to speak, withheld
from consciousness."[3] Jung saw the dream as an image of the
dreamer's unconscious psychic situation, expressed in symbolic
terms that could be unravelled to reveal an underlying
meaning.

In this particular dream, Jung saw the house as representing an image of his own psychological space, with the room on the upper story referring to the conscious level with its experiences of everyday life. Below were the strata of the unconscious, retreating into successively greater depths, each one being farther removed from personal experience and embodying more and more of the collective nature of mankind in which all individuals participate. The deepest layer to which the dream allowed him to penetrate displayed the most primitive aspect of his own psyche. The skulls were decaying images of the primitive aspects of his own nature, far removed from conscious functioning, but still contributing their substance to the fundamentals of his individual personality. Jung thought that those skulls were as much a part of his psychological heritage as remainders of the genetic patterns of our ancestors are a part of our biological heritage. The latter is apparent in our physical structures, while the former is manifested in dreams and images and visions and, paradoxically, in "new" ideas.

The dream proved an important factor in bringing Jung's growing awareness of the collective aspect of the psyche into conflict with Freud's more personalistic approach to the dream. Many years later Freud was able to integrate into his own theory, his realization of the role of the "archaic heritage" in the life of the individual. At this time, however, the disparity between the approaches of the two men to the dream was a source of crucial conflicts. These served to stimulate Jung's own unconscious processes. He questioned: "On what premises is Freudian psychology founded? To what category of human thought does it belong? What is the relationship of its almost exclusive personalism to general historical assumptions?"[4]

By 1914, several of Freud's closest collaborators, including Jung, had broken away from the Vienna circle in order to work in settings where they could treat their own patients without being bound by what seemed to them a rigid orthodoxy. None of the dissenters challenged Freud's assumption that dreams were meaningful phenomena, but all of them

disputed to some extent the specific kinds of meaning he ascribed to dreams and the techniques he employed to interpret
them. Jung was dissatisfied with the emphasis Freud placed
on wish fulfillment, and also with what seemed to him to
be Freud's overvaluation of the sexual aspect of the unconscious.

Not that Jung denied the importance of the unconscious
wish in the formation of dreams. He recognized the role of
this factor, and saw how exploring the element of the unfulfilled wish could often lead the investigator back to the antecedent factors behind the formation of a particular dream. He
had some skepticism about the use of this approach as a standard technique, however, for he felt that the analyst and
analysand need not engage in a long and distracting search
for the origin of the dream when the immediate situation
in which the dream took place could provide all the information necessary to proceed with diagnosis and treatment.

An example from my own practice will show how a dream
which was brought to the second analytic session enabled me
to move in on the problem of the analysand without first
recovering irrelevant sexual details of the patient's childhood.
Alex, twenty-nine, had drifted from job to job over the past
several years. In discussing his jobs, there was always something wrong with the employer or with "conditions." His objective seemed to be to make as much money as possible while
expending as little effort as possible. In his sex life he was always haunting the dating bars for a good-looking girl whom he
could get into bed as quickly as possible. He had come into
analysis with the statement that life was empty and meaningless for him, that he was bored, and that he was afraid to
get married because he had never stayed with anything he
had started. He came to me for help saying, "I hope you
can do something for me."

I did not accept Alex unequivocally in the initial session.
I told him that we would give it a three-month trial to see
if he was able to make the kind of commitment that an analytical relationship requires. He returned the following week
for the second session, and brought this dream: *I am fooling*

around with a bolt that is about three inches long and a quar-
ter of an inch in diameter. I have a nut but can't seem to
find the way to get the nut and bolt together and I ask you
to help. You place your hands on mine and show me how,
by patient and careful movements, I can get them to fit to-
gether perfectly.

The symbolism of the nut and bolt was "obvious" to Alex.
He was sure that the root of his difficulties was his inability
to find the right way to get along with women. This was,
in his eyes, the result of a long history of failure with women;
it probably stemmed from his early problems with his mother,
he said. This was in fact why he had decided to come to
a woman analyst. He felt that if he could somehow re-enact
his early history with an analyst who would substitute for
his mother, that he might be able to get to the bottom of
his inability to find sexual fulfillment on a stable basis. He
had pinned his hopes on me; I was the one who would help
him. He saw the dream as expressing his "unconscious" wish,
that my help, my laying on of hands, would solve his
problems.

I realized what Alex was up to. He wanted to take control
of the process, and to lead it back to the events of childhood
where we could spend many sessions reviewing his early history including all his childhood frustrations. I suspected that
when this did not produce quick results he might follow his
characteristic pattern, saying, "I tried analysis, but it just
didn't work out. I know why I can't get along with women,
but that doesn't really help to change things." Alex was like
so many people who seek psychotherapy in order to absolve
themselves of the responsibility for their failure to come to
grips with their own reality. The act of sitting with an analyst
is supposed to work a miracle. You come and talk about yourself, you reveal your secrets, you pay your bills, and you wait
for something to happen. There is little or no change, and
heaven knows you have tried, so it must be the analyst's fault.

I followed the practice described by Jung of looking into
the context of the dream itself, instead of moving back in
time to try to find the supposed "cause" of Alex's difficulties.[5]

This is based on the principle that the dream really means what it says. The unconscious presents a point of view which enlarges, completes, or compensates the conscious attitude. Through the dream it supplies the missing elements of which the ego is unaware, thus exercising its function of striving toward wholeness.

To discover what is missing from the conscious viewpoint, it is helpful to *amplify the associations* to specific elements of the dream itself. This means to widen the associations by bringing to them analogous material from myth and fantasy which has the power to illuminate the dream symbolism. Even in Alex's very brief dream there were numerous such elements. I was interested, first of all, in the associations that he would bring to the material of the dream.

I asked him what he thought "fooling around" meant. He supposed it meant playing with something, not taking it very seriously. I asked him whether he thought fooling around was purposeful activity. No, he felt it was idle or aimless. We explored some other meanings. To fool is to speak in jest, to joke, to tamper with something carelessly or ignorantly. It can also mean to deceive another person, or to take advantage of him. As these meanings came out, I could see that Alex was growing distinctly uncomfortable as he considered the role the dream portrayed him in.

The next elements of dream material were the nut and the bolt. Alex was sure that the bolt was a penis and the nut was a vagina. And clearly the root of his problem was that he couldn't get the two together properly. Or was it?

Jung's research had led him to say: "The sexual language of dreams is not always to be interpreted in a concretistic way . . . it is, in fact, an archaic language which naturally uses all the analogies readiest to hand without their necessarily coinciding with a real sexual content . . . As soon as you take the sexual metaphors as symbols for something unknown, your conception of the nature of dreams at once deepens . . . So long as the sexual language of dreams is understood concretistically, there can be only a direct, outward and concrete solution . . . There is no real conception of, and attitude to, the problem. But that immediately becomes possible when the concretistic misconception is dropped."[6]

I asked Alex to try to free himself of the stereotyped interpretation and to consider what a bolt really was. He knew, of course, that a bolt was a metal pin used to fasten things together, and usually secured by a nut.

I asked him, "Is this all you can think of in connection with a bolt?"

He thought awhile, and then mentioned a thunderbolt, or a bolt of lightning.

"What do these images mean to you?" I asked him.

"They mean great power, something I can't manage, it's out of my control. Energy is all bound up in that."

"Anything else?"

"You can bolt a door. The bolt is what fastens it, keeps it closed, keeps out intruders."

We then moved on to look at the associations occurring to Alex around "nut." The nut in the dream was the kind of nut which has internal screw threads and fits on a bolt.

I asked him what the purpose of a nut was.

"To connect something to something else, or to tighten a connection."

"Is there anything else that the word 'nut' means to you?"

This brought a wealth of associations from Alex. "A nut is a kind of fruit or seed, its kernel is a seed. Also, a nut is something hard—when you have a real problem you say that you have a hard nut to crack. Or, in business, the nut is how much you have to make before you can begin to show a profit."

"Anything else?" I asked him.

"Well, nuts are testicles. That certainly fits in with the sexual theory."

"Maybe so," I replied, "but notice also that nuts as testicles have something in common with nuts as fruit-bearing seeds, they both carry the potentiality for germination into something new. That's not exactly unrelated to sex."

This was clearly something he had not thought of, he said. I wondered aloud why it had not occurred to him, and he quickly realized that his ideas about the sex act had very little to do with procreation, in fact it held very little meaning for him beyond immediate pleasure. Little by little the dream was beginning to yield up clues to the source of Alex's difficulties. These sources were not in the past, but were ongoing, giving rise each morning to problems he would experience before the evening.

I did not permit him to get off the track by letting him free-associate to the associations. Since the dream is a self-portrait of the unconscious at a given moment, I find that the best way to understand it is to fix my total attention upon it, and to establish the context. I bear in mind that Jung wrote: "Free association will get me nowhere, any more than it would help me to decipher a Hittite inscription. It will of course help me to uncover all my own complexes, but for this purpose I have no need of a dream—I could just as well take a public notice or a sentence in a newspaper. Free association will bring out all my complexes, but hardly ever the meaning of a dream. To understand the dream's meaning, I must stick as close as possible to the dream images."[7] I have found that this course makes for immediacy in the relationship of analyst, analysand and dream material.

The next part of Alex's dream consisted of the words *you showed me how* . . . A typical mode of operation in the dreamer was demonstrated here. He was always expecting the other person to perform the magic. The analyst was to be no exception. Everything would work out if the analyst would just take the dreamer's hands in hers and show him how to do what had to be done. Alex was prepared to play a passive role again, as usual.

The dream says that the way to resolve the problem is by "patient and careful movements with my hands." He has to learn a different way of functioning from the way in which he has been approaching problems in the past. The old way is "fooling around." The alternative that is presented is "by patient and careful movements." By its versatility, the hand distinguishes man from lower animals and makes possible all sorts of specifically human accomplishments.

The dream brings into awareness the message from the unconscious, that in his habitual conscious approach to his problems Alex is only half serious. He is not as interested in the
meaning of what he does, as he is concerned with deceiving
someone, or taking advantage. Sexuality is a part of his problem, but not the whole of it, and it would be a mistake to
overemphasize this. What is more important than a concretistic approach is the joining of the disparate elements of the
dream into a chain. This cannot be done carelessly; no
amount of struggling or forcing will do it; but if the task
is approached with care and delicacy, it can be accomplished
quite easily. Openness to the implications of the associations
is needed. Locked into the components of the dream is the
natural power of the psyche to restore its own balance. Our
task in interpretation is to free that power.

We can move through the entire dream and relate to the
associations to Alex's life situation. In this way the dream
serves as a diagnostic tool. It opens up to exploration several
possible avenues for therapy.

An important aspect of this sort of approach to dreams
is that the major portion of responsibility for bringing up material that would lead to interpretation rests with the analysand and his unconscious. When the analyst offers interpretations, these always have a tentative quality. "Understanding
a dream" requires agreement between the analyst and the
analysand. It must grow out of the dialogue between the two,
and it must be *felt* as valid by the analysand, it must "click"
with him. Otherwise the analyst's pronouncements are mere
intellectualizations. The analysand may follow what the
analyst is saying, but the words will have little effect upon
him.

There is the further danger, if interpretation is a unilateral
function of the analyst, that the analyst's own projection onto
the patient may be mistaken as the message of the dream.
Unless the analyst can say, "I think it may be like this; what
is *your* reaction?" there is no way for the analyst to check
as to whether he is really on the right track. If the analyst's
interpretations are allowed to go unchallenged, if the analy-

sand is led to believe that any objection on his part will be treated as a mechanism of defense against a truth he is expected to recognize, the analysis stands in grave danger of being controlled by the preconceived notions or theoretical scheme of the analyst. The questionable "results" which stem from the impositions of the analyst's interpretations depend largely on suggestion. The analyst in the dialogue imposes his ideas on the analysand, a process which can easily lead to dependence of the analysand upon his analyst. This is a condition which I usually try to avoid, and, certainly, in the case of a man like Alex, whose problems were complicated by his need to get as much help as he could from external sources while making the minimal contribution from his own inner resources.

Jung stated the case very clearly, "The analyst who wishes to rule out conscious suggestions must therefore consider every dream interpretation invalid until such time as a formula is found which wins the patient's assent."[8] The whole point of dream analysis is to teach the patient eventually to become independent of the therapist, by acquiring the ability to carry on the dialogue with his own inner aspect which has a therapeutic quality, that is, with "the therapist within."

The dream images themselves point to the causes of the dream, that is, to the immediate events that preceded the dream and provided material for its formation. By tracing the causal material backward we can bring about the recollections of an earlier time. Through systematic inquiry concerning antecedent events it is sometimes possible to return the patient to a childhood trauma, and to recapture with him the intensity of feeling which accompanied the incident. When repressed feelings which have been contained for a very long time break through into consciousness a tremendous emotional release may occur. Pent-up feelings of anger and hostility burst forth with unimagined fury. It is like a copious bowel movement after a long period of constipation; hence Freud's term, "catharsis." It does a great deal for the individual at the moment, and helps to deal with the emotion of the past, but it does not necessarily imply any promise for the future.

Understanding the cause of a neurosis is not enough to explain its nature, and it is surely not effective in transforming the neurosis into a productive and rewarding aspect of being. Nor is belated railing against the evildoing parents. The *causalistic* point of view is insufficient; a second viewpoint must be brought into play. This second view is called by Jung the *finalistic* standpoint. By *finalistic* he means to suggest that the neurosis can be seen as striving for a purpose, an end or goal.

"All psychological phenomena," Jung says, "have some such sense of purpose inherent in them, even merely reactive phenomena like emotional reactions. Anger over an insult has its purpose in revenge; the purpose of ostentation over mourning is to arouse the sympathy of others, and so on."[9] In a wider sense, the neurosis, and the dream which carries its message, has, as its purpose, the drive toward individuation. This involves correction of some conscious attitude that prevents the individual from more fully realizing his total capacity. When normal productive means of achieving one's purpose are blocked off, neurosis develops as an effort to find a way over or around the obstruction. Neurotic symptoms often direct a person's attention to his inner development through the medium of dreams.

Steven brought a nightmare to his analytic session which was so full of horror that he was deeply shaken for several days after it occurred. He could hardly bear to read it to me, and broke into tears as he did so, more than once. He could have looked at the dream from the causalistic point of view without coming close to the meaning of it. But in the end he was able to take a finalistic view of it, and the effect was transformative. I present the dream in its entirety, not because the details need to be discussed here, but because anything less than the total presentation of the dream would diminish its impact.

The scene seems to be in an open area. There is a brick structure with two openings on one side and on the opposite side from it are two more openings. In each of these openings is fitted a long, heavy iron box that slides on rollers into the hole in the brick wall. In the opening scene my aunt has crawled into one box and is pushed into the wall. On the inside of the brick walls is a hot fire. My aunt had been told that she had cancer of the lungs and that she was going to die anyway and this would be an easier death than by cancer. I found this very horrifying, but didn't question it.

Then I am told the same thing about myself and am again horrified because now I'm supposed to follow my aunt. However, I want to check with another doctor because I just had a chest X ray and no one reported cancer then. Before this, however, I was standing at the furnace thinking I had incurable cancer of the lungs and I thought I must take the furnace as the way out. After I thought about it, I decided to get some X rays somewhere else, or to ignore the whole thing. As I am hurrying to get X rays somewhere else, my Dad runs up from behind and hands me the keys to his car and the papers in his pockets. I am glad to see him. He too has cancer of the lungs, he says, and is preparing to go to the furnace. It is as though this is what one has to do. I tell him there is not much point in his handing over his things to me because I've been told I have the same thing. He insists, though, and I accept. I go to get an X ray done elsewhere and my father goes toward the furnace. The brick walls to the furnaces are only one layer thick of non-firebrick, with a rather thin layer of concrete on the top. The fire in such a construction would be hot enough to kill one, but not hot enough to cremate one, which would appear to be what the furnaces are for.

We need to know that the patient had been suffering for a long time from a depressive neurosis. He had feelings of great personal inadequacy, feelings which restricted him from attempting new relationships or from accepting challenging opportunities in his work. He had grown up as the third and youngest child in an unloving household. His mother had been a strict disciplinarian, using the authority of religious doctrine as the basis for her unloving, moralistic rigidity. The best that young Steven could hope for was to be saved from hellfire if he would behave as his mother required him to do. There was never any commendation or appreciation of his efforts that he could remember, but he stood in constant terror of his mother's anger and rejection should he displease her. His father was cool and distant. While he did not necessarily support his wife in her zealous attitudes, he did not take Steven's part either. Steven's brother and sister were older than he, and did not show much interest in him. He thought that they were the favored ones, that he had been born late and was probably unwanted. He tried in vain to justify his existence before his parents, but he never felt that he had been able to do so. The pain in Steven was evident in the lines on his face, the expression in his eyes and in his carriage. When he first came into analysis he had been taking large amounts of antidepressant medication for a long time and had become something like a zombie—a certain vacancy of expression was superimposed over his suffering face.

During the course of analysis, Steven began to face his buried angers and to give voice to them. Each confronting experience was accompanied by a burst of relief; then a reactive depression would set in, in which he was filled with guilt and shame. The analytic relationship, specifically the transference aspect of it, carried him. Here his expectations that he would be punished or rejected for expressing his feelings were not met, instead his expressions were seen as indications that attitudes can change and that change is acceptable. During this time Steven gradually stopped taking the antidepressants, and concurrently his dream life increased in activity and in the powerful way it affected him. The above dream was the climax of a series.

Reading the dream, Steven could hardly manage to get his words out. At the point of relating where his father appears and tells him that he has cancer and is preparing to go to the furnace, Steven broke into uncontrollable tears. "You don't know the worst of it," he cried, "you don't know where this led me." He managed to pull himself together enough to read the rest of the dream, then quietly wept until it was all out. Then he told me what he understood of the dream: "I interpreted it to mean, I am going to have to think for myself.

I cannot accept what people have told me, that my life is hopeless, that I am dying inside and that it may as well be all over. I will have to find out what is in me, or it will be a wasted life—I must, else I will die and burn in hell. But you don't know where the dream leads—the meeting with my father . . ." Here he could hardly go on. But he soon continued, "*He* didn't make it, but he thought *I* could. The last time I saw him, a few weeks before he died, I realized for the first time that under his cool, critical attitude—there was love there. It came too late." Steven recalled the last days of his parents. His father had, indeed, softened in his attitude toward him. And later, when his mother was terminally ill she had called Steven to her bedside. She had given him two goblets from her wedding crystal, and six silver iced-tea spoons. Similar cherished items were given to his brother and sister. But for Steven there was a special gift, the small hand-carved table that his mother's parents had brought with them from Austria when they had come to settle in America, the only remainder from the life in the old country. Steven realized from this that he, the youngest child, had been selected to carry on; that in her way, his mother had indeed loved him, although she was unable to let him know until the end of her life.

We could have reviewed the dream from the causalistic point of view, but it is doubtful whether anything particularly new or helpful would have been revealed. To retrace the agonies of his childhood, to reiterate his anger and helplessness, would have been counterproductive. It made more sense to look at the dream from the finalistic point of view. To what purpose did the dream guide him, what was its meaning for the future? His "sickness" was associated with the "sickness" in his family; he had apparently fallen heir to the orientation toward life and its problems that was characteristic for his family. But, stop, the dream seems to say, notice that just because someone has told you that you are doomed to go the way of the others in your family, you need not accept your fate without questioning it. The dream dramatizes the unconscious revulsion against the passive conscious attitude that Steven had held up until this time—the attitude that he had been irreparably damaged in his youth and would never get over it.

The dream tells him that his father, though dead in reality, still exists as a psychic factor in him. The father *in him* once exerted control and dominated him, and, likewise, did the mother, in a different way. That father element was weak and dependent; it stemmed from the example of a man who was not able to take responsibility for his own life, much less for the rearing of his son, Steven. But now it was time for the father to go, to be deposed from his position, and the son was to take over. The keys to his car were handed over—the dream was saying that Steven was to gain the instrument from the father, which would enable him to take control of his own life. He had to let the hated father go into the furnace and be burned, not destroyed, but transformed into spirit. The confidence of the father spirit in Steven had been unconscious until this time. It now passed into consciousness via the dream. The purpose of the dream, then, was to let the father go, in one sense, and in another sense to allow Steven to assume the power of the father as his own. The keys and the papers point to this.

Discussion of this dream helped Steven to make its contents his own, to assimilate them into consciousness with an active resolve to carry forward the meaning and purpose that were seen in it, first by him, and secondly in the dialogue of analysis. I had very little to say after Steven gave his own interpretation. More important than anything that was said in the exchange, were the feelings that passed between us in those intense moments. Steven, who had always been reserved, could not be reserved with me any longer. The dream broke through all that. We were able to be in it together, for I, too, was profoundly moved by the horror of the dream and I shared the intensity of his reaction. What was unsaid between us seared more deeply than the actual verbal communication. The dream was full of the inescapable fact of death as the end of life, the tenuousness of life, and the importance of embracing the time that is left—each of us—and loving that time and being committed to use it well. There is no room for self-pity in this brief span, we both knew that, nor for regrets about the unlived past. The future is too swiftly upon us; but today we know what our task is and, therefore, today we must address ourselves to it.

There are moments in analysis when feelings overflow the brink of tears. Sharing this with the analyst is very different from experiencing it alone. Many people ask, why can I not interpret my own dreams? If, after all, the information that is needed is all embedded in my own psyche, why should it be necessary to come to someone else for help in interpreting my dreams? It is true that the work of analysis is directed toward helping the analysand not only with interpretations of specific dreams, but also with gaining an understanding of the dream process so that he can discover the essential meaning in his own dreams. The difficulty is that the dream comes from outside one's conscious orientation, and one often cannot assess the value of the interpretation solely on the basis of one's own work on it. It takes a long time of diligent work in relating to the unconscious before one is able to step aside from his conscious standpoint. Exploring a dream with a person skilled in interpretation, who is able to participate in the dream with one aspect of his being and at the same time remain outside of it with another, may bring the necessary objectivity. The analyst is trained to exclude his own projections from the interpretation of a dream, to leave out his own wishes, his own moral judgments.

Frequently, analysands want to discuss their dreams with their husbands or wives or close friends. Much as I dislike some esoteric aspects of analysis, there are occasions when it is absolutely necessary to maintain silence, and my feeling is that this is especially true of the "virginal dream" (the dream as it freshly appears, without having been exposed to anyone). To tell it prematurely to another person is to break the special relationship between the ego and the unconscious, a relationship that is carried by a slender bridge that can only be walked alone. I am reminded of the tradition of the earliest Jewish mysticism, having to do with the vision of God's appearance on the throne, as described by Ezekiel. The Jewish mystic, in contemplating the "throne world" as the center which embodies and exemplifies all forms of creation, is interdicted from speaking about these most sacred matters.[10] There are some things, he is told, that may be discussed in groups of ten, some things in groups of five, and some may not be told to more than three; some things are to be told only to one other, and there are some which may not be uttered at all.

For the tension to be kept between consciousness and the unconscious, it is vitally important that the material be held in and contemplated, that the full feelings associated with it be experienced in all their strength and not dissipated in idle conversation. The very fact that the dream is not told to the analyst immediately as it occurs, but that the analysand has an interval of time to turn it over in his thoughts and to extract from it all that he possibly can, means that he brings his dream to the analytic hour in all its purity, and even intensified by his contemplation. In my experience I have found that those analysands who allow their dreams to work on them in solitude are likely to be the ones who find their analyses most productive. As they learn to maintain the tensions of their dreams, they also learn to live with the tensions of their lives. They learn to express their feelings in the right time and in the right way, after filtering them through the discrimination and differentiation that powers a sensitive ego which has developed a partnership with the unconscious.

Occasionally, I have the experience that an analysand may not wish to discuss a dream with me. Recently an analysand brought a dream which, he said, had very deep meaning to him, not fully understood, but so strong that he did not feel he could deal with it. He wanted me to know about it, but he said that he would show it to me only on the condition that I would promise not to say anything about it. I respected his wish, and he handed me the dream to read after the session was over. I did so, and I hold the dream and all my thoughts about it in confidence. It is important to him that I know what it was about, and that I give him the right to live with it, while I do the same. Perhaps there will come a time when he will wish to discuss it. That will be his decision.

So far, in speaking about dreams, we have dealt mainly with single dreams. The reason for this was that the dreams were used to illustrate particular points. However, dreams do not occur generally as isolated psychological events, even when they appear to. They may be regarded rather as emerging evidence of the ongoing unconscious processes. Certain themes may be followed through series of dreams. Each dream may have its own meaning, yet take on far more significance in the light of its position with respect to other dreams. So it is necessary for the analyst to keep the "dream history" of the analysand in mind just as much as it is necessary to keep the ongoing life history before him.

The dream series that follows will show not only how dreams may be related to one another, but also how they may, in turn, direct the process of psychotherapy itself. This is possible because so much of emotional disturbance is due to a lack of correspondence between the conscious orientation and the unconscious purposes. It is necessary that the unconscious make known its own direction and we must allow it an equal voice with that of the ego, if each side is to be able to adapt to the other. As the ego listens, and the unconscious is encouraged to participate in the dialogue, the unconscious position is transformed from that of an adversary to that of a friend with a somewhat differing but complementary point of view. This process is what James Hillman has aptly called "befriending our dreams."

There will follow, greatly abbreviated, a series of four dreams, which belong in turn to four important aspects of the analytic process. The dreams took place over a long period of time, with many other dreams between, but these nevertheless show a cohesiveness of theme. The first dream is *diagnostic*, describing the situation that needs to be corrected, the "neurosis," if you will. The second dream has to do with *prognosis*, it suggests what can happen as a result of treatment. The third dream deals with the *method of treatment*. The fourth has to do with the *resolution of the transference re-*

lationship, a necessary element in the conclusion of analysis. This fourth dream is not my analysand's; it is my own. I think it admissible here, because I strongly feel that the analyst is part of the process, rather than being either an observer or the one who makes it happen. The analyst's unconscious material, then, is not excluded from the process.

Nicholas came into analysis shortly after he had accepted an important position which required him to pull together his life work, including all his education and his previous experience. He was to be in charge of a large project which involved a number of people. A high degree of talent and creativity would be demanded from him as director. He had been encouraged by friends and associates to seek the position, and he had applied for it despite a strong personal feeling that he was insufficiently qualified. When he was given the post he reacted with a depression that had within it elements of panic. He came into analysis appearing calm and well possessed, but this was altogether persona. Here is his initial dream: *I am climbing a rocky cliff made of shale and loose rocks. I have to put my foot into rough depressions and holes, and grab onto protuberances of rock. Sometimes rocks break loose and go hurtling down into the valley. I am afraid of losing my balance, or of starting a huge landslide.*

This dream offers a diagnosis of the situation. He is aiming much too high, and he is not comfortable with the task or with his own ability to master it. He feels vulnerable, and is fearful of falling from the place to which he has come through so much effort. He may lose his balance and come crashing down at any moment. Or, even if he hangs on, the people in the valley below him are in danger—he can destroy them in a moment by an accident, a miscalculation. But, judging from the way in which he was climbing, he was not concerned for anything but his goal. As we discussed the dream it became apparent that his only concerns were ego concerns.

The conscious attitude of Nicholas, which was that he must go ahead and do his job to the best of his ability and no matter who gets hurt in the process, was shown by the dream to be an unproductive attitude. The whole thing might easily collapse if he were to go ahead and try to build on the present basis.

All of this would appear to be an external interpretation. Jungians hold that the external situation (in the world) generally reflects the inner situation of the individual. When we are feeling calm and secure and smoothly functioning on the inside, it is nearly certain that things will go well for us or, if they take a bad turn, that we will be able to cope with that and even to extricate something of value from an apparently unfavorable circumstance. On the other hand, if we are "at odds with ourselves," with the conscious and unconscious parts running at cross purposes, we tend to make a mess of even the most favorable of circumstances. The external situation in which we find ourselves is merely our way of looking at the "box" which we call experience, from the outside. We could also look at the box from the inside and call it subjective experience. But the box, "experience," is neither inner nor outer, it is that which joins together the outside and the inside. For the purpose of indicating something about the dream series, we will for the present look at these dreams from the external or objective side.

The second dream in the series: *I am standing alone at the foot of a huge mountain. It is of unimaginable size and I am so small. A footpath winds its way up on the lower slopes and disappears behind a rise in the distance. I do not know if I will live long enough to climb that mountain, but at least I will begin.*

This is a prognostic dream. Nicholas has come down from his precarious position of the first dream and his feet are on solid ground. The dream reflects the coming change in his attitude. He is beginning to realize that he will have to reorganize his work, and even before that, his attitude to the work. He must not be in too big a hurry, as he has been in the past. He must not try to salvage the mistakes of the past, but must go back and begin again on a sounder basis. The task is enormous, it is the fulfillment of his whole life, but it is not important that he concern himself too much about the end result. He has to be prepared for a long and arduous time ahead—no man would start out on the kind of journey the dream presents without making sure that he is in good health. This means total good health, physically and psychologically. The dream suggests that the only way to go is upward, and that the process will require more attention than the goal.

It may well be asked here whether dreams predict the future. Jung has answered this question by saying that dreams are no more prophetic than a meteorologist who predicts the weather. What the dream does is to present a reading of the unconscious, so to speak, and if we are able to discern its message we have a basis for expecting that, on the basis of certain conditions present, there is a good chance of certain occurrences taking place in the natural course of events. The dream then, while not actually predicting the future, can be an aid in helping us to realize what forces are in motion and in what direction they are going.

The third dream: *I have reached a plateau high in the mountains. Before me stretches a calm, smooth mountain lake. Seated crosslegged with his back toward me is a man whom I do not know. He is facing the lake, immovable.*

The dream left Nicholas with a peaceful feeling. He felt, upon awakening, like taking the time to make a small drawing of the scene. He did, and he taped it to his bedroom mirror where he could see it often, so that he would be reminded of the dream and the feeling it engendered. The dream seemed to have two functions. The first was to compensate the one-sided attitude of consciousness, which from time to time became obsessed with the responsibilities of work and with other problems, and made it difficult for Nicholas to concentrate his energies. The dream showed a thoughtful figure, representing perhaps an unconscious demand, perhaps a repressed wish, for distancing himself from pressing problems and finding perspective and restfulness. The second function of this dream was to suggest a method of treatment. It clearly indicated that meditation of some sort would be helpful for Nicholas. He could find the necessary balance for his life if he would set aside time from his busy schedule for quiet reflection. He should turn his back on the upward struggle, gazing instead over the smooth waters, in which he himself could be revealed.

Other dreams reiterated this message in varying ways. Nicholas began to recognize the importance of taking time for those practices which would provide for him a temporary separation from the demands of his external life, and then allow him to return with new energy and vigor. He followed the attitude prescribed by the dream, and though there were better times and worse times, he gradually gained the capacity to return at will to the high mountain plateau when it was necessary to view his situation from another prospective.

The fourth dream was my own. It occurred near the end of the analysis, and let me know that my role in Nicholas' development was nearly finished. My dream: *I have climbed to the top of a snowy mountain with Nicholas. We look down and see some men and machines cutting a hole in the ice, maybe for fishing. It is noisy. But atop the mountain the sun is warm. I lie back in the snow and enjoy the sun. Nicholas remains standing.*

I have said that this fourth dream had to do with the end of analysis which requires the dissolution of the transference relationship. The dream points to the unconscious relationship between analyst and analysand, from the point of view of the analyst. This is more properly called "countertransference." Countertransference in orthodox psychoanalysis was thought of as dangerous, a condition which the analyst should by all means try to avoid. He was advised to remain remote and objective and not to allow his personal feelings to enter into the analytic relationship. In contrast to this view, it is accepted as a matter of course by Jungians that in an analysis extending over a long period, with intense emotional involvement, that the analyst will participate in depth and not purely out of the conscious position. This is confirmed when the analyst dreams of a patient and, in fact, may be helpful in letting the analyst know what is going on between himself and the patient, far better than if his judgment were based on thinking alone. The analyst must, therefore, consistently pay attention to his own dreams. And, when he is unable to understand a dream that seems important to him, he may be obliged to discuss it with a colleague who will help him achieve the necessary objectivity.

As I regarded the foregoing dream, I had to recognize that Nicholas and I had gone as far as we could together. We had reached a stage of development which had seemed impossible when we first began our work together. I say "we" because I, too, grew in the process of this difficult analysis. The problems and difficulties which were brought to the analysis were by no means entirely solved, but the means for dealing with them were at hand. Nicholas' panic was gone and a relaxed but ready attitude took its place. It was time for me to withdraw from the relationship. I thought of how far Nicholas had come. Some words of Jung's on the goals of analysis came to mind. They seemed relevant to the image of Nicholas standing there in the sunshine:

> The greatest and most important problems of life are all in a certain sense insoluble. They must be so because they express the necessary polarity inherent in every self-regulating system. They can never be solved, but only outgrown. . . . This "outgrowing" . . . on further experience was seen to consist in a new level of consciousness. Some higher or wider interest arose on the person's horizon, and through this widening of his view the insoluble problem lost its urgency. It was not solved logically in its own terms, but faded out when confronted with a new and stronger life-tendency. It was not repressed and made unconscious, but merely appeared in a different light, and so, did indeed become different. What, on a lower level, had led to the wildest conflicts and to panicky outbursts of emotion, viewed from the higher level of the personality, now seemed like a storm in the valley seen from a high mountain-top. This does not mean that the thunderstorm is robbed of its reality, but instead of being in it one is now above it.[11]

Jung has suggested two ways of approaching a dream, and they are not necessarily mutually exclusive. One is to analyze the dream on the *objective level*. Every character in the dream may be taken as the person in real life, and the events and relationships in the dream may be seen as referring to real life events and relationships. The dream is seen as the reaction of the unconscious to what is happening in the conscious life of the dreamer. Or, the dream may either be confirming or objecting to some action in which the dreamer is involved. If it is a prognostic dream, it may represent the attempt of the unconscious to work out the solution of some problem in the dreamer's life situation.

Another way to take the dream is on the *subjective level.* Here we can interpret dream figures as personified aspects of the dreamer's own personality.[12] A person whom the dreamer knows in his daily life may appear in his dream as the embodiment of an archetypal element of the unconscious. In this case the dream figure is to be taken as referring to some aspect of the dreamer himself. Subjective-level interpretations are indicated in dreams where the dream figures evoke more emotion than one would expect from their role in the waking life of the dreamer. Steven's cremation dream is a case in point. When Steven meets his father, who is about to go to the ovens for a quicker death than that from cancer, we may be sure that the subjective interpretation—father as an internalized aspect of Steven—comes closest to the meaning of the dream.

Sometimes there are no recognizable or familiar characters in a dream. Then it is nearly impossible to interpret the dream in any way except subjectively. If the dream figures, however, can be associated to actual events in the life situation, it is simpler and usually more helpful to interpret the dream objectively. A subjective level interpretation is necessary in cases where the objective level interpretation does not strike the dreamer as relevant or meaningful.

The strange Kafkaesque dream of Edith, a middle-aged woman, may serve to illustrate this point further. *I am being chased by those who would exterminate my race. I have friends among my enemies—who would protect me by beating me lightly, in order to avoid the more destructive beating. Also, I have enemies among my friends, who would betray me. Alas. I awaken feeling that something in my life has changed.*

In exploring this dream with her on the objective level I found it necessary to raise first the question of "race." Edith is Jewish, so I asked if perhaps she felt in some way discriminated against because of her Judaism. She did not respond to this probe with any particular feeling, for she was not aware of ever having suffered for this reason. There had been no event that she could think of in recent days that would have provided any basis for the content of the dream. As to friends among her enemies, she thought of some men in her business firm who were immediately above her. They would often help her in various ways, so that she had gained a reputation for excellence which she thought was better than she deserved. Enemies among her friends might refer, she conjectured, to other women on her same level who may have been jealous of her accomplishments. But somehow this objective level interpretation of the dream did not seem significant to the dreamer—it did not correspond to the strong feelings she experienced when she awakened from the dream.

Reading the dream from a subjective point of view brought quite different results. "Race" was seen to refer to the dreamer's character: Edith was an energetic and ambitious woman with high aspirations. There were inner obstacles which she felt were working against her: personal feelings of insecurity, intuitive insight into the sensitivities of others which sometimes inhibited her action, and a tendency to become distracted from something on which she was trying to concentrate. These qualities of personality were "enemies" in her eyes, yet the puzzling dream urged her to examine them and to see whether each in its way might serve as an impetus to growth. Accepting these aspects of her nature might be the "lighter beating." In the individuation process the "more destructive beating," that is, failure due to unconsciousness of her weaknesses, would be avoided. Feeling insecure would lead her to seek out and work on the less developed talents; intuitive insight could help her in establishing better relationships; and the tendency to become distracted, if not repressed, might allow her to enjoy a wider range of interests and aspirations. So these were "friends among my enemies."

Edith had then to consider the "enemies among my friends, who would betray me." These seemed to refer to characteristics of her own which appeared to be productive in nature, but which she had a tendency to carry to excess. They were such qualities as energy, which could become compulsivity; ambition, which could become greed; singleness of purpose, which could become ruthlessness. All these inner qualities displayed her characteristic way of being which, as it happened, were also reflected in her current life situation. Naturally Edith had been totally unaware of these forces underlying her behavior. In working through the dream with the analysand, I had the distinct feeling that it was not the objective life situation which precipitated the dream, but the contrary: the condition of the unconscious which is portrayed so graphically in the dream is the same condition which, quite unknown to the dreamer, created the life situation which she was currently experiencing. The confirmation that the subjective interpretation was valid in this case came as the dreamer recalled that her ongoing life problem was not an isolated one but bore a resemblance to other situations which had come up before—all in response to the ongoing character problems which the dream indicated.

Much more could be said about the process of dreaming. We could discuss how dreams are classified, or how they may be systematically approached.[18] But all this would be theorizing. What we do in the analytic process is to carry on a dialogue with the dream, instead of trying to make it conform to a theory. The few general principles that have been illustrated above may be helpful to suggest avenues of approach to the dream. The important thing is to record the dream, to pay attention to it, and to allow the dream to speak for itself. It is not even absolutely necessary that the dream be understood. As in the most helpful of human relationships where much can transpire which is not fully understood, so with dreams. This or that element reveals something that was not known before, or one is reminded of some quality or capacity that he had all but forgotten. And there is always the possibility that more of a dream's meaning will be revealed as time passes.

The dream has been called everything from a "temporary psychosis" to the "gateway to the treasure-house of the unconscious." Much of what we see when we close our eyes at night depends upon the attitude with which we go to sleep. And much of what we do by day may be affected by the attitude we bring to our dreams.

12

DREAMING
THE DREAM ONWARD:
ACTIVE IMAGINATION

Dreams may be a source of potential strength and wisdom, but unfortunately they present their difficulties and problems too. For one thing, I do not find that it is always possible to understand dreams. Often they are unclear and it seems that no amount of reflection and examination will produce the feeling of having come to the essence of the dream. Dreams may have to be shelved until some future time when they may become clearer—meanwhile we can keep them in view and turn them over in our thoughts, now and again.

Since dreaming is a spontaneous function of the unconscious, we cannot, by any conscious efforts, "cause" dreams to appear—much less can we command dream content that will serve our needs at any given moment in time. It seems as though the unconscious were like the vault of a great bank in which is stored all the wealth inherited from our ancestors and in which we, as individuals, also have deposited our own coin. All of this treasure is said to belong to us, to be at our disposal, but the trouble is that we cannot withdraw it on demand. We have to wait until the guard at the door is ready to open up, and we must be present at that moment and ready to receive what is offered to us. We cannot withdraw more than what the guard may decide to give us. This may be more than we need at this particular moment, or it may not be enough. Or we may wait in vain, and nothing comes. The ego-aspect of the human personality is weak and powerless against the guard-aspect who bars the door to the vault of dreams.

Not only dreams have their vagaries. Other secrets of the unconscious may be equally inaccessible to the ego and its capacity to deal with them. In the course of analysis we need to find other approaches to that chaotic underworld which intrudes into our lives when we least desire it and often eludes us just when we try to penetrate its depths.

Looking at this problem from the standpoint of the ego, we can see two kinds of situations that demand some different modes of relating to the unconscious other than the straightforward analysis of dreams. The first situation occurs when the individual's ego is barricaded against the unconscious, when there is little sense of flow, of fresh ideas, of genuine expression or even perception of feelings. In this situation, dreams may be completely absent, or they may be so fragmentary and superficial that they are practically valueless. The second situation is the opposite: here the ego actively attacks the unconscious, stimulating it to produce more contents —dreams and fantasies and a tendency to act out in bizarre behavior—than the ego can deal with in any creative or productive way.

A different way of working with the unconscious may be suggested by the unconscious itself, instead of coming from the ego standpoint. The unconscious may spontaneously flood the ego with contents—such as anxieties, fears, obsessive ideas, visions—that threaten the very survival of the ego position. Or—and in a sense this is a less apparent but more excruciatingly painful situation—the unconscious becomes isolated from the conscious ego, and leaves the individual feeling disconnected from anything which might possibly have meaning or importance to him.

These are, of course, gross categories of possibilities. They are meaningless in themselves, but they provide a framework for the discussion of certain human experiences in analysis which give rise to a third element, less transitory and rambunctious than the dream, which may be utilized in the therapeutic process. This third element, called *the transcendent function*, belongs neither to the ego sphere nor to the unconscious, and yet possesses access to each. It stands above them, participating in both. It is as though ego and unconscious were points at either end of the baseline of a triangle. The third element, at the apex of the triangle, transcends both the point of the ego and the point of the unconscious but is related to each of them. The transcendent function's emergence grants autonomy to the ego and also to the unconscious by relating to both of them independently, and in doing so, unites them.

How this works in the several situations involving strained or disharmonious relations between the ego and the unconscious can best be seen by considering what happened in several cases in which the transcendent function came into play. Maureen's analysis required facing a central problem in which the ego was barricading itself against the onslaught of the unconscious.

Maureen came into therapy with me after she had been discharged from a mental hospital. She had been admitted there six months previously, after she had slashed her wrists with a razor, and now the psychiatrist who had been treating her in the hospital had refused to continue seeing her on an outpatient basis. When she first came to see me she looked and behaved like a frightened little girl of about twelve, although her chronological age was nineteen. She would curl up in the corner of a large chair in my office, as if she would have liked to disappear. Yet she answered every question I put to her in the beginning with clarity, although I noted the absence of any show of feeling. She told me that she had been told by her former doctor not to call him any more, and that she felt that he had rejected her, "just like everybody else." It came out that her father, a successful businessman, had interests which kept him away from home most of the time while Maureen was growing up; he was always either working, or sailing his boat, or flying his plane. Her mother had been at home, but Maureen remembers little about her until the birth of a brother, when Maureen was about three-and-a-half years old. Following this, her mother had become severely depressed and had to be hospitalized. Mother and the new baby had disappeared from the home at the same time. Actually, the baby was taken by an aunt, but Maureen thought that her mother had chosen the baby and left her behind. Maureen's grandmother came to take care of her, and her father was rarely home during the three-month period until her mother returned. Maureen remembered her mother from that time on as cold and unfeeling. She expressed only hatred for this mother who had left her when she was little. It was not surprising to learn that her mother had told her, "You were born without trust," and Maureen, in telling me this, said she knew it was true.

It was nearly impossible for Maureen to communicate with me in any depth. I had to pull the facts of her life from her bit by bit. She had few recollections of her past, and these few could only be brought to the surface through much energetic questioning on my part. Not that she was unwilling, but she seemed to be blocked off from any relationship with her life up to this point. So, for the most part she would sit in the chair with eyes averted, picking at her fingernails and answering my questions and observations with brief, often monosyllabic responses if she spoke at all.

But she did try to communicate. Once, just before she left my office, she gave me a poem she had found somewhere. It read:

> the other
> one laughs
> is worried
> under the sky exposes my face and my hair
> makes words roll out of my mouth
> one who has money and fears and a passport
> one who quarrels and loves
> one moves
> one struggles
>
> but not i
> i am the other

who does not laugh
who has no face to expose to the sky
and no words in his mouth
who is unacquainted with me with himself
not i: the other: always the other
who neither wins nor loses
who is not worried
who does not move

the other
indifferent to himself
of whom i know nothing
of whom nobody knows who he is
who does not move me
that is i

I knew that she was trying to explain to me how she felt, and that the poem she had come across said what she would have liked to have been able to say. It was clear that there were two figures in conflict within her, the ego, which was represented by a very small girl who could not make herself heard, and a bigger, older, wiser person. We began to talk about these two, and although Maureen was not too responsive, I had the feeling that I was beginning to reach her.

Often, however, she would sit through the hour hardly saying anything. Then at the end of the hour she would become clinging and begin to bring out what had obviously been on her mind all along. She would attempt to extend the hour this way, and to get control of me—she must have sensed that I would not want to play the part of the rejecting mother by sending her off just when she wanted to talk to me, which was of course true. Furthermore, she must have known that I did not want to miss these bits of communication at last so tantalizingly dropped. It is always amazing to me how certain patients are able unerringly to zero in on the therapist's own weaknesses and sensitive points! I could see Maureen was making it nearly impossible for me to act as a mediator between herself and her unconscious material, and it was clear to me why her former therapist had been eager to refer the case. Maureen was doing whatever she could to make her therapy hours with me ineffective.

One day she was even more withdrawn than usual. She admitted that she was afraid to speak out. At the end of the hour she cried a little, and just as she was getting ready to leave she pulled a note out of her pocketbook and handed it to me. In her neat schoolgirl handwriting, she had written:

Telephone booths are such blissful places to hide in. I guess the problem with the little girl is that she doesn't want to be mothered by the big girl—the big girl has no feelings or emotions—she is cold and hard and efficient and maybe brave—but the little girl doesn't want to grow up without feelings and is afraid of what the big girl could do to her—little girls are a nuisance—they reduce efficiency and get in the way—they have feelings and needs that big girls want no part of—and when they're neglected they scream—but sometimes after something screams loud enough and long enough, it just gives up and withdraws into a corner too hurt to react—that is what this little girl has done—and she is sitting in the corner refusing to grow—the big girl likes it this way except for the nuisance involved, because as long as she sits in the corner no one will ever know her or love her—little withdrawn girls are much less of a nuisance than growing girls—growing girls need mothers and the big girl doesn't want to be a mother—she scarcely knows what one is—and growing girls scream continually, they never stop—so the little girl out of necessity will stay little and reasonably quiet—and the big girl will maintain her coldness to protect herself.

Here was the whole story of herself and "the other." Maureen had clearly shown what her feelings were, growing up as she did, which meant not really growing up emotionally. She told me how, in the hospital, she had been allowed to regress to the age of six or seven and how she had loved being free and uninhibited, and being able to crayon all over the bathroom walls. Now, she said, she still wants and needs to be a little child, to withdraw from responsibility. But there is also the "big girl." The original model for this figure may have been Maureen's mother, but the big girl is also an aspect of Maureen, the person she is expected to become and in one sense has already become, although she is not yet able to assume the responsibility and the mature attitude that would be appropriate.

What she had written was more than idle fantasy, it was a conscious attempt to bridge the gap between the conscious "little girl" sense of herself and the frightening image of the "big girl" with all of her big demands and requirements. Maureen, who had not gotten any help from her dreams, had stumbled upon the rudiments of the transcendent function as a way to gain a position outside of the inadequate ego position, and also outside of the power of the unconscious. It was that aspect which could stand over the big girl and the little girl and view them both, as well as the relationship between them. As we talked about the telephone booth paper, Maureen began for the first time to be able to acknowledge her fears openly, but she was obviously still terrified by much more than she was saying. It seemed to me a good time to help her embark on the kind of interaction between ego and unconscious that makes use of imagination to perform the work of the transcendent function.

Imagination, employed in this way, is not the same as fantasy. Jung has called this use of imagination by the term *active imagination*, to distinguish it from the ordinary passive imagination which is nothing else than a self-propelling fantasy. Active imagination is entered into consciously, in an effort to engage the unconscious in dialogue with the ego. And, since the unconscious is not limited in its expression to verbal intercourse, the varieties of approach to it are many. Words presented great difficulty for Maureen, therefore her active imagination needed a medium that would permit uninhibited flow of thoughts and feelings in both directions, from the unconscious to consciousness, and from the ego to the unconscious. I thought of the crayons she had enjoyed so much at the hospital. They had given her freedom to express her passive fantasies, without any attempt to direct them in any way. Now perhaps we could move to the next step, active imagination, in which she might give the unconscious a chance to speak for itself, and provide some material for the ego to work on. I suggested that instead of our usual session, perhaps Maureen would like to sit at the table with me and do some drawing. She agreed to do this, and was even somewhat eager. I suggested to her that she draw a picture which would represent the way she felt about herself at that very moment.

While she was drawing I reflected on what had happened to her during the past two months since she had started to work with me. She had secured a clerical position and was doing routine office work, fitting into the office very much like a part of a machine. She was efficient, bland, and compulsive about getting her work done. Her employer was well satisfied with her work. She had made no friends, and she always came straight home from work to her small apartment where she spent her time alone until she returned to the office the next day.

Soon Maureen's picture was done. It showed a large stick figure in a running position, with a round head, and a crowd of smaller similar figures off to the right apparently running also, with one of their number out in front. I asked her about the drawing. Her response was, "I'm running away. Everyone is chasing me. If I stop running they will trample me. The only way for someone to communicate with me is if they can run faster than I." Maureen's self-portrait was pitiful, with her painted smile, her face devoid of personality, her sexless body without weight or substance, just something to support the head, and something that can run away. The crowd of people represented to her just "they," everyone outside herself. In other words, "they" referred to the terror of the unconscious. It is a nameless terror, but it has the shape of other human beings. In a new way Maureen was able to see both herself and what she was afraid of.

It did not seem important to try to analyze the meaning of the feelings that came up. It was more important that we looked at the picture together and felt that something in her was capable of expressing itself, and it might not have to be in words. We agreed that pictures could help us to find out more about herself, and especially about that part which was so hard to reach. To seal the compact I gave her the box of crayons to take home "in case you feel like letting the other side of yourself say something more to you."

To the next session Maureen brought two pictures. The second picture was almost like the first one that she had made in my office, but there were significant differences. For one thing, the large figure which represented her idea of herself (the ego figure) was now carrying a box of crayons. Maureen had titled the picture "Running with Crayons." I sensed that the crayons were the visual representation of the transcendent function, that they were incorporated into the picture as the thing that would enable the unconscious contents to flow over into consciousness. In another way, the crayons represented my own role as mediator in the process. It is the analyst who carries the transcendent function for the patient in the beginning, as a rule, showing the analysand the way to make use of the new movements that develop once the process is set in motion. Facing the unconscious is facing all the agonies of the past that have been conveniently forgotten, and for some people it is just to avoid this that neurotic symptoms have been invented. So, in order to ward off the dangers that have long been feared, the analysand needs someone to go through it with him, namely the analyst. In Maureen's picture, all this is represented by the crayons. Moreover, perhaps the crayons were a magical protecting amulet for her.

Another difference between this picture and the first one was that in the first picture the ego figure had been drawn with hesitating, sketchy lines. In this one, the lines were clear and definite. And, interestingly enough, the crowd in the second picture was smaller than it had been in the first.

The third picture showed her running head-on into a fence or grill. "They" were still following after, but the crowd was a little smaller still than the one in the previous drawing, and no single figure was out in front. The title of this picture was "Wanting Free." I had asked her how long the little girl could keep on running away. She had put this question to the unconscious when she had started to draw. Here was the answer that came: "One day you will come up against something that will stop you from running. Wanting free means wanting to be able to stop running. That is what you want, and you may as well recognize it." I saw this picture as hopeful. It was the first expression of the idea that things could possibly change, that there might be any point in "wanting."

In the analytic session, I suggested that perhaps Maureen would like to try something even freer than crayons, to give the unconscious the freedom it seemed to be asking for. We took out finger paints and she selected a rich golden yellow which she overlaid with brilliant red. Then with her fingernails she made circle after circle in a spiraling movement over and over, spiraling around a center. When she was finished she had a primitive form of a mandala, a spontaneous representation of the motif of centrality. I had the feeling that this picture pre-formed the pulling together of the conscious and unconscious elements of her personality into a cohesive whole. It seemed as though the unconscious was offering an image, a glimpse of the self in sun colors nearly blinding in their brilliance. It was particularly striking as an expression coming from this quiet, inconspicuous girl who liked to hide in telephone booths or sink into the corners of chairs. The picture was exciting, it was an experience, and it was not necessary to say much about it. Without interpretation it had a strong effect on Maureen, and I felt it with her.

After this, things went along fairly well for a while. The fears were less than they had been, and Maureen began to become a little more verbal. She talked about her work and her day-by-day experiences. She began to take an interest in decorating her apartment. Still I knew the fears were present even though she did not speak of them very much, and I did not prod her to do so. I tried to remain as close as possible to the level of her feelings, and to let her know that I was reacting *with* her as well as reacting *to* her. During this time she brought out many details of her life and they began to assume a pattern which corresponded to the pictures that were coming from those quiet hours when she would sit down at home with her crayons and trace out the images that would come to her. She brought the drawings to her sessions. Gradually "they" began to diminish in size and at last they lost their legs and arms. The running was less frantic in a picture called "Running to her friend, Gray Mouse." At this time she told me that her bedroom was filled with stuffed animals that she had collected for years, and that she often talked to them. To the next session she brought an armful of them to show them to me. It was apparent that they, too, had been helping her to cope with the unconscious contents which frightened her so much. And her telling me this, revealing this secret, showed the degree to which I was carrying the transcendent function for her. I felt that her dependence upon me was growing far too great, even though this dependence had made it possible for Maureen to establish a relationship that allowed her to express her feelings. There was always much reserve in her way of being with me, almost as though the more she could speak about herself the more she became afraid that she would overcome her neuroses, that she would be "cured," and that she would have to go out into the world without the support of the therapist, facing the unknown all alone. She wanted me as the mother she would have wanted to have, and she tried to force me into the role of mother by constantly asking me for advice and for special little favors in a childish way.

There came a time when she told me that she was thinking of moving to share an apartment with a girl with whom she had gotten acquainted at work. This took me somewhat by surprise and I responded that it appeared that she was getting ready to interact with someone on an ongoing basis. I knew the moment I said it that it was the wrong thing to have said. At the end of the session she just sat in the chair and would not leave. The next several sessions were especially difficult. She seemed to lose ground. At last she attacked me furiously:

Maureen: "You're trying to bust it all up."

Therapist: "Bust what up?"

It came out that she was in the position of trying to defend her fortress. I realized that it was being defended against the old mother image which she feared, the one who also represented a hostile world which regarded her presence in it as an intruder. I was trying to break her fortress down, by encouraging her, by expressing my confidence that she was getting better and might not need it. The deeper fear, underlying all the other fears, now emerged. That was the horrible, empty feeling that there might be nothing in the fortress after all her trouble—this was what she was so desperately trying to defend against. That is what she was feeling when she said, "I cannot put my gun down when you are also holding your gun."

When she next came she was tense and distant, really quite out of touch. She said, "I don't want to talk, I feel too flipped-out." When I suggested that she might prefer to paint what she was feeling, she readily agreed. She made one finger painting after another, always the stereotype of the stick-figure girl-ego, always running. Finally I encouraged her to show me what the girl was running from. She painted furiously, a painting in which the figure in front is about to be overtaken by the one approaching from the rear. She stared at the picture and said coldly, "One of them will have to be killed!"

This marked the beginning of the most crucial period in the therapy. Maureen was testing me and she even went so far as to make a gesture in the direction of another suicide attempt, which was obviously not genuine. She thought I would hospitalize her and thereby reject her as her mother had done. I did not. I asked her whether I could trust her to continue working on her problems and not give up. She said yes, and I did trust her. Gradually she began to trust me again, and this time it seemed that she was involved in therapy in a different way than she had been previously. The pictures had helped her to feel that she had some way of reaching the unconscious and looking into it. She did not have to close herself off from it any longer.

One day she brought a drawing which she titled "Sometimes the mind runs faster." She said that she had taken out her crayons and then had put a question to the unconscious, "Why do I become afraid?" Then she had let her imagination find an image. What now appeared before her was the same figure, but this time the head was separated from the body and was running ahead of it. "They" had retreated far into the background. I asked her what was happening in the picture, and she laughed. "My fantasy life runs ahead of me, it disconnects from me as a person, and I am always struggling to keep up with it. It looks as though what I am running from is not those others, whoever 'they' are, but I am running to keep up with what is in my head."

Then she wanted to fingerpaint again. The painting she made was the last of this series. The figure was seated. She saw what she had painted and knew that she was able at last to stop running. She would allow to happen whatever would happen. She had become aware that—just as her pictures had in a sense created themselves—there were forces in her which needed expression and that would follow her relentlessly like her own shadow no matter how she might try to avoid them. One cannot avoid what is part of one. The pictures provided a point of view that was able to transcend her ordinary awareness and also to avoid capitulating to the unconscious. She had objectified the struggle, and so could deal with it in a new way.

From this point in the analysis, Maureen began to have dreams, and the spiral of individuation took another turn.

Active imagination is, more than anything else, an attitude toward the unconscious. It cannot be said to be a *technique* or even a *method* of coming to terms with the unconscious, because it is a different experience for each person who is able to use it. The common feature of all varieties of active imagination is its dependence upon a view of the unconscious that recognizes its contents as containing innate structures (archetypes) which inevitably define the potentialities and the limitations of the personality. Through the use of active imagination, Analytical Psychology works in specific ways that differ from the approaches to the unconscious employed by other psychotherapeutic methods.

Gerhard Adler, a Jungian analyst who has written extensively on active imagination, summarized this difference:

The root conception which gives the approach of Analytical Psychology its specific character, and which indeed forms the foundation on which its whole technique is built, is the absolute directedness and seriousness with which it accepts the reality of the unconscious and its contents as an essential part of the whole personality. For the unconscious is, as Jung has so often pointed out, not merely . . . nothing but repressed sexuality or repressed will to power; but, as the matrix of the conscious mind, it is the really potent and creative layer of our psyche. The unconscious contains all the factors which are necessary for the integration of the personality. It possesses, as it were, a superior knowledge of our real needs in regard to their integration and the ways to achieve them. Only when the unconscious is understood in this way as the "objective psyche," containing all the regulating and compensating factors which work for the wholeness of the personality, does it make sense to advise a patient to face his unconscious in such a direct and forceful manner.[1]

Active imagination is not without its dangers. Unlike dreams, which are self-limiting, since we eventually wake up, active imagination may become extremely fascinating and may even pull the individual so strongly toward the unconscious that the ego position may be endangered. In a well-defended ego the danger is not so great, for the individual constantly brings into consciousness what he discovers, and relates it to his own thoughts or circumstances. This was the case with Maureen at the start, yet even with Maureen there was a period of grave risk when she felt that one of the two figures of her painting would have to be killed.

Charles was a graduate student in psychology, and a part-time occupational therapist at a mental hospital. He was at the opposite extreme from Maureen when it came to approaching his own unconscious processes, as well as those of everybody else. If Maureen barricaded herself against the unconscious, Charles wanted to dive in head first. He had taken LSD on two or three occasions and he smoked marijuana from time to time, but, of late, more rarely, as he realized that he had at hand more unconscious material than he could begin to understand and that it was more important to derive some meaning from it than simply to pile ecstasy on top of ecstasy. His dreaming was full of collective unconscious material. There was clearly too much to deal with already and when he broached the subject of his wanting to try active imagination,

I hesitated. Yet it seemed clear that Charles for all his interest in fantasy, was nevertheless a person with a clearly defined view of himself as one who was solid and well balanced. In a way he regarded himself almost as *too* well balanced, and this suggested to me that he had been trying to fit his dreams and fantasies into a plan dictated wholly from the conscious point of view. He was interested in finding out just how the psychological mechanisms he was studying worked out, and every aspect of behavior had to be accounted for theoretically and in practice.

He enjoyed becoming involved in long personal discussions with his friends in which intimate details of each other's lives were exposed and "explained" by his facile reasoning. Charles had found it necessary to explore the emotional life history of every companion, no matter how brief the relationship. He did not become deeply involved personally, and he failed to feel any ongoing sense of obligation to those whose feelings he had exposed when they had been with him. In fact, he seemed to be less than aware that the encounters had left any residue as far as other people were concerned—they certainly did not leave any with him. His attitude in personal relationships was, one might say, "pseudo-clinical," a combination of clinical curiosity without an accompanying sense of responsibility.

In his studies, Charles was careful to master the subject matter which was assigned. His papers and research projects were carried out in a highly professional manner. He conformed to the standards of style and content that were required, and he also managed to psych out his professors and give them the content they wanted, even when they were not aware that this was what they were looking for. In short, it looked as though Charles was sailing through graduate school without a worry.

Underneath appearances, things were not so smooth. Charles felt under constant pressure to produce, to find out, to relate to women. He was always figuring out how, he was always manipulating in his head; and after any experience he had a compulsive need to fit it into place in the mental picture of his own psychological structure. It may be asked, wasn't Charles attempting to do what we have been talking about all along, to gain a greater degree of self-knowledge? Superficially, it did appear that way. But he was not guided by the aims of the self in the sense of moving toward a sense of the fitting place of the ego in the total psyche, much less in the sense of his place as a human being within a field among other human beings. Rather, it seemed that his goal lay in the direction of ego mastery over the self on one hand, and toward his own domination of other people's psychological space, on the other. Charles's preoccupation with unconscious material seemed to be an effort to escape from a dry, superior, intellectual approach, and yet his very way of viewing this material was from a stance of a superior controlling ego. It was out of this truly paradoxical situation that he broached the subject of attempting some active imagination.

I suggested that painting would be a good medium for him, since he had studied painting in the past and he had enough technical skill so that he would not be discouraged by the obsessive character of his perfectionist needs in other areas. I suggested that he take a good long look at himself in the mirror, and then without any notion of what he would paint, to simply address the canvas and let it reply to the touch of his brushes. The canvas might become the ground upon which a representation would appear; I could not say more than that for I did not know any more than he what might come out of it, if, indeed, anything would come at all.

To the next analytical session Charles brought a large painting. I was struck at once by the color of the background, a vibrant yellow, shimmering as though one were looking directly into the sun. It was a picture of two men. One was a pale, sunken-chested, potbellied, slightly slumped man with pinkish-white skin. He resembled Charles, but was a weaker and older-looking version. The other had the appearance of a Neanderthal man, a little shorter than the first man, with shaggy hair, earth-toned skin, and heavy muscular structure. The two men, both naked, stood facing one another, looking each other in the eye. Charles told me: "The painting was spontaneous, and so it was very mysterious when that ape-man appeared. I can remember I started painting a hunched-up oval-like image, and out he came."

Here was a clear expression of a situation in which the conscious side with its self-image had become separated and dissociated from that aspect of the unconscious that touches the most primordial, the archetypal layer of the psyche. The man of the well-developed intellect had seen for the first time a primitive side which could not and did not interpose the process of rationalization when instinctive behavior was indicated. The dark man was non-rational, at least according to the preconceived notions of the white man as to what rationality is. Consequently, the dark-man-aspect had been rejected as having nothing of value to offer to this sophisticated student. It was seen by him as "illness," and not any illness he could discover in himself. It was, rather, the illness of the world, which was concentrated in the mentally disturbed— those who were not as "balanced" as he regarded himself to be.

It had made good sense for him to work as occupational therapist with these unfortunate people whom he saw as so underdeveloped in comparison with himself. But when the most primitive of all men appeared on his own canvas, face to face with an older and sadder image of himself, there was no possibility of avoiding the evidence that these were two elements of a single psyche. The glowing yellow light pervaded the picture with a feeling of clarity. No escaping the implications of this picture!

Then Charles did a lot of painting on his own, without any suggestions from me. He would just sit aimlessly before his table, letting images come up and then transcribing them to paper. One was a painting he called "Africa." It was a large design something like a map of the continent of Africa, broken into many pieces of all different shapes and colors. Of this he said, "I made layer upon layer of overlapping colors. All I can remember of that evening was the feeling that what I needed to do was build and change, I needed constant change."

This marked the beginning of a long series of experiments with painting which were allowed to "paint themselves" in a way which seemed nearly automatic. During this period,

Charles felt a growing dissatisfaction with his work as occupational therapist. He faced the hopelessness of ever accomplishing anything with the patients. He was not able to see
them through day by day, but could only work with them
for an hour or two a week when they came to the O.T. room.
It irked him that the psychiatrists regarded what he was doing
as "busy work," and did not pay the slightest attention to it.

Around this time Charles had quite a few dreams dealing
with conflicts between men—between brothers, or between
himself and an enemy soldier or someone criminal or uncontrollably impulsive or in some other way socially unacceptable.
He learned to recognize these figures as aspects of the ape-
man, and gradually was able to see that although this character was not compatible with his conscious image of himself,
that he nevertheless had some valuable qualities. First, there
was great strength and endurance in the ape-man. He would
not easily be dissuaded when he had determined to do something. There was an absence of indecision. There was a strong
capacity to sniff out a situation instinctively, to sense the total
environment and to be able to react to it directly and spontaneously. Charles, as he saw himself, in contrast, was flabby
and rather weak physically. He had to rely on his will and
his reasoning to assure his supremacy. His skill was all learned,
and the only way he could stay ahead of other people, he
had felt, was to learn more, and to develop more skills in
exploiting his learning to his own advantage. It became apparent that he was missing in his life much of the vitality
that the ape-man stood for, and that this vitality was encapsulated in the unconscious, waiting to be experienced if only he
could accept it in an unprejudiced way. He began by getting
into closer touch with his own body by allowing himself to
experience his physiological sensations in a more conscious
way, to face his own sensations with an open curiosity, and
to allow himself to reflect on his experiences and to give some
expression to them. The mode of expression could be of any
sort, but it would be necessary to go beyond pure reflection
and carry his psychic experience either into artistic form, verbal form, or into physical activity.

Throughout this period the image of the ape-man appeared from time to time in dreams. One day Charles decided that it was time to have a direct confrontation with this shadow figure in active imagination. But, as he later reported, he did not know how to go about it. A verbal encounter would be impossible, for the ape-man would be able to utter only guttural sounds. He thought of dancing with the ape-man—dancing is also a form of communication. But when he came to it, it did not happen that way at all. He sat alone in a room with a pencil and paper on the table before him. The ape-man appeared and sat on his left, beside him at the table.

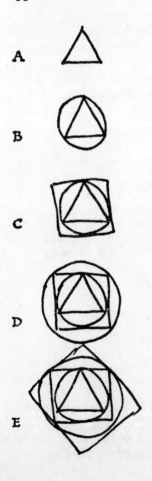

Charles picked up the pencil and drew a triangle on the blank sheet of paper. Then he put the pencil down.

The ape-man reached over and picked it up. He then drew a circle around Charles's triangle, and replaced the pencil on the paper.

Charles drew a square around the ape-man's circle.

The ape-man once more encircled the square.

Now Charles drew a larger square, this one at a forty-five-degree angle to the one he had drawn the last time.

Now the ape-man made a cross.

Charles responded with a cross of his own, but it disturbed him; it was not "neat"; the corners did not meet the corners of the triangle. It seemed to him that they should have.

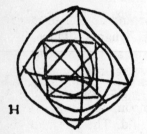

The ape-man once again encircled the whole drawing

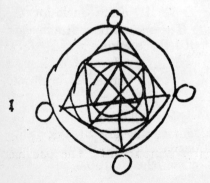

Now Charles made four small circles.

Charles was left with a sense of well-being.

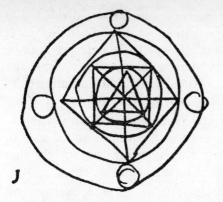

J

The ape-man encircled the whole once more, then disappeared.

The drawing finally created by the two was a mandala circle, corresponding to many symbols for wholeness which are often used for focusing the attention in meditation. His mandala called for some meditation from us, and we turned to the composition of the parts. Charles brought forth his own associations, and I suggested some amplifications, beginning with the initial triangle.

[A] "It is a form which we do not find anywhere in nature. It is like an arrowhead, moving, dynamic. Three is a masculine number, the triangle is like the arrangement of the male genitals. Three is the holy trinity. Again all male.

[B] The ape-man encircles the triangle. The circle is a natural form, we see it in the sun, moon, in flower forms, many places throughout the natural world. The ape-man belongs to nature.

[C] This is squaring the circle. It means enclosing the mystery of nature. The square stands for a fourth added to the masculine trinity. The fourth is something other, it may stand for earth, perhaps the devil, or shadow, or perhaps it brings the feminine into the picture. A mandala begins to emerge.

[D] Again, nature encompasses everything.

[E] A new square now, and this one is composed of triangles like the one that Charles started with. The one has become four.

[F]   The one that has become four is now divided into quarters. This time the ape-man has turned from his game of always encircling, and has attempted the straight lines of the civilized man. He begins to assimilate something from the other. The unconscious is affected and somehow altered by the interaction between these two figures.

[G]   Charles, as ego figure, is disconcerted when the unconscious aspect comes closer to consciousness and begins to function in a conscious way, that is, using the straight line which is not of nature but of human construction.

[H]   The primordial circle form is restated. Nature will remain constant, even though it enters into the area of the ego. Charles does not need to feel threatened by the nearness of his instinctual side.

[I]   As if to confirm this, Charles ventures into the ape-man's scheme. He makes four circles at the point where his own square touches the ape-man's circle.

[J]   The whole is encircled by the ape-man and the mandala is complete. There is a new sense of relatedness between Charles' conscious ego and the rough primordial figure. The conscious position has not been relinquished, nor has the other been repressed. Charles experienced a sense of well-being as the symbol acted to help him find a connection with his own unknown depths. He did not forget this image; at times he could reflect upon it and regain the feeling of inner harmony that came to him when he first meditated upon it."

A couple of months later Charles experienced still another encounter with the primitive man. This one came in the form of a dream.

I saw the ape-man carrying me with the greatest of ease high up on his hands, very gently. I felt very secure. Then he put me down and we stood face to face and embraced each other. He drew a picture of the dream.

I asked Charles, "What could be the meaning of the erection that both of them experienced in the dream?"

"There is an exhilarated feeling on the part of the ego figure. He has gained his manliness through his relationship with the other one, the primordial man who is for him the representation of a potency he did not know he possessed. Not alone sexual potency, though that was part of it, but potency in the sense of the vigor and drive to carry through what he intended with energy and delight."

We looked closely at the picture, and I noted, "The primordial man is stocky, built close to the ground."

Charles: "He gains power from his knowledge of the earth and the ways of nature. He takes her as she is, he does not have to try to subdue her, he accepts her and he finds it easy to be in harmony with her. He gets power from her, this is his carrying power, and this is what can carry the man of today if he allows himself to trust it and rest easy with it."

"Then the ego side is able to assimilate some of the energy of the unconscious?"

"Yes," replied Charles, "and the ego side also gives something. He gives to the primordial energy a delicacy of expression which he has acquired through his long experience with the culture and the arts, through his education, his training, his personal discipline. So, through the union of the pale man and the cave man the possibility of a newly created point of view comes into being. It is a great and exciting challenge for both of them, nearly an ecstasy, and their readiness to experience this union of opposites is symbolized by their erections."

It was clear that the sexual element of the dream, and in fact of the whole encounter between the two, was to be understood as a metaphor for the creative act of synthesizing conscious attitudes and unconscious contents. Here symbolism that appeared in sexual images did not refer to a problem that was primarily sexual, nor did it specifically suggest homosexuality. Intimate relationship had to occur between these two male figures, who represented ego and shadow, the opposing aspects of the masculine nature within a single human being.

Through these encounters Charles learned the nature of the potential which had been previously locked up in the unconscious. Gradually he was able to establish a two-way transactional relationship between his critical, evaluating, and controlling ego, and the energetic spontaneous, and irrepressible archaic man within him. Where, in the beginning, I had served as the primary mediator for the transcendent function, Charles now took over that role more and more often.

I can imagine that the reader who has never participated in this kind of experience may be asking himself, why in the world when there is so much trouble everywhere that needs attention should a grown man be spending his time having imaginary conversations with some prehistoric character, and engaging in paper and pencil games with him? What practical purpose does it serve?

I would not want to suggest that any practical purpose is served directly, nor is that the intention behind active imagination, dream analysis or any other analytic procedure we may decide to use. Through the process, if seriously undertaken, transformations of the personality do occur. Narrow attitudes become broadened, one-sidedness gives way to the capacity to view a situation from several positions, aggression is replaced by productive activity, and passivity becomes receptivity. The changes are often subtle, but they go deep, and the one who experiences them knows that he is living in a different way than he did before. This difference may not be readily evident to people who know him, for often he has hidden his self-doubts and insecurities well enough from public view; but *he* knows, and this is what is important.

In the case of Charles the analytic work and specifically the active imagination led him to withdraw the projections he had made on the patients with whom he was working in the mental hospital. He no longer looked upon them as subhumans and himself as a superior being. Of course he would never have admitted, early in his analysis, that this is what he had been doing; but his very attitude of hopelessness toward what he was trying to do and the patronizing way he spoke about the patients gave away his real view of them. His manner of distancing himself from his patients by standing over them and observing them and waiting for the psychiatrists who never came, was evidence enough that he was acting out in his work the split in himself between the natural intuitive energetic side and the cool professional side. One side was projected onto the patients, who were "hopeless," and the other side was projected onto the psychotherapists, who stood for an idealized version of his own ego.

As the alien sides within himself became friends, he began to deal with his O.T. patients in a new way, as though seeking out their potential for change, regardless of how deeply buried that potential might be. He no longer had to wait for the psychotherapists who would never come; *he* was the person who was there, and he began to be fully there in a way that was different from before.

The case of Charles illustrates an important point, not only with respect to active imagination, but also to the whole of Analytical Psychology. The source of change, of transformation, in the individual comes from within the individual himself, rather than from any outside agent. There is no dictum in Analytical Psychology that the environment must or should shape the individual, nor is there the implication that the behavior of the individual ought to be modified to conform with the environment or its demands. Analytical Psychology does not seek to achieve a race of happy, productive sheep. People are troubled in a troubled world; they do not cry " 'Peace,' when there is no peace." Nor does this psychological view suggest that individuals submit to any external authority which is given the power to determine what kind of activity or behavior is acceptable and what is not. Analytical Psychology casts its lot with the champions of individual freedom and offers another source of guidance than that of the political or psychological despot, however "benevolent" he may be. That other source is the inner mystery, the unconscious, which has its own individual way of manifesting itself to every man and woman who is open to see it. Active imagination is one of many ways in the analytic process which teach an individual to develop his own capacity for relating to the interlocking worlds of soul and society.

Active imagination is not always a long and involved process. Sometimes it comes as a flash, a momentary experience

to which an individual gives himself, draws the meaning out
of it, and is changed by it.

Such a moment came to Clara at a crucial time in her
analysis. Clara was a woman in her early thirties who had
never married, although she was charming and intelligent and
attractive. Certain attitudes instilled in her early childhood,
as well as events in adolescence, left her with a pathological
fear of intimacy, so that her sexual drives were thoroughly
inhibited. While she was in analysis it became possible to
lessen the strength of these inhibitions, and in time the possibility of a close relationship with a certain man appeared
on the horizon. She had one or two erotic dreams, and then
the dreams stopped, or she stopped remembering them. She
put off taking any active steps toward encouraging the relationship with the man. I had written in my notes after her
last analytic session: "An arid session. She is in a rut. Can't
move out into life enough. Inertia. Finds it hard to get up
in the morning."

When Clara came to the next session she was obviously
eager to tell me something. It was about a waking fantasy
that she had experienced the day before: "I was standing over
the sink, peeling something. All of a sudden the water started
coming up in the drain in a kind of rush. It was spouting
out. I had a feeling of panic, of loss of control. I was afraid
of getting inundated. Then I thought, what's the use of getting excited, all it can do is overflow. The word 'unconscious'
floated through my mind."

What seemed to be the difficulty underlying the "aridity"
of our last sessions, was Clara's fear that she would be overwhelmed by the unconscious, that is, by her own deeply buried sexuality. She had attempted to stop the flow, but in discussing the matter with me in her previous analytic session
the unconscious had evidently been stimulated to the point
that it released some of its contents. This was experienced as
the gushing waters. What was especially interesting was that it
appeared in such a humdrum place, so near at hand, and
furthermore, that the unconscious provided its own balance.
It seemed to say, "Let it happen, at least something in your

life will be moving, and it may not be as dangerous as you believe." The interaction with the symbolic presentation came as Clara found a way to accept the message in the flow of water upward from the deeper levels of her being. She saw it as permission to avoid imposing controls upon any spontaneous responses she might have. She could anticipate that now some blockage between herself and the unconscious had been dissolved, and she could also expect that this greater freedom would reflect in her dealing in interpersonal situations as well.

Active imagination may provide access to a person who is deeply depressed, when no amount of "rational conversation" can have an effect. There is a certain kind of depression, in which the individual feels desperately alone and helpless to face his tasks and responsibilities. Such a person was the middle-aged professional woman whom we will call Dolores. Her isolation appeared to her to be a separation from the world of people, but, as I saw it, underneath her feeling of isolation was the real problem, the unconscious had drawn away from consciousness and had ceased to stimulate and nurture the ego. Therefore, Dolores projected everything outside; she had problems with her aged father, she suffered from stomach ulcers, she had "financial problems" which were completely unrealistic in view of her more than adequate income, but mostly she complained that she felt no zest for life, she was always weary; she regarded herself as being without love and without purpose.

Dolores had suffered for many years from periodic depressions. Several years ago she had gone to Zurich for a summer and there she was able to undergo a few months of Jungian analysis. She had improved considerably at the time. Now the depression had returned full force, and she was not able to return to her former analyst. She came to me for help, and circumstances were such that it was vitally important to bring her out of the depression as rapidly as possible. Four sessions were arranged on four successive days. I counted on her previous experience in Jungian analysis to provide us with a common frame of reference so that we would be able to move into the problems without having to spend much time communicating our basic premises to one another.

In the first session she talked about her history of depressive episodes. She told me that it seemed to her as if some of the most dramatic changes in her life had come out of her attempts to handle depression and boredom. In this way she went to college, went into the Peace Corps, and went to graduate school. In a way, she said, her trip to Zurich had a similar motivation. One reason she felt so depressed and desperate now, was that she could see no place to run, just an endless procession of days leading eventually to retirement which she both anticipated and dreaded. She asked, "What will I do when I am left entirely upon my own resources? I can hardly tolerate being alone for a day now—how will I ever face a lifetime of being alone?"

I tried to help her to get down into her feelings and to let me know how it was. I did not allow her to put up her knowledge and experience in Jungian therapy as a barrier between us; in fact, I dismissed her theoretical framework completely. In this first session her feeling of having no place to escape was intensified. When she left, I suggested that between now and the next day she should examine her feelings and put them down in some way, either by writing or drawing.

In the interim she did both. She had written, "Perhaps I was expecting instant relief from all the tension I have been under, but I was disappointed to continue feeling badly today, especially nauseated and as if I would throw up any minute. This is disconcerting and makes it hard to concentrate."

She had also drawn a picture, and brought it to me. I asked her to describe what she saw there. She said, "It's me, it's how I feel. I'm sitting alone, in my cage and that is all there is, nothing inside the cage but me, and nothing outside it. That's all there is."

I looked at the picture carefully. The figure was seated, her head bent over and resting on her knees, her arms forward, hands clasped about her ankles. The color she had chosen was a flat, monotonous blue. There was a horizontal black bar at the top and bottom, and vertical lines between. I wanted to know better how Dolores felt, so I sat myself down on the floor and took the position of the figure in the painting. As my head dropped forward onto my knees, I automatically closed my eyes. It was a position of complete passivity. Even if I had been seated in the midst of the most beautiful garden, I would not have known it. The position made it impossible for me to experience anything outside of my sense of being by myself.

When I had let the feeling work on me and had some sense of it, I then asked Dolores how she could be sure that she was, in fact, in a cage. Had she examined it carefully? It had no back, after all, and no sides. Perhaps it was only the front of a cage, that she had mistaken for an entire cage. Perhaps there were ways to get out that she had not seen because she had not looked for them.

It all seems so obvious when looking back to it. But at that moment Dolores was amazed to discover that she was not in a cage at all. She could get up and walk around the edges and be free of it. She felt as though she had experienced a revelation! Anyone could, of course, have told her that her problems were not real, that they were "all in her head," but this was quite different. The information came from herself, from her own drawing and from the implications of the drawing which she was able to discover. There is a great difference here. When the insight comes from a friend, an adviser, or a therapist, it comes from "just another person who doesn't understand." The patient has a right to respond, "Yes, I know that I ought to change my ways, but if I could change them I would. That's just the trouble, I can't change, that's why I am coming to you." The analyst does not take the viewpoint which opposes that of the patient's ego in order to impose the new view. The new view can and will come from the unconscious itself, given the enabling situation in which it can happen. The analyst's role is to follow the emerging contents of the unconscious and, only when it is necessary, help the analysand to recognize what is happening.

When Dolores appeared for her third session she announced

that she was feeling a great deal better. "The last session," she said, "was like a cold shower—it woke me up to a few things." She had made two pictures and now wanted to explain them to me. The first showed a vast horizontal blue plane resembling the curvature of the earth. Upon it stood a tiny black female figure very much alone, with arms outstretched. Above were huge black-gray clouds.

Dolores had broken out of her self-imposed prison. She seemed very small, facing the immensity of her problems, which were symbolized in the great foreboding clouds. But she was free—at least for the time being—frightened, perhaps, but free.

The second picture, also done in blue and black, was devoid of any human life. The black curvature of the earth was seen, this time more like a gentle hilltop. From it rose a straight tree, a scraggly pine with only two branches and, on top, a crown that could have been of leaves except that they were not differentiated, so that all one could see was the tree's blackness silhouetted against the sky. The sky was infused with a blue light, in the midst of which gleamed one star. At the bottom of the picture Dolores had lettered in these words:

> A lonely God—enthroned in lonely space
> Created us as we are—
> As single as a tree—
> As separate as a star.

The second picture had come as an interaction between Dolores's conscious attitude and the first picture, which had represented her unconscious fears and hopes. She stood before immensity, and enjoyed the freedom of being there, even though it terrified her. The third picture showed her the wonder which she was capable of contemplating once she could accept her loneliness as an aspect of the human condition, even as an aspect fashioned in the image of God. From this point of view, "lonely" loses some of its agonizing texture and becomes "single," that is, individual, and also "separate," that is, differentiated from all others and, therefore, unique. To accept this is to take another step on the way to individuation.

She told me, "I felt much more at ease today, both inwardly and outwardly. Through these pictures some contact must have been made with the unconscious. I have not suffered from tension and nausea as I did the first days."

I asked her if she knew what had happened.

"I am not at all sure," she replied. "Perhaps it was your direct confrontation of my own responsibility for my mental state—the cold shower I mentioned. Whatever it was, it has enabled me to look more favorably on my total life situation."

We then went on to discuss the specific problems with which she was faced, and her attitude was indeed much more open to new possibilities of solution than it had been before.

Little needs to be said about the last session with Dolores. Her final picture told it all, unmistakably. The elements of the previous picture were all there, but this picture was entirely different. The ground had become a grassy meadow reflecting the blue of the sky and the yellow sunshine. The tree was there, but it was not the same tree. It was now a strong tree with many branches, an old tree, solid and substantial. Sunlight and shadow played on the trunk, which was rounded and dimensional, not flat as before. Most exciting was the crown of the tree, full of many-colored leaves in great joyous clusters, interspersed with pink blossoms. The sky was light blue with gentle, white clouds floating across, and in this sky four birds were flying—separate, alone, yet belonging where they were and sharing their condition with each other.

Dolores's mood had changed to match the picture. She was ready to move back into life and to become active again. I do not mean to suggest that any problems had actually been solved, only that she was able to view her problems in a different way. This was a first step toward dealing with the objective situation, the next step would have to be taken by her, and in her own setting of everyday living. This is where the transformations of analysis are tested anyway. Statistics be damned, the only validation that I know for the analytic process is the validation which is stamped on the life of the individual who has experienced it.

The unconscious has many ways of communicating with
the ego besides through visual imagery such as we have seen
in these examples of active imagination. Some people are able
to personify the figures of the unconscious and engage them
in conversation. These figures may have appeared in a dream
without yielding up the meaning of the dream in a way in
which the dreamer is able to understand it. The dream figure
may then be called upon while one is in the waking state,
and actively confronted. In this form of active imagination
a true dialogue between the ego and the unconscious may
take place. The conscious side states its position vis-à-vis the
dream, or asks the question that the dream has evoked. It
then suspends all critical judgment and allows the unconscious
an equal opportunity to express itself. Often words will come,
or ideas, which have meaning, and to which the ego may
respond. And so it is possible to carry on a conversation with
a dream figure or some other unconscious aspect such as the
anima or some representation of her.

It may seem to some that this is a way of manipulating
the unconscious, that the power of suggestion is a strong element here. Those who have been able to enter successfully
into the kind of dialogue that is true active imagination know
that it is something different from suggestion or "seeding the
unconscious." The material that comes forth when the controlling tendencies of the ego are suspended is often what
is least expected or wanted. The impact with which these
"new" ideas come forth indicates that they have their own
autonomy and are not at all a reflection or distortion of the
conscious position.

What is important is that the dialogue between the ego
and the dream figure be transcribed onto paper so that it
can later be analyzed, very much as a dream or a picture
from the unconscious is analyzed. Only then can the greatest
value be derived from the assimilation of the unconscious
contents.

There are many other ways of getting into active relationship with the unconscious. In *Memories, Dreams, Reflections*,
Jung described some of the methods he discovered which were

for him doorways into the unconscious. In every case there was some tangible product into which his emotions could flow freely, and which could later be regarded not only from the side of the emotions that produced it, but also from his rational side. He described how, as a child, he used to spend many hours "playing passionately with building blocks." He recalled how he built little houses and castles with bottles to form the sides of gates and vaults. When he was a man, he built a retreat house for himself at Bollingen far down the Lake of Zurich from the house in which he lived with his family. The shape and form of the house was dictated by his inner needs, and with the passage of years new parts had to be added as he himself grew.

Jung also carved in stone; the ring of the chisel against the rock gave shape to his emotions during some of his most difficult times. He wrote of the help he found through stone carving after the death of his wife and how this work helped him to shape the contents which poured forth from the unconscious so that he could later express them in words in a series of important writings. There followed a period of introspection and objectification through the successive phases from idea to stone to the word. Nor was this all. There were periods when he inscribed and painted manuscripts, and at other times he wrote out his inner experiences by hand in beautifully illuminated books. He painted murals on the walls at Bollingen. His imagination was not a matter of the head—his whole person was involved in it; every skill and craft he could master was enlisted in its service.

If we take our inspiration from Jung, we will find many avenues through which we may pass in the quest of the mysteries of our own inner natures. Jung was an innovator and much of what he did was to venture into new areas which had never been related specifically to the task of psychological healing. It would not be in the spirit of Jung to slavishly copy Jung, to attempt to do what he did in the way that he described. The spirit of Jung, it seems to me, demands that we utilize the means and skills, the techniques and devices that are natural for us as individuals to use in our encounters with the unconscious. Writing and the graphic arts are available to everyone, but we need not be limited to these. New media offer new vehicles for the expression of the archetypal images. Experimenting with still photography, for example, offers many possibilities, and motion pictures even more. Videotaping, single and multiple voice recording, lighting effects, and electronic music could be added to the list. It may be thought that the technical difficulties would get in the way of the pure expression, but there were technical difficulties in stone carving also. The very difficulties become part of the creative process and part of the challenge to the imagination. In this way, the tools of the material world may serve the needs of the human spirit for expression.

An analysand of mine had heard about active imagination and asked me if I would tell her a little about it. What I told her, briefly, was this: Active imagination is not a confrontation of the ego and the unconscious directly. It entails getting *outside* of the ego position and yet not letting the unconscious take over the control either. The task is to assume the role of the transcendent function, which means being able to give equal credit and equal opportunity for free expression to both the ego and the unconscious. If the ego takes control and forces, it doesn't work; it is a fabrication. If you have to ask yourself whether it is really the unconscious that is speaking, then it is not. On the other hand, if the ego gives way to the unconscious completely, then there is the danger of getting lost in it. I see no virtue in encouraging yelling, screaming, crying, panic—I see no particular virtue in inducing a psychotic episode, however temporary. The potentiality for it is present in everyone, and a skillful therapist can bring it to the surface quite easily. (Often an unskillful therapist does so even more easily, and also unwittingly.)

I personally believe in keeping functioning people functioning. Therefore I do not remove the support of the orientation to the real world. I am often reminded of a passage in William Blake's *The Marriage of Heaven and Hell*, in which Blake and his infernal companion look into the "infinite Abyss" (hell, the unconscious), "till a void boundless as a nether sky appear's beneath us, & we held by the roots of trees . . . hung over this immensity." I, too, feel strongly that in our katabases we must be held by the roots of trees, that is, by our connection with the real world. That is just the danger of uncontrolled use of psychotomimetic drugs—that they may cut off the connection with the objective world, especially in cases where the ego is not sufficiently solidly based to begin with. I believe that active imagination is to be employed with utmost care and respect for the volatile nature of the unconscious.

Another analysand of mine, one who had himself traveled the way of active imagination into considerable depth, expressed with great sensitivity what his active imagination had meant to him. He wrote in his notebook:

It is possible to allow oneself so to be, that is, to be unraveled for the sake of affirming who one is. When the parts are separated and untangled one can experience each in itself and from that attentive focus upon the parts, realize more fully the ingredients of the self. One can do this even in the midst of relating considerately to others. Granted this is no easy task; perhaps it is better to remove oneself to the mountains for the duration of the dangling period. It is an art to accomplish this while in the midst of responsible relationships to others, an art that can only be known after the dreadful, beautiful looking within process that, if practiced properly, may lead to the control of one's madness to the right degree.

13

RELIGION:
AND OTHER APPROACHES
TO THE UNKNOWABLE

When the easy concept fails—that man is nothing but his own conscious personality—it becomes necessary to face the proposition that "individual consciousness is based on and surrounded by an indefinitely extended unconscious psyche."[1] Jung's psychology, as we have seen, is based on the need he perceived to explore these indefinite extensities of the psyche, and to penetrate them—which he did, perhaps more deeply than any other psychologist or psychotherapist had done before. Since he regarded the unconscious as far more than a bundle of instincts plus the residues of individual consciousness, he could not imagine the unconscious as bound up in any single individual. As a psychotherapist he did not assign one unconscious to his patient and another to himself, with the possibility of connecting them through a chain of associations or bridging them by the transference. Rather, he saw that each man's consciousness emerges like an island from the great sea in which all find their base, with the rim of wet sand encircling each island corresponding to the "personal unconscious." But it is the collective unconscious—that sea—that is the birthplace of all consciousness, and from there the old ideas arise anew, and their connections with contemporary situations are initiated.

Realizations such as these were growing in Jung in the last

years of his close association with Freud, and especially while he was pursuing his study of Miss Miller's fantasies, which he was to publish in his book *The Psychology of the Unconscious.*[2] In working on the amplification of these fantasies, Jung discovered their rootedness in non-personal experience. The themes of the fantasies paralleled themes of creation myths which Jung discovered through his research as having been manifested in various ancient civilizations in widely separated parts of the world. Everywhere man has yearned to know of his own psychic beginnings; and he has fashioned myths and legends, songs and rituals, to express his awareness of his individual littleness in a world whose magnitude impresses and eludes him. The study of comparative religion, legend and folklore, led Jung to reconsider the events of his own childhood and youth. They all had seemed so personal to him at the time, but now proved to be only ingenious new scenarios based on ageless archetypal plots.

While Jung was in his residency at Burghölzli, his chief, the disciplined and demanding Professor Bleuler, had required him to concentrate on psychiatric treatment of mental patients and on conducting the Word Association studies. During his association with Freud, his desire to carry the new psychoanalytic theory into his own practice and research in order to validate it empirically took up most of his attention and thereby imposed limitations on his personal search. Whatever feelings Jung may have had during these years (1900–13) about the necessity of going beyond the province of the methodical researcher and theoretician, his responsibilities and loyalties held him in check. His conscious efforts were directed toward widening his experience and knowledge in areas to which he had committed himself both publicly and in the intimate circles of his professional associates.

The unconscious, however, did not fail to make its autonomous tendencies known to Jung whenever he turned his attention to it. I do not mean that he recognized the unconscious only in his patients, or in the clinical reports of others. The primary opening to the unconscious was through the aperture of his own consciousness, through his dreams and visions and the products of his imagination. Nevertheless, until his open break with Freud in 1913, Jung was firmly based in consciousness and, I believe, basically committed to the primary therapeutic goal of the growth and development of the ego personality. There were other voices calling him, and he listened, but he did not address himself fully to the confrontation with the unconscious until after he realized that he could never be as sure as he thought Freud was, that truth was truth, or that scientific investigation would sooner or later be able to expose the mysteries of the psyche.

After his separation from Freud and his withdrawal from the psychoanalytic circle, Jung found himself isolated from most of his former colleagues. He had no interest in justifying his position or winning adherents to it. The years from 1913 to 1917 were for Jung a period of inclining his ear toward his inner voices and allowing them opportunity for full expression. He voluntarily entered into the dimension of the nonrational, submitting himself to emotions over which he had little control. In the grip of strong affect, he suffered the experience of observing the contents of the unconscious as they formed themselves into images and as they became personified. Some of the figures that arose before him in his vision or imagination, had their source in the history of ancient civilizations, some in myth and legend, some in epic poetry, and some in the Bible. Each being had its own symbolic import: for example, Salome appeared as the anima figure who was "blind because she does not see the meaning of things," and Elijah, "the figure of the wise old prophet represents the factor of intelligence and knowledge."[3] Characters flooded into awareness, bringing confusion more than clarity.

A turning point came with the appearance of the figure who was to become Jung's *psychagogue*, the instructor of his soul in matters of the unconscious. The opening to the unconscious which preceded the appearance of the Philemon figure came in a dream which he described as an epiphany:

There was a blue sky, like the sea, covered not by clouds but by flat brown clods of earth. It looked as if the clods were breaking

apart and the blue water of the sea were becoming visible between them. But the water was the blue sky. Suddenly there
appeared from the right a winged being sailing across the sky.
I saw that it was an old man with the horns of a bull . . .[4]

Jung accepted this presence as a guiding spirit, at times
as real as a living personality. Jung wrote of Philemon:

[He] brought home to me the crucial insight that there are
things in the psyche which I do not produce, but which produce
themselves and have their own life. Philemon represented a force
which was not myself. In my fantasies I held conversations with
him, and he said things which I had not consciously thought
. . . He said I treated thoughts as if I generated them myself,
but in his view thoughts were like animals in the forest, or people in a room, or birds in the air, and added, "If you see people
in a room, you would not think that you had made those people,
or that you were responsible for them." It was he who taught
me psychic objectivity, the reality of the psyche.[5]

The encounter with Philemon gave Jung the impetus to
continue with his experiment, and later, as he looked back
upon what had happened he was not quite sure whether he
had been doing the experimenting or whether the experiment
had been done *to him*. At any rate, he had committed himself
into the hands of the unknown, and his experiences were filled
with terror and wonder. He recorded the fantasies scrupu-
lously, in order to be able to get some sort of grasp of them,
to be able to face them in the clear light of reality and to
try to understand what meaning might lie behind them.

At times during this period, Jung was so overcome with
emotion that he feared that he might be in danger of losing
his psychic balance altogether. The writing down of the material helped to keep it under control, since once it was objectified he could then turn his mind to other things, secure
in the knowledge that the unconscious material was safe from
loss or distortion. During this strained and difficult period
of his life he never withdrew from his routine of active work
and relatedness to his family. Life with his wife and children
proved to be a stabilizing influence, as also was his psychiatric

practice. He forced himself to move back and forth from the conscious position with its distinct, if temporal, demands— to the unconscious one. Gradually he attained a capacity for granting each position its important role in his life and, when it was necessary, to allow the interpenetration of the one by the other.

He had discovered the practice of active imagination. In principle, it was the same discovery that many people have made in the course of their struggle toward individuation. Only Jung was the pathfinder who introduced active imagination into the area of psychotherapy. He had the courage to state that psychotherapy cannot be defined altogether as a science. In making a science of her, he said, "the individual imagines that he has caught the psyche and holds her in the hollow of his hand. He is even making a science of her in the absurd supposition that the intellect, which is but a part and a function of the psyche, is sufficient to comprehend the much greater whole."[6]

The word *science* comes from the Latin *scientia*, which means knowledge, and therefore is identified with consciousness and with the intellectual effort to draw into consciousness as much knowledge as possible. But, with our psychological concept of the unconscious, and with all the evidence that has emerged to justify its reality, it is necessary to recognize that there is a very large area of human experience with which science cannot deal. It has to do with all that is neither finite nor measurable, with all that is neither distinct nor—potentially, at least—explicable. It is that which is not accessible to logic or to the "word." It begins at the outermost edge of knowledge. Despite the continuing expansion or even explosion of information, there will forever be limits beyond which the devices of science cannot lead a man.

It becomes a matter of seeing the "created world" in terms of a "creating principle." This is difficult when we conceive of ourselves as being among "the created" and hence being unable to comprehend that which was before we existed and which will continue after the ego-consciousness with which we identify ourselves no longer exists in the form in which we know it. We cannot, however much we strive, incorporate the unconscious into consciousness, because the first is illimitable and the second, limited. What is the way then, if there is a way, to gain some understanding of unconscious processes? It seemed to Jung, as it has to others who have set aside the ego to participate directly in the mystery, that the risk of entering into the unfathomable sphere of the unconscious must be taken.

It is not that Jung deliberately sought to dissolve the more or less permeable barrier between consciousness and the unconscious. It was, in effect, something that happened to him—sometimes in dreams, and sometimes in even more curious ways. Under the aegis of Philemon as guiding spirit, Jung submitted himself to the experience that was happening to him. He accepted the engagement as full participant; his ego remained to one side in a non-interfering role, a helper to the extent that observation and objectivity were required to record the phenomena that occurred. And what did occur shocked Jung profoundly. He realized that what he felt and saw resembled the hallucinations of his psychotic patients, with the difference only that he was able to move into that macabre half-world at will and again out of it when external necessity demanded that he do so. This required a strong ego, and an equally strong determination to step away from it in the direction of that super-ordinate focus of the total personality, the self.

However, we must remember that it was with no such clearly formulated goal that Jung in those days took up the challenge of the mysterious. He was experiencing and working out his fantasies as they came to him. Alternately, he was living a normal family life and carrying on his therapeutic work with patients, which gave him a sense of active productivity.

Meanwhile, the shape of his inner experience was becoming more definite, more demanding. He found himself besieged from within by a great restlessness. He felt that the entire atmosphere around him was highly charged, as one sometimes senses it before an electrical storm. The tension in the air seemed even to affect the other members of the household; his children said and did odd things, which were most uncharacteristic of them. He himself was in a strange state, a mood of apprehension, as though he moved through the midst of a houseful of spirits. He had the sense of being surrounded by the clamor of voices—from without, from within—and there was no surcease for him until he took up his pen and began to write.

Then, during the course of three nights, there flowed out of him a mystifying and heretical document which began: "The dead came back from Jerusalem, where they found not what they sought." Written in an archaic and stilted style, it was signed with the pseudonym of Basilides, a gnostic of the second century after Christ. Basilides had belonged to that group of early Christians which was declared heretical by the Church because of its pretensions to mystic and esoteric insights and by emphasis on direct knowledge rather than faith. It was as though the orthodox Christian doctrine had been examined and found too perfect, and therefore incomplete, since the answers were given in that doctrine, but many of the questions were missing. Crucial questions were raised in *The Seven Sermons of the Dead*; the blackness of the nether sky was dredged up; the paradoxes of faith and disbelief were laid side by side. Traces of the dark matter of the *Sermons* may be found throughout Jung's works which followed, especially in those which deal with religion and its infernal counterpoint, alchemy. All through these later writings it is as if Jung were struggling with the issues raised in the dialogues with the "*Dead*," who are the spokesmen for that dark realm beyond the understanding of man; but it is in Jung's last great work, *Mysterium Coniunctionis*, on which he worked for ten years and completed only in his eightieth year, that the meaning of the *Sermons* finally finds its definition. Jung said that the voices of the *Dead* were the voices of the Unanswered, Unresolved, and Unredeemed. Their true names became known to Jung only at the end of his life.

The words flow between the *Dead*, who are the questioners, and the archetypal wisdom which has its expression in man,

who regards it as revelation. It is not accepted that God spoke
two thousand years ago and has been silenced ever since, as
is commonly supposed by many who call themselves religious.
The authors of the New Testament attempted to combat this
attitude, as Paul says in his Epistle to the Hebrews (I:1),
"God who at sundry times and in divers manner spake in
time past unto the fathers by thy prophets, hath in these
last days spoken unto us by his Son . . ." Revelation occurs
in every generation. When Jung spoke of a new way of understanding the hidden truths of the unconscious, his words were
shaped by the same archetypes that in the past inspired the
prophets, and in the present are operative in the unconscious
of modern man. Perhaps this is why he was able to say of
the *Sermons*: "These conversations with the dead formed a
kind of prelude to what I had to communicate to the world
about the unconscious: a kind of pattern of order and interpretation of all its general contents."

I will not attempt here to interpret or explain the *Sermons*.
They must stand as they are, and whoever can find meaning
in them is free to do so; whoever cannot may pass over them.
They belong to Jung's "initial experiences" from which derived
all of his work, all of his creative activity. A few excerpts
will offer some feeling for the "otherness" which Jung experienced at that time, and which was for him so germinal. The
first *Sermon*, as he carefully lettered it in antique script in
his Red Book, begins:

> *The dead came back from Jerusalem where they found not what
> they sought. They prayed me let them in and besought my word,
> and thus I began my teaching.*
>
> *Hearken: I begin with nothingness. Nothingness is the same
> as fullness. In infinity full is no better than empty. Nothingness
> is both empty and full. As well might ye say anything else of
> nothingness, as for instance, white it is, or black, or again, it is
> not, or it is. A thing that is infinite and eternal hath no quali-
> ties, since it hath all qualities.*
>
> *This nothingness or fullness we name the pleroma.*

All that I can say of the *pleroma* is that it goes beyond
man's capacity to conceive of it, for it is of another order

than man's consciousness. It is that infinite which can never be grasped, not even in imagination. But since we, as people, are not infinite, we are distinguished from the *pleroma*. The first *Sermon* continues:

> *Creatura is not in the pleroma, but in itself. The pleroma is both beginning and end of created beings. It pervadeth them, as the light of the sun everywhere pervadeth the air. Although the pleroma pervadeth altogether, yet hath created body no share thereof, just as a wholly transparent body becometh neither light nor dark through the light which pervadeth it. We are, however, the pleroma itself, for we are a part of the eternal and the infinite. But we have no share thereof, as we are from the pleroma infinitely removed; not spiritually or temporally, but essentially, since we are distinguished from the pleroma in our essence as creatura, which is confined within time and space.*

The quality of human life, according to this teaching, lies in the degree to which each person distinguishes himself from the totality of the unconscious. The wresting of consciousness, of self-awareness, from the tendency to become submerged in the mass, is the task of the individuated person. This is the implication of a later passage from the *Sermons*:

> *What is the harm, ye ask, in not distinguishing oneself?*
> *If we do not distinguish, we get beyond our own nature, away from creatura. We fall into indistinctiveness . . . We fall into the pleroma itself and cease to be creatures. We are given over to dissolution in the nothingness. This is the death of the creature. Therefore we die in such measure as we do not distinguish. Hence the natural striving of the creature goeth towards distinctiveness, fighteth against primeval, perilous sameness. This is called the* principium individuationis. *This principle is the essence of the creature.*

In the pleroma all opposites are said to be balanced and therefore they cancel each other out; there is no tension in the unconscious. Only in man's consciousness do these separations exist:

> *The Effective and the Ineffective.*
> *Fullness and Emptiness.*

Living and Dead.
Difference and Sameness.
Light and Darkness.
The Hot and the Cold.
Force and Matter.
Time and Space.
Good and Evil.
Beauty and Ugliness.
The One and the Many . . .

These qualities are distinct and separate in us one from the other; therefore they are not balanced and void, but are effective. Thus are we the victims of the pairs of opposites. The pleroma is rent in us.

Here lies the germ of the concept marking the necessity of ever looking to the unconscious for that compensating factor which can balance the one-sided attitude of consciousness. Always, in the analytic process, we have searched the dreams, the fantasies, and the products of active imagination, for the elements that will balance: the shadow for persona-masked ego, the anima for the aggressively competitive man, the animus for the self-effacing woman, the old wise man for the *puer aeternis,* the deeply founded earth-mother for the impulsive young woman. The traditional Christian ideal of attempting to live out only the so-called higher values and eschewing the lower is proclaimed disastrous in this "heresy." The traditional Christian ideal is antithetical to the very nature of consciousness or awareness:

When we strive after the good or the beautiful, we thereby forget our own nature, which is distinctiveness, and we are delivered over to the qualities of the pleroma, which are pairs of opposites. We labour to attain to the good and the beautiful, yet at the same time we also lay hold of the evil and the ugly, since in the pleroma these are one with the good and the beautiful. When, however, we remain true to our own nature, which is distinctiveness, we distinguish ourselves from the good and the beautiful, and therefore, at the same time, from the evil and ugly. And thus we fall not into the pleroma, namely, into nothingness and dissolution.

Buried in these abstruse expressions is the very crux of
Jung's approach to religion. He is deeply religious in the sense
of pursuing his life task under the overwhelming awareness
of the magnitude of an infinite God, yet he knows and accepts
his limitations as a human being to say with certainty anything about this "Numinosum," this totally "Other." In a
filmed interview Jung was asked, "Do you believe in God?"
He replied with an enigmatic smile, "I *know*. I don't need
to believe. I know." Wherever the film has been shown an
urgent debate inevitably follows as to what he meant by that
statement. It seems to me that *believing* means to have a firm
conviction about something that may or may not be debatable.
It is an act of faith, that is, it requires some effort. Perhaps
there is even the implication that faith is required because
that which is believed in *seems* so preposterous. Besides, it
is not necessary to acquire a conviction about something if
you have experienced it. I do not *believe* I have just eaten
dinner. If I have had the experience, I *know* it. And so with
religious belief and religious experience. Whoever has experienced the divine presence has passed beyond the requirement
of faith, and also of reason. Reasoning is a process of approxi-
mating truth. It leads to knowledge. But *knowing* is a direct
recognition of truth, and it leads to wisdom. Thinking is a
process of differentiation and discrimination. In our thoughts
we make separations and enlist categories where in a wider
view of reality none exist. The rainbow spectrum is not composed of six or seven colors; it is our thinking that determines
how many colors there are and where red leaves off and orange
begins. We need to make our differentiations in the finite
world in order to deal expediently with the fragmented aspects
of our temporal lives.

The *Sermons* remind us that our temporal lives, seen from
the standpoint of eternity, may be illusory—as illusory as
eternity seems when you are trying to catch a bus on a Monday morning. Addressed to the *Dead*, the words are part of
the dialogue with the unconscious, the pleroma, whose existence is not dependent on thinking or believing.

*Ye must not forget that the pleroma hath no qualities. We cre-
ate them through thinking. If, therefore, ye strive after difference or sameness, or any qualities whatsoever, ye pursue thoughts
which flow to you out of the pleroma; thoughts, namely, concerning non-existing qualities of the pleroma. Inasmuch as ye
run after these thoughts, ye fall again into the pleroma, and
reach difference and sameness at the same time. Not your thinking, but your being, is distinctiveness. Therefore, not after difference, as ye think it, must ye strive; but after your own being.
At bottom, therefore, there is only one striving, namely, the
striving after your own being. If ye had this striving ye would
not need to know anything about the pleroma and its qualities,
and yet would come to your right goal by virtue of your own
being.*

The passage propounds Jung's insight about the fruitlessness
of pursuing philosophizing and theorizing for its own sake.
Perhaps it suggests why he never systematized his own theory
of psychotherapy, why he never prescribed techniques or
methods to be followed. Nor did he stress the categorization
of patients into disease entities based on differences or same-
nesses, except perhaps as a convenience for purposes of describing appearances, or for communicating with other therapists. The distinctiveness of the individual man or woman is
not in that which has happened to him, in this view, nor is it
in what has been thought about him. It is in his own being,
his essence. This is why a man or woman as therapist has
only one "tool" with which to work, and that is himself. What
happens in therapy depends not so much upon what the
therapist does, as upon who he is.

The last sentence of the first *Sermon* provides the key to
that hidden chamber which is at once the goal of individuation, and the abiding place of the religious spirit which can
guide us from within our own depths:

*Since, however, thought estrangeth from being, that knowledge
must I teach you wherewith ye may be able to hold your
thought in leash.*

Suddenly we know who the *Dead* are. We are the dead.
We are psychologically dead if we live only in the world of

consciousness, of science, of thought which "estrangeth from being." *Being* is being alive to the potency of the creative principle, translucent to the lightness and the darkness of the pleroma, porous to the flux of the collective unconscious. The message does not decry "thought," only a certain kind of thought, that which "estrangeth from being." Thought—logical deductive reasoning, objective scientific discrimination—must not be permitted to become the only vehicle through which man may approach the problematic of nature. Science, and most of all the "science of human behavior" must not be allowed to get away with saying "man's attitudes are not important, what is important is only the way in which man behaves." For if a man's behavior is to be enucleated from his attitudes he must be hopelessly split in two, and the psyche which is largely spirit, must surely die within him.

That knowledge . . . wherewith ye may be able to hold your thought in leash must, I believe, refer to knowledge which comes from those functions other than thinking. It consists of the knowledge that comes from sensation, from intuition, and from feeling. The knowledge which comes from sensation is the immediate and direct perception which arrives via the senses and has its reality independently of anything that we may think about it. The knowledge which comes from intuition is that which precedes thinking and also which suggests where thinking may go; it is the star which determines the adjustment of the telescope, the hunch which leads to the hypothesis. And finally, the knowledge which comes from feeling is the indisputable evaluative judgment; the thing happens to me in a certain way and incorporates my response to it; I may be drawn toward it or I may recoil from it, I love or I hate, I laugh or I weep, all irrespective of any intervening process of thinking about it.

It is not enough, as some of the currently popular anti-intellectual approaches to psychotherapy would have it, merely to lay aside the intellectual function. The commonly heard cries, "I don't care what you *think* about it, I want to know how you *feel* about it," are shallow and pointless; they miss the kernel while clinging to the husk. *To hold your thought in leash,* that seems to me the key, for all the knowledge so hard-won in the laboratory and in the field is valuable only in proportion to the way it is directed to the service of consciousness as it addresses itself to the unconscious, to the service of the created as it addresses itself to the creative principle, to the service of man as he addresses himself to God.

Jung's approach to religion is twofold, yet it is not dualistic. First, there is the approach of one man to God and second, there is the approach of the scientist-psychologist to man's idea-of-God. The latter is subsumed under the former. Jung's own religious nature pervades all of his writing about religion; even when he writes as a psychotherapist he does not forget that he is a limited human being standing in the shade of the mystery he can never understand.

Nor is he alone in this. Margaret Mead has written, "We need a religious system with science at its very core, in which the traditional opposition between science and religion . . . can again be resolved, but in terms of the future instead of the past . . . Such a synthesis . . . would use the recognition that when man permitted himself to become alienated from part of himself, elevating rationality and often narrow purpose above those ancient intuitive properties of the mind that bind him to his biological past, he was in effect cutting himself off from the rest of the natural world."[7]

I have discovered in my analytic practice and also in my capacity as a teacher, that many people come to Jung knowing that he is one psychologist who takes seriously the need people have to find some correspondence between their rational thoughts and activities, and the dimension of their lives to which the rational does not seem to apply: the area of feelings, of love, and of awe. How Jung's approach to these questions actually works in the lives of individuals may be illustrated by quoting from a paper titled "Potentials for the Application of Jungian Psychology to Religion," written by one of my students:

> I came into this class with a vague notion that Jungian psychology would be helpful in the task of relating psychology and

religion. As the class progressed that expectation was richly fulfilled. My task in the Religion and Personality field is to discover what psychology and religion have to do with each other. Jung has offered one approach to that task which I find helpful and stimulating for my own thought.

One of the reasons why there has not been to date a convincing psychology *of* religion (there has been an ample supply of modern attempts to do psychology *and* religion) is that both psychologists and theologians have ignored the important place of myth and symbol in the life of man and in religion. It is precisely here that Jung makes a unique and significant contribution.

Once one accepts his theory of the archetypes, one must deal with myth and symbol. And once the cosmic and cultural dimensions of the archetypes are understood as well as their personal dimensions, we are immediately thrown into contact with the numinous aspects of life which many psychologists and historians of religion agree constitute religion. If we apply Jung's theory of archetypes to our understanding of religion, we are then forced to deal with the structure of the psyche, and Jung's structural categories (e.g., the conscious, the unconscious, archetypes, shadow, anima, animus, self, etc.) are meaningless outside his theory of the dynamics of the psyche which includes such concepts as individuation, psychological typology, and the tension of opposites. Any of these structural or dynamic dimensions can not only throw light on how the theologian understands man in relationship to God, but also can force him to re-evaluate the role and structure of the Church itself.

What Jung is attempting to understand and elucidate is, as the student quite correctly supposed, a psychology *of* religion. He puts the religious experience of the individual man, which comes about often spontaneously and independently, into place with the religious systems that have been evolved and institutionalized in nearly every society throughout history.

In psychotherapy, the religious dimension of human experience generally appears after the analytic process has proceeded to some depth. Initially, the individual has come for help with some more or less specific problem. He may admit to a vague uneasiness that what is ailing may be a matter of his own essence, and that the "symptoms" or "problems" he is facing could be outcroppings of a deeper reality—the shape of which he does not comprehend. When, in analysis, he comes face to face with the figurative representation of the self, he is often stunned and shocked by the recognition that the non-personal power of which he has only the fuzziest conception, lives and manifests itself in him. Oh, yes, he has heard about this, and read about it, and has had it preached to him from intricately carved pulpits, but now it is all different. It is the image in his own dream, the voice in his own ear, the shivering in the night as the terror of all terrors bears down upon him, and the knowing that it is within him— arising there, finding its voice there, and being received there.

> It is not in the least astonishing, [Jung tells us] that numinous experiences should occur in the course of psychological treatment, and that they may even be expected with some regularity, for they also occur very frequently in exceptional psychic states that are not treated, and may even cause them. They do not belong exclusively to the domain of psychopathology but can be observed in normal people as well. Naturally, modern ignorance of and prejudice against intimate psychic experiences dismiss them as psychic anomalies and put them in psychiatric pigeonholes without making the least attempt to understand them. But that neither gets rid of the fact of the occurrence nor explains it.[8]

In our reading of Jung we find that in attempting to understand the numinous experience, a man looks to those earlier and collective metaphysical ideas which have been associated with religion, and more specifically, the religion into which he happens to be born. He tends to develop a concept of "God" based on the concept held by his fathers, or his educators, or his community. Jung says, "It seems to me at least highly improbable that when a man says 'God' there must in consequence exist a God such as he imagines, or that he necessarily speaks of a real being. At any rate he can never prove that there is something to correspond with his statement on the metaphysical side, just as it can never be proved to him that he is wrong."[9]

Nor is there any more hope that the God-concept advanced

by the various religions is any more demonstrable than that expressed by the individual as "my own idea." The various expressions that have been given voice about the nature of transcendental reality are so many and diverse that there is no way of knowing absolutely who is right. Therefore, as Jung saw it, the denominational religions long ago recognized that there was no way to defend the exclusivity of their "truth" so, instead, they took the offensive position and proclaimed that their religion was the only true one, and the basis for this, they claimed, was that the truth had been directly revealed by God. "Every theologian speaks simply of 'God,' by which he intends it to be understood that his 'god' is *the* God. But one speaks of the paradoxical God of the Old Testament, another of the incarnate God of Love, a third of the God who has a heavenly bride, and so on, and each criticizes the other but never himself."[10]

Such insights as this do not come only from reading the philosophers and the psychologists. They arise even more vividly out of the personal experience of the individual. Essentially this is where they find their true meaning—every other exposition of these ideas merely points in the direction of their meaning. I can illustrate this statement with an example from my practice. A young woman was studying theology, and was preparing to take her examination for the master's degree. A few nights before the exam she had the following dream: *I walk into the classroom to pick up my M.A. exam. They are printed on the backs of psychedelic posters. The exam question is, "Write a critical exposition of the play, 'Fools.'"*

That was the name of a play, she told me, that had been recently put on by the university faculty. It had flopped. As she gave her further associations to the dream, she said that while she had been preparing for the exams the phrase kept recurring in her mind, "The fool hath said in his heart that there is no God." She expressed her resistance to the *over-objectivity* that characterized the professors in her department. No personal religious experience was ever discussed in the classroom. She observed that the study of Comparative Reli-

gion—which seems to be a screen behind which can be established the one true faith—derives its rationale by purporting
to determine what is valid and what is not, and ranking ideas
in hierarchies.

The dream seems to be saying essentially that on one side
she is being asked to look critically at the "play," the postur-
ings of the theological faculty, who are acting the roles of
fools. She has to deal with her recognition that they speak
the lines which justify God, when God is not justified in their
own experience. On the other side are the blazing colors of
the psychedelic posters which express the breaking up of light-
waves into hues and forms to delight the eye—the ineffable
is brought into the realm of human experience. She is faced
with both, they both belong to the same sheet of paper, which
is given to her as her task to make meaningful.

She can approach this task with either her intellectual function or with her spiritual function. Or, she can attempt to
bring both to bear on the problem; she can at one time think
and also "hold her thought in leash." If she chooses the second
alternative, she will follow the example of Jung in his exposition of the religious side of the psyche, placing side by side
the individual experience of the divine and the collective expression of it, with the many symbols and myths and rituals
that attach to it.

A basic principle of Jung's approach to religion is that the
spiritual element is an organic part of the psyche. It is the
source of man's search for meaning, and it is that element
which lifts man above his concern for merely keeping his species alive by feeding his hunger and protecting himself from
attack and copulating to preserve the race. Man could live
well enough on the basis of the instincts alone, the naked
ape does not *need* books or churches. The spiritual element
which urges man on the quest for the unknown and the unknowable is the organic part of his psyche, and it is this which
is responsible for both science and religion. The spiritual element in man is expressed in symbols, for symbols are the
language of the unconscious. Through consideration of the

symbol, much that is problematic or only vaguely understood can become real and vitally effective in our lives.

The symbol attracts, and therefore leads the individual on the way of becoming what he is capable of becoming. That goal is wholeness, which is integration of the parts of his personality into a functioning totality. Here consciousness and the unconscious are united around the symbols of the self. The ways in which the self manifests are numerous beyond any attempt to name or describe them. I choose the mandala symbol as a starting point because its circular characteristics suggest the qualities of the self (the pleroma that hath no qualities). In principle, the circle must have a center, but that point which we mark as a center is, of necessity, larger than the true center. However much we decrease the central point, the true center is at the center of that, and hence, smaller yet. The circumference is that line around the center which is at all points equidistant from it. But, since we do not know the length of the radius, it may be said of any circle we may imagine, that our mandala is larger than that. It is "smaller than small and bigger than big." The mandala, then, as a symbol of the self, has the qualities of the circle, center and circumference, yet like the self of which it is an image, it has not these qualities.

Is it any wonder then, that the man who was not a man should be chosen as a symbol of the self and worshiped throughout the Christian world? Is it at all strange, when considered symbolically, that the belief arose that an infinite spirit which pervades the universe should have concentrated the omnipotence of his being into a speck so infinitesimal that it could enter the womb of a woman and be born as a divine child?

In his major writings on "Christ as a Symbol of the Self"[11] Jung has stated it explicitly:

In the world of Christian ideas Christ undoubtedly represents the self. As the apotheosis of individuality, the self has the attributes of uniqueness and of occurring once only in time. But since the psychological self is a transcendent concept, expressing the totality of conscious and unconscious contents, it can only be described in antinomial terms; that is, the above attributes must be supplemented by their opposites if the transcendental situation is to be characterized correctly. We can do this most simply in the form of a quaternion of opposites:

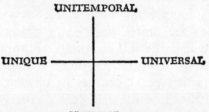

UNITEMPORAL

UNIQUE ——————— UNIVERSAL

ETERNAL

This formula expresses not only the psychological self but also the dogmatic figure of Christ. As an historical personage Christ is unitemporal and unique; as God, universal and eternal. . . . Now if theology describes Christ as simply "good" and "spiritual," something "evil" and "material" . . . is bound to arise on the other side . . . The resultant quaternion of opposites is united on the psychological plane by the fact that the self is not deemed exclusively "good" and "spiritual"; consequently its shadow turns out to be much less black. A further result is that the opposites of "good" and "spiritual" need no longer be separated from the whole:

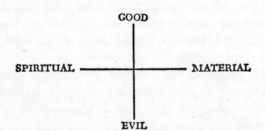

GOOD

SPIRITUAL ——————— MATERIAL

EVIL

This *quaternio* characterizes the psychological self. Being a totality, it must by definition include the light and dark aspects, in the same way that the self embraces both masculine and feminine, and is therefore symbolized by the marriage *quaternio*. [See chapter 9 on Animus and Anima, supra] . . . Hence individuation is a "mysterium coniunctionis," the self being experienced by a nuptial union of opposite halves and depicted as a composite whole in mandalas that are drawn spontaneously by patients.[12] [We recall how beautifully this was expressed in the active imagination of the patient Charles and the ape-man.]

We have seen how, in analysis, the image of the self often manifests very early and provides the impetus for the entire process. It may come in a dream which is only partly understood, and remains in a prenascent state until its time has come. This was the experience of Vincent, whose dream was discussed in chapter 10, Circumambulating the Self. The dream is repeated here, to show how the religious significance of a dream sometimes only begins to emerge after it has been carried to its maturity: *I am walking with a woman slightly older than myself along a mountain path. It is a glacial idyllic scene by moonlight. I am also somehow watching myself. We come to some huge gray boulders. They are blocking our path. We stop, and she turns to me and looks at me. We are engaged in pleasant conversation. Suddenly she turns extremely ugly. Her face takes on a greenish color and she gets very old. I realize there is only one way to help the situation and that is to have intercourse with her. My penis enters her vagina, then goes through her body and into the rock behind her. Then she disappears and I am alone, having intercourse with the rock.*

The setting is surely referring to the aspect of the unconscious farthest from consciousness—the cold, colorless moonlight speaks of the mysterious side of life; the mountain, of the heights of the spirit. The woman companion has two aspects, the one "slightly older than myself" referring to the anima as reflecting initially the experience of the personal mother and, later on, the transference relationship with the analyst. In any case it is this aspect of the anima that leads him to the boulders. Then, suddenly, the unique and unitemporal poles of the quaternio shift into their opposites: The woman becomes old and ugly; her face takes on a greenish color. She is ageless, yet in being available for intercourse she offers youth to youth, with the possibility of a creative union. The greenish color that comes over her is the color of nature which, out of the glacial stillness of the night, brings the shocking suggestion of fertility and rebirth. The effect upon the man is to infuse him with a miraculous potency, so that his virile member is able to penetrate her and not only her, but through her and into the rock! "Hence, individuation is a 'mysterium coniunctionis,' the self being experienced as a nuptial union of opposite halves." Through the anima the individual has become united with his transpersonal self, as symbolized by the stone.

The stone, or the *lapis*, is a central symbol in the literature of alchemy. The search into the various aspects of its meaning occupied Jung in scholarly research throughout much of his life. He understood the alchemical opus as a process which at one time was an attempt to transform base materials into an incorruptible substance (gold, elixir, panacea, treasure hard to attain, pearl of great price, lapis), and to transform the original base nature of man into its spiritual potentiality in which it would find its union with the divine, which was called the *lapis philosophorum*, the philosopher's stone, and by many other names. The alchemical opus, understood symbolically as many of the medieval alchemists did understand it, was recognized by Jung as a striking parallel to the process of individuation.

The pre-form of this insight appeared in the first of the *Seven Sermons of the Dead* where it is said, "the striving of the creature goeth toward distinctiveness, fighteth against primeval, perilous sameness. This is called the *principium individuationis*." Man is caught in the struggle between the opposites; the stone is fixed and incorruptible. The individuation process is an *opus contra naturam*; it is a struggle against the natural, haphazard way of living in which we simply respond first to the demands made upon us by the circumstances of our environment and then to those of inner necessity, paying the most attention to the side that is most insistent at any given time. Individuation leads through the confrontation of the opposites until a gradual integration of the personality comes about, a oneness with oneself, with one's world, and with the divine presence as it makes itself known to us.

The beginning of the alchemical process parallels the legends of creation, the consolidation of a world out of formless chaos. In alchemy the opus starts out with a *massa confusa*, a teeming, disordered conglomeration of what is called *prima materia*. It goes through a series of transformations, all described in the most abstruse language, in a lore that predated Christianity and extended into the seventeenth century. We seldom get much of an idea of how the work was actually done, what materials were used and what results were achieved. Jung says, "The alchemist is quite aware that he writes obscurely. He admits that he veils his meaning on purpose, but nowhere,—so far as I know—does he say that he cannot write in any other way. He makes a virtue of necessity by maintaining either that mystification is forced on him for one reason or another, or that he really wants to make the truth as plain as possible, but that he cannot proclaim aloud just what the *prima materia* or the *lapis* is."[13] This is in a tradition of refusing to make easily available material that has been acquired only with great difficulty, on the grounds that the quest is at least as important as the goal, or that the importance of the goal rests on the energy and commitment that has been involved in the quest.

Jung cites one of the oldest alchemical tests, written in Arabic style: "This stone is below thee, as to obedience; above thee, as to dominion; therefore from thee, as to knowledge; about thee, as to equals." He comments on the passage:

[It] is somewhat obscure. Nevertheless, it can be elicited that the stone stands in an undoubted psychic relationship to man: the adept can expect obedience from it, but on the other hand the stone exercises dominion over him. Since the stone is a matter of "knowledge" or "science," it springs from man. But it is outside him, in his surroundings, among his "equals," i.e., those of like mind. This description fits the paradoxical situation of the self, as its symbolism shows. It is the smallest of the small, easily overlooked and pushed aside. Indeed, it is in need of help and must be perceived, protected, and as it were built up by the conscious mind, just as if it did not exist at all and were called into being only through man's care and devotion. As against this, we know from experience that it had long been there and is older than the ego, and that it is actually the *spiritus rector* (guiding, or controlling spirit) of our fate.[14]

The study of Jung's extensive writings on religion and alchemy, of which the above lines give only the merest suggestion, led Vincent into a consideration of his own potentiality for realization of the promise of his dream. He was able to apply the universal and transcendent themes, inherent in the anima and the stone, to his personal life, and through them to gain the broader perspective that was needed in order to face the difficulties in his path with energy and equanimity.

One may well ask, Why did Jung become so involved with the arcane material of alchemy with all of its pseudoscientific pretensions, its inchoate philosophical speculations, its dubious conclusions? Why did he not utilize more the symbolic presentations of the orthodox religions, the well-ordered logic of the Church Fathers and the disciplined precepts of the non-Christian religions? To be sure he did not overlook these latter, but however well versed in the "establishment philosophies" he may have been, there is no doubt that the subject of alchemy held him fascinated. What was it that managed to draw his attention from the academic or conventionally accepted intellectual position to the opposing one, at which people tended to look askance? What was it that had long ago pried him away from his medical studies to attend the séances where S.W. fell into trance states and described her visions? What was it that had him spending his nights at Burghölzli, after a full day of research and psychotherapy, poring over the possible meaning behind S.W.'s apparently hysterical performances? What led Jung to jeopardize his psychiatric career just as it was beginning, in order to join forces with the doctor from Vienna whose radical theories were bringing down the criticism of practically every prominent European psychiatrist? And again, when Freud was well established and regarded, what was it that led Jung to leave the group, and to pursue an analytical approach that intensified the roles of religion and myth in the field of psychology just as the field of psychology was struggling to enter the arena of the sciences as a respected junior member?

Perhaps the answer to these questions is intimated in Jung's writing concerning the Sacrament of the Mass. In his account of "Transformation Symbolism in the Mass"[15] Jung described the acts in detail and commented on the symbolic significance of the sequence of the transformation rite: the oblation of the bread, the preparation of the chalice, the elevation of the chalice, the censing of the substances and the altar, the epiclesis, the consecration, the greater elevation, the post-consecration, end of the canon, breaking of the host, consignatio, commixtio and conclusion. He tells us: "the uttering of the words of the consecration signifies Christ himself speaking in the first person, his living presence in the *corpus mysticum* of the priest, congregation, bread, wine, and incense, which together form the mystical unity offered for sacrifice. At this moment the eternal character of the one divine sacrifice is made evident: it is experienced at a particular time and in a particular place, as if a window or a door had been opened upon that which lies beyond space and time."[16] "The Mass thus contains, as its essential core, the mystery and miracle of God's transformation taking place in the human sphere, his becoming Man, and his return to his absolute existence in and for himself."[17]

Jung then makes the statement that although the Mass is a unique phenomenon in the history of comparative religion, its symbolic content is rooted in the human psyche. Therefore, it may be expected that we would find similar patterns of symbolism both in the history of earlier peoples and in the contemporary non-Christian world. He does, indeed, find examples of religious rites which come very close to Christian practices, and he describes those of the Aztecs, in particular, that of the *teoqualo,* "god-eating," as recorded by a missionary in the early sixteenth century. He then reviews in alchemical literature some parallel rites of transformations as depicted in visions and practices, in myths and rituals and in allegorical

392 BOUNDARIES OF THE SOUL

legends. He deals at length with the visions of Zosimos, a natural philosopher and alchemist of the third century, whose works have been preserved, though in a corrupt state. He relates a number of Zosimos's dream-visions, all of which, Jung says, appear to go back to the same dream—in which Zosimos observes a priest who becomes split into the figures of the sacrificer and the one who is sacrificed. As the sacrificed, he submits voluntarily to the torture through which he is transformed. But as sacrificer he is pierced through with his own sword and is ritually dismembered. As the priest stands before him high on an altar, Zosimos hears a voice from above say to him, "Behold, . . . I have completed the ascent up the steps of light. And he who renews me is the priest, for he cast away the density of the body and by compelling necessity I am sanctified and now stand in perfection as a spirit (*pneuma*)."[18]

Jung studiously compares in all details the visions of Zosimos with the sacrifice of the Mass, the crucifixion and the resurrection. At last he comes to this interpretation:

> Looked at from the psychological standpoint, Christ . . . represents a totality which surpasses and includes ordinary man, and which corresponds to the total personality that transcends consciousness. We have called this personality the "self." Just as, on the more archaic level of the Zosimos vision, the homunculus [a mannikin that is produced by an alchemist in a vessel or flask] is transformed into *pneuma* and exalted, so the mystery of the Eucharist transforms the soul of the empirical man, who is only a part of himself, into his totality, symbolically expressed by Christ. In this sense, therefore, we can speak of the Mass as the *rite of the individuation process.*[19]

It seems to me that in his essay, "The Lapis-Christus Parallel," in *Psychology and Alchemy*, the true position of Jung vis-à-vis the opposition between orthodox Christianity and alchemy is made clear. There is Christ; and there is the stone. Christ comes to earth, is born and lives for man, dies and is sacrificed for the sake of man's salvation. The stone, the precious body, is concealed in the *prima materia*, the confused mass; and it is man, symbolically represented as the alchemist, who must save the stone from dissolution in matter. The Christian received the spiritual benefits of the Mass for himself personally, to improve the circumstances of his existence in the widest sense. But the alchemist performed his labors for the perfection of the precious substance, not merely for himself, but more importantly for the King (which is his symbol for God), or for the King's Son. As Jung points out, the alchemist "may play a part in the *perfectio*, which brings him health, riches, illumination, and salvation; but since he is the redeemer of God and not the one to be redeemed, he is more concerned to perfect the substance than himself."

Now we begin to discover where, in Jung, there comes the parting of the ways. As a religious man he can say "I don't need to believe in God, I *know*." He can accept Christ and the meaning of Christ in his personal life as the One through whom he is redeemed. This is given to him, through the grace of God, and he does not question it. For him Christ is truly a symbol of the self, the most congruent symbol of the self for him, in terms of his rootedness in the Christianity of his fathers. For a Jew, or a Hindu, for example, the self would be expressed in different symbols.

As a psychotherapist, however, Jung approaches his patient with an open attitude, an attitude that says, "Here is a man before me whose nature is unknown to me. The nature of the contract to which we will commit ourselves is also unknown to me. And the goal, the end of the process, is equally unknown." Therefore the alchemist becomes a guiding symbol for Jung as he takes up the task of tinkering with the human soul. The consulting room is symbolically represented by the alchemist's laboratory. From this it can be seen how the alchemical opus parallels the individuation process.

As though Jung recognized the possibility of projecting his own unconscious contents into the symbolism of alchemy, he was careful to make it clear in speaking of the alchemist: "One should not suppose for a moment that he presumes to the role of redeemer from religious megalomania. He does so even less than the officiating priest who figuratively sacrifices Christ. The alchemist always stresses his humility and begins his treatises with invocations to God. He does not dream of identifying himself with Christ; on the contrary, it is the coveted substance, the *lapis*, that alchemy likens to Christ."[20]

Jung's alchemical studies, drawing as they did from the fields of archaeology and comparative religions, led him time and time again to face the importance of the role of astrology in the history of human consciousness. It was characteristic of Jung, when he became interested in a subject to pursue his research with thoroughness and zeal, and the lore of astrology was no exception. If Jung's interest in alchemy had led to misunderstanding on the part of the general public, his interest in astrology has had an even more confusing effect. Hard-nosed scientists asserted that Jung's scientific respectability was called into question when he investigated a field such as this, which lies outside the area of what is considered by them to be proper subject matter for experimental research. On the other side, many people who wanted to give an air of authenticity to their assertions about the validity of astrological predictions have tried to persuade an unwitting public that Jung was a "true believer" in astrology as a predictive instrument. I am quite convinced that he was not, and I would not even raise the question in this book, except for the fact that it has often come up in my practice. Here is another instance of people hearing a half-truth or a patently fraudulent statement about Jung, and then coming to a Jungian analyst because they think he will understand such things, or that he will support their beliefs.

When the question does come up—and it usually comes up in the form, "What did Jung *really* think about astrology?" —I do not dismiss it lightly. I believe that the query belongs to the questioner's search for meaning in his life, and that probably he has gotten lost between the world of the senses and the world of symbols, and needs to find a workable re-orientation. Perhaps, in a wider sense, a similar subjective condition inspired Jung to study the astrological symbols and their relationship to man's psychological and religious history. Since I could not speak directly with Jung about this, I can only base my conclusions on my reading of his extensive writing on the subject. In his chapter on "The Sign of the Fishes," in *Aion*, he amplified and interpreted the astrological symbolism connected with the theme of Christ as the fish (pisces). He dealt with the archetypal basis for the development of and belief in astrology in his essay, "Synchronicity: An Acausal Connecting Principle," in *The Structure and Dynamics of the Psyche*. This essay also contains a report on a research project directed by Jung for the purpose of testing certain astrological hypotheses. A personal and subjective view of astrology, its uses and abuses, may be found in Jung's *Memories, Dreams, Reflections*. Other references to the subject of astrology are scattered throughout the speculative-philosophical portions of Jung's writings.

I believe that by quoting a passage from Jung here, we may get the flavor of his objective scientific investigations into the tenets and folklore of astrology as a historical phenomenon. Appreciating this open and inquiring attitude on the part of Jung will prepare us for an understanding of his psychological observations concerning man's belief in the power of the stars to influence his life. Jung writes in *Aion*:

A direct astrological aspect of Christ's birth is given us in Matthew 2:1 ff. The Magi from the East were star-gazers who, beholding an extraordinary constellation, inferred an equally extraordinary birth. This anecdote proves that Christ, possibly even at the time of the apostles, was viewed from the astrological standpoint or was at least brought into connection with astrological myths . . . Since this exceedingly complex question has been discussed by those who are more qualified than I, we can support our argument on the well-attested fact that glimpses of astrological mythology may be caught behind the stories of the worldly and other-worldly life of the Redeemer.

Above all, it is the connections with the age of the Fishes which are attested by the fish symbolism, either contemporaneous with the gospels themselves ("fishers of men," fishermen as the first disciples, miracle of loaves and fishes), or immediately afterwards in the post-apostolic era. The symbolism shows Christ and those who believe in him as fishes, fish as the food eaten at the Agape, baptism as immersion in a fish-pond, etc. At first sight, all this points to no more than the fact that the fish

symbols which had always existed had assimilated the figure of
the Redeemer; in other words, it was a symptom of Christ's
assimilation into the world of ideas prevailing at that time. But
to the extent that Christ was regarded as the new aeon, it would
be clear to anyone acquainted with astrology that he was born
as the first fish of the Pisces era.[21]

It is clear from this passage that Jung was acquainted with
the history of the primitive science or pseudo-science of astrology as it was long before the appearance of Jesus. Astrology
is the ancient art or science of divining the fate and future
of human beings from indications given by the positions of
the stars, sun, moon and planets. The belief in a connection
between the heavenly bodies and the life of man has played
an important part in human history. From man's earliest written records, recovered from the sands or caves of Babylonia,
through the studies and speculations of Greece and Rome,
from which it spread into Jewish, Arabic and Christian lore
in the West, and Chinese and Indian culture in the East,
astrology has had an uninterrupted history of five thousand
years. In earlier days, as much as now, men have always wanted
to "predict and control" their environment. Always men have
used what they believed to be the best means available to
accomplish this end, and always men have believed that the
knowledge and techniques of their own day were based upon
the authority of all previous knowledge, and incorporated current discoveries and observations, hence were "true," while
the beliefs of an earlier day were "myths" in the sense of
being primitive or naïve.

In Babylonia, as well as in Assyria as a direct offshoot of
the Babylonian culture, astrology had taken its place in the
official cult as one means the priests had for ascertaining the
will and intention of the gods. At its base is the indisputable
fact that man's life and welfare were largely dependent on
phenomena in the heavens: the fertility of the soil depends
upon the sun shining in the heavens and the rain that comes
from the heavens. Likewise, the disasters caused by storm and
inundation were seen as originating in the heavens. From this,
the conclusion was drawn that the great gods had their seats

in the heavens. It was a natural step for the priests, who corresponded to the scientists of a later day, to perfect a theory of accord between the phenomena observed in the heavens and occurrences on earth. The movements of the sun, moon and planets conveyed to the more intelligent mind the conception of a rule of law and order in the universe as against the more popular notion of chance and caprice. The sun, moon and planets became identified with the gods, and the concepts of ruling gods and ruling planets became hopelessly indistinguishable.

The predictive element in astrology grew out of a belief that the stars and planets did indeed rule not only the abstract nature, but also the lives of men. Therefore, it was important to man's control of his fate to discover ways of foreseeing what these ruling bodies were likely to do next. Man's only way of dealing with what is both unknown and the unknowable, is to project the contents of the unconscious, in terms of his own hopes and fears, upon the incomprehensible object of his concern. By ascribing human tendencies and human characteristics to the various planet-gods, men were able to account for the vagaries of fate. The character of the ruling bodies and the relations between them would then be seen as characterizing or influencing events taking place on earth. It is a matter of simple observation to recognize that the moment of a child's birth corresponds in time with a specific configuration of heavenly bodies. In a time when little was known about the many and diverse factors contributing to the development of the individual temperament, it was believed that the ruling constellations determined the dimensions of the nascent personality.

Modern science has shown that the correspondence of the stars and other natural elements and forces with events and human personality are not related in the simple, causalistic way that the ancients believed they were. But, as we all know, and as ecologists are constantly pointing out, there is a correspondence, there is a very evident relationship between man and his larger environment. The more we discover about this relationship, the more we are able to withdraw our projections of unconscious contents. The process of projection, that is, making subjectively determined, yet reasonable, suppositions about the unknown, is the first step toward going ahead to test the suppositions, the hypotheses, and eventually to withdraw those suppositions that are proved to be basically projections.

In his essay on *Synchronicity* (Jung's term for meaningful coincidences of events separated in space and/or in time),[22] Jung examined some of the beliefs surrounding apparently related incidents which seem to have no causal connection. These incidents could be, for example, the coinciding of a patient's dream with an actual event corresponding to its occurring at the same time some distance away, it could be ESP phenomena—response to some event that does not become known through any sense; it could be a horoscope reading which corresponds to the observed character of the individual or his self-image, or an astrological prediction which seems to be borne out in subsequent events. The possibility of finding meaning in these correspondences had tantalized Jung for many years. The beginning of his serious study goes back to the days when Albert Einstein was developing his first theory of relativity. During this time he was a guest on several occasions for dinner in Jung's home. In a letter on Einstein and synchronicity, Jung wrote: "It was Einstein who first started me off thinking about a possible relativity of time as well as space, and their psychic synchronicity."[23]

The study of meaningful coincidences could not be complete for him without a careful scrutiny of astrology. Since there was a lack of legitimate scientific data either validating or invalidating the correspondence of predictions based on horoscopes with subsequent events, Jung undertook an astrological experiment in the hope of finding out for himself how accurate such predictions might be. The proposition to be tested was the astrological assumption that certain individuals, as characterized by their horoscopes, will be predisposed to marry certain other individuals. The experiment is described in detail, and carefully worked out with statistical analysis comparing the horoscopes of married couples with those of non-married couples. The results of the experiment greatly abbreviated, were given by Jung as follows: "Although our best results . . . are fairly improbable in practice, they are theoretically so probable that there is little justification for regarding the immediate results of our statistics as anything more than chance . . . From the scientific point of view the result of our investigation is in some respects not encouraging for astrology . . . there is little hope of proving that astrological correspondence is something that conforms to law."24

Astrology has never been proved to be a valid means for predicting events or characterizing an individual. Nor did alchemy ever succeed in transforming base metals into gold. Yet these two precursors of modern science provide us with a wealth of data concerning the psychological nature of man and his symbols. Taken literally, astrology and alchemy have little meaning for modern man; for they belong to a world in which beliefs were based on the appearances of things, and the appearances of things have changed. What was believed to be true in those days is no longer believed. But taken symbolically they provide us with a history of the development of consciousness through an ever changing panoply of archetypal images. These images point backwards to the unknown and unknowable, to the archetypes of the collective unconscious. The symbolic representations that man constructs, in astrology and elsewhere, connect him with his roots in the past, from which he draws the strength for growth.

In recent years, ever since the Beatles met the Maharishi Mahesh Yogi and found peace and bliss—if not for life everlasting, then at least for a year or two—Americans have been turned on to the mysterious East. This rediscovery of ancient truth has led many of these people, most of them in their teens and twenties, into fads and fantasies inspired by the pilgrims from the Orient, and a smaller number to a serious study of Hinduism, Taoism and Zen Buddhism. In their reading, they often discover that Jung had taken a similar path many years before, and had learned a great deal about Eastern religions and philosophy both through study and through his travels in India. If they have read his essays on Eastern religion in *Psychology and Religion*[25] they have some feeling for the great respect Jung had for much of the sacred teaching of the Orient. Also, they will have some understanding of his views on the potential effects of certain traditional Eastern ways of thinking upon the Western mind. All too frequently, however, Jung's writings have been misunderstood or only partially understood. His interest in Eastern religious thought and certain practices associated with it—like his interest in séances, in alchemy, or in astrology—have been incorrectly construed as a wholehearted and literal endorsement for use by Western man today.

During the period of greatest fascination with psychedelic drugs among college students and college drop-outs in the late 1960s, Tibetan mysticism was seized upon as a model or ideal to be sought within the psychedelic experience. Cecelia, whose case was discussed in Chapter 2, above, was one of these. *The Tibetan Book of the Dead*[26] had been available to the English-speaking reader since it was compiled and edited by W. Y. Evans-Wentz in 1927. It only became a best-seller on campuses from Harvard to Berkeley when Leary, Metzner and Alpert publicized it in their efforts to provide instant illumination for American youth through LSD. Their book, *The Psychedelic Experience: A Manual Based on The Tibetan Book of the Dead* contains in its introductory section, "A Tribute to Carl G. Jung." Jung is presented, quite correctly, as one who understood that the unconscious could, and in extraordinary states did, manifest itself in hallucinations such as have been called "The Magic Theatre," and "The Retinal Circus," where energy is transformed into strangely frightening bodily sensations, "wrathful visions" of monsters and demons, visions of the earth-mother, boundless waters, or fertile earth, broad-breasted hills, visions of great beauty in which nature flowers with an intense brilliance that is not known to ordinary consciousness. Messrs. Leary et al., suggest that *The Tibetan Book of the Dead*—in which these images are described in exquisite detail so that the living may recite the text (or oral tradition) to the dying or newly dead person in order to guide him on his path into the realm of Spirit—

is not a book of the dead after all. It is, they assert, "a book of the dying; which is to say a book of the living; it is a book of life and how to live. The concept of actual physical death was an exoteric façade adopted to fit the prejudices of the Bonist tradition in Tibet . . . the manual is a detailed account of how to lose the ego; how to break out of personality into new realms of consciousness; and how to avoid the involuntary limiting processes of the ego . . ."27 In this sense, they identify "personality" with the conscious ego state, a state which in their view must be put aside in order to break into new realms of consciousness. They suggest that Jung did not appreciate the necessity for this leap into the unknown, since, in their words, "He had nothing in his conceptual framework which could make practical sense out of the ego-loss experience."28

But here these purveyors of imitation psychosis by the microgram (which occasionally, unfortunately, turns into the real thing), are the ones who miss the point, who misread Jung completely. Jung did know what it was like to come to the edge of ego-loss experience. His commitment had long been to the inner vision, but however close he came to total immersion in it, he felt that it was important, for Western man at least, to maintain some contact with the ego position. To lose this entirely, it seemed to Jung, would be unconsciousness, madness or death. For him it was impossible to conceive of that state, described in *The Tibetan Book of the Dead* as the attainment of the Clear Light of the Highest Wisdom, in which one is merged with the supreme spiritual power, without the paradoxical conclusion that there is something left outside to experience the "conceiving." That something is ego-consciousness, which of course is not present in an unconscious state, in psychosis or after death, because ego-consciousness is by definition a term which describes our awareness of our nature and identity vis-à-vis that which "we" are not.

Jung explains his own difficulty, which is perhaps the difficulty of the Westerner, to realize what the Tibetan Buddhist calls *One Mind*. The realization of the *One Mind* (according

to Jung's reading of *The Tibetan Book of the Great Liberation*) creates "at-one-ment" or complete union, psychologically, with the non-ego. In doing so, *One Mind* becomes for
Jung an analogue of the collective unconscious or, more properly, it is the same as the collective unconscious. Jung writes:

> The statement "Nor is one's own mind separable from
> other minds," is another way of expressing the fact of "all-
> contamination." Since all distinctions vanish in the uncon-
> scious condition, it is only logical that the distinction between
> separate minds should disappear too . . . But we are unable
> to imagine how such a realization ["at-one-ment"] could ever
> be complete in any human individual. There must always be
> somebody or something left over to experience the realization, to
> say "I know at-one-ment, I know there is no distinction." The
> very fact of the realization proves its inevitable incompleteness.
> . . . Even when I say "I know myself," an infinitesimal ego—
> the knowing "I"—is still distinct from "myself." In this as it were
> atomic ego, which is completely ignored by the essentially non-
> dualist standpoint of the East, there nevertheless lies hidden
> the whole unabolished pluralistic universe and its unconquered
> reality.[29]

Jung, for all his metaphysical speculations, was in the first
place and the last essentially a psychotherapist, and his life
was devoted to discovering the means through which he could
help individuals to know their lives as rich in meaning in
this world, namely, the world of consciousness. This world
may be immeasurably deepened and enhanced as we have seen
throughout our reading of Jung, by the data of the unconscious. Of utmost importance is it that the unconscious material flow into consciousness, and furthermore, that material
from consciousness flow into the unconscious, adding new elements which dissolve, transform and renew what has been
present all along. But the most important thing, from the
Jungian point of view is that the ego may not *fall into* the
unconscious and become completely submerged, overwhelmed.
There must always be an "I" to observe what is occurring
in the encounter with the "Not-I."[30]

Thus, when Jung says of *The Tibetan Book of the Dead*

"it is a book that will only open itself to spiritual understanding, and this is a capacity which no man is born with, but which he can only acquire through special training and special experience"[31] I do not believe he meant that we should indiscriminately take a pill that enables us to shed the ego like an old snakeskin and slither newborn into the waters of the unconscious. Like the devotees of the hallucinogenic drug experience, he was interested in expanding the arena of consciousness, but, unlike many of them, he was also aware of the danger that in doing so, in bursting the boundaries of consciousness, consciousness itself could be lost.

This was why he favored the method of "active imagination" for his own patients, and why this method is widely used by analytical psychologists today. Admittedly, it is a slow process, this establishing of an ongoing dialogue with the unconscious, but we accept that. Confronting the unconscious for us is not an "event," but rather a "condition" in which we live. It is serious business, it is play; it is art and it is science. We confront the unknown at every turn, except when we lose the sense of ourselves (ego) or the sense of the other (the unconscious).

In my work with analysands, questions often come up about the relationship of active imagination to the practices of yoga and Eastern meditation. Students and analysands come to recognize that the dialogue between the ego and the unconscious, through the agency of the transcendent function in all its symbolic expressions, bears a certain resemblance to the symbolism of Tantric yoga in India and Tibet, lamaism, and Taoistic yoga in China. Yet Jung, who had immersed himself in the study of all of these for over half a century, beginning when they were quite unknown in the West except to a few scholars, did not advocate the adoption of these methods as a whole in the West, nor even their adaptation to our occidental modes and culture. The reason for this, as I have come to believe through study of Jung's writing, is that a psychotherapy based upon a psychology of the unconscious, a psychotherapy which is the "cure of souls" is, indeed, the "yoga" of the West.

Jung has pointed out that an uninterrupted tradition of four thousand years has created the necessary spiritual conditions for yoga in the East. There, he says, yoga is

the perfect and appropriate method of fusing body and mind together so that they form a unity . . . a psychological disposition . . . that transcends consciousness. The Indian mentality has no difficulty in operating intelligently with a concept like *prāna*. The West, on the contrary, with its bad habit of wanting to believe on the one hand, and its highly developed scientific and philosophical critique on the other, finds itself in a real dilemma. Either it falls into the trap of faith and swallows concepts like *prāna, atman, chakra, samādhi*, etc., without giving them a thought, or its scientific critique repudiates them one and all as "pure mysticism." The split in the Western mind therefore makes it impossible at the outset for the intentions of yoga to be realized in any adequate way. It becomes either a strictly religious matter, or else a kind of training . . . and not a trace is to be found of the unity and wholeness of nature which is characteristic of yoga. The Indian can forget neither the body nor the mind, while the European is always forgetting either the one or the other . . . The Indian . . . not only knows his own nature, but he knows also how much he himself is nature. The European, on the other hand, has a science of nature and knows astonishingly little of his own nature, the nature within him. For the Indian, it comes as a blessing to know of a method which helps him to control the supreme power of nature within and without. For the European, it is sheer poison to suppress his nature, which is warped enough as it is, and to make out of it a willing robot . . .[32]

He concludes his discussion with the warning:

Western man has no need of more superiority over nature, whether outside or inside. He has both in almost devilish perfection. What he lacks is conscious recognition of his inferiority to the nature around and within him. He must learn that he may not do exactly as he wills. If he does not learn this, his own nature will destroy him.[33]

The reasonable question at this point would be, "How do we learn this?" Perhaps I can approach it by telling about a brilliant young psychotherapist. Hannah worked in a university setting, treating student-patients. She was also attending graduate school and expected to get her degree "some day," but had never seemed in too much of a hurry about it. When Hannah came into analysis, she was immersed in some intense relationships with close men and women friends, in the Women's Liberation movement, and more than one demanding campus activity. She was feeling increasingly fragmented, expending herself in every direction, attempting to bring her knowledge and will to bear, first on this problem, then on that. As she felt under more and more pressure, she became increasingly assiduous about seeking out various new ways of dealing with the situations and conflicts that arose in her personal life and her work.

One "panacea" followed another. For a while there was yoga. But only by the hour, for there was always someplace to rush off to, someone who needed her, or some obligation she had promised to fulfill. The need she felt to socialize expressed itself in a round with encounter groups. Then she would feel too extraverted, so she would try meditation for a while. The passivity she came to in meditation turned her attention to her body—there was where the problems were impressed, encapsulated, she came to believe. A course of bio-energetics would follow, giving her an opportunity to attack physically each part of the body in which the impress of the psychic pain was being experienced, and to have it pounded or stretched or pushed or pulled into submission. Other techniques, ranging from attempts to control alpha waves in the brain through bio-feedback training, all the way to the scheduled rewards of behavior modification therapy, were attempted by Hannah in the attack on her own nature. In the race to gain control over herself she had failed to learn that man may not do exactly as he wills, and consequently her own nature was destroying her.

In the course of our analytic work, I did not tell her that her own nature, if she continued to heed it so little, would destroy her. I watched with her, the experiences she brought to the analytic sessions, and the effects that these experiences

were having upon her. We talked about the high hopes with
which she was accustomed to approach each new method or
technique. She was interested in analyzing the results of her
activities, but always impatient to go on to something else, always wanting to try a new way. For a while she was nearly
hysterical between her enthusiasms and disappointments. It
was just at this time that Hannah announced her desire to establish and organize a "crisis center" on campus where people
who were suicidal, or in some other way desperate, could come
for immediate help. The whole proposition was so untimely
in view of her own tenuous situation, her own near desperation, that it was not difficult for me to help her come to
the realization that the first "crisis patient" would be, or indeed, already was, herself. It was then that she began to become aware of the necessity to look at the crisis within herself,
to see what was disturbed there.

But looking within was not so easy. That which was within
was so cluttered by all the appurtenances, the many personas
she was used to putting on for various occasions, that it was
difficult to find out who the "who" was behind all its guises.
This involved looking at her behavior, and also at her attitudes, not as something which she initiated in order to create
an effect, but in a different way. Strange to say, because she
had never thought of it in just that way, she had to discover
that her ego was not the center of the universe! But it was
far more than a new way of thinking. Thinking, in fact,
scarcely entered into it. Perhaps it came to her just because
necessity made her shift her perspective, and perhaps a factor
was the analytic transference itself, through which the patient
observed and experienced the therapist as one who resisted
using her own ego to enforce change upon the patient. It
was a slow process, the process of change, and mostly it went
on under the surface, below the matters that were actually
discussed in the session. Occasionally hints of it emerged in
dreams; sometimes they were acknowledged, sometimes that
did not seem necessary.

Then there was a vacation for Hannah, a chance to get
away from external pressures and to hike in the mountains

and sleep under the open sky. Returning, at the beginning of the semester, Hannah announced that she was going to spend a little more time studying, that she was going to limit her other activities to those she could carry on without feeling overburdened. During the past two years, she admitted, she had coasted through graduate school without reflecting on her activities, without seeing what she was experiencing under the wider aspect of the history of human experience. Now she wanted to learn, and to do it at a relaxed and unhurried pace.

In the next weeks I noticed a growing calm in Hannah. At last the day came when it could be expressed. She came into my study, sat down, and was silent for a few moments, and she then told me: "Something important happened to me this week. I discovered what 'the hubris of consciousness' means. Oh, I had read many times that the intellectual answers are not necessarily the right answers, but this is not what it is. It is on a much different level than that. It means —one can hardly say it, for if I do I will spoil it, and I don't want to do that. The striving after awareness—as though awareness were something you could 'get' or 'have,' and then 'use' is pointless. You don't seek awareness, you simply *are* aware, you allow yourself to be—by not cluttering up your mind. To be arrogant about consciousness, to feel you are better than someone else because you are more conscious, means that in a similar degree you are unconscious about your unconsciousness."

Hannah had dreamed that she was in a small boat, being carried down a canal, in which there were crossroads of concrete, which would have seemed like obstacles in her way. But the boat was amphibious, and when it came to the concrete portions it could navigate them by means of retractable wheels.

She took the dream to portray her situation—she was equipped for the journey on which she was embarked, and she was being guided along, within certain limitations, in a direction the end of which she did not foresee. It was not necessary for her to make the vehicle go; all she had to do was to be there and go with it, and she would have time to spare to observe the scenery and learn what she could from everything around her. She was a part of all that, and not any longer one young woman out to save the world, or even a part of it. She *was* a part of it, and she did not even have to save herself. As she became able to hear with her inner ear the harmony of nature, and to see it with her inner eye, she could begin participating with it and so cease fighting against nature.

She was now experiencing the sense of "flowing along" as a bodily experience, in a body that was not separate from the psychic processes that experienced it. But she would never have known the smoothness, the ease, the utter delight of "flowing along" unless she had come to it as she did, through the confrontation with its opposite, the futile exercise of beating herself against insuperable obstacles.

Obviously, this particular way of coming to a harmonious ego-self relationship is not appropriate or even possible for everyone. Each person must find his own individual way, depending on many inner and outer circumstances. Hannah's case is important, however, in that it exemplifies a certain sickness of the Western world, which seems to affect the ambitious, the energetic, the aggressive, and the people who achieve "success," in the popular sense of the word. These are also the people who become, more frequently than not, weary, depressed, frustrated, dependent on medicine and alcohol and drugs to handle their moods, sexually unfulfilled, and who sometimes even admit to being "neurotic." Unlikely as it may seem, their problem is essentially a religious one; for it has to do with that "hubris of consciousness" which prevents man from looking beyond himself for the solution to his problems and for the meaning that lies hidden in all that he does, and sees, and is.

14

WE WERE BORN DYING

When the late-winter sun burns the snow off tree branches and buds begin to swell, we anticipate that in due time there will be tiny yellow green leaflets, then pale leaves greening as summer progresses, which will turn red or golden in autumn, and that before the winter returns they will become dry and brittle and subject to the merciless wind which tears them off and blows them away. Nor are we surprised, though, when some leaves drop before they are fully grown, nor when some are blown off or chewed up by insects when they are fully ripe and strong-looking, nor that there are always a few that, shriveled and brown, cling tightly to the twig in the face of autumn storms and winter winds, until the new buds gently nudge them aside.

I have observed in the course of my work, and also in the events in my personal life, that nature has an inexorable way of proceeding that is, at the same time, unpredictable as to details. We enter into life, but despite the actuarial tables and the learned doctors' prognoses there is no way of knowing whether we shall die in the spring or the summer of life or cling to our last breath in the icy cold of winter. Only one thing is certain, life proceeds onward toward its goal, which is death, and it is the knowledge of that fact which determines much that we do, and the choices that we make. I heard a television announcement the other day asking for contributions to aid research on a fatal children's disease. The sentence that caught my attention was, "Did you know that some children are born dying?" I started for a moment and then I knew why the words had stabbed me—I know that *all* children are born dying, *we are all born dying!* This is the central fact of life, of analysis; it is the core of the individuation process.

In the beginning we lie curled up, unconscious, in the maternal womb. We grow there until it is time to be born, and then emerge to begin the circular journey which takes us through childhood and youth upward to the mid-point of life, then slowly, softly downward through the years of maturity, toward a gradual or sudden surrender of the ego to the unknowable—to the darkness in the womb of earth, the matrix of the unconscious. At every stage of life, the individuation process is going on. In some people it is pure nature expressing herself spontaneously, while in others it is highly cultivated. Since in every life the same goal is reached, and what lies beyond remains a mystery, the process is the only thing that matters. The sooner we realize it, the sooner we identify with the flowing stream (or any other metaphor of process which presents itself), the more likely we are to be able to become free of pointless struggles and fruitless conflicts. Thus, we liberate our energies for that collaboration with nature, which is self-realization in the highest sense. And yet, wanting self-realization is a modest desire, saving us from the exhaustion which comes from the effort of striving itself—no matter what we are striving for.

Jung, in his old age, was able to look back and reflect: "My life as I lived it had often seemed to me like a story that has no beginning and no end. I had the feeling that I was a historical fragment, an excerpt for which the preceding and succeeding text was missing."[1]

Hannah, the analysand who discovered the capacity in her to flow with life, was consciously involved in individuation while she was still young, on the very edge of her career. She had come to an attitude not so very different from the one Jung expressed, an attitude which would support her through the exigencies of her life—and they would be many, because she was curious and adventurous and unafraid.

Engaged in this same ubiquitous search was Byron, an analysand of mine. He was a social worker who had at one time intended to become a minister, but had left the seminary just before ordination. He gave as his reason his perception that the life of a cleric necessitated a rigid patterning and adherence to a creedal structure which he did not believe was possible for him. In the course of his battling inwardly against the traditional doctrines, he had lost the sense of his own personal contact with God. So then he had to ask, what is the battle all about? Are we fighting over the color of the Emperor's New Clothes?

In his daily work, Byron struggled over the practical problems of food, clothing and shelter for low-income families. The task was discouraging; he could never provide enough of whatever was needed in material things, and in matters of the spirit they asked nothing and he offered nothing. He became depressed and gradually withdrew from his casual friendships, maintaining only one or two close relationships. For the most part he felt very much alone, and especially as he was approaching his thirty-third birthday.

The time was of great symbolic importance for him. Thirty-three was the age at which Jesus died, having accomplished all that he could during his life. Byron reflected on his own life: what had he done in his thirty-three years? What if he were to die now, what would have been the meaning of his life? The idea of death began to haunt him. More and more he thought about the possibility of dying—at times it was appealing, at other times ghastly and horrifying.

On the eve of his birthday Byron decided to confront his fear and fascination with death, with the help of as much marijuana as he could manage to smoke. He had used marijuana occasionally in the past, but only a few puffs, and this time he determined that it would be different—he wanted to go into the feelings that had frightened him, and he would loose the barriers that had until this time prevented his doing so. He would go into the feelings and come out again, and

he would then deal with what he had experienced. To make
sure of this he would write down everything he saw and heard
and felt.

He related, afterward, how he did this, stoned on grass,
holding onto his pen with all his strength, forcing the letters,
the words, to flow out of it like a thin stream of blood from
his fingers, and with all the pressure and all the pain. Under
the heavy dosage of the drug, he had begun to write:

> DEATH IS AN ORGASM
> the final one.
> Is the death-wish nothing more than a giant fuck pretasted?
> So too the sacrament of the altar
> a pre-taste of bliss, of glorious bliss?
> What is so gorgeous as ORGASM? COSMIC ORGASM?
> The final fuck-up is a fuck-out of existence

Clutching the pen to direct its vibrations, he set forth his
experience:

> I finally held it to the breaking-point—until I collapsed—
> A foretaste of the real, the GOD-DAMNED real (!!!!) thing.

Then in carefully lettered words, the letters growing larger
as they progressed down the page:

> To have gone there and come back is to have a call, I sup-
>   pose . . .
> But to say WHAT!!???
> Not just that one was there!!!
> Is there an answer!!!!??????

Words from the rock opera floated up at him:

> JESUS CHRIST SUPERSTAR said
> that to learn how to die one only has to die.

The poem of life and death took shape in a hazy way as
the blue smoke thickened:

> It all began tonight by picturing myself underwater
> as I was holding the smoke . . .
> Swimming, swimming, holding my breath . . . YES, that's
>   where

I began to taste of death and liked it . . .
begin the orgasmic experience of life . . .
downing the half (or more)—dying . . .
this repeats itself as one dies in orgasm—now with a
woman, a thought, a friend, a vision . . . then in the final one.

. . .

ANXIETY experienced to pt. of panic—
Then acceptance of it overcoming it.
Getting beyond ego and ego-loss.

. . .

The period of the mystics co-incides
with that of ars moriendi,[2]
whether they coincide or not.

. . .

When the heat of death burns the insides of your veins,
you're beginning to see glory.
To learn HOW to die (in glory) you only have
to die (willingly) . . .
You give yourself back to God . . . What could be more sexual
in the spiritual sense than to return from whence we came?

. . .

33 was experienced
orgasmically—
Now starts the second half—a half that is already
beyond death (a little), willing to die and from thence
beginning to transcend death (a little).

. . .

Able to get back to Holy of Holies . . .
to see the problems of wearers of the cloth . . .
Kept from their orgasm with the world, forced to fuck
the Church, which became
for them the Real Presence of Death . . .
fuck the Church, die to death . . .
that you may die to life and capture willingly
the life that willing death has to offer.

. . .

Learn to die that you may live again.

. . .

Death is the ultimate assurance of a tranquil end . . .
the everlasting extension of the utterly embracing silence
that follows one's intercourse . . .

think then of the depth of bliss in the silence following
one's intercourse with death.

. . .

He who penetrates through beyond death . . .
begins to taste of a life that can know no end.
ONE EXISTS in the afterglow of death, NO MORE:
one LIVES (and creatively!)

. . .

What message can I bring from beyond death . . .
If I'm called to preach that. . . .
Then WHAT (!) am I to say?
A vision of light at depth, of the darkness,
at the deep end of the shaft . . .
It opens up—

Here a sketched circle, within it a great burst of light, exploding, shooting out in all directions.

JESUS CHRIST superstar MESSAGE:
TO CONQUER death, you only have to die . . .
He then proceeded to do just that . . .
TO DIE . . .
and by doing so
conquer it . . .
commending Himself to the Father . . .
that should have ended orgasmically—on a
high (or RISING) tone,
not on a spirit trailing
off to the depths.

. . .

At the end Byron had felt exhilarated, as though the long
tense quiet search for the mystery of death were ended. The
tone of the cry at the crucifixion should not be weak and resigned, he averred, but forthright and courageous. This death,
the death of Jesus Christ incarnate in him, in his contemporary life, in "Jesus Christ Superstar," was the death of his
own spiritual frustration, leaving as residue the jaded, dejected,
unfruitful ego-part, encapsulated in ennui, disorientation, anxiety and isolation. The way was made open for rebirth, into
the second half of life.

"Writing the notes under the influence of pot," he said later, "I was feeling that this was the most important thing I would ever do—to capture these ecstatic moments for all time . . . the sense of eternity must not fly away, I must get them down . . . the pen was a strong, electric, resistant thing, I was hanging on to it for dear life. The feeling of falling and falling . . . the panic that goes with every muscle tensing up in the fear of falling . . . then at some point the fear turns into an acceptance of falling. So let me fall, and then the body can go limp and it doesn't feel bad anymore."

He said, "The point is not to solve the problems of the world, nor even to resolve them; what seems to be right is to dissolve the problem, break it down into tiny particles as a detergent breaks down grease, and then assimilate the substance of the problem. The individual must become able to do that."

Continuing, "You have to let the inner voice tell you what to do. The New Testament says, the Holy Spirit will give you the words. If you let yourself fall into your own resources, then the kinds of conflicts you feel on the conscious level are transcended."

What can the analyst do in the face of the powerful matter surging up out of the depths? I could only be there, be there and let him know that he was not mad but had tapped the source of the archetypal vision, which is timeless, and in which death is not an end, but merely an incident.

There is not much more to say about Byron. His work on himself has now fully begun. The ego boundaries are broken through and he no longer feels bound by his daily chores and responsibilities. Outside, out in the world, it doesn't appear that he has changed very much. No objective measure would pick up what has happened, is happening. But Byron knows, and I know, that everything *is* different. Death and resurrection belonged to a concept before, and now there is no longer any need for him to *believe* in death and resurrection. It is his reality, as every cell in his body bears witness.

Psychological death and rebirth was experienced by another man in my practice, an older man, Julian, who is well into the second half of life. It manifested itself in two dreams. Here is the first: *Our way of getting there at all is full of difficulties. It is furtive, sub-legal, via boats, smuggling, sneaking, avoiding authorities, being chased—somehow I feel on the side of the officers, yet I help the hoods. After climbing through intricate alleys, rushing up stairs, leaping rooftops, we find ourselves in the labyrinthine, plush-carpeted and gilt interiors of a nineteenth-century-style opera house like La Scala. We are always being rushed about from this to that loge for a glimpse of this or that elaborately dressed person. I am trying to arrange a secret rendezvous—is it Lola?—of complicated proportions. Everywhere are glimpses of luxury—in architecture, interiors and dress.*

Then, suddenly, it all begins to fall apart—columns and walls split and disintegrate before my eyes. The rich decorations and costumed people all collapse and melt away in clouds and showers of paste, chalk, plaster. It is as though all had been made of chalk masks, a pretense of overwhelming proportions. How could I ever have taken it all for real? Pillars, balconies, ornate frescoes crumble and fall into total ruin and final catastrophe. I, too, fall with a thunderous clatter. I awake with fear and trembling.

The dream accurately depicted Julian's precarious psychological state, although the reality of it, until this time, had remained relatively unconscious to him. He was a successful business executive, as measured by conventional standards—he had made a lot of money and lived in a fine house; he did all the proper things like dressing his wife elegantly and inviting the right people to his parties. He pretended to be interested in social reforms, and spoke a good deal about morality and justice. But it had all been a front, a persona which did not fit the person behind it. That person had been an exploiter of the weak, an opportunist of sorts. He had carried on shoddy romantic affairs which had been damaging both to the women involved and to his wife. Inside of all the splendor and artistry that his appearance displayed—the opera house of the dream—was decay and dust. "Gilt" covered it all, could this have been a play on the word? For all his savoir-faire,

Julian was feeling the overwhelming burden of having lived a false and mean life. And, suddenly, when he looked in the mirror, the years of dissolution stared back at him and he knew that he was sick inside. This was what had brought him into analysis. All that he had struggled to attain over the years seemed empty and unimportant. If only he could feel like a decent person, if only he could get free of the burden of the bad deals and chicanery and lies and infidelity.

And yet, he had not faced the real truth until this dream. The real truth is, of course, the fact of death. The fact is that he must now look around himself and see the hollow splendor that he had built up while in the process of sacrificing his own integrity, and ask himself, "Is this all there is?"

In his youth, Julian had wanted to be an artist. Early he had become discouraged—for one thing, he was convinced that he wasn't sufficiently talented to become outstanding, for another he was unwilling to struggle financially when there was a chance that he could follow a more lucrative profession. But always he had told himself, "Someday when I have enough money I'll buy a small house by the seashore and take vacations and long weekends off to go there and paint." There had never been enough time for that and there had never been enough money.

Now, at fifty, time was getting ever shorter; he could expect at best another twenty years or so. On the other hand, tomorrow or today might be his last. Panic was setting in—there had to be another way to live, there had to be a way to get out of the way things were now.

I thought of what Jung had said in his essay on "The Stages of Life":

Thoroughly unprepared, we take the step into the afternoon of life; worse still, we take this step with the false assumption that our truths and ideals will serve us as hitherto. But we cannot live the afternoon of life according to the programme of life's morning; for what was great in the morning will be little at evening, and what in the morning was true will at evening have become a lie. I have given psychological treatment to too many people of advancing years, and have looked too often into the

secret chambers of their souls, not to be moved by this fundamental truth.[3]

Before the advent of Julian's dream of destruction, he had
been aware that his life internally was a shambles, but he
felt that there was little hope of accomplishing any radical
change. The problems seemed insurmountable, he was en-
meshed in the complicated structure of his own construction,
there was no way of getting out. "Labyrinthine" was the word
the dream supplied, and it was well chosen. The dream
showed him that it could collapse, all and all, suddenly and
completely. In his own soul the event had already been
foreseen.

We talked about the meaning of the dream, but said nothing about how life could change in practical terms. That
happens, it occurs, when the inner situation is right for it.
The dream had indicated that the inner situation was clearly
bound to change now—we needed to observe it and to be
ready to follow the lead of the unconscious. In a way, Julian
had come to the same point which Byron had reached: the
point of having to let himself fall, to simply let go and fall,
fall into his own resources, and let go of the conflicts that he
had been grappling with on the conscious level.

A few days after the dream of destruction, Julian had another dream: *I am at some kind of double funeral. Two
women are dead. I say to Bill that the mothers (deceased)
looked nice—in a kind of conventional funeral remark. He is
angry because one of the women was not his mother, the other
was. He wanted all the compliments. I walk up to the woman
who was not Bill's mother to look at her, and she turns, rises
up, looks fresh and exceedingly healthy, and gives a tremendous, defecating blast. Two doctors come in and remark that
she has soiled the sheets. The deceased now lives in a kind
of vigorous exuberant health.*

Julian had some associations to the dream. He told me:
"I had read before of Martin Luther's moment of great transformation: it had happened on the monk's toilet, and he who
had been chronically constipated suddenly experienced this

tremendous defecating blast; at the same time his psyche experienced a renewal, he no longer spoke and wrote in a stilted way, but in a vigorous, expressive German."

The double funeral, the two women, puzzled him. One was known, but the one who was restored to life was unknown. The latter must mean then, the soul-woman, the anima who represents the life of the unconscious and its guiding spirit. It is she who is apparently dead, and yet the dream tells the dreamer very clearly that she is only blocked and *apparently* dead, the excrement of her life—his soul's life—has been contained too long, it has putrefied, it has poisoned her, it has brought on the appearance of death. Still, in its very putrefaction the micro-organisms come powerfully alive and create the explosive situation within. Either the foul stuff has to be expelled, or the corpse is really a corpse. The unconscious shows what must happen and furthermore, by presenting the whole image in the funeral scene, it becomes clear that there is really nothing to lose. This re-emphasizes the scene of the previous dream, when the building collapses and consequently is seen to have been nothing but a decayed shell anyway.

The "doubling" motif appears again, with the two doctors who come in. We conjecture that this may refer to the analytic process, and that seems right. I am not the one who heals, nor is the patient—we both belong to the healing moment—but we are there, basically, to note what occurs. Perhaps this scene also suggests that we are not supposed to congratulate ourselves. That theme came up when the shadow-figure, Bill, "wanted all the compliments." It is clear from the role of the doctors—just being there and paying attention to what has happened—that they do not *do* anything. The situation has been recognized, it has been faced. And from the very depths of the unconscious, the change has come, and burst into the world. When it comes out there is much noise and it is ugly and it stinks, but it is possible for dead woman, now rid of her rotting feces, to live anew. Perhaps she will guide Julian in returning to some of his earlier interests, painting, for instance, when the time is right. The other dead woman, pristine and properly peaceful, is dead for all time.

The death-in-life experiences which we call *psychological death*—in contrast to *organic death*—have been described in two men, one in his thirties and one in his fifties. For both of these, the specter of organic death was somewhat distant; each felt the inevitability of it, but neither felt it pressing so close that he was without hope. They were ill-prepared for death, both of them, but they were prepared to prepare.

It would be possible to relate many cases in which death is feared or denied, or where there is protest against the fact of death, by an individual for himself or on behalf of some-one close to him. We all know such cases, and we are well enough acquainted with their pitiable nature.

I want to bring to a close this discussion of analysis in the Jungian mode with a report on the case of an older man, approaching seventy years of age, who has lived his life in knowing awareness of the fact we have posited here: *We were born dying.*

Abraham is a judge, a Roman Catholic, and a philosopher. Reared in the tradition of the Church, he has spent much time on and off during his lifetime in the study of the writings of the Church Fathers and mystics. Also, contemplative "in-fused" prayer has been for him at certain periods a direct meeting with the *spiritus rector*, the divine guide within. But at other times, he had been tempted to involve himself in various schemes and projects that clashed with his personal idealism, and he had given in to the proffered temptations on many occasions. He made and lost several modest for-tunes, made them through questionable dealings and lost them through greed. There were also some inconsequential love affairs which made him feel slight in his own eyes. Al-ways, when he went through a period of reverses, he had found his way back, through withdrawal from his more extra-verted activities and meditation. He would be able to get himself into better order, and begin to function again in a more integrated way, with his philosophical grounding and his activities of the day finding a closer harmony. But it was life full of distraction and allurements, with which he had constantly to come to terms in one way or another.

At the time he came into analysis he was preparing to retire. There would be a modest pension, little money had been saved otherwise. His wife had been urging him to go back into the private practice of law, but he had made the decision not to do so. He was interested now in composing his thoughts, reading, writing, taking long walks and enjoying his small garden. Life was like a flower that has stood the heat of the sun throughout the long day and now, at evening, he was willing to see the petals begin gently to draw up while dusk approached.

He had been ill for a week, with one of the chronic complaints that afflict the aging, and had stayed home in bed. By Friday he was feeling better and several friends had come in over the weekend to visit.

On Monday when Abraham came to analysis, he told me that he had felt that his visitors over the weekend had been mainly "business friends." "They totally dried me up—maybe it was partly the medicine I was taking. We were having conversations about certain judicial matters. When they left I wanted to get back to the quiet mood of the sickness, the thoughts I had had then, the meditation. So, after a short rest, I began to organize my thoughts, and I would like to relate them to you."

He then proceeded, and I will try to put down the gist of what he said from my recollection and from the notes I made after the session was over. Here is the essence of it:

"I am feeling less uptight. I'm not trying specifically to cling to insight or meaning. I have felt in a double bind—the temptation to expand, to capitalize on my efforts all these years, or to withdraw, into a smaller and yet—in an inner sense—an infinitely wider existence.

"I had an insight. Part of the meaning of the double bind is that I have been trying consciously to loosen up—to put myself through a regimen of inner discipline. Now it seems to me that the more you consciously try to interfere with natural behavior, the more you tighten up. It is not 'let go'—

that is too active; what is necessary is just to 'let be'—let
myself be, principally, as well as the world.

"I remember when I was engaged on a day-to-day pursuit
of detachment. My goal was to loosen the grip of my desires.
It required a certain amount of will, this detachment—it was
like using a stiff wire scrubbing brush on my psyche.

"I've always been goal-directed. I think basically that is
where the real desert of my life has been. As I look back on
it, living in the present moment—in *fact*, practicing the sacrament of the present moment—was an illusion, a *fiction* to
conceal the unconscious motivations that obsessed me. I was
no less goal-directed, no freer nor less bound than before; it
was, in fact, purely spurious.

"I'm reminded—some one of the great spiritual voices (St.
Teresa?) was speaking of the ascent of the ladder, La Scala,[4]
saying, the soul is like an infant constantly demanding the
mother's breast, and peevish and irritable if it is deprived
of it. St. Teresa said that we try to *do* too much—like children
we constantly want to love, to crave, spiritual experience.

"Our thinking in terms of past events, field events, are
futile things; we become blinded with historicism and overlook the fact that the purely historic events may be futile—
because the event occurring in the field was perceived im-
properly—therefore we may have derived a false meaning.
Thus only through this mysterious organ in the psyche that
we call intuition are we at all able to arrive at a meaning of
what we have lived through, and the extent to which we have,
in participating in it, falsified it.

"Examining ourselves from an internal viewpoint and not
from a standpoint that is culturally determined, we are able
to work out meanings to relate what we then were to what
we are now. Even Heraclitus[5] never believed altogether in
the flux, since he thought there was a persistence in 'becoming.'

"I feel that the real meaning of my life is to find a freedom
from fear and the 'false anxieties' that have obsessed me
since childhood."

Here I asked Abraham what he meant by "false anxieties."

He continued: "If an anxiety does not equate in some form of causal relationship to some contemporaneous aspect of life —if, in fact, its structure is almost fetishistic, I say it is 'false.' I am not referring to *Angst*, to which we are all subject, but to the shames and fugues that have beset me all my life.

"For the first time in my life I have confronted my own ambiguity. [Here he referred to some writing he is doing in an attempt to clarify these matters.] I think everyone somewhere knows that the real source of *Angst* is not the existential *Angst*, but a coming to awareness of a basic ambiguity, an ambiguity that lies behind the appearances.

"The great paradox is ambiguity and freedom—the ambiguity that lies between the polarities of determinism and free will—and it is within these polarities that we have to choose our standards, our ethos, both as relates to our personal lives and our view of the world.

"So you see, I have had an insight."

We could stop here, and leave the matter of Abraham with the assumption that he was able to live out his days holding in his psyche the tension of the opposites, polarities in balance, as he proceeded on the path to the inevitable final goal. But somehow life is not like that; just when one thinks he has acquired knowledge and understanding, the spiral of individuation takes another turn, and there are new problems, new difficulties. A person seems to be in much the same place as before, but he looks upon his situation from another level, with more distance, more perspective, and so there is a difference from the way it was.

The events in Abraham's life were such that he did not take the rest he had anticipated. A few months after the experiences related above, a very important political position was offered to him. It promised to make use of all his talents, his lifetime of acquired skills and knowledge. He had been reluctant to take on the new responsibility just at the time he was preparing to retire, but he was urged and pressed by those who said he was the only man for the job, and that he was badly needed. At last he gave in.

The responsibilities of his new position were indeed de-

manding. He missed a couple of analytic sessions, saying that
something important had come up. Then he suspended his
analysis for a while, telling me that the work he had gotten
into was just too much, and that during the period of adjust-
ing to the additional requirements that were placed upon
him he was feeling that he simply could not give adequate
attention to his analysis. He stayed away for a few weeks,
then telephoned and asked to return to me for regular
sessions.

The first few sessions after he came back were frightful
and discouraging. He had lost most of the calm which had
characterized the last sessions before he had taken the new
position, and especially the one which I have described. He
was tense, nervous, fidgety, chain-smoking—anything but composed. He complained about the pressures of work, about
his physical health, his aches and pains. He expressed a longing for the deeply grounded peace he had known only a few
months before, but which now seemed out of reach. Even his
dreams had been affected; he described them as "drenched
in grays, blacks, and the soapy colors of street lights seen
through a slight fog."

I noted that Abraham would now come into each session
in an agitated state, sometimes with trembling hands, obviously suffering. There was little I could do for him except
to feel his feelings with him, and to let him know that I was
as much a participant in his suffering as another human being
could be, while at the same time maintaining the objectivity
that would be necessary if I were to help make it possible for
clarity to enter his situation. By the end of each session his
level of anxiety would be greatly reduced, and he would have,
if nothing more, the courage to face a few more days of stress
and disquietude.

Then one day he came in more vibrant than I had seen
him in a long time, saying he had had an experience which
began as a dream, but was more than a dream, for it encompassed a strange and powerful vision. He began with the
dreaming part: *I am in a building, looking out over a parapet.
The building starts to move—the movement is toward the*

East. Streets with pedestrians and cars are passed. The build-ing functions like a train.

Then, he told me, he became suddenly aware that he was no longer dreaming. The light in his room had changed, from the usual twilight or half-lit night, to full daylight. This is how he said it was:

With the light, suddenly the numinosity appears. I am no longer on the other side, the dreaming-ego side, the side that belongs to "my" unconscious. I have left this behind. I have crossed over. I am in another world.

"What strikes me as not only significant, but also stupefy-ing, is that I lost consciousness of the dreaming-I. Phenomeno-logically, there was no longer an *I* to perceive, on this side of the dream screen. I recall rubbing my hands, my face; engaging in those traditional reassurances of a personal sub-stance and saying quite distinctly—'I am awake, I am really here.'

"There was a real division between the two sides of the screen. First, I was here, this side in the reality of the uncon-scious; then I was there, fully conscious, but with no screen in front of me, no sense of awareness of the dreaming-I look-ing. I was conscious and I was engaged in another world. Still, there persisted the ego sensation: perception was or-ganized; the other world in which I so briefly found myself was multi-valued, yet at the same time I perceived a difference in the energy gradients; there was unity and multiplicity. They existed together and they did not exist together. I was conscious of no change, either before or after. I was one place, then the other, by a sort of quantum leap."

From this new state, which was not dreaming, but another sort of consciousness from that which we experience as a shal-low skin on the surface of the unconscious, the vision of light faded and darkness returned. Then the dream continued:

The building of the earlier part of the dream now becomes a train. The train is shunted at a siding. I walk into another building. It is a courthouse, but it has a small chapel on the first floor as you go in. [He later realized, upon reflecting, that it was similar in arrangement to the courthouse into which he was planning to move the next week.] *The chapel was Catholic. There was a center aisle and rows of benches sharply descending on either side of the aisle. The chapel would not seat forty people. I genuflect. I have an armful of umbrellas, suitcases, and a topcoat. I attempt to sit down and I find the bench occupied by another person; she has packages of her own strewn around, but helps me arrange mine. I say that I will sit on the next bench below. I turn and look at the woman. She has a long crooked nose like a certain opera star, which I had always felt was unfortunate, a narrow razor-edge face and beautiful kind eyes, lovely hair, and a magnificent, full-breasted body. I am sexually attracted to her and realize at once and fully that I could wind up in bed with her.*

There is another fragment to the dream—a moment when I realize that in the back of the chapel someone has stolen my topcoat.

We analyzed the dream, or rather he analyzed the greater part of it, for his understanding of himself over the long years of search and contemplation had made it possible for him to draw meaning out of the seemingly meaningless symbols of the unconscious. I give you basically what he said about the dream, expressed as it was in the atmosphere of intense dialogue, questioning, wondering, answering, absorbing. My own contributions are present also, but the process has been so much a mutual endeavor all along that it is not easy to sort it out in terms of whether the material originated with him or with me. This mutuality had been evidenced in a long series of synchronistic events that had occurred between us— we both would think of the same book at the same time, or he would telephone me just when I was pondering one of his dreams—so that it seems fully believable that we were united on an unconscious level by some archetype which was constellated in our way of being-with one another.

To return to the dream—Abraham remembered that the dream of the moving building was a recurrent theme. He experienced it as a structure, an internal structure that carried him along. He said, "The building seems to me to be the

space-time continuum congruent with the perceiving ego. I
am moving through historical time. I notice that I am being
transported. I have not placed this mechanism in motion.
This is a streaming motion over which I have no control,
that does not frighten me, which I tolerate fully, which I do
not question. This is very different when compared to my
inching-progress in 'real' time, when every circumstance seems
to 'gall my kibe.' I am assured of something extraordinary
about this movement."

I asked him about "the East."

"I am moving toward the East. The building is carrying
me. The East evokes thought of Spirit, of William Blake and
the gnostics, the alchemists, the direction in which men turn
in prayer—Mecca, Jerusalem, the rising sun."

So this is the direction into which the unconscious guided
him at this important moment in his life! And, when he was
turned toward the East, being moved from within, he had a
sudden experience of the Holy. He described this so I could
nearly see and feel it.

"Suddenly the dream becomes numinous, I mean to say,
filled with a sense of the presence of divinity. I realized,
while within the core of sleep, that I had not had a numinous
dream. Now the numinosity was signified by the appearance
of light.

"What really startled me about the dream," Abraham continued, "was that, when I made the effort of recall, the faint
hum of the body disappeared. Sometimes I can almost sense
my body's recumbency as a recollected secondary factor after
the dream content is recalled. I have often had the impression
that the body was a stage upon which the dream was enacted.
Direction, in terms of dream movements, seem to result in
an orientation so precise, in terms of the four quadrants, that
the direction or the understanding of it must have a very
ancient archetypal organization."

Looking back over the records of his dreams over the past
few months he saw that over and over again the action upon
the inner screen was oriented with precise reference to the
cardinal points of the compass without fail. Abraham, as

dreamer, always knew the direction, whether East, West, North or South, which he assumed in the dream. With reference to this dream, he explored the symbolism of the East for the deeper meaning it would provide through the process of amplification:

"In Blake, the East is the seat of the emotions. If the movement is toward the West, the East becomes the seat of Ulro, Hell; the West is the location of the spirit. Yet other and contrary values have been assigned in astrological and gnostic literature to these compass points. Perhaps they can only be interpreted within the context of the actual present of the individual. I mean all this in terms of a system of symbols neither absolute nor random. I must apply to them that homespun system of probability theory—common sense. This is coupled with intuition, which leads me more surely. Emotions are, in a sense, the spirit of the body, the pervasive odor of sacrificial meats, rendered upon the coals of the altar to the utterly other, whether it be the other self, or God."

As Abraham accepted this interpretation provisionally, a great deal of meaning emerged from the matrix of the unconscious events. He was able to see the unconscious (the building) carrying him toward an antinomy of emotional balance (eastward) against the stream of the rational westward movement which might have seemed to overwhelm him in this particular moment in time and space in which he was engaged as he moved into a new phase of endeavor. He could now see that the non-rational in his life was opposed to the rational; the movement East was the opposition of the unconscious, a corrective maneuver to allay a headlong flight into the rigid frame of work and obligation.

Halfway between the sections of the dream came the moment of light—the identification with a balanced world of light and color. The ensuing dream spoke clearly of the balance of opposites, in showing to Abraham's dreaming mind that neither the one extreme nor the other was wholly satisfactory. The *being-there* experience was a prefiguration of individuation, the actual attainment and, also, the indication of the path that lay between the polarities. This was the meaning of the experience of the moment of awakening: the attainment of a new state; the placement of this experience within the linear, therefore rational and dreamlike experience.

Abraham described how his sudden break with this world was recaptured from the frozen depths of the dream, at the time that he made the active effort of recall. There was a remarkable and totally inexplicable break between one part of the dream and the other; and again, when he returned to the dream state. He said, "I immediately had the impression of being in another framework; not of time or space, but something totally altered. Nor was there any rejection or nausea or anxiety. It was a state that I accepted totally, calmly, as though it were predestined."

It was impossible not to attribute this complete capacity for acceptance of the unknowable to some prognostic element; probably deeply rooted biologically, related to the dissolution of organic systems. It is necessary to interpret these rare experiences on different levels at the same time, as they should be interpreted, particularly with persons well past the median of life.

To return to the text of the dream: The building which seems to be a train, or like a train, brought up several associations. One, especially, dipped unexpectedly into the dreamer's childhood, to a recollection of his father's last days. His father had been ill in the hospital, and when he was recovering from an injection of morphine he had begun to talk about riding a freight train (moving from west to east) and how he was going to jump off at the place where his house approached the tracks. The hospital was the train, the freight train; he was wanting to get out of bed in order to go home. He was obviously hallucinating, and yet he was *there*. He died not long after.

Abraham commented on a quite other use of the word "train," the French use—*en train*—which means to set to work, to get going, to start, to put in hand, to begin, to throw into gear, to make ready . . . as, *mettre en train*.

Putting it all together, he saw that there were coincidences at different levels, and within different segments of the dream, spaced linearly, so that the whole might be seen as a totality: the emotions, balance, yielding to the will of God, work, the reminder from his father's hallucination—that the bottom is all hallucination, in a normal sense, or a universal sense of Maya; that the visionary light was a partial experience of individuation—perhaps an unconscious satori. This latter was reinforced by the loss of the topcoat—perhaps one of the layers of the ego.

The woman was also present in the small and sacred place. When Abraham came in he was heavily laden with all sorts of impedimenta. She helped him, with great good humor, to arrange the various articles. He was totally paralyzed by the multitude of the burdens—a typical response to his complicated life situation. He described the other figure as a representation of the analyst, and his reactions to her as follows:

"The woman herself was divided into two parts: one part, her face, was very unpleasant—ugly and distorted. He emphasized the word *distorted*. The eyes, the hair, were transcendently beautiful; the face, in all its crooked, mean distortions with its crooked, long nose, seemed not so much as an absolute block, but as a dam posited between the upper and the lower parts of her. Nothing impeded my sexual response to the body. My immediate reaction to this on awakening was that the ugliness was only a mask, and that this served as a psychological deterrent, splitting the analyst in a very realistic way between the upper and the lower poles. Concealed behind this mask must be the repressions which had been rejected by the conscious mind.

"I do not believe in the *censor* of Freud," Abraham continued, "nor in a lot that flows from it. Nevertheless, I do feel that much that he has interpreted and ascribed to this automation is a result of factors that arise elsewhere, as is the case in this dream. The dream itself obviously has reference to the transference of patient to analyst. I cannot see the transference as a neurosis, nor shall I ever. I further believe that if you have a male-female relationship, you can only have a male-female reaction."

The distortion in the image of the woman was very sensible.

The analyst had been idealized by the patient. She had received the projection of the anima of the patient, she reflected beauty and wisdom, and her expressiveness, which meant so much to him was symbolized by the opera star, a singer, which is, of course, a homonym for the analyst's name: Singer. But the analyst was also a person, a very human person, who was in reality unable to measure up to the image in the psyche of the patient. The dream apprised him of this, by diminishing the overvalued physical appearance and the attraction of the woman for him. This was the way the dream denied to the patient and the analyst a full resolution of their relationship. The patient was responsive to the analyst on an unconscious level, as the dream showed, but the patient and the analyst were separated in terms of the aesthetic value—the distortion of the analyst's face. The analyst had to be decapitated to reach the patient; the patient had to be blinded to reach the analyst. Thus, it was clear that the transference was meant to be an inner relationship, assimilated to the patient, and not to be lived out in an objective relationship, as a love affair.

Working through this dream became a profound experience for Abraham. It was no less so for me, for it deepened my understanding of the process and brought me closer to the experience of living toward death as I moved slowly through the experience with my patient.

In the weeks that followed, Abraham regained the calm that he had known before, but this time it was deeply grounded in its archetypal basis and would not easily be moved. In the sessions that followed, the insights and feelings became as friends; Abraham could reach into them and take hold of them, even in the midst of his busy days and his worldly responsibilities.

Little by little his attitude toward his work changed. He found that he could do what was necessary without always feeling that what he accomplished was insufficient. He was content with expending his best efforts, and he had come to realize that those efforts would naturally be forthcoming as he also took time for his work on himself, his dreams, and his contemplative practices. Gradually he began to delegate portions of his work to other people. He sought out younger men who would be able to assume the tasks which he himself had been doing and who would be able, when the time came, to relieve him of his responsibility. His analytic work became increasingly important to him. Much of it was done without the analyst's help, although he continued to come in and discuss some of the events of his inner life which he felt needed clarification.

Then one day he brought a dream which he did not understand, and which troubled him deeply. This is the dream: *I am married. I have one child, about eighteen months old, barely walking. I take him by the hand and tell him that we will have an adventure. We find ourselves by a gigantic concrete sewer pipe. A small boat is at the landing. We get into the boat and take off, beginning to descend. We go deeper and deeper. I am paddling, steering the boat. We finally emerge in clear water. Someone tells us to get out, that the water is clear, it is rainwater, not sewage. We walk through the shallows to the shore. We are suddenly in a busy arcade. There are many stores. Much business is being transacted. A woman tells me that the business is finished. I can go back up. I take the child in my one arm and pull the blanket over his head and begin to swim upstream. I am not aware of any cold. I feel quite warm. We arrive in a room far above. Another woman takes the child from me and I disrobe to my shorts and dry myself. Shortly another woman comes to me and tells me the child is dead. I exclaim that it is impossible. She says that he has died through exposure to the cold in the water. I am horrified and grief-stricken. I fall to my knees and ask God to give him back to me. I pray.*

Feelings of grief and loss pervaded the days between the dream and Abraham's coming to analysis. It seemed incomprehensible to him—after all his suffering and struggling to come to consciousness—that this child, this gift of God, should be taken from him. What was the symbolism of the child, the symbolism of the rest of the dream?

It had been about eighteen months since Abraham's sickness, when he had found the time to reflect upon his life as he had lived it in the past, goal-directed in his professional work and even goal-directed in his spiritual pursuits. This was the period during which the insights came which had their fruition in his change of commitment—from goal to process. Also, during this time there had been the swing away from the inner life, and the many distractions that brought the opposite pole into the foreground of his attention. And then the movement back in the other direction, but in a less violent, more tenable way. And now there is a child of eighteen months, the child who has grown from that time of new beginnings until this.

The concrete sewer pipe is a conduit of sorts, through which he must go with the child, through the filth and debris which has been in his life and sloughed off from his life, to the place where the water is pure rain water. The past has been clarified, through his working on it, his willingness to look at it carefully and see the meaning in it. But again he finds himself in the hustle and bustle of the marketplace—this refers to his intensification of his professional life. In time he is told that the business is finished. This can be nothing else than a prefiguration of the end of life, his life. He can go back up. There is to be another transformation, but this time there is no vessel to carry him, he must swim through the waters. And, in those waters he is not aware of any cold. The waters are the waters of the unconscious, the final journey to the room "far above," which to the Catholic would signify the eternal abode. Upon arriving here he is told that the child is dead; and he cannot believe it, he cannot accept it.

Throughout this dream there has been a woman near him. In the beginning of the dream it is said that he is "married." There has been in his life the experience of the *coniunctio oppositorum*, the meeting of the opposites. He has come to terms with his feeling side as well as his intellectual side. In the long years Eros has come to rest beside Logos, so that the sacred marriage, called by the ancients the *hieros-gamos*, has occurred. The women whom he meets at various stages of his journey are guides through the mysterious regions of the unconscious; as such they are manifestations of the anima, who brings a man to the depths of his own soul.

But the child, who is the child whom he must give up in the end? We have learned that historically the appearance of a divine child heralds a new development, or an era of important change. In most legends and myths the advent of the child is hailed with joy and celebration. Not so in Abraham's dream. When the dream became fully articulate upon waking, Abraham was overwhelmed by the recollected grief and yet at the same time he was shocked into intense attention. That attention had not wavered very long, he kept returning and returning to the dream.

As we talked about the dream, the meaning of the child emerged out of the shade of sorrow. In the end a man must lose that which is most precious to him, that to which his whole life has been devoted. The treasure is consciousness; it is the ego's final sacrifice to the self. This sacrifice must be offered before the ultimate moment when man merges with the unconscious and stands before his God.

Abraham falls to his knees and asks God to give him back the child. He prays.

It is the prayer that may not or may be answered.

It belongs to the unknowable.

NOTES

INTRODUCTION

1. C. G. Jung, *Memories, Dreams, Reflections.*
2. Ibid., p. 4.
3. Ibid., p. 84.
4. Ibid., p. 32.
5. *Lehrbuch der Psychiatrie,* 4th Edition, 1890.
6. *Structure and Dynamics of the Psyche,* C. W. 8, p. 353.
7. Werner Heisenberg, *Physics and Philosophy,* p. 31.
8. Ibid., pp. 55–56.
9. *Memories, Dreams, Reflections,* p. 147.
10. *Psychiatric Studies,* C. W. 1, p. 3.

CHAPTER 1
Analyst and Analysand

1. *The Practice of Psychotherapy,* C. W. 16, pp. 53, 54.
2. Adapted from *Structure and Dynamics of the Psyche,* C. W. 8, p. 377.
3. James Hillman, *Suicide and the Soul,* p. 101.
4. See Chapter 9: Anima and Animus: Will One Sex Ever Understand the Other?
5. Gerhard Adler, "Methods of Treatment in Analytical Psychology," in *Psychoanalytic Techniques,* Benjamin B. Wolman, ed., p. 340.

6. Arthur Janov, *The Primal Scream, Primal Therapy: The Cure for Neurosis.*

7. V. Meyer and Edward S. Chesser, *Behavior Therapy in Clinical Psychiatry,* p. 215.

8. Horace B. English and Ava C. English, *A Comprehensive Dictionary of Psychological and Psychoanalytical Terms.*

9. *The Practice of Psychotherapy,* C. W. 16, p. 164.

10. Gerhard Adler, op. cit., p. 344.

11. "Psychology of the Transference," in *The Practice of Psychotherapy,* C. W. 16, p. 178.

CHAPTER 2

Complexes by Day and Demons by Night

1. Sigmund Freud, *The Psychopathology of Everyday Life.*

2. *The Archetypes and the Collective Unconscious,* C. W. 9, i.

3. *The Structure and Dynamics of the Psyche,* C. W. 8, p. 315.

4. *Psychiatric Studies,* C. W. 1.

5. Ibid., p. 24.

6. Ibid., p. 39.

7. Ibid., p. 56.

8. Eugen Bleuler's article "Upon the Significance of Association Experiments," in C. G. Jung, *Studies in Word Association,* pp. 1–7, passim.

9. Ibid.

10. *Psychogenesis in Mental Disease,* C. W. 3, p. 41.

11. "A Review of the Complex Theory," in *The Structure and Dynamics of the Psyche,* C. W. 8, p. 92.

12. Ibid., p. 93.

13. Ibid.

14. Ibid., p. 96.

15. J. E. Cirlot, *A Dictionary of Symbols,* pp. 328–29.

16. Exodus 15:25.

17. Mircea Eliade, *Images and Symbols,* pp. 37–38.

18. In *Civilization in Transition,* C. W. 10.

19. Ibid., p. 50.

20. Ibid., p. 72.

21. "The Psychological Foundations of the Belief in Spirits," in *The Structure and Dynamics of the Psyche,* C. W. 8, p. 311.

22. Ibid., pp. 311–12.

23. Ibid., p. 312.

CHAPTER 3
From Associations to Archetypes

1. *Memories, Dreams, Reflections*, p. 148.
2. Ibid., p. 150.
3. Letter quoted in *Two Essays on Freud and Jung*, by Jolande Jacobi, p. 25.
4. *The Archetypes and the Collective Unconscious*, C. W. 9, i, "Concerning the Archetypes with Special Reference to the Anima Concept," p. 58.
5. Sigmund Freud, "Leonardo da Vinci and a Memory of His Childhood." Referred to by Jung in "The Concept of the Collective Unconscious," *The Archetypes of the Collective Unconscious*, pp. 44–49.
6. *Der Mythus von Der Geburt des Helden*, published in the series, *Schriften zur angewandten Seelenkunde*, Vienna: F. Deuticke, Heft 5, quoted in Freud, *Moses and Monotheism*, p. 7.
7. Sigmund Freud, *Moses and Monotheism*, pp. 7–11.
8. C. G. Jung, "The Psychology of the Child Archetype," in *The Archetypes and the Collective Unconscious*, C. W. 9, i, p. 152.
9. Ibid., p. 153.
10. "The Psychological Aspects of the Kore," in *The Archetypes and the Collective Unconscious*, C. W. 9, i, p. 183.
11. See also *Psychological Types*, Part II, Def. 26; "The Archetypes of the Collective Unconscious," "Concerning the Archetypes with Special Reference to the Anima Concept," "Psychological Aspects of the Mother Archetype," "The Psychology of the Child Archetype," and "The Psychological Aspects of the Kore," all in *The Archetypes and the Collective Unconscious*, C. W. 9, i; Commentary on *The Secret of the Golden Flower*, in *Alchemical Studies*, C. W. 13. For alternate sources see the complete list of Jung's *Collected Works* at the end of this volume.
12. Glover, *Freud or Jung*, pp. 21–22.
13. "The Personal and Collective Unconscious," in *Two Essays in Analytical Psychology*, C. W. 7, p. 65.
14. Ibid.

CHAPTER 4
Are Archetypes Necessary?

1. Jolande Jacobi, *Complex, Archetype, Symbol*, p. 31.
2. William Blake, *Visions of the Daughters of Albion*, p. 191.
3. Jones, *The Life and Works of Sigmund Freud*, Vol. 1, p. 29.
4. *Memories, Dreams, Reflections*, p. 168.
5. Alfred Lord Tennyson, *De Profundis*, in *Victorian and Later English Poets*, James Stephens, Edwin L. Beck and Royall H. Snow, eds., p. 187.
6. *Memories, Dreams, Reflections*, p. 167.
7. "The Sacrifice," in *Symbols of Transformation*, C. W. 5, pp. 416–17.
8. Ibid.
9. Ibid., pp. 417–18.
10. *Roche Report: Frontiers of Clinical Psychiatry*, March 12, 1969.
11. Ibid.
12. "Archetypes of the Collective Unconscious," in *The Archetypes of the Collective Unconscious*, C. W. 9, i, p. 5.
13. Ibid.
14. Ibid., pp. 4–5.
15. Joseph Campbell, *The Masks of God: Primitive Mythology*, p. 30.
16. N. Tinbergen, *The Study of Instinct*, pp. 7–8.
17. Campbell, loc. cit.

CHAPTER 5
Analysis and the Counter-culture

1. *Memories, Dreams, Reflections*, p. 175.
2. "The Confessions of Lieutenant Calley," by First Lieutenant William L. Calley, Jr., interviewed by John Sack, in *Esquire*, November, 1970.
3. Jung, *Psychology and Alchemy*, C. W. 12, p. 34.
4. The New York *Times* Magazine, June 1, 1969.
5. Ibid.
6. Ibid.
7. Chicago *Sun-Times*, August 12, 1970, p. 64.

8. *Behavior Today*, June 22, 1970.
9. The New York *Times* Magazine, June 1, 1969, loc. cit.
10. *Civilization in Transition*, C. W. 10.
11. Ibid., p. 51.
12. Ibid.
13. Ibid.
14. Ibid., pp. 54–55.
15. In *The Idea of the Holy*.
16. "The Autonomy of the Unconscious," in *Psychology and Religion*, C. W. 11, p. 7.
17. Ibid., p. 8.
18. Jung, *Psychological Types*, p. 600.
19. Theodore Roszak, *The Making of a Counter-Culture*.
20. Ibid., p. 156.
21. "The Undiscovered Self," in *Civilization in Transition*, C. W. 10, p. 257.
22. Ibid.
23. *Psychological Reflections*, p. 149.
24. "The Swiss Line in the European Spectrum," translation in part from *Civilization in Transition*, C. W. 10, pp. 486–87, and in part from the excerpt in *Psychological Reflections*, pp. 155–56.
25. *Civilization in Transition*, C. W. 10, p. 488.

CHAPTER 6
Individuation: The Process of Becoming Whole

1. *Two Essays in Analytical Psychology*, C. W. 7, p. 171.
2. *The Secret of the Golden Flower*, p. 83.
3. Ibid.
4. Jolande Jacobi, *The Way of Individuation*, p. 19.

CHAPTER 7
Psychological Types: Key to Communications

1. *Two Essays in Analytical Psychology*, p. 18.
2. Ibid., p. 24.
3. Ibid., p. 26.
4. Ibid., p. 27.
5. Ibid., p. 31.

6. Ibid.
7. Ibid., p. 34 f.
8. Ibid., p. 39.
9. Ibid., p. 40.
10. Jung's analysis of their differences are to be found in the first of the *Two Essays in Analytical Psychology.*
11. Cited in *Psychological Types*, p. 9.
12. Ibid.
13. Ibid., p. 513.
14. Ibid., p. 516.
15. Gerhard Adler, "Methods of Treatment in Analytical Psychology," in Benjamin B. Wolman, *Psychoanalytic Techniques.*

CHAPTER 8
Persona and Shadow

1. *Two Essays in Analytical Psychology*, C. W. 7, pp. 155–56.
2. Ibid., p. 156.
3. *Aion*, C. W. 9, ii, p. 8.
4. *Two Essays in Analytical Psychology*, C. W. 7, pp. 158–59.
5. Ibid., p. 159.
6. Ibid., p. 161.
7. Ibid., p. 162.
8. *Über die Energetik der Seele und andere psychologische Abhandlungen*, Zurich: Rascher, 1928, p. 158.

CHAPTER 9
Anima and Animus: Will One Sex Ever Understand the Other?

1. *Nihongi* translated by W. G. Aston, and cited in Mircea Eliade, *From Primitives to Zen*, p. 94.
2. *Two Essays in Analytical Psychology*, C. W. 7, p. 188.
3. Erich Neumann, *The Great Mother*, p. 3.
4. Ibid.
5. Cf. Erich Neumann, *The Great Mother, Amor and Psyche;* M. Esther Harding, *The Parental Image, The Way of All Women, Women's Mysteries;* Emma Jung, *Animus and Anima;* Eleanor Bertine, *Human Relationships, Jung's Contributions to Our Times;* Joseph Campbell, the four-volume

series, *The Masks of God*, also *Hero with a Thousand Faces*.

6. *Saturday Review*, April 25, 1970.

7. *Women in the University of Chicago*. Report of the Committee on University Women, May 1, 1970 (prepared for the Committee of the Council of the University Senate), p. 29 f.

8. *Two Essays in Analytical Psychology*, C. W. 7, pp. 204–5.

9. U.S. Office of Education estimates based on a probability sampling of teaching faculty who taught at least one degree-credit course in Spring 1963, and who were employed full time by a United States university or four-year college during the entire academic year 1962–63, cited in the *Women in the University of Chicago* report, p. 71.

CHAPTER 10
Circumambulating the Self

1. Edward C. Whitmont, *The Symbolic Quest*, p. 216.

2. The "I" and the "Not-I."

3. *Psychology and Alchemy*, C. W. 12, p. 304. For further study of alchemy in Jung's works, see the entire book, *Psychology and Alchemy*, also see *Alchemical Studies*, C. W. 13; *Mysterium Coniunctionis*, C. W. 14; *The Secret of the Golden Flower*, and "The Psychology of the Transference" in *The Practice of Psychotherapy*, C. W. 16. Also see Chapter 13, below.

4. *The Perennial Philosophy*, pp. 3–4.

5. William Blake, *A Song of Liberty*.

6. The archetype of the divine child is discussed by Jung in his essay "The Psychology of the Child Archetype," in *The Archetypes and the Collective Unconscious*, C. W. 9, i.

7. Cf. also Bacchus, Dionysus.

8. Mary-Louise von Franz, *The Problem of the Puer Aeternus*.

9. *Ibid*.

10. A full discussion of this archetype and the preceding one appears in James Hillman's essay, "Senex and Puer: An Aspect of the Historical and Psychological Present" in *Eranos-Jahrbuch* XXXVI/1967, Zurich: Rhein-Verlag, 1968.

11. *The Archetypes and the Collective Unconscious*, C. W. 9, i, p. 263.

12. William Blake, "Proverbs of Hell," from *The Marriage of Heaven and Hell*.

13. *Two Essays in Analytical Psychology*, C. W. 7, p. 225.

14. Cf. *Aion*, C. W. 9, ii, p. 22 and "The Psychology of the Transference" in *The Practice of Psychotherapy*, C. W. 16.

15. *Aion*, loc. cit.

16. Ibid., p. 23.

17. The reader is referred especially to the following volumes of the *Collected Works*: the entire book *Two Essays in Analytical Psychology*, C. W. 7; the last three essays in *The Archetypes and the Collective Unconscious*, C. W. 9, i; all of *Aion*, C. W. 9, ii; sections throughout *Psychology and Religion: West and East*, C. W. 11; *Psychology and Alchemy*, C. W. 12; *Alchemical Studies*, C. W. 13; *Mysterium Coniunctionis*, C. W. 14; and "The Psychology of the Transference" in *The Practice of Psychotherapy*, C. W. 16.

18. Cf. Jung, *The Secret of the Golden Flower*, p. 99 f.

CHAPTER 11
Understanding Our Dreams

1. *Freud and Psychoanalysis*, C. W. 4, p. 25 ff.

2. *Memories, Dreams, Reflections*, p. 158.

3. Ibid., p. 161.

4. Ibid.

5. "The Practical Use of Dream Analysis," in *The Practice of Psychotherapy*, C. W. 16.

6. "General Aspects of Dream Psychology," in *The Structure and Dynamics of the Psyche*, C. W. 8, pp. 263–64.

7. "The Practical Use of Dream Analysis," in *The Practice of Psychotherapy*, C. W. 16, p. 149.

8. Ibid., p. 147.

9. "General Aspects of Dream Psychology," in *The Structure and Dynamics of the Psyche*, C. W. 8, p. 241.

10. Gershom Scholem, *Major Trends in Jewish Mysticism*, p. 44.

11. Jung, *The Secret of the Golden Flower*, pp. 91–92.

12. Jung, "General Aspects of Dream Psychology," in *The Structure and Dynamics of the Psyche*, C. W. 8, p. 266 ff.

13. Cf. Jung's essays, "General Aspects of Dream Psychology," and "On the Nature of Dreams," in *The Structure and Dynamics of the Psyche*, C. W. 8.

CHAPTER 12
Dreaming the Dream Onward: Active Imagination

1. Gerhard Adler, *Studies in Analytical Psychology*, pp. 60–61. For a fuller treatment of active imagination, see Gerhard Adler, *The Living Symbol*, and C. G. Jung, "The Transcendent Function," in *The Structure and Dynamics of the Psyche*, C. W. 8.

CHAPTER 13
Religion: and Other Approaches to the Unknowable

1. Jung, *Psychology and Religion: West and East*, C. W. 11.
2. Revised and later published in the *Collected Works* as *Symbols of Transformation*, C. W. 5.
3. *Memories, Dreams, Reflections*, p. 182.
4. Ibid., pp. 182–83.
5. Ibid., p. 183.
6. *Psychology and Religion*, C. W. 11, p. 84.
7. "Five Who Care," *Look* magazine, April 21, 1970.
8. *Mysterium Coniunctionis*, C. W. 14, p. 547.
9. Ibid., p. 548.
10. Ibid.
11. *Aion, Researches into the Phenomenology of the Self*, C. W. 9, ii, p. 62 f.
12. Ibid.
13. *Psychology and Alchemy*, C. W. 12, p. 277.
14. *Aion*, C. W. 9, ii, p. 167.
15. *Psychology and Religion: West and East*, C. W. 11, pp. 201–96.
16. Ibid., p. 214.
17. Ibid., p. 221.
18. Ibid., pp. 226–27.
19. Ibid., p. 273.
20. *Psychology and Alchemy*, C. W. 12, pp. 338–39.
21. *Aion*, C. W. 9, ii, pp. 89–90.
22. In *The Structure and Dynamics of the Psyche*, C. W. 8, pp. 417–531.

23. Letter to Dr. Selig dated 25 February, 1953, in *Spring*, 1971, p. 127.

24. *The Structure and Dynamics of the Psyche*, C. W. 8, p. 475.

25. *Psychology and Religion: West and East*, C. W. 11 contains psychological commentaries on *The Tibetan Book of the Great Liberation* and *The Tibetan Book of the Dead*; "Yoga and the West," the "Foreword to Suzuki's Introduction to Zen Buddhism," "The Psychology of Eastern Meditation," "The Holy Men of India: Introduction to Zimmer's *Der Weg zum Selbst*," "Foreword to the *I Ching*" and his "Commentary on *The Secret of the Golden Flower*: a Chinese Book of Life."

26. W. Y. Evans-Wentz (compiler and editor), *The Tibetan Book of the Dead*, with a psychological commentary by Dr. C. G. Jung.

27. Timothy Leary, Ralph Metzner, and Richard Alpert, *The Psychedelic Experience: A Manual Based on the Tibetan Book of the Dead*, p. 22.

28. Ibid.

29. "Psychological Commentary on *The Tibetan Book of the Great Liberation*," in *Psychology and Religion*, C. W. 11, pp. 504–5.

30. Cf. M. Esther Harding, *The "I" and the "Not-I."*

31. *Psychology and Religion*, C. W. 11, pp. 525–26.

32. Ibid., p. 533.

33. Ibid., p. 535.

CHAPTER 14
We Were Born Dying

1. *Memories, Dreams, Reflections*, p. 291.

2. *Ars moriendi*, the art of dying, was one of the favorite subjects of philosophers and theologians during the Renaissance. Many treatises were written to instruct the soul in the manner of dying. An oriental example would be *The Tibetan Book of the Dead*, which was referred to in chapter 13.

3. *The Structure and Dynamics of the Psyche*, C. W. 8, p. 399.

4. How different the meaning of the same symbol when it appears to two different people! (Cf. Julian's dream, p. 416). A patient once told me, "I have been doing some thinking about the Freudian apparatus: the choice and insistence upon arbi-

trary meanings, is, on the whole, and with the whole person observed, something like treating the patient with a gypsy dream book. So little comes from the patient and so much from the analyst. I suspect the long silences and the apparent blocking are unconscious ploys to divert the conscious mind from those meanings which surface from the unconscious dream experience to a system of references which accords with the symbolic dictionary."

5. Heraclitus (c. 540–475 B.C.) was said to be in a real sense the founder of metaphysics. He believed that the fundamental uniform fact in nature is constant change. He thus arrived at the principle of relativity: harmony and unity consist in diversity and multiplicity. The senses are "bad witnesses"; only the wise man can obtain knowledge. This attitude is implicit in the *Seven Sermons of the Dead*, cf. chapter 13, supra.

LIST OF WORKS CITED

BOOKS

ADLER, GERHARD: *Studies in Analytical Psychology*. New York: G. P. Putnam's Sons (1966).

——: *The Living Symbol*. New York: Pantheon Books (1961). Bollingen Series 63.

BAKAN, DAVID: *Sigmund Freud and the Jewish Mystical Tradition*. New York: D. Van Nostrand Co. (1958).

BERTINE, ELEANOR: *Human Relationships*. New York: Longmans, Green and Company (1958).

——: *Jung's Contributions to Our Times*. New York: G. P. Putnam's Sons (1967).

BLAKE, WILLIAM: *The Complete Writings of William Blake, with all the Variant Readings*, edited by Geoffrey Keynes. London: The Nonesuch Press (1957).

CAMPBELL, JOSEPH: *Hero with a Thousand Faces*. New York: Pantheon Books, Bollingen Series 17 (1949).

——: *The Masks of God: Primitive Mythology*. New York: Viking Press (1959).

CIRLOT, J. E.: *A Dictionary of Symbols*. New York: Philosophical Library (1962).

ELIADE, MIRCEA: *From Primitives to Zen*. New York: Harper & Row (1967).

——: *Images and Symbols*, translated by Philip Mairet, from the Librairie Gallimard, 1952, London: Harvill Press (1961).

ENGLISH, HORACE B., and AVA C.: *A Comprehensive Dictionary of Psychological and Psychoanalytical Terms.* New York: Longmans, Green and Company (1961).

EVANS-WENTZ, W. Y., compiler and editor: *The Tibetan Book of the Dead.* Oxford: A Galaxy Book; Oxford University Press (1969).

FRANKL, VIKTOR: *Man's Search for Meaning.* New York: Washington Square Press (1969).

FREUD, SIGMUND: The Standard Edition of the *Complete Psychological Works,* translated from the German under the General Editorship of James Strachey, in collaboration with Anna Freud, assisted by Alix Strachey and Alan Tyson. London: The Hogarth Press and the Institute of Psycho-Analysis (1968).
Vol. IV: *Interpretation of Dreams.*
Vol. VI: *The Psychopathology of Everyday Life.*
Vol. XXIII: *An Outline of Psycho-Analysis.*
Vol. XXIII: *Moses and Monotheism.*

———: *Moses and Monotheism.* New York: A Vintage Book (1939).

GLOVER, EDWARD: *Freud or Jung.* Cleveland, Ohio: A Meridian Book, World Publishing Co. (1963).

HARDING, M. ESTHER: *The "I" and the "Not-I."* New York: Pantheon Books, Random House, Bollingen Series 79 (1965).

———: *The Parental Image, Its Injury and Reconstruction.* New York: G. P. Putnam's Sons for the C. G. Jung Foundation (1965).

———: *The Way of All Women.* New York: G. P. Putnam's Sons (1970).

———: *Women's Mysteries.* New York: G. P. Putnam's Sons (1971).

HEISENBERG, WERNER: *Physics and Philosophy.* New York: Harper and Brothers (1958).

HILLMAN, JAMES: *Suicide and the Soul.* New York: Harper & Row (1964).

HUXLEY, ALDOUS: *The Perennial Philosophy.* New York: Harper Colophon Books (1970).

JACOBI, JOLANDE: *Complex/Archetype/Symbol in the Psychology of C. G. Jung.* New York: Pantheon Books, Bollingen Series 57 (1959).

———: *The Way of Individuation.* New York: Harcourt, Brace & World (1967).

JANOV, ARTHUR: *The Primal Scream, Primal Therapy: The Cure for Neurosis.* New York: G. P. Putnam's Sons, 1970.

JONES, ERNEST: *The Life and Work of Sigmund Freud*, 3 vols. New York: Basic Books (1953).

JUNG, CARL G.: *Collected Works*. Princeton: Princeton University Press, Bollingen Series XX. Edited by Sir Herbert Read, Michael Fordham, M.D., M.R.C.P., and Gerhard Adler, Ph.D. Translated by R. F. C. Hull.

Vol. 1: *Psychiatric Studies* (1957).

Vol. 3: *Psychogenesis in Mental Disease* (1960).

Vol. 4: *Freud and Psychoanalysis* (1961).

Vol. 5: *Symbols of Transformation* (1956).

Vol. 7: *Two Essays on Analytical Psychology* (1953).

Vol. 8: *The Structure and Dynamics of the Psyche* (1960).

Vol. 9, i: *The Archetypes and the Collective Unconscious* (1959).

Vol. 9, ii: *Aion: Researches into the Phenomenology of the Self* (1959).

Vol. 10: *Civilization in Transition* (1964).

Vol. 11: *Psychology and Religion: West and East* (1958).

Vol. 12: *Psychology and Alchemy* (1953).

Vol. 13: *Alchemical Studies* (1967).

Vol. 14: *Mysterium Coniunctionis* (1963).

Vol. 16: *The Practice of Psychotherapy* (1954).

——: *Memories, Dreams, Reflections*, recorded and edited by Aniela Jaffé. New York: Pantheon Books, a division of Random House (1963).

——: *Modern Man in Search of a Soul*. New York: A Harvest Book, Harcourt Brace & Co. (1933).

——: *Psychological Reflections*, selections edited by Jolande Jacobi. New York: Harper Torchbooks (1961).

——: *Psychological Types*. London: Routledge & Kegan Paul (1959). (Now available in the *Collected Works* as Volume 6.)

——: *Psychology of the Unconscious*. London: Kegan Paul, Trench, Trubner (1922).

—— et al.: *Studies in Word Association*, authorized translation by Dr. M. D. Eder. New York: Russell and Russell (1969).

——: *The Secret of the Golden Flower: A Chinese Book of Life*, translated and explained by Richard Wilhelm with a Commentary by C. G. Jung. New York: Harcourt, Brace & World (1965).

——: *Über die Energetik der Seele und andere psychologische Abhandlungen*. Zurich: Rascher (1928).

JUNG, EMMA: *Animus and Anima*. New York: The Analytical Psychology Club of New York (1957).

KRAFFT-EBING: *Lehrbuch der Psychiatrie*. 4th Edition (1890), cited in Jung, *Memories, Dreams, Reflections*.

LEARY, TIMOTHY; RALPH METZNER; and RICHARD ALPERT: *The Psychedelic Experience, A Manual Based on the Tibetan Book of the Dead*. New Hyde Park, New York: University Books (1964).

LEVI, EDWARD H.: *Points of View*. Chicago: A Phoenix Book, University of Chicago Press (1969).

McGLASHAN, ALAN: *A Savage and Beautiful Country*. Boston: Houghton, Mifflin (1967).

MEYER, V., and EDWARD S. CHESSER: *Behavior Therapy in Clinical Psychiatry*. New York: Science House, 1970.

NEUMANN, ERICH: *Amor and Psyche: The Psychic Development of the Feminine*, translated by Ralph Manheim. New York: Pantheon Books (1956). Bollingen Series 54.

——: *The Great Mother*, translated by Ralph Manheim. New York: Pantheon Books (1955). Bollingen Series 47.

PLATO: *The Republic*. Chicago: Encyclopedia Britannica, Great Books of the Western World, Vol. 7 (1955).

RANK, OTTO: *The Myth of the Birth of the Hero*. Vienna: F. Deuticke, Heft 5 (1909).

ROSZAK, THEODORE: *The Making of a Counter-Culture*. Garden City, New York: Doubleday & Company, Inc., Anchor Books (1969).

SCHOLEM, GERSHOM G.: *Major Trends in Jewish Mysticism*. New York: Schocken (1961).

STEPHENS, JAMES; EDWIN L. BECK; and ROYALL H. SNOW: *Victorian and Later English Poets*. New York: American Book Company (1937).

TINBERGEN, N.: *The Study of Instinct*. London: Oxford University Press (1951).

VON FRANZ, MARY-LOUISE: *The Problem of the Puer Aeternus*. New York: Spring Publications (1970). A private limited edition.

WHITMONT, EDWARD C.: *The Symbolic Quest*. New York: G. P. Putnam's Sons (1969).

WOLMAN, BENJAMIN B., editor, *Psychoanalytical Techniques*. New York: Basic Books, Gerhard Adler article, "Methods of Treatment in Analytical Psychology" (1967).

PERIODICALS

Behavior Today, June 22, 1970.

Chicago *Sun-Times*, August 12, 1970, p. 64.

GREELEY, ANDREW M.: "There's a New Time Religion on Campus," The New York *Times* Magazine, June 1, 1969.

HILLMAN, JAMES: "Senex and Puer: An Aspect of the Historical and Psychological Present," *Eranos-Jahrbuch* XXXVI/1967, Zurich: Rhein-Verlag (1968).

JUNG, CARL G.: "Letter to Dr. Selig dated 25 February, 1953," *Spring*, 1971.

MEAD, MARGARET: "Five Who Care," *Look*, April 21, 1970.

OTTO, HERBERT A.: "Has Monogamy Failed?" *Saturday Review*, April 25, 1970.

Roche Report: Frontiers of Clinical Psychiatry, March 12, 1969.

OTHER SOURCES

JACOBI, JOLANDE: *Two Essays on Freud and Jung*, Zurich: C. G. Jung Institute (1958). A pamphlet privately printed.

JUNG, CARL G.: *Seven Sermons of the Dead*, an unpublished manuscript privately circulated by Dr. Jung.

Women in the University of Chicago, Report of the Committee on University Women (May 1, 1970). Prepared for the Committee of the Council of the University Senate.

INDEX

Aborigines, 73. *See also* Archaic (primitive) man and archaisms

Academic pressures, analysis and counter-culture and, 121 ff.

"Accidents," trickster archetype and, 289

Active imagination, 337–65, 371, 376, 403

Adler, Alfred, 39; and Individual Psychology, 180, 181–82

Adler, Gerhard, 343

Affect(s), repression and, 102–3. *See also* Emotions; Feelings

Aggression (aggressiveness), 217–18, 354

Aion (Jung), 395–96

Alchemy, 131, 273–74, 373, 388–94, 399

Alienation, 81–82, 89

Alpert, Richard, 41

Amnesia, periodic, xxxii

Analysand. *See* Analysis (analytical process)

Analysis (analytical process), 1–36, 37 ff. (*see also* Analytical Psychology; Psychotherapy; specific aspects, concepts, individuals, kinds); active imagination and, 337–65; animus-anima concept and, 247–69 (*see also* Anima; Animus); availability and accessibility of analyst to analysand and, 173–75; complexes and demons and, 38–83 (*see also* Complexes; Demons); and death and rebirth, 410–34; dreams and, 16–17, 21–34 *passim*, 307–30 (*see also* Dreams); and individuation process, 155, 157 ff., 173 ff. (*see also* Individuation process); initial session, 19 ff.; and knowledge of, and search for self, 272–302 (*see also* Self; specific aspects, concepts); and personas and shadows, 209–27; and psychedelics, 140–47; relationship between analyst and analysand and, 15–36, 173–75 (*see also* specific aspects); screening for, 15–16; and therapy, defined, 19–21; and transcendent function, 332–37 ff.

Way of Individuation. *See* Individuation process

Weltanschauung, Jung and, 4–7

"Will to power," 181–82. *See also* Power instinct (power-complex)

Wisdom, 280–81, 288, 298, 377–79. *See also* Knowledge

Wise man archetype, 298

Wishes, unconscious, dreams and, 304, 306–7

Witchcraft, 32–33; counter-culture and, 131 ff., 139

Witch-doctor (shaman), 32–33

Women-men relationship (*see also* Love; Marriage; Sex[ual-

ity]; specific aspects, kinds): animus-anima concept and, 229–69, 295–97 (*see also* Anima; Animus; specific aspects); dreams and, 307–20; masculinity and femininity and problems in, 229–69; psychological types and, 193–94, 199–208

Women's liberation movement, 261, 264–65

Word association, 53–57, 86–87

Yantra symbol, 300

Yoga, 399, 403–4

Zosimos, 392

THE COLLECTED WORKS
OF C. G. JUNG

Bollingen Series XX. Published by Princeton
University Press. Princeton, New Jersey

10. *Civilization in Transition* (2nd edition, 1970)

The Role of the Unconscious (1918)
Mind and Earth (1927/1931)
Archaic Man (1931)
The Spiritual Problem of Modern Man (1928/1931)
The Love Problem of a Student (1928)
Woman in Europe (1927)
The Meaning of Psychology for Modern Man (1933/1934)
The State of Psychotherapy Today (1934)
Preface and Epilogue to "Essays on Contemporary Events" (1946)
Wotan (1936)
After the Catastrophe (1945)
The Fight with the Shadow (1946)
The Undiscovered Self (Present and Future) (1957)
Flying Saucers: A Modern Myth (1958)
A Psychological View of Conscience (1958)
Good and Evil in Analytical Psychology (1959)
Introduction to Wolff's "Studies in Jungian Psychology" (1959)
The Swiss Line in the European Spectrum (1928)
Reviews of Keyserling's "America Set Free" (1930) and "La Révolution Mondiale" (1934)
Complications of American Psychology (1930)
The Dreamlike World of India (1939)
What India Can Teach Us (1939)

Appendix: Documents (1933–38)

11. *Psychology and Religion:*
West and East (2nd edition, 1969)

WESTERN RELIGION

Psychology and Religion (The Terry Lectures) (1938/1940)
A Psychological Approach to the Dogma of the Trinity (1942/1948)
Transformation Symbolism in the Mass (1942/1954)
Forewords to White's "God and the Unconscious" and Werblowsky's "Lucifer and Prometheus" (1952)
Brother Klaus (1933)
Psychotherapists or the Clergy (1932)

THE COLLECTED WORKS OF C. G. JUNG

Child Development and Education (1928)
Analytical Psychology and Education: Three Lectures (1926/1946)
The Gifted Child (1943)
The Significance of the Unconscious in Individual Education (1928)
The Development of Personality (1934)
Marriage as a Psychological Relationship (1925)

18. *Miscellany* (in preparation)

POSTHUMOUS AND OTHER MISCELLANEOUS WORKS

19. *Bibliography and Index* (in preparation)

COMPLETE BIBLIOGRAPHY OF C. G. JUNG'S WRITINGS
GENERAL INDEX TO THE COLLECTED WORKS